Liberal and Illiberal Nationalisms

Also by Ray Taras

CONSOLIDATING DEMOCRACY IN POLAND

DEMOCRACY IN POLAND (*with Marjorie Castle*)

HANDBOOK OF POLITICAL SCIENCE RESEARCH ON THE USSR AND EASTERN EUROPE: Trends from the 1950s to the 1990s

IDEOLOGY IN A SOCIALIST STATE: Poland 1956–83

LEADERSHIP CHANGE IN COMMUNIST STATES

LE DÉBAT LINGUISTIQUE AU QUÉBEC (*with Donat Taddeo*)

NATIONAL IDENTITIES AND ETHNIC MINORITIES IN EASTERN EUROPE

NATIONS AND POLITICS IN THE SOVIET SUCCESSOR STATES (*with Ian Bremmer*)

NEW STATES, NEW POLITICS: Building the Post-Soviet Nations (*with Ian Bremmer*)

POLAND: Socialist State, Rebellious Nation

POLITICAL CULTURE AND FOREIGN POLICY IN LATIN AMERICA: Case Studies from the Circum-Caribbean (*with Roland Ebel and James Cochrane*)

POSTCOMMUNIST PRESIDENTS

THE ROAD TO DISILLUSION: From Critical Marxism to Post-Communism

UNDERSTANDING ETHNIC CONFLICT: The International Dimension (*with Rajat Ganguly*)

Liberal and Illiberal Nationalisms

Ray Taras
Tulane University
New Orleans

First published 2002 by
PALGRAVE MACMILLAN
Houndmills, Basingstoke, Hampshire RG21 6XS and
175 Fifth Avenue, New York, N. Y. 10010
Companies and representatives throughout the world

PALGRAVE MACMILLAN is the global academic imprint of the Palgrave Macmillan division of St. Martin's Press, LLC and of Palgrave Macmillan Ltd. Macmillan® is a registered trademark in the United States, United Kingdom and other countries. Palgrave is a registered trademark in the European Union and other countries.

ISBN 0–333–96119–6

This book is printed on paper suitable for recycling and made from fully managed and sustained forest sources.

A catalogue record for this book is available from the British Library.

Library of Congress Cataloging-in-Publication Data

Taras, Ray, 1946–
    Liberal and illiberal nationalisms / by Ray Taras.
        p. cm.
    Includes bibliographical references and index.
    ISBN 0–333–96119–6
    1. Nationalism. 2. Nationalism—History. I. Title.

JC311.T37 2002
320.54—dc21
                                                        2001059848

10   9   8   7   6   5   4   3   2   1
11   10   09   08   07   06   05   04   03   02

Printed and bound in Great Britain by
Antony Rowe Ltd, Chippenham and Eastbourne

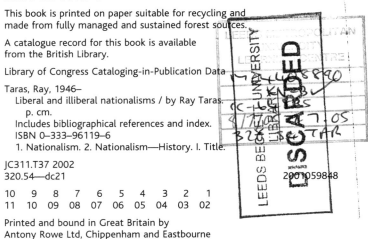

Contents

List of Figures

Acknowledgments

In researching and writing this book, the largest debt I have incurred is to two university research centers which provided me with a wealth of intellectual resources and first-class facilities. During 1987–88 I was a visiting scholar at the Davis Center for Russian Studies, Harvard University. Among the inspiring seminars I participated in during that year, the Tuesday-night ethnicity discussion group organized and led by Lis Bernstein, the Center's deputy director, was particularly valuable in shaping my thinking about nationalism. I am grateful to Tim Colton, director of the Center, and Roman Szporluk, director of the Harvard Ukrainian Research Institute, for letting me take part in many stimulating lectures, seminars, and conversations in the corridors.

During spring semester of 1999, I was visiting professor at the School for Postgraduate Research on Interculturalism and Transnationality (SPIRIT for short), Aalborg University, Denmark. The five-month tenure did indeed provide a rich intercultural and transnational experience, compelling further refining and reformulating of my assumptions about nationalism and identity. Ulf Hedetoft, the School's director, helped in countless practical ways but, above all, in sharing his erudition.

A number of other institutions provided opportunities to carry out study visits to countries forming part of the book's case studies. The Ramakrishna Mission Institute of Culture in Golpark, Calcutta, offered research facilities and a hospitable home-away-from-home in India. A Canadian Government Faculty Enrichment Grant allowed me to develop my research on Quebec politics. A home base at Haifa University, Israel, in 1998 served as a springboard for conducting research on politics in that country. An Andrew W. Mellon Faculty Field Research Grant enabled me to travel to several Latin American countries in search of anti-Americanism. The Committee on Research, Tulane University, awarded several travel grants to conduct additional study visits.

For their valuable comments on and lively discussion of specific issues raised in various parts of this book, I would like to thank the following specialists: Susanne Baier-Allen, Center for European Integration Studies, Bonn; David Carment, Carleton University, Ottawa; Marjorie Castle, Tulane University; Flemming Christiansen, University of Leeds; Sanjin Dragojevic, University of Zagreb; Malene Gram, Aalborg University; Francois Grin, University of Geneva; John Hall, McGill University; Marta-Lisa Magnusson, Suddansk University; Bo Petersson, Lund University; Melita Richter, Center for International Ethnic Research, Trieste; Richard Rose, University of Strathclyde; Bill Safran, University of Colorado; Muhammad Siddiq, University of California, Berkeley; Daniel Skobla, Warsaw University; Irina Stakhanova,

Bowling Green State University; Michael Taylor, University of Washington; Barbara Tornquist-Plewa, Lund University; Edmund van Trotsenburg, University of Klagenfurt; and Hakan Yavuz, University of Utah. I am also grateful to Rajat Ganguly, University of East Anglia, for assistance with parts of Chapters 2 and 4. Although they still couldn't prevent me from generating hermeneutic and factual imperfections, whatever strong points there are in the study result from their input.

I dedicate this book to my dear daughter Gabriela.

Introduction: New Millennium, Old Nationalisms?

The plurality of nationalisms

Academics and policymakers alike are searching for new understandings of world conflict in the first years of the new millennium, especially in the aftermath of the September 2001 terrorist attacks in the United States. The East–West ideological struggle has become consigned to the history of the twentieth century. The North–South economic divide remains salient to world politics but efforts have been made to remedy its symptoms through the panacea of globalization. Eclipsing conflicts based on these two axes in many parts of the world is the struggle between what are viewed as illiberal forms of nationalism which include religious extremism, and Western liberal ideas. A large body of excellent and intriguing scholarship has been published on this subject over the past decade.

Many nationalist movements are indeed illiberal, but not all are. Conversely, anti-nationalist forces have often proved to be the reactionary illiberal element. As the great historian of colonialism, C.L.R. James, bluntly stated three decades ago, in pre-independence West Indies 'those suspected of anti-nationalism are usually rich whites and their retainers'.[1] What has changed since then? Today nationalism takes many forms; it is widespread, highly differentiated, yet fixated on internal homogeneity. To remain anti-nationalist under all circumstances would itself constitute profound chauvinism. It is not nationalism's ethnic dimension that sets it apart from other forms of collective identity but its diverse character: 'it is both a vehicle for "ethnic" identity and political identification, for ideological modernization and ardent traditionalism, for rationality and passion, for past nostalgia and future hope, for anonymity and familiarity, for the most respectable and the most despicable values at the same time'.[2]

Nationalism may be unpredictable, then, but it is also reassuring. Cultural theorist Svetlana Boym observed:

> The seduction of nationalism is the seduction of homecoming and total acceptance: one doesn't even have to join the party; one simply belongs. Nationalist ideology mobilizes the nostalgia for the old Common Place lost and individual nostalgias and family histories, and it also proposes a plan of action for the purification and rebuilding of the collective home. It offers a comforting collective biography instead of a flawed individual story full of estrangements and disappointments; it promises to recover the blissful childhood of a nation, without the alienation and loss experienced in adult years.[3]

There is far more to nationalism, then, than ethnonationalism.[4] Some forms of nationalism are employed to justify the maintenance of empires and others to attack immigrants. Some underpin movements of secession and irredentism while others seek to unify anti-Western or anti-modernity sentiments in various parts of the world. Some attract diasporas back to the homeland, others expel the legal citizens of a state. The present age is not one of political nationalism, therefore, but of political and cultural nationalisms. The life expectancies of the various forms differ.

Nationalism was the most powerful and recurring political idea of the nineteenth and twentieth centuries and it starts off the twenty-first century in a lead position. Nationalism was the central organizing principle of the modern state system; it has had a great impact on peoples in all modern societies; and it shapes the international order at the millennium's turn. Defining the collective self remains a major function performed by nationalism even as it serves as a source of friction affecting the world system. The study of nationalisms, its effects, and its durability, continues to have urgency today.

Structure of the study

This book studies nationalisms in a disaggregated form, at the most general level distinguishing between those attached to a statist project and those that go beyond the state. This is not a contentious typology and has been explicit or, more often, implicit in much research on nationalism. In trying to distract scholars from the *idees fixes* of civic versus ethnic nationalisms, for example, sociologist Rogers Brubaker drew an analytical distinction between 'state-framed' and *counter-state* understandings of nationhood and forms of nationalism. In the former, "nation" is conceived as congruent with the state, as institutionally and territorially "framed" by the state; in the latter, it is conceived in opposition to the territorial and institutional frame of some existing state or states'.[5] Brubaker was quick to avoid any normative hierarchy for the two, asserting that each can be liberal and civic in orientation. But when it came to explaining counter-state nationalisms, Brubaker revisited very traditional categories: 'counter-state definitions of nation may be based on territory, on historic provincial privileges, on distinct political histories prior to incorporation into a larger state and so on'.[6]

In this book I adopt traditional categories making up nationalism, such as territory and history and link them to the idea of home. 'The singularity of nationalism rests in its tenet that a marriage must take place between culture and politics and that this union must be sanctified on a native land.'[7] What is a native land, a home? 'Our home is where we belong, territorially, existentially and culturally, where our community is, where our family and loved ones reside, where we can identify our roots, and where we long to return to when we are elsewhere in the world.'[8] It is therefore an affective rather than cognitive construct, and more than just legal citizenship is required to belong to it. Accordingly, 'home as belonging to a nation is a structured set of emotions and attitudes, shaped by an imagined oneness of political and pre-political, contemporary and historical, rational and cosmological orientations'.[9] A settled territory is not automatically a home. Instead, '[a] homeland emerges not when it has been inhabited but when it has been mapped'.[10]

Chapter 1 examines the historical evolution of nations – the many different ways that nation-building occurred, the territories people settled and called homes, the languages they adopted for use in these homes, and the different types of nationalism that followed. The state made its appearance at different points in time and the modern nations of today differ greatly in terms of histories as states. While the Napoleonic wars two centuries ago were a milestone in the development of political nationalism, countries followed distinct paths to nationhood and used nationalism in often divergent ways.

In Chapter 2, I examine the conceptual tools used for understanding nationalism. What has the term meant, which factors shape it, what other phenomena are related to it, what functions does it perform? The review of the scholarly literature and of contrasting typologies and schools of thought reveals the extraordinary richness and, at the same time, avid contention about the subject.

In order to study the varieties of contemporary nationalisms empirically, I have selected contrasting case studies built around four principal themes, each involving a particular understanding of home.[11] The first deals with the linkage between *nationalism and empire* – the problem of the conversion of the nation-state to the nations-state, or the multinational home. In Chapter 3 I consider the role played by nationalist movements in taking Russia out of the Soviet empire and India out of the British empire and, subsequently, how the new nations-states have themselves occasionally behaved imperially when confronted with their own separatist movements. Behaving imperially involves the construction of ethnically-spacious homes. Corresponding nationalisms – a great Russian and secular Indian one – have been propagated to bind ethnically and linguistically diverse peoples. The chapter compares the success of the two imperial projects in achieving this goal.

A second theme is how nationalism can lead to secessionist movements— the breakup of states and construction of *multiple homes*. Chapter 4 focuses on two contemporary separatist movements: the struggle of the historic Zulu nation to govern itself rather than be governed by South Africa, and the efforts of Quebec sovereigntists to separate from Canada. Identity politics undergird both movements. Difficulties defining who Zulus and Quebecers are reveal how political or ethnolinguist criteria are applied in order to ensure exclusionary understandings of the nation. The title of the chapter, 'home writ small', refers to both the attempt to carve out a small state out of a larger parent one and the restriction of the national home to a narrow community.

The third theme addresses radical nationalisms, those disaffected with existing political structures and seeking the transformation of the national state rather than the creation of a new one. The goal of right-wing fundamentalist movements is to construct a *uninational home*, whether based on racial or religious grounds. Chapter 5 analyses the rise of right-wing nationalism in two advanced Western-type democracies which recently have undergone rapid demographic transformation, Germany and Israel. In the first a loose association of groups, most of them outside of mainstream politics, has fought to secure the racial purity of the country. In the second a combination of religious fundamentalists, establishment political organizations, and right-wing extremists has struggled for a purist view of spiritual home. The actors, poles of conflict, and methods used differ in the two cases. This chapter attempts to link these factors to contrasting understandings of nation and home.

The final theme is the effort by pan-nationalist movements to construct a *transnational home*. While we normally identify transnationality with a democratic project like the building of a European home, pan-nationalist movements grounded in anti-modernity and anti-Westernism try to do much the same thing and create solidarity among disadvantaged nations. Chapter 6 considers two case studies; the endeavor to realize an Islamic commonwealth based in large part on anti-Westernism, and the struggle for pan-Latin Americanism based on the ideology of anti-dependency and anti-Americanism on that subcontinent. Because they target Western hegemony such movements are frequently depicted as especially militant. Indeed, the terrorist attack on the US in 2001 confirmed that anti-Westernism may represent the most virulent variant of nationalism today. The chapter explores the weaknesses and strengths of such pan-nationalisms.

The final chapter examines the connection between nationalisms, constructions of home, and conflict. Imagining home can prove divisive and lead to nationalist unrest.[12] I do not make a causal argument for this, but at the same time I propose that disputes over what is home and who its titular residents are cannot be resolved by the adoption of magic formulae like multiculturalism and civic nationalism. In the hands of politicians and their ideologues, these have become mantras rather than solutions. Reordering political power seems the practical and prudent way to allay the fears of most types of nationalists, yet it is what leaders are often reluctant to do.

Reaching beyond Western approaches

The originality of this study, I hope, lies not only in this analytical framework but also in the attempt to be crosscultural, by the use of contrasting case studies, and intercultural, by a focus on regional and hemispheric (though not global) processes. Let me explain why I believe this approach is needed.

Much of the theoretical discourse on nationalism has been Eurocentric, even more specifically, *Mitteleuropa*-centric. There have been noteworthy exceptions, as I point out in Chapter 2. Even when research is not Eurocentric, many scholars inherently adopt a hierarchy of nationalisms that is transparently normative. Michael Billig has exposed this bias by contrasting the developed West's 'banal nationalism' that is supposedly modern, enlightened, and rational, with the alien, backward, irrational, and violent nationalisms of others.[13] The bias is long-standing. Hans Kohn, for example, put forward the view that Western nationalism is grounded in the ideas of free will, citizenship, and social contract developed by Jean-Jacques Rousseau, while Eastern nationalism comprises the more primordial organic, cultural, and communitarian notions admired by Johann Gottfried Herder.[14] One Swedish scholar observed how 'closely tied to the dichotomy of extremism/banality are the dichotomies of irrationality/rationality, primordiality/modernity and ethnicity/civicness'. Furthermore, '[t]he civic/ethnic dichotomy is dangerously close to this self-righteous "us" and "them" picture of the free and enlightened citizens of the "West" and the culturally trapped collectivities of the "East"'.[15]

The emphasis placed since the Cold War on 'European' values – human rights, religious and political freedoms, democracy, tolerance, and equality of opportunity – is designed to hammer home the inferiority of the Other. The term European 'values' is consciously used in preference to 'ideals' to imply that Europe has succeeded in internalizing such norms, the many twentieth-century European wars notwithstanding. To be sure, other books have sought to expose what can be called the 'new Eurocentrism'. But it is alarming when even postcolonial literature focuses on celebrating difference rather than empowering the disadvantaged. The study of nationalism has become a battleground between Western and non-Western value systems.

Hopefully in keeping with a more enlightened and egalitarian spirit that a new century should bring, it seems appropriate, then, to examine Western and non-Western nationalisms alongside each other. In organizing the empirical analysis in this way, I wish to indicate which nationalisms pose the most serious threat to the stability of states and the well-being of peoples in the new century, which have a limited life expectancy, and which nurture a disadvantaged people's identity and interests.

In sum, this book is an exploration of the diverse manifestations of contemporary nationalisms: imagining different types of home, benign and malign types, conflict-generating and consensus-making, centered on the state and extending beyond it, ideological and action programs. I recognize that nationalisms are not the sole explanation for most of what happens in politics. The mobilizing potential of different nationalisms is also not constant across time and space. Other factors – economic interests, international organizations' bureaucratic imperatives, leadership idiosyncracies – may reduce the salience of identity politics in the future.

My study strives for parsimony in a field where both generalization and thick descriptions abound. I set out to link *theorie* and *empirie*. I also recognize that it is through making sense of both the minutiae and the momentous side of nationalisms that this book can contribute to the extensive literature on this subject.

1
Nations and Nationalisms Historically

Introduction

Most historians accept that nationalism was first harnessed as an instrument of politics at the time of the French Revolution – staged in the name of *les peuples francais* – and the wars waged by Napoleon shortly afterwards. But the antecedent, more protracted process of nation-making that led up to the events in France has proved a murkier subject. In ancient Rome the word *natio* meant birth or descent; Cicero, for example, had the aristocracy in mind when employing *natio*. By the twelfth century it referred to a racial group, and for Adrian Hastings '[t]here is in fact overwhelming evidence that "nation" was regularly used in the Middle Ages in the Vulgate sense of a people distinct by "language, laws, habits, modes of judgment and customs" – to use an almost defining phrase of Bernard, first Norman Bishop of St David's, when describing the Welsh as a "nation" to the Pope about 1140'.[1] But the word was devoid of any real political significance.

Perhaps surprisingly, then, the English, not the Welsh, are singled out by many historians as being the first historic nation. One reason for this may have to do with what Dutch-born historian Ian Buruma has dubbed *Anglo-mania*: an admiration for all things English, a long-standing fashionable and influential current among European (Goethe and Voltaire) and even some American intellectual circles – not to mention the English themselves.[2] Accordingly English academic Hastings made the bold claim that the later fourteenth century 'represents the very latest point at which it is plausible to claim that the English nation-state had gelled so decisively that no imaginable circumstance could later have diverted English society into some quite other form'.[3]

The process in England that led 'from rabble to nation', in Russian-born Liah Greenfeld's characterization, occurred two centuries later:

> At a certain point in history – to be precise, in early sixteenth-century England – the word 'nation' in its conciliar meaning of 'an elite' was

applied to the population of the country and made synonymous with the word 'people.' This semantic transformation signaled the emergence of the first nation in the world, in the sense in which the word is understood today, and launched the era of nationalism.[4]

In searching for the origins of the nation-state, Ernst Haas, a long-time government professor of the University of California, Berkeley, stated simply that '[t]his story began in England toward the end of the sixteenth century'.[5]

Yet English precociousness was belied by legal practice: 'The concept of nationality did not appear in English law before the 1914 British Nationality Act. Personal allegiance to the Crown remained predominant.'[6] And if England was really already a nation in the sixteenth century, it was only in the eighteenth century that groups anywhere came to be described as being nationalistic, and only in 1789 did the word nationalism appear in print, in French. Swedish political scientist Patrik Hall has succinctly summarized the contrasting claims that scholars have made about nationalism:

> The date of the birth of nationalism has been stretched from sixteenth century England (Greenfeld 1992) over seventeenth century England (Kohn 1944), the French Revolution (O'Brien 1988), the German Romantic era (Kedourie 1985) and industrialism (Gellner 1983), to the period of imperialism (Hobsbawm 1990), to mention just some of the more notable datings.[7]

Clearly only a case-by-case study can reveal the distinct paths and different time frames marking the emergence of nationhood and nationalism.

When we inquire into the birth of nations, we are inclined to search for breakthroughs in the adoption of a national language, the flourishing of a national culture, or the emergence of a national character. In this chapter I review some key junctures in the linguistic, cultural, and psychological development of several large Western nations. At the outset, it is important to underscore that 'the ontology of national formation has been a relatively untheorized shadow-area, traversed in the main either by idealists who imbue it with the force of a primordial essence or by historians who seem resigned to documenting its outer reaches'.[8] This is illustrated by theorists' resistance to confront the relationship existing between language, culture, character, identity, and nationhood. Generally the issue is dodged by asserting that once a sense of nationhood is in place – and not the emergence of the other factors – nationalist ideology can come into being. Nationalist ideology is usually understood as the fundamental principles justifying actions and behavior and promoting the values and interests of a particular nation.

Nationhood and language

One of the foremost historians of nationalism, Hans Kohn, was persuaded that before the birth of modern nationalism a feeling of nationality was prevalent among many peoples. It was largely unconscious, poorly articulated, and did not shape the actions and aims of groups in a permanent way. 'It was no purposeful will welding together all the individuals into a unity of emotions, thoughts, and actions.'[9] Kohn's intriguing study of early nations has fallen out of fashion in recent years and more recent scholarship has focused instead on the more manageable conceptualization of nations after 1789 or, at the earliest, from the late Middle Ages on. If we are to dismiss Kohn, let us at least become familiar with his narrative.

Language was accepted as a natural fact and throughout the Middle Ages was not regarded as a political or cultural determinant. Its perceived insignificance was evident when the Arabs swept across the Mediterranean world at the end of the first millennium and chose not to impose their language on conquered peoples. On the contrary, Omar forbade Christians from learning Arabic and Muslims from learning foreign languages. On the other hand, like English today, Arabic proved an irresistible force in many countries and it spread quickly among Greeks, Visigoths, Persians, and Berbers.

The first use of the vernacular by a pope was in 1095 at Clermont when Urban II called for a crusade to wrest the Holy Sepulcher from 'the wicked race'. He was referring to the Persians, thereby displaying European ignorance of the fact the Arabs had conquered them four centuries earlier. Vernacular languages developed rapidly from the fourteenth century on, in many places coinciding with the rise of anti-ecclesiastical national movements. For Hastings, the anti-universalist breakthrough in early modern Europe was the product precisely of the *Christian* thrust to vernaculize: 'a very strong case can be made for the claim that the single most effective factor was the desire of many Christians, clerical and lay, to translate the Bible or produce other works conducive to popular piety'.[10]

The ascendancy of the vernacular at this time still had few political consequences. In the Middle Ages some of the first to write in their vernacular languages, like Christine de Pizan in French or Petrarch in Italian, did indeed paint stereotypes of their own nations as well as of others. But in the hands of such great writers, even the humorous or mocking construction of national stereotypes was largely devoid of political motives.

It took another three centuries for language to become the major determinant of a nation. The process was indirect: emergent national literatures became the basis for nascent popular cultures in which an increasing number of people participated. These popular cultures stood in opposition to the old Latin culture of the elites and had therefore a transformative character. To be sure, new linguistic barriers arose between different nations, but they were in part at least cancelled out by the emergence of ideas – Descartes' new term for thought – common to all Europeans. By the beginning of the seventeenth century, Europeans might speak, read and write different languages, but they increasingly had just one way of thinking and a sense of belonging to a common Republic – *La Republique des Lettres*. Still, the role of language in nation-making was critical, and the relationship was most clearly mapped out by the German writers Johann Gottfried Herder (1744–1803) and Johann Gottlieb Fichte (1762–1814).

It is easier to trace the development of national languages than it is to identify the emergence of nationhood. As I have suggested, the two are only vaguely related, for having a common language does not by itself guarantee that a shared sense of nationhood will be attained. Conversely, today as in the past, there are nations who possess no language distinctly their own. The Swiss have four languages – a version of German, Italian, French, and Romansch. By contrast, most Latin American states have one 'national' language, Spanish, though of course many indigenous groups continue to speak their native tongues.

If language has not necessarily served as the primary determinant of nationhood, the early historians of Western civilization pointed to the significance of differences in the *character* of peoples. Homer's epic *The Odyssey* underscored the peculiarities of the many peoples encountered by the protagonist, while the ancient Greek historians Herodotus and Thucydides pointed to the salience of different characters found in the city-states and beyond. Roman Emperor Julian attacked the universalism of Christianity and specifically poured scorn on the Biblical story of the Tower of Babel, which alleged that national – in particular, linguistic – distinctions were dysfunctional. He contrasted the freedom-loving Teutons of his day with the submissiveness of the Orientals, and juxtaposed the incestuous behavior of the Persians with the harsh Greek condemnation of it.

But attributing a national character to a nation has always been a slippery exercise. If it does exist, it is mutable over time and not permanent. The Mongols under Genghis Khan were known for their warlike qualities, but by the sixteenth century, with their conversion to Lamaist Buddhism, they had become pacifist and pious. The character and collective mentality of groups are often formed by factors having little to do with racial or ethnic origin. We can speak of the distinctive character of separate socio-occupational groups such as peasants, bureaucrats, and soldiers; of rural and urban characters; of a Protestant, Catholic, or Jewish mind set; and, of course, of gender-based character. Character may even be tied to the type of education and training young people undergo, for example, whether it is Talmudic, Jesuit, or Confucian, and whether it is primarily scientific (Euclidian) or humanist (classical) in its orientation. Clearly, if it exists at all, national character is the result of complex social conditioning and socialization rather than an innate set of genetically-transmitted attributes.

The universal nations of antiquity

It is conventional to begin the study of modern nations with European coun-tries governed by various dynasties in the late Middle Ages. But Kohn drew attention to a much earlier period that was influential in shaping modern civilization, so let us follow his approach here (see Figure 1.1). We can agree that the Western world, and the Judeo-Christian tradition which shapes it, is founded on two great civilizations of antiquity – those of the Greeks and the Israelites. These were the peoples of ancient times with a strong sense of history. As Kohn put it,

> With them the natural group-sentiment of tribalism – which animated the ancestors of the Jews and of the Greeks, in common with all other ethnic groups – became a guiding factor of spiritual life, a new conscious-ness which gave every member of the group the knowledge of a special mission entrusted to it and distinguishing it from all other peoples.[11]

It was the spread of group sentiment across social classes that distinguished ancient Greece and Israel from the many other civilizations of antiquity. Kohn pointed to how the

> feeling of a peculiar dignity and mission in other countries was confined to the rulers, kings or priests, investing them, and them alone, with divine origin or with special wisdom and pride, making them superior to all the other members of their people and setting them apart in a class.[12]

While other peoples faded into obscurity, the Greeks and Jews endured, largely because their cultural vibrancy proved much stronger than their political, racial, or geographic continuity. Both peoples exhibited clearly-defined characteristics but these differed greatly and in some instances were binary opposites. The artistic and philosophic temperament of the ancient Greeks stood in relief to the spirituality and messianism of the Israelites. Jews were defined by their calling from God. Yahweh was the guarantor and agent of unification and of the reconciliation of multiplicity with unity. The mission of the Jewish people was to serve as a messenger for the unification of humanity, as expressed in the Psalm's dictum 'Make my heart one'. By contrast, Greeks arrived at this reconciliation through contemplation and love of wisdom ('philosophy'). They were certain that all men would em-brace virtue if they could only contemplate it.

Where the Greeks cultivated the philosophy and science of history, Jews did not develop history as a science but instead undertook historical action. All human action acquired historical meaning and value because men were related to God. History itself became the way of God, and the Jewish God was the God of the historical deed: 'I am the Lord your God who brought

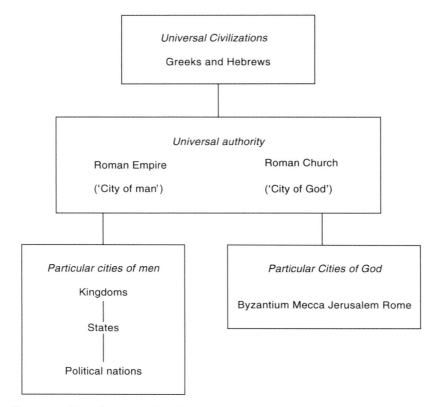

Figure 1.1   From the universal to the national

you out of the land of Egypt, out of the house of bondage.' The Pentateuch underscored the need to arrive at a historical consciousness: 'Only take heed to thyself, and keep thy soul diligently lest thou forget the things which thine eyes have seen, and lest they depart from thy heart all the days of thy life: but teach them to thy sons and thy sons' sons.' Shared memories and ambitions were to undergird Jewish national consciousness, just as much later they were to shape the national consciousness of other peoples.

Three characteristics of nationalism originated with the Israelites: the notion of a chosen people; consciousness of national history; and national messianism. The covenant constituted the Jews as a people. The first covenant God made, with Noah, was to stop the shedding of human blood. The second, with Abraham, was designed to found a new nation and give the Israelites a new land. The third covenant was between God and the whole people of Israel: 'If ye keep my Covenant – but only on this condition – ye shall be mine own treasure from among all peoples.'

Consciousness of their history forged the Israelites into a community. Many scholars from the seventeenth century on have identified 'the Jews as the example par excellence of nationalism in ancient times . . . . The Jews are indeed an outstanding example, inasmuch as for a certain period they (being an indigenous population) actualized their political nationalism, that is, they created a Jewish state'.[13] This was from 164 to 67 BC, when the Roman conquest began. Consciousness of their trials under the Pharaoh was also critical. In the nineteenth century, French writer Ernest Renan asserted that 'national sorrows are more significant than triumphs because they impose obligations and demand a common effort'.[14] The Old Testament served as a record of the Israelites' suffering under Egyptian bondage; the need to resist assimilation on which Joseph, the Pharaoh's administrator, reneged; their discovery of an identity during the exodus under the idiosyncratic leadership of Moses; and their later glory under Kings David and Solomon.[15]

The emergent Jewish nation understood messianism in both a national and universal sense. Out of Zion, the prophet Isaiah claimed, would go forth the law. The Kingdom of God was centered on the Jewish people but it also represented religious salvation for all humanity. Genesis includes God's promise that 'in you will be blessed all the families of the earth'. A universal kingdom of peace and justice would follow. As the famous biblical passage asserts, peoples would beat their swords into ploughshares and their spears into pruning hooks. Thus 'Israel's nationhood, its selection by God, was recognized and proclaimed, not as an end in itself, but as the means to a greater universal end'.[16] The convert St. Paul was especially zealous in proclaiming God's salvation of all who have faith.[17]

As with the ancient Hebrews, so the Greeks, too, had a strong sense of their distinctiveness and superiority as a people. Rather than being located at the very beginning of their history, as with the Jews, for Greeks this sentiment grew with their history. The war against Troy, vividly described in *The Iliad*, was presented as the first great conflict between two worlds different from each other in racial makeup and culture. Because it did not live under the rule of law, the barbarian world was regarded as inferior and as much more unreconcilable with Hellenic civilization than the gap between Jews and Gentiles, which was bridged by the fact that God created all men in His own image. The learned Socrates called for the complete subjugation of the enemy whenever Greeks fought barbarians (termed *polemos*), including their annihilation or, in other circumstances, their abduction into slavery. Aristotle wrote: 'some men are by nature free and others slaves, and for this latter slavery is both expedient and right'. Hellenic imperialism was thus justified as being in the interest of the enslaved as well as the conqueror.[18] By contrast, wars between Greek states (*stasis*) were regarded as merely factional and required swift reconciliation.

Political nationalism remained out of the grasp of the Greeks, whose focus of identity was the city-state. The Delphic oracle, the Olympic games, and the

Persian wars were the circumscribed occasions when Greek civic feeling was broadened. To be sure, in the fifth century BC the Sophist philosophers moved beyond city-state and Hellenic identities and championed the natural equality of men (the subordinate status of women was not questioned). Slavery was seen as unnatural and a result of conquest. But Aristotle and most Greek political thinkers disagreed with panhumanism understood so inclusively.

Paradoxically, universalism could be promoted by the quest by a great power for world domination. Persian kings such as Cyrus, Camyses, and Darius conquered much of the world known to them and their policy was to recognize the religious distinctiveness of conquered peoples. They acknowledged the pantheon of indigenous gods. In consequence, apart from the great Persian god Ahuramazda, these rulers sought the favor of the Babylonian god Marduk and of the Egyptian Re, Osiris, and Amon. The need to establish internal cohesion within a large dominion persuaded the Persian kings to construct an original, universalist synthesis.

In 334 BC Alexander the Great crossed into Asia Minor in his endeavor to create a world empire, at least, the world as he knew it. His noble objective was to unite all men in a peaceful order based not on race or blood ties but a community of spirit and civilization. This idea was also taken up by Stoic philosophers, in particular, Zeno. In his *Republic* Zeno outlined a world state in which all men belonged to the same community; Aristotle's posited republic was parochial by contrast. At this time increased cultural exchange between Asia Minor and Egypt led to a reappraisal of barbarian civilization and a reconsideration in political thought about the nature of citizenship. It was now argued that any person who reflected the qualities of Hellenic civilization was to be considered a Greek. As with the Hebrews, then, the shift from racial to cultural consciousness had been completed. Greek civilization became a rational and human civilization corresponding to the rational human mind that transcended racial origins.

We have recounted how, over time, Greeks and Jews moved from material, racial conceptions of themselves to more all-embracing spiritual and cultural ones. Before antiquity had ended, Greek and Jewish thought had accepted the values of universalism and humanism and hailed every man as a part of humanity, wherever he came from. Kohn pointed to the inherent paradox of this transformation: '[i]t is significant that in antiquity only the two nationally conscious peoples developed a conscious cosmopolitanism and universalism.'[19] Thus the peoples of Hellas and Judea assumed historical importance precisely because they had surmounted their ancient narrow nationalisms and proclaimed a universalistic message for all humanity.

The Roman Empire and church in the development of nations

The Roman Empire became heir to the universal imperial ideal of Alexander. Cicero captured the heterogeneity of the empire when he described Rome as 'a city composed of all the nations'. For him Stoic philosophy centered on all *humanitas*. The Romans possessed greater political energy than the Greek city-states and were able to assimilate the peoples of Gaul, the Iberic peninsula, and northern Africa. Julius Caesar revived Alexander's imperial idea and accepted that obedience to the Emperor – rather than the race or *ethnos* of subject peoples – would ensure fair, if not always equal treatment. The limitations of the old city-state, where a citizen was a stranger in any city but that of his origin, disappeared. Reason united men into a community, and Roman common law brought peoples together. Latin became the official language of the empire and served as the language of politics, even if the educated classes still preferred Greek.

Christians now appropriated for themselves the mission formulated by Israel and sought the fulfillment of Israel's history. But they were not satisfied to be one religion or one spiritual nation among others. The God of Christianity was the jealous God of Judaism: 'Thou shalt have no other Gods before me.' The Roman church challenged the empire for the right to insist on universalism and was ultimately to emerge triumphant. In 1095 Pope Urban exhorted Christians to undertake a Crusade: 'Let no attachment to your native soil be an impediment: because, in different points of view, all the world is exile to the Christian, and all the world his country.'[20] The great theologian Thomas Aquinas (1226–74) also contended that all Christians formed one people and their division into states was of little importance.

A sense of community of language and homeland emerged in the Middle Ages, though narrower nationalist sentiment still did not form part of the communal mind.[21] As German historian Hagen Schulze succinctly put it, 'in the early middle ages and at their height, people lived simultaneously in the Roman Empire and in a totally different, archaic world'.[22] Conflict was central to this world. Kohn concluded that

> [t]he main conflict of the Middle Ages was not between universalism and the desire of separation of individual groups, but between two forms of universalism, *Sacerdotium* and *Imperium*, a struggle unknown in the Eastern Church and unknown in Islam, where universalism remained a reality much longer than in Western Christianity.[23]

In this same period, national development in the non-Roman world took a different course. In the Byzantine empire, the church was organized along, and helped to define, emergent national lines. Autonomous, or autocephalous, churches appeared throughout the area, for example in Armenia, Constantinople, and Syria. Its largest branch, the Greek Orthodox church, was directed by a patriarchate organized as a state ministry of the Byzantine empire. Since the Greek church developed in the cradle of ancient civilizations, it was sensitive to long-standing distinctions. The final schism between Byzantinium and Rome which deepened between 1009 and 1054 was fueled by disparaging stereotypes of Greeks and Romans (that included their Teutonic protectors) of each other.

In turn, the apogee of Islam in the eighth century welded all Muslims into a rapidly-growing community, or *umma*. Historian Philip Hitti noted pointedly how '[t]he year 732 marked the first centennial of the Prophet's death. His followers were now the conquerors of an empire extending from the Bay of Biscay to the Indus and the frontiers of China, from the Aral Sea to the upper Nile'.[24] Like the Byzantine church, Islam continued to recognize differences stemming from religion (infidels), status (slaves), gender (women), and nation. The fifth sura of the Qur'an explains why and how these differences work: 'To every one of you We have appointed a right way and an open road. If God had willed, He would have made you one nation; but that He may try you in what has come to you' (5:48).[25] The Qur'anic injunction 'O mankind, We have created you male and female, and appointed you races and tribes, that you may know one another' (49:13) emphasizes the desirability of differences.

Under the Umayyad caliphate that began in the Christian year 661 in Damascus, the Arab state was largely national. It also had a branch in Cordova, Spain, from 929 to 1031. But the rise of the Abbasid dynasty in Baghdad in 750, which shifted Islam's cultural center from Arabia to Persia, produced a gradual obscuring of national divisions. Still further removed from Europe, the religious and social systems found in Hinduism, itself struggling against Islamic influence, served as insurmountable obstacles to the formation of a greater Indian nation.

In theory, the Roman church set itself above national distinctions. But with the crowning of Charlemagne in 800, the struggle for political power between Pope and Emperor had peaked. The appearance of rival pretenders to the papacy complicated this conflict and added national differences to the religious ones. From the thirteenth to sixteenth centuries the church continued to insist on its oneness and universality even while being forced to countenance national distinctions. The theological foundations underpinning unity were articulated by Aquinas: 'Though one distinguishes peoples according to diverse dioceses and states, it is obvious that as there is one Church there must also be one Christian people.'[26] The spiritual unification promoted by the church delayed the emergence of a sense of nationhood in European countries. But when its administrative structure came under challenge, it hastened a wider process of fragmentation.

For historian E.H. Carr, the first period of nationalism involved 'the gradual dissolution of the medieval unity of empire and church and the establishment of the national state and the national church'.[27] In its administrative structure the church was now organized along national lines even while Rome continued to serve as the capital of all Christianity. Almost inadvertently, then, it was the church that first regarded English, French, and German peoples as national units rather than as mere collections of tribes. Everything in the Middle Ages continued to be defined by religion, and the very symbols of distinct national experiences were religious. National saints included St. Denis for France, St. Patrick for Ireland, St. Stanislas for Poland, St. Stephen for Hungary, and St. Wenceslas for Bohemia. In time saints, together with folk heroes, kings, and warriors, 'became national heroes, the common heroes of ethnic collectivities'.[28]

Reform movements that sprang up within the church, as in the cases of John Wycliffe in England and Jan Hus in Bohemia, contributed further to national differentiation. In a similar way, secular authorities' attempts to exert greater influence over the Papacy, as when the Avignon popes became an instrument of French policy, served to reinforce the national character of the Roman church in particular lands. Despite this process of partial 'nationalization' of the church, the combination of universalism from above and town and guild autonomy from below inhibited any rapid growth of national consciousness.

From a historical perspective, the countervailing tendencies within the church towards unity and differentiation were not evenly matched. There seemed to be an inexorable, centrifugal force that promoted particularism. As early as the thirteenth century the Holy Roman Empire was described by Henri Pirenne as 'anarchy in monarchial form...which had neither common laws, common finances nor a common body of functionaries.... Compared with France and England, it seemed amorphous, illogical, almost monstrous'.[29] Church synods began to make regular use of the concept of nation, witnessed most vividly in the general council held at Constance from 1414–17 that dealt with the papal schism. The council confronted the historic question of which group really constituted a nation. Despite, or perhaps because of, the English victory at Agincourt in 1415, French ecclesiastics became locked in a dispute with English bishops over the right of England to be represented as a nation in Constance. The advocate of the French king claimed that English representatives should not enjoy the sweeping right to exercise a quarter or a fifth influence over the general council's proceedings and, therefore, over the affairs of all Christendom, on the flimsy grounds that England constituted a major nation. England could not be treated as the equivalent of France, Italy, Spain, or the *natio germanica*, to which hitherto England as well as Scandinavia and, of course, most German-speaking lands belonged. After all, the French delegate contended, France contained eleven provinces, England had only two.

One uncharitable recommendation put forward by the French was for this upstart fifth nation, the English, to disappear altogether and be absorbed into the German nation. The English protested vigorously:

the glorious kingdom of England is recognized to have been no less endowed by divine favor than the kingdom of France in antiquity or reputation, let alone in ancient and broad faith, dignity and honor. It is at least equal in all respects: in royal power, in numbers of clergy and people, in material wealth.[30]

An early understanding of the meaning of nation was contained in the formal English protest note of March 1417:

> But, surely, these two nations are equivalent, in right, in reason and on the basis of much documentary evidence. Everything necessary to being a nation with an authentic voice as a fourth or fifth part of the papal obedience, just like the French nation, [is there], whether the nation is understood as a people (*gens*), distinct from another by blood relationship (*cognationem*) and association (*collectionem*) or by difference of language, – which is the chief and surest proof of being a nation, and its very essence, either by divine or human law.[31]

Given their quarrel over each other's national legitimacy, it is ironic that both France and England emerged as the first two autonomous nations of the Middle Ages.

The early sessions of the council of Constance were taken up by renewed condemnation of the 'pseudo-Christian' Wycliffe's heretical articles on the ecclesiastical hierarchy, and also with an eyewitness account of the execution of the 'heresiarch' Hus in 1415. Both men's writings had inspired national religious reform movements and the synod felt threatened by their questioning of established authority seated in Rome.

Apart from the church, the first medieval universities in Europe were being founded at this time mainly along national lines: Cordova, set up in the principal mosque during the reign of Caliph Abd-al-Rahman (912–61); Bologna, established in 1088; Paris, created in 1200; Naples, the first to receive a charter in 1224; and Prague, founded in 1348. Students in most of these universities were organized into associations representing territorial divisions. But let us not exaggerate this rise of national units; the centralizing power of kings through most of Europe from around 1500 forced loyalties and identities to be directed towards the sovereign state. Officials of the Holy Roman Empire, the church, merchants, and bureaucrats shared a common interest with the king in promoting the growth of a centralized state.

Still, feudal fiefdoms continued to distract the masses from identification with any one patrimonial state. Feudal relations were often so complex that conflicting loyalties to different lords were common. Certain rights belonged to one lord, others to another. In addition, loyalty to one's rank (nobility, knighthood) or to one's town overrode solidarity based on a broader principle. Kings were persuaded to create parliaments not because of their fondness for democratic or national ideals but in order to secure cross-cutting representation from different areas.

At this point let us consider the idea of national aspirations as a way of measuring the growth of nationhood. Writing in 1943, Frederick Hertz observed how '[n]ational consciousness consists in the combined striving for unity, liberty, individuality, and prestige'. National aspirations consist of

(1)   The striving for national unity comprising political, economic, social, religious, and cultural unity, community and solidarity.

(2)   The striving for national freedom, which comprises independence from foreign domination or interference, and internal freedom from forces regarded as un-national or derogatory to the nation.

(3)   The striving for separateness, distinctiveness, individuality, originality, or peculiarity. The most significant example is the value attributed to a separate national language.

(4)   The striving for distinction among nations, for honor, dignity, prestige and influence, which easily becomes a striving for domination. The striving for distinction is, probably, the strongest of all four aspirations, and seems to underlie them all.[32]

From our account of the painfully-slow process of nation formation in Europe, it becomes apparent that while some objective qualities of a nation – language, culture, memory, territory – began to emerge, national aspirations had not yet crystallized. Having national goals or aspirations posits that some system of like states has emerged and that they compete to strengthen their respective unity and freedom. A British study from 1939 noted this fact:

There also seems to be implicit in the word 'nation' the idea of a multiplicity of units organized on a similar principle. The national State is a unit in a world of other national States, more or less commensurable with it in size and possessing similar attributes. These are the considerations which justify the view that 'nations' in the modern sense of the word did not emerge until the close of the Middle Ages.[33]

In short, even if early forms of literary nationalism had made an appearance in the fourteenth century, magnates still went to war against each other and showed no loyalty to the nations from which they originated. In their turn, the masses were still far from experiencing any sense of larger community. Becoming a nation was to be very much a random process, with little or no path dependence evident. The very understanding of the word *natio* was confused or inconsistent, referring in succession to a group of foreigners, a community of opinion, an elite, a sovereign people, and a unique people.[34]

It was only with the Treaty of Westphalia in 1648 that an international state system came into being, and it was only with the French Revolution and its slogan of liberty, equality, and fraternity that quintessentally national goals were identified.

To conclude this section on nation formation during the Holy Roman Empire, brief consideration needs to be given to the role of empires in nation-building (a subject discussed at length in Chapter 3). Conventional wisdom has it that empires are the graves of many nations because they annex, absorb, and assimilate many different peoples. But Hertz has made the case that early empires were in fact the cradles for, and even nourished, emergent nations:

> Modern national and democratic opinion is apt to judge Empires severely as destroyers and oppressors of free, peacable nations, actuated by lust of power. Nevertheless, it cannot be ignored that it was the empire-builders who probably first created territorial states and political institutions which became the cradles of nations.[35]

The view of empires as the cradle of nations was exemplified in the twentieth century by systems as different from each other as the Habsburgs and the Soviet Union. But in the late Middle Ages it was not the establishment of rival imperium but the centralization of power by monarchs that marked an irreversible break with the universalism proclaimed by the Roman church. Centralizing monarchies were to serve as cradles of nations.

Renaissance and national awakenings

One view of the Renaissance is as a movement of aristocratic individualism confined mainly to a small group of literate people. Such new individualism, when combined with growing secularization in many societies, represented a new challenge to the universalism of the church and, indirectly, contributed to the rise of national consciousness. Reinhold Niebuhr argued that the precarious unity of Western civilization was easily undermined by this combination in conjunction with the Reformation's refutation of papal absolutism:

> The force of universal cohesion was not the empire but the church; and it used an authority drawn not from the meaning of a community but from a dimension of human existence transcending the community. When the legitimacy of this form of authority was challenged..., the doom of the unity of the western community was a foregone conclusion, which the Renaissance and the Reformation elaborated – the one protesting against papal pretension in the name of the dignity of rational man, and the other in the name of the majesty of God.[36]

The rise of humanist thought identified human nature as the source of values, not divine revelation. It also recognized cultural differences among national groups.[37] By returning to ancient Greece and Rome for meaning, humanism aroused an awareness in the Italians of their connection with the Romans. A copy of Tacitus' long-lost *Germania*, which idealized the old Saxons, was discovered in a German monastery and published in Italian in 1455, evoking a national awakening. More and more people learned about their national histories. The invention of the printing press broadened intellectual life and added a further crack in the crumbling universalist edifice.

British historian Hugh Seton-Watson found that '[i]n the process of formation of national consciousness, and in movements for national independence and unity, there has been in each case a different combination of certain constantly recurring forces: state power, religion, language, social discontents and economic pressures'.[38] Nation formation is a quintessentially idiosyncratic process and so we follow the conventional approach and examine countries individually.

We start with a brief account of some of the often overlooked peoples in Europe who, in different ways, began to create the rudiments of a national state from the time of the Renaissance. These include Italy, the Czech state, and Spain, each of which contributed to the rise of modern nationalism but is usually overshadowed by developments in Europe's historic great powers. We then turn to the larger countries which have received considerable attention from scholars on nationalism: France, Germany, England, and Russia.

Non-classic nation builders

Italy provides the best example of how the precocious development of a type of literary nationalism did not necessarily lead in short succession to political nationalism. The great poet Dante never even conceived of the political unity of Italy. He had praise for Tuscany and Florence, of which he was a citizen, but admitted that 'many nations and peoples use a more delightful and useful language than the Italian'.[39] In his youth four languages were prominent in Florence: Latin for scholarly works, French for literature, Provencal for aristocratic love songs, and Italian for democratic treatises. Francesco Petrarca (1304–74) is often regarded as the first Italian nationalist but his influence was limited to literary circles. In 1347 Cola di Rienzo made an attempt to unify Italy under Rome but ruling circles and the masses greeted it with indifference and incomprehension. Thus Italy remained disunited except in the vision of a handful of poets.

Perhaps the first writer who saw political power located primarily in the secular state was Marsilius of Padua. Attacking the cupidity and corruption of clerics, this citizen of an important city-state rediscovered in the free communes of Italy the revival of the classical conception of the state as *polis* and *civitas*. His idea was to subject all public affairs to the will of one authority, creating in the process the sovereignty of the legislator. In his view, the affairs of the church should be placed in the care of the state. Marsilius was not an early proponent of nation-building, then, but of state-building. He underscored the separation and superiority of the state in relation to the *Civitas Dei*,or *Sacrum Imperium*.

Niccolo Machiavelli (1469–1527) is a better known forerunner of Italian nationalism. Religious universalism as represented by the Papacy had no appeal for him. The state was an end in itself and he therefore supported its political unity. The glory of classical Rome lay in the virtue of its citizens, that is, their political energy and skills, their ambition and heroism, and their self-sacrifice and devotion to the seat of the empire. Christianity, by contrast, exalted the humble and contemplative virtues such as charity and humility. Also for Machiavelli, the rivalry among states evoked the pressing need for recognizing *raison d'etat*, or reasons of state. The state was an organism that had to be judged by a standard of morality unknown at the individual level. Leaders and power, not societies and their identities, fascinated Machiavelli.

Italy, of course, had a long way to go to achieve nationhood and political unity. As one writer noted, '[i]t was in fact the political instability of Italy in the fifteenth and sixteenth centuries that made the country a kind of proving ground where various political models might be tested: it is hardly surprising that the leading political theorists of the age were Italian'.[40] In some respects Italy had a parallel in the Slavic world which was fragmented into numerous principalities most speaking closely-related languages. Especially among the Western Slavs – Czechs, Poles, Slovaks – there seemed no reason why their histories should not have converged. But Poland became politically tied to non-Slavic Lithuania while Slovakia was linked with non-Slavic Hungary. In turn, the Hussite wars fought in the Czech lands in the fifteenth century, though unconnected to the effort to establish a national Czech state, were provoked by the belief that the reform-minded Czechs were the most Christian of peoples. Already a century earlier, the distinctiveness of a Czech character was captured in an anonymously-authored chronicle *Dalimil*.

Even with their religious defeat, Czech artisans were able to capture city government from German burghers and many German towns in Bohemia came under Czech control. As a result, the Czechs became the first people in Central Europe to develop a middle class – a breakthrough that has resonance today. In 1615 the Bohemian Diet went so far as to enact a law prohibiting the employment of non-Czech-speaking officials. The law had more to do with safeguarding the exclusiveness of the Czech dominant class than with embodying a form of Czech proto-nationalism, but its unintended consequence was the consolidation of a small Western Slavic people and, in spite of Karl Marx's affirmation to the contrary, their transformation into a historic nation.

If the many peoples living in Italy and Central Europe did not become the vanguard of nation formation that was beginning in Europe, on the Iberian peninsula we might expect to encounter a case of precocious nation-making. For Spain the year 1492 ushered in a period of unparalleled greatness. Indeed, in some respects Charles V's dynastic imperialism represented the last mani-festation of medieval universalism. But with far-flung exploration and con-quests, a wave of national pride and a sense of national mission took hold in Spain in the fifteenth and sixteenth centuries. The Inquisition begun in 1478 persecuted Moors, Jews, Lutherans, humanists and other 'heretics' and estab-lished a unity of jurisdiction over all of Spain. State and church became inseparable and efforts were made to achieve a unity of loyalty and faith. Ultimately, however, Spain remained a decentralized despotism loosely united by a common kingship. Even as Spain expanded overseas, its own kingdoms and provinces were largely separate from each other. In practice, the empire constituted a loose confederation of autonomous states, each retaining its traditions and privileges, rather than domination by one nation over many peoples. The closest to a dominant state was Castile, having considerably greater military and economic weight than Aragon (the foun-dations for a union between the two crowns was formed through the mar-riage of Ferdinand of Aragon and Isabella of Castile in 1469), Granada (annexed in 1492), and Navarra (annexed in 1515).

Classic nation builders

France

One of the earliest works of European literature was *Chanson de Roland*, written in French in the late eleventh century describing some of the military exploits of Charlemagne. Following the battle of Bouvines in 1214, royal power was expanded and institutions of state were created. Schulze is cat-egorical: '[t]he first modern state to come into permanent existence in Europe was France.'[41]

As we have seen, at the council of Constance in the fifteenth century, France laid claim to the role of arbiter on the matter of which people constituted a nation. The growing sense of national unity was expressed in the works of poets such as Robert Blondel, Alain Chartier, and Eustache Deschamps. But towering above them all was the slight figure of Jeanne d'Arc (1412–31), arguably the historical character most responsible for the emergence of the modern nation. Setting aside the many legends and myths that have de-veloped over time, enough of the Jeanne d'Arc story is true to cast her – and not French kings – as the first true representative of the emergent French nation. Her Armagnac party was at war with the English and their allies in France, the Burgundians. The transcript of her trial and interrogation un-equivocally revealed her precocious sense of nation and nationalism: 'You Englishmen, who have no right in this kingdom of France, the King of Heaven sends you word and warning, by me Jehanne the Maid, to abandon your forts and depart into your own country, or I will raise such a war-cry against you as shall be remembered forever.' Asked by ecclesiastics if God loved the French more than the English, she cleverly replied that God wanted the English to stay in their own lands. The perfidy of the English that led to her cruel execution was a crucial catalyst in bringing the peoples of France together. What stood out was 'the "patriotic" determination of Jeanne d'Arc amidst the wavering loyalties of her compatriots, many of whom saw nothing wrong in being ruled by the English branch of the royal family'.[42] As recently as in the Second World War, Charles de Gaulle used her standard, the Cross of Lorraine, as the symbol of Free France.

The Estates General convening at Tours in 1484 discussed an embryonic notion of French patriotism advanced by Guillaume de Rochefort and Jean de Rely. It was to be centered on the king, of course, but it was also connected, inevitably and not for the last time, with France's supposed dual inheritance of the rational order and the legality of the Roman Empire. French myth-making claimed that Charlemagne had conquered Spain from the Saracens, liberated Rome and Italy, and baptized and subjugated Germany. Without doubt he, together with the Caliph Harun al-Rashid of the Arab Islamic world, were the two great emperors of the ninth century. Frankish kings thereafter made universalistic claims. The interconnected goals of *unitas imperii* and *unitas mundi* had been proclaimed by a succession of popes, and had also been identified by the Hohenstaufen dynasty that ruled the Holy Roman Empire from 1152 to 1250. Now these missions were accepted by the Frankish kings.

But it was with the Renaissance that the concepts of *la patrie* and patriot-ism, a new and more profound veneration of *le pays*, was developed. The term first appeared in an essay written in 1539, the year in which Francis I ordered that all legal acts had to be issued in French (much to the dislike of the Provençals). The king attacked the twin pillars of medieval society, the church and the feudal nobility, and thereafter French kings strove for abso-lute power. A people constituted under such dynastic government was bound to develop a collective consciousness and will quickly.

As if these inherited legacies were not enough, the French also took up the mantle of the Greeks and Romans and reasserted the linkage between cul-tural vitality and political aspirations. Jean Bodin (1530–96) wrote of the organic structure and historical individuality of nations. His theory of sover-eignty averred that supreme and indivisible legislative power, vested in the monarchy but limited by natural law and the traditions of France, was pivotal for national unity. Colbert was the first important statesman to make the effort to promote the political integration of France.

La patrie became associated primarily with political liberty. Patriotism established reciprocity between rulers and subjects, the land and its people, and so France's inhabitants shared the country's destiny. Like *patrie*, the nation implied a free and sovereign people and the term was adopted by those opposed to royal absolutism. Louis XIV tried to confiscate the concept for his own purposes, however: '[l]a nation ne fait pas corps en France; elle réside tout entière dans la personne du roi', that is, the nation resides entirely in the personage of the king.[43] Louis also sought to appropriate the Crown of Charlemagne for the French dynasty.

As elsewhere at this and later times, the liberty of citizens of France took second place to the unity of the nation. The importance attached to political unity, as opposed to political freedoms, distinguished many of its political thinkers. Montesquieu contended that states and societies were not the product of contract (as social contract theorists like Hobbes and Locke believed) but were maintained by organic solidarity. Each political system had its particular mentality, each constitution had to conform to the spirit of its people and this was how organic solidarity was achieved. This logic led Montesquieu to the view that large states, in which such solidarity was more difficult to attain, could only be governed despotically. For him a federation of smaller republics served as the best guarantor of both democratic and national interests. The effort to marry democratic interests with national ones had to wait for the French revolution of 1789, which had little connection with the institutional matter of federating small states.

Germany

From the outset German national development, in sharp contrast to that of France, was hampered by weak royal authority. The first flickering of a German consciousness in the masses was the peasant revolt staged in Luther's name in 1524–25, quickly crushed by the princes and nobles. Luther himself was largely indifferent to political issues and stressed how only the inner life of men and the subjective state of the soul mattered. While his attack on the 'Antichrist' in Rome and his campaign for religious reform had resonance among many Germans, Luther did not directly trigger an expanded German consciousness. For him the German nation consisted of its bishops and princes. On the other hand, his translation of the Bible into German did advance Protestantism as well as establishing a standard for written German.

After the Thirty Years' War, prospects for German unification dimmed as more than 300 territorial states emerged. Schulze emphasized, then, that '[t]he unity of the German nation was initially purely linguistic and cultural'.[44] An important figure in the German romantic movement, Johann Gottfried Herder, parlayed this fact to great advantage. Germany's greatest contribution lay in its language and literature which anyway constituted the soul of a nation. States and constitutions were of secondary importance. Herder was also a 'cultural ecumenical' and believed that every people, no matter how small and backward, possessed beauty and goodness. His thought exerted a strong influence on the cultural revival of Slavic nations as well as of Germany.

In addition to his immense contribution to Western philosophy, Immanuel Kant (1724–1804) is also viewed as a father of German liberalism, though he personally considered himself to be a citizen of the world. Indeed, the positive quality he recognized in the German-speaking people of his time was their supposed cosmopolitanism. National passion had no place, he argued, where reason prevailed, and German lands were to constitute the abode of reason. By contrast, in his famous 1808 *Reden an die deutsche Nation*, Fichte was more 'constructivist', seeking to awaken the German nation through educational expansion. He exalted German language and culture but also ascribed a political mission to this nation. The German people were destined to bring about the religious and moral regeneration of humanity, for only Germans had maintained a linguistic continuity and allowed various social classes to take part in the development of its culture. Fichte and, later, Georg Wilhelm Friedrich Hegel (1770–1831), felt that the political disintegration and demoralization of a nation could only be prevented by a strong ruler. When Hegel witnessed Napoleon's victory over Prussia in Jena in 1806, he hailed it as 'convincing proof that civilization defeats crudeness'.[45]

For Hegel it was the state, not the nation, that embodied reason and morality. As Hertz wrote: 'Hegel's philosophy was incompatible with the fundamental beliefs of nationalism. He judged a nation according to the degree of reason which its State and civilization represented, he was alien to the German national aspirations of his time, and sharply rejected political romanticism.'[46] Of course, the anti-German, anti-nationalist thrust of Hegel's work appealed to Marx, who also deprecated the emergent nationalism of his own country. Both Marx's political and economic positions were challenged by Friedrich List, who believed that the way for Germany to catch up with England, France, and America was by becoming an economic power in its own right.[47]

According to German historian Hagen Schulze,

> [i]t was precisely because there were so many untested and wholly Utopian theories about the reality of a German nation, her boundaries and internal order, that German nationalism became so attractive.... Nationalism was open to all kinds of content; it could be made religious, Liberal, democratic and egalitarian.... in short, it formed the ideal vehicle for every kind of anti-establishment creative idea.[48]

The collapse of the German revolution in 1848–49 ended the dream of constructing a liberal all-German nation-state, but Europe shared some of the blame in this. For, as Schulze emphasized, '[e]very attempt to found a German nation-state at the expense of the European balance of power established in 1815 foundered against the determined opposition of other European states'.[49]

England

As we have reported, for a number of scholars the first nation, 'God's first-born', was England.[50] The Anglo-Saxon chronicler Bede referred as early as

731 to a *gens anglorum* in his ecclesiastical history of the English people. In 1362 English replaced Anglo-Norman as the language of parliament and the courts. Matthew of Westminster felt compelled to write that 'whoever was unable to speak the English language was considered a vile and contemptible person by the common people'.[51] The end of the Hundred Years' War, lasting from 1337 to 1453, and the rise of the house of Tudor, which reigned from 1485 to 1603, served as catalysts for the emergence of the English nation. The Hundred Years' War had been fought not on a national but dynastic principle but unintended consequences may invariably follow such convulsions: dynastic wars could indirectly stimulate national consciousness.

England's defeat of France and subsequent withdrawal from the continent removed the need for strong centralized authority, which increased the power of Parliament and the spread of common law. Henry VIII established the Anglican Church, which used English as the liturgical language. He united England and Wales, and took the title of King of Ireland. He uprooted the vestiges of feudal power in England and built a strong navy. English etatism began to develop around the person of the king but Kohn also observed that 'England was the first country where a national consciousness embraced the whole people. It became so deeply ingrained in the English mind that nationalism lost its problematic character with the English.'[52] Being an island with a Celtic fringe also brought a sense of Englishness into relief.

The reign of Elizabeth brought England literary greatness, captured in Edmund Spencer's national epic *The Faerie Queene* (Elizabeth being this queen), and also scientific discovery. By the seventeenth century it was the scientific spirit that, arguably, defined England as much as Shakespeare's plays or the High Anglican Church. The Puritan Revolution blazed a trail for new liberties that encompassed wider sections of society. Religious, political, and social nationalism began to develop among its inhabitants, surpassing the more restricted etatist patriotism of the Renaissance and the absolute monarchies. Puritanism laid stress on individuals' responsibility for the salvation of the community through strict observance of God's laws. It also served to emphasize England's independence from Rome and, in the process, antagonized Catholic powers like France and Spain. Puritanism came to reflect the national aspirations of England and other Protestant nations. It also contributed to the rise of democratic, liberal values which were to become incorporated into the idea of the national mission.

The poet John Milton inquired: 'Why else was this Nation chosen before any other, that out of her as out of Sion should be proclaimed and sounded forth the first tidings and trumpet of Reformation to all Europe?'[53] He identified the English people with the cause of individual liberty, symbolized by the ideas of the English Revolution of the seventeenth century. Oliver Cromwell appeared to be a great champion of liberty in the political sphere.

Although he regarded the causes of liberty, a free church, and a free state as supranational, Cromwell presided over the transition from religious medievalism to middle-class and trade interests in England and to the breakdown of absolutism. For a time he was able successfully to combine religious, political, and social aspects in an expanded notion of England's national mission.

The birth of English nationhood was inseparable from the rise of the middle classes. The new liberalism, optimism in man, unshakable faith in reason, and growing acquisitiveness that developed out of capitalism engendered a spirit of progress and self-assurance in the country. Writers considered the relations between government and society, and John Locke (1632–1704) understood the nation as the reign of law, government by consent, and the natural rights of man. In the *Treatises of Government*, he celebrated private property and its enjoyment in safety and security, and argued how liberty was founded upon property. Loyalty to a government was contingent on whether it was good, that is, if it provided legal security for private property. England's rise to conscious nationhood was linked with the state's role as guarantor of individual liberty and happiness. Kohn concluded: 'A nation had come into being, directing its own destiny, feeling responsible for it, and a national spirit permeated all institutions.'[54]

Many writers took up the task of defining Englishness. In the eighteenth century, the English statesman Lord Bolingbroke introduced the notions of patriotism and the patriot king – a fusion of traditional with more nationalist understandings of monarchy. In his essay 'Of National Character', Scottish philosopher David Hume asserted that mixed government and the freedom enjoyed by all classes and religions combined to inhibit the emergence of a national character. The English 'of any people in the universe have the least of a national character, unless this very singularity may pass for such'.[55] Lacking in a readily-identifiable national character, subscribing to a low-key form of patriotism, and emphasizing individual liberties over collective interests seemed, paradoxically, to be the qualities that made England the first modern nation.

Russia

If England constituted the first modern nation in Europe, Russia represents one of the last to attain nationhood. Rather than resurrecting a distinct, historic identity that had been suppressed for three-quarters of a century, the collapse of the Soviet Union at the end of 1991 only intensified the search for a Russian national identity that never had time to emerge. This may appear surprising given that Russian peoples were converted to Christianity as early as 988. But uncertainties about identity were already embedded in Vladimir's conversion in that year. The Kievan Rus state that emerged was neither unambiguously proto-Russian nor Ukrainian. Russia's historical starting point is located in the capital of what is today a separate country.

This may for Americans be analagous to the American Revolution occurring in Toronto.

Under Ivan III (1440–1505) Muscovy Rus was turned into a centralized administrative state. In 1480 it was liberated from Mongol rule and during the reign of Ivan the Terrible it expanded eastward and southward into Siberia, Kazan, and Astrakhan. Ivan the Terrible was crowned Tsar in 1547 and established a system of autocracy that was to endure for four centuries. But Russia's Time of Troubles followed soon after the end of Ivan's reign and led to attempts by foreign rulers to seize the throne in Moscow. A new dynasty centered on the Romanov family came to the country's rescue. It gave Russia two of its greatest rulers, Peter the Great (1672–1725) and Catherine the Great (1729–96). Many historians consider that Russia would never have become a nation without these two monarchs. As Greenfeld writes: 'Two autocrats can be held directly responsible for instilling the idea of the nation in the Russian elite and awakening it to the potent and stimulating sense of national pride: these were Peter I and Catherine II'.[56] A Russian saying sums up their respective contributions: where Peter gave Russia a body, Catherine gave it a soul.

Many of Peter's reformist edicts began to use the notion of fatherland (*otechestvo*), symbolizing the expansion of the Russian state to subsume the uneducated and backward groups in society. Peter elevated the spoken Russian language to a new status, one more important than the written Old Slavonic used by the Orthodox church. But the emperor was attracted by the West and even considered making Dutch (he had served as a ship's apprentice in Holland for a time) an official language. Later, Catherine looked to the West, too, mostly to France and its *philosophes*. The language of her court was French but she made sure that she learned Russian as well. Both Peter and Catherine wanted Russia to become part of a modernizing Europe.

If these rulers created the structural conditions necessary for forging a Russian nation, it was the sizable nobility that was most receptive to the ideology of nationalism. 'The protracted crisis of identity within the nobility, similarly to the development in other countries, rendered this elite stratum sympathetic to the nationalist ideas that had been forcefully promoted by Russia's energetic despots, Peter and Catherine the Great.'[57] But just as it appeared that all key political actors in eighteenth-century Russia sided with the nationalist program, a schism broke out between those who saw the path to greatness as having to be modelled on the West, and those who were certain Russia's greatness lay in its indigenous attributes and institutions.

The latter tendency, usually called Slavophilism, was driven by what Greenfeld understood as *ressentiment*, or existential envy of the West:

> The recognition of Russia's inferiority led the sensitive Russians among the educated elite (and those were the people who both experienced the

crisis of noble identity most painfully and were the first to turn to national identity) to the realization that having the West as a model must inevitably result in self-contempt.[58]

Logic required that they take pride precisely in Russia not being Western, and some Slavophiles rejected altogether a European identity for the country. With its Orthodox church, Russia was seen as the last preserver of the original form of Christianity. Slavophiles also singled out the village commune, where individual identity was subsumed under a collective one, as a uniquely Russian institution that gave the nation superior organization over the West. Slavophiles were the greatest propagators of the Russian national idea which, Greenfeld tells us, consisted of a nation '(1) defined as a collective individual, (2) formed by ethnic, primordial factors such as blood and soil, and (3) characterized by the enigmatic soul, or spirit'. She added:

> The spirit of the nation resided in the 'people', but, rather paradoxically, was revealed through the medium of the educated elite, who, apparently, had the ability to divine it. The rejection of the common thinking individual, which expressed itself in the glorification of his opposite, the community, also led to the emphasis on special, uncommon individuals.

This explained how 'the adoration of the "people" frequently found its counterpart in elitism and contempt for the dumb masses.'[59]

Russia's efforts to identify with the West had many positive aspects, argued the Slavophiles' opponents, categorized as the Westernizers:

> It was the West, the encounter with the West, that ushered Russia into the new era in which it became aware of itself as a nation; it was Russia's originally successful incorporation into the West which gave its patriots the first reasons for national pride, and it was before the West that they experienced it.[60]

Russia's subsequent development as a nation has revealed the persistent tension between competing visions of its natural place in the community of nations. In the twentieth century, Bolsheviks were roughly divided into Slavophiles (Stalin, Brezhnev) and Westernizers (Trotsky, Gorbachev). Post-Soviet political leaders have disagreed about whether to reconstruct 'Fortress Russia' or to integrate into the Western political and economic order. But there is an even more fundamental debate about the meaning of Russian national identity, as Svetlana Boym has noted: 'There is still, in present-day Russia, a great urge to find a single, all-embracing narrative – national, religious, historic, political, or aesthetic – to recover the single dramatic plot with devils and angels, black and white swans, hangmen and victims, that would explain Russia's Past, Present, and Future.'[61]

The Westphalian state system

I have sought to tease out the many factors that promoted the formation of separate nations in Europe. The process of nation formation, whether in Catherine's Russia or in France under the ancien regime, owed considerably to the influence of the Enlightenment. Kohn was emphatic about the connection:

> The era of Enlightenment which spread with French influence witnessed the height of cosmopolitanism and the beginnings of nationalism; the exaltation of the individual and a new sense of national unity; an enthusiastic faith in the future and an awakening of interest in the past of the peoples, their customs and folkways; an unquestioning acceptance of reason as the guiding principle of man and world and an appeal to the forces of the heart.[62]

Mark Juergensmeyer went further in stressing the distinctiveness of the Enlightenment, asserting 'I prefer to speak not of one "Western civilization" but of two: Christendom and Modernism. The former refers to social and political values shaped by Christianity, and the second to those values shaped by the Enlightenment and the secular philosophic tradition labeled "Philosophia"'.[63] Over time, Christendom's universalist project fell victim to Modernism's interest in peoples and their folkways.

The coupling of the Enlightenment's noble project with the energy and exhilaration of nationalism seemed to justify optimism in future political development. Unfortunately, as David Miller summarized, '[n]ations are hugely unequal in their capacity to provide for their own members'.[64] A new axis of conflict arose at the same time that old ones were being made obsolete.

At the beginning of the seventeenth century the national states of Western Europe continued to regard themselves as parts of one Christian polity. The unity of Christian Europe remained considerably stronger than any of the national divisions that had appeared. With the Treaty of Westphalia in 1648, concluded to provide protection for the individual state or principality, a balance of power system, or 'just equilibrium', was established. The notion of sovereignty became important but had unexpected consequences. Alfred Cobban explained:

> The rise of the idea of sovereignty was not altogether favorable to the continued growth of nation states.... It emphasized the rights of government, and so intensified the process of unification in nation states which were already set in that path; but it also militated against the development of the process where different political entities prevailed, as in the petty states of Germany and Italy, or the great dynastic empire of the

Habsburgs. The process of formation of nation states therefore experienced a setback at the end of the Middle Ages, from which it did not recover until the nineteenth century.[65]

Without the glow of religious or nationalist sentiment the state was a 'cold monster'. The state began to emancipate itself from the church, leading to a depoliticization of religion and, related to this, an end to the threat of renewed religious wars. *Raison d'etat* – the interests of the state – formed the rationale for state actions. In an effort to impose some order on the emergent state system, Hugo Grotius elucidated an early version of international law.[66]

In his influential book *Imagined Communities*, Benedict Anderson highlighted the contrast between the murky contours of the state before the seventeenth century and its status today:

> In the modern conception, state sovereignty is fully, flatly, and evenly operative over each square centimetre of a legally demarcated territory. But in the older imagining, where states were defined by centers, borders were porous and indistinct, and sovereignties faded imperceptibly into one another. Hence, paradoxically enough, the ease with which pre-modern empires and kingdoms were able to sustain their rule over immensely heterogeneous, and often not even contiguous, populations for long periods of time.[67]

With the Westphalia peace, etatism crowded out nationalism, the dynasty took the place of religion, and loyalty was transferred to the prince. The state became the maker of nations and national identities, not the other way around. As Anthony Smith noted about England and France, many scholars argued that

> in these and other cases the state actually 'created' the nation, that its activities of taxation, conscription and administration endowed the population within its jurisdiction with a sense of their corporate identity and civic loyalty.... The extension of citizenship rights and the build-up of an infrastructure that linked distant parts of the realm and vastly increased the density of communication networks with the state borders drew more and more areas and classes into the national political arena and created the images of national community.[68]

The state also began to control economic life. Mercantilism was an economic theory that recognized wealth as an instrument of state power. It was an economic counterpart of political etatism in that its aim was to increase the greatness of the nation, not just the profits of its merchant class. Mercantilism served as the ideological framework within which intense competition between European states took place.

Earlier we referred to the equivocal relationship between language and nation. Before the era of general primary education, it was difficult to identify spoken national languages. The literary idiom was confined to a small group and, as Anderson put it, 'a particular script-language offered privileged access to ontological truth'.[69] While administrative vernaculars were in use prior to the sixteenth century, Anderson hypothesized: 'nothing suggests that any deep-seated ideological, let alone proto-national, impulses underlay this vernacularization where it occurred'.[70] Print capitalism created 'languages-of-power', 'unified fields of exchange and communication', and 'that image of antiquity so central to the subjective idea of the nation'.[71] The mythical language of the *Volk*, as Herder would write about, had not come into existence, but it had been given a kick-start. Anderson concluded: 'the convergence of capitalism and print technology on the fatal diversity of human language created the possibility of a new form of imagined community, which in its basic morphology set the stage for the modern nation'.[72]

But the process of linguistic unification was still very incomplete. As late as 1789, for example, half of all Frenchmen could not speak French, and even though efforts were undertaken to develop a standardized idiom out of a multiplicity of spoken dialects, in 1863 more than one-fifth of schoolchildren in France did not understand French and one-half still considered it to be a foreign language.[73] Moreover, which dialect was chosen as the basis for a national language was often arbitrary. In the illuminating case of Norway, Landsmal (or Nynorsk), based on a number of local dialects, was promoted in reaction to the excessively-Danicized Riksmaal – the language spoken by two-thirds of the population and used by writers such as Knut Hamsun, Henrik Ibsen, and Sigrid Undset in the late nineteenth century. A language could be grafted onto a nationality, therefore, as a result of an arbitrary political decision rather than of a natural, historical process. Counterintuitively, such a grafted language could actually consolidate the nation-building process.

It is spurious, then, to view language as the primary determinant of nationhood. Myth-making about language may in some cases be as important as the language itself in shaping a nation's history. Taking issue with Irish poet Seamus Heaney's supposed cultural nationalism underpinning a Gaelic revival, one writer contended: 'The hankering after a lost state of monoglossia, a period when linguistic purity represented most clearly, and indeed guaranteed, cultural purity, was ... a common reflex of nationalism. In particular the lamenting references to an epic golden age when language and land were tied together in easy unity is a familiar rhetorical trope of this type of thinking.'[74] Another essayist argued how '[t]he one big advantage of speaking Dutch or Danish, or even German or Bengali, is that one is forced to be proficient in at least one other language if one is going to function in the modern world'.[75] Political and cultural ideas can carry as much weight as language in forging and preserving a nation.

A new way to nationhood: the US

It was in America that many of the European ideals of the age of Enlightenment were put into practice. In 1770 Abbe Raynal praised the liberty, religious tolerance, and prosperity of the inhabitants of the British colonies. The English tradition of liberty, rational laws, and active participation by everyone in the commonweal brought prosperity to the colonists and a new sense of nationhood. The colonies revolted less because they were oppressed and more because they wanted to expand the considerable freedoms they had already acquired. The revolution was the result less of a reaction to English tyranny and more because the settlers were already among the freest of people.

Several key factors shaped the character of the new nation that arose from among the English colonies of North America. The English tradition of common law and constitutional liberties was one. The colonists stressed rational, universal, natural rights that had originated in English political thought, for example, in the writings of Thomas Paine. The arrival of immigrants from the continent, of lower class background and a multiplicity of religions, inhibited the growth of class or religious hierarchy. Many were from nations that had an antipathy towards England, such as the Irish, Scots, and Germans. Initially the diverse background of settlers held back the process of integration as local loyalties, creeds, and racial strains remained influential. In the 1770s there was little territorial unity and the different colonies remained separated politically.

The Puritan spirit in America evoked comparisons with the ancient Israelites. Even though it resonates with hyperbole, the struggle for civic liberty against an oppressive colonial power did engender a new nation that was the product of the will of its people, not the result of common ancestry, loyalty to a monarch, nor geographic compactness. In the process Americans also emancipated themselves from their own European past. Benjamin Franklin eloquently testified to this: 'Here individuals of all nations are melted into a new race of men, whose labors and posterity will one day cause great changes in the world.'[76]

Because of its diversity, a centralizing power was required to maintain American federalism. Alexander Hamilton strove to create strong national government which would guarantee the United States 'a national character and policy'. The new constitution overcame the isolationism of the 13 colonies and created the basis for commerce and prosperity. It also forged a nation based on truths held 'to be self-evident, that all men are created equal, that they are endowed by their Creator with certain unalienable Rights, that among those are Life, Liberty and the Pursuit of Happiness'.

Thomas Jefferson gave the new nation an ideological foundation to complement political independence. Opposing conservative groups which wanted to reinstitute the rigid social order of European states, he advocated a new egalitarianism and popular democracy. A representative of the liberal, humanist nationalism of the eighteenth century, Jefferson stressed public allegiance to the national idea as the prerequisite for the nation's existence. His patriotism was devoid of exclusiveness and stressed the strength of diversity. As a southerner he shared the views of northern advocates of emancipation in stopping the future importation of slaves, and he also supported a liberal, humanitarian policy towards the native Indian peoples. Identifying agriculture as the foundation of the new nation's economic life, he cherished the ideal of self-contained communities imbibed with civic virtue and moral happiness. For Jefferson, America's nationhood also had universal significance. Its form of government was 'a standing monument and example for the aim and the imitation of the people of other countries'.[77]

No nation is created exclusively as a result of the existence of a national language but, in the end, few can do without one. Noah Webster sought to develop an American language and an American fashion. This was the converse of the process in Europe where culture and ideology had preceded national independence.

This American nationalism infused with the spirit of the Enlightment was rattled by the war of 1812. A more aggressive, imperial nationalism appeared, reflected in James Madison's stark exhortation to conquer Canada because it involved 'a mere matter of marching'. This second war against Britain raised Americans' consciousness of their nationality, even though their new capital, Washington, was burned down and their armies driven out of Canada.

Both wars against Great Britain, together with the civil war of 1861–65, consolidated American nationhood, as well as its borders, in a way consistent with Michael Howard's assertion: 'It is hard to think of any nation-state, with the possible exception of Norway, that came into existence before the middle of the twentieth century which was not created, and had its boundaries defined, by wars, by internal violence, or by a combination of the two.'[78]

American nationhood did not develop in a purely linear fashion, however. The result of the civil war was renewed political unification, but its causes had revealed how the American nation-building project had fallen apart less than a century after independence. With hindsight, it is possible to claim that the civil war and reconstruction forged a stronger sense of nation. At the time, it was just the opposite view that prevailed.

Economic interests shaped American nationalism from the outset of the republic. With time the Jeffersonian ideal of self-contained, self-governing rural communities was seen as a fetter on the development of a strong national economy. Hamilton's advocacy of manufacture, commerce, and tariffs was a better basis for the creation of a strong economy. American economic nationalism was spurred by the Napoleonic wars which cut the continents off from each other.

The conquest of the west after 1815 marked a phase of rapid imperial expansion. Mass killings and cleansing of Indians, in the view of some historians, was almost genocidal in scope.[79] In turn, the Louisiana purchase reflected both secret diplomacy and anti-democratic methods: inhabitants – many French-speaking with a distinct culture and lifestyle – were never asked their opinion about annexation.[80] Wars with Mexico led to further territorial conquests. In defense of the US, citizens in the new territories generally shared in the equality and freedom obtaining in the expanding country.

In contrast to European nation-making, then, the American nation arose not as the product of natural factors of blood or soil, nor as a product of shared memories. It was based on a universal idea, which meant that everyone could be included in it. We are well aware of the widespread impact that the American Revolution had on many other countries. The political and national awakening of the French nation followed closely on the heels of the American Declaration of Independence. In Central Europe, Poland attempted to stave off partition by drafting a democratic constitution in 1792 in the spirit of the American document. Writing of Poland, Jean-Jacques Rousseau believed that large independent states with recognizable national communities had the right to remain independent: 'It is making fools of people to tell them seriously that one can at one's pleasure transfer peoples from master to master, like herds of cattle, without consulting their interests or their wishes.'[81] This, too, was one of the lessons learned from the American experience of building a nation.

The French Revolution and liberal nationalism

Up to the eighteenth century and, in some parts of the world beyond it, nations had become equated with kingdoms or principalities whose subjects were identified by their loyalty to a dynasty. Cobban noted how '[b]y the eighteenth century, in fact, most of the cultural and linguistic significance had been emptied out of the word nation. It merely meant the state considered from the point of view of the ruled rather than the ruler'.[82]

French political thinkers developed new ideas about government, its institutions, and the organization of nations. Where Voltaire stressed the importance of creating a civilized society based on a common sense of citizenship, Rousseau wrote that government had to be based on the general will, the people, thereby introducing the notion of popular sovereignty. He acknowledged the centrality of public education that underlay popular legitimate government. The state's role was to assure liberty and happiness for its inhabitants. But, conversely, the virtue of its citizens allowed the state to perform its role. Only from free states where each citizen felt an active responsibility for the commonweal could the state draw strength.

Liberty and justice formed the basis of the state for Rousseau, then, not the integrating force of nationalism. But he was a believer both in the rationalist secular state and in national civic feelings which bound individuals together in a community. For him, the merging of private individuality in the collective organism of a national state was the way to restore the original goodness of man. In distinct ways, Voltaire and Rousseau were precursors of nineteenth-century liberal nationalism.

The revolutionaries who overthrew Louis XVI did so in the name of the people, the French nation. Rousseau's followers hoped to achieve fraternity and unity by suppressing privilege and by invoking rights and liberties. For them, therefore, nationalism was both a revolutionary and democratic ideology. The equation 'nation = state = people' implied that many such nation-states would come into being as a consequence of popular self-determination. As the French Declaration of Rights of 1795 put it: 'Each people is independent and sovereign, whatever the number of individuals who compose it and the extent of the territory it occupies. This sovereignty is inalienable.'[83]

During the revolutionary and Napoleonic wars lasting from 1792 until 1815 France attacked and occupied many European countries. Napoleon's empire differed from that of Charlemagne or Charles V in that it was based on a Diocletian model, as Napoleon himself asserted: all conquered peoples were to introduce French laws and administration and pay tribute to France. The aim was the destruction of other nations even though Napoleon announced – and many Europeans believed – that he was the champion of oppressed peoples. He assumed that, like religion (*cuius regio, eius religio*), national loyalty could be switched by the will of the emperor. One explanation for Napoleon's ruthlessness is that as a Corsican with a distinct accent, he was himself an outsider in France: 'At odds with the identity of his host nation, he drew on literature and art to forge his sense of reality.'[84] Not to mention military campaigns.

Of course the struggles of nations against invading Napoleonic armies reflected a national principle of their own. Most of the national movements of the nineteenth century – Italians, Germans, Poles, South Slavs, Greeks – were at least incidentally stimulated by and a response to revolutionary France and Napoleon. Next, nationalist ideas spread to Latin America, and in the early nineteenth century Simon Bolivar undertook the task of establishing the independence of New Grenada from Spain.

The explicitly political doctrine of nationalism thus emerged out of the French Revolution. For Carr, this second period of nationalism extended from Napoleonic times to the outbreak of the First World War in 1914. This period 'succeeded in delicately balancing the forces of "nationalism" and "internationalism"; for it established an international order or framework strong enough to permit of a striking extension and intensification of national feeling without disruption on any wide scale of regular and peaceful international relations.'[85] Kohn's remarks on the rise of nationalism in this period are also instructive: 'The great voices of former ages – Aquinas,

Erasmus, Voltaire – spoke for Christendom or Europe; Bentham, Rousseau and Kant were concerned with mankind; but in the nineteenth century the European society and the European mind lost the oneness of the preceding age and dissolved into conflicting groups and culture patterns.'[86]

A related explanation for the rise of nationalism was offered by Lord Bryce in 1901, when he linked it to the decline of religion. 'Nationality' was

> a sentiment comparatively weak in the ancient world and in the Middle Ages, and which did not really become a factor of the first moment in politics till the religious passion of the 16th and 17th centuries had almost wholly subsided, and the gospel of political freedom preached by the American and French Revolutionaries had begun to fire men's minds.[87]

Of primary importance for democrats in the nineteenth century was how sovereign people became entitled to a state that they would govern. For nationalists, it was how new political entities would be derived from the prior existence of distinct communities. Neither was a straightforward task. The 'ethnographers' nightmare', the often-cited case of Macedonia before the First World War, illustrated how complex a process creating states on the basis of the existence of nations was. On the other hand, regarding the nation as sovereign implied transferring a sacred, quasi-divine character to it from kings and centralized state authorities. After all, throughout the Middle Ages the state was conceived of as a divine institution in which the sovereign was God. For the nation to take on a sacred authority and mission was a quantum leap.

Agreeing with Walter Bagehot that 'nation-making' was the chief characteristic of nineteenth-century politics, Hobsbawn summed up the often-contradictory developments in the 'era of triumphant bourgeois liberalism' from 1830 to 1880:

> the European balance of power was transformed by the emergence of two great powers based on the national principle (Germany and Italy), the effective partition of a third on the same grounds (Austria-Hungary after the Compromise of 1867), not to mention the recognition of a number of lesser political entities as independent states claiming the new status as nationally based peoples, from Belgium in the west to the Ottoman successor states in southeast Europe (Greece, Serbia, Romania, Bulgaria), and two national revolts of the Poles demanding their reconstitution as what they thought of as a nation-state.[88]

In 1848 democratic nationalist uprisings occurred among Czechs, Danes, Hungarians, Germans, and Italians, while Poles rose up against Russian rulers in 1831 and 1863. Historian John Breuilly was drawn to the contrast between the 'unification nationalism' of Germans, Italians, and Poles, and the 'separatist nationalism' of peoples subjugated to the Habsburg or Ottoman empires: Czechs, Hungarians, Romanians, Serbs, Bulgarians, and Greeks.[89]

In the year the civil war broke out in the United States, Italy became a unified state, the process only completed in 1870 with the inclusion of Rome. Giuseppe Mazzini (1805–72) believed that the small nations of Europe would be merged into or federated with larger ones. Italy, like Germany and the Slavs, was expected to form such a federation. As important as political unity was for Mazzini, it was his emphasis on moral unity that caused him to be regarded as a champion of democracy throughout much of Europe. As one historian wrote of Mazzini's contribution:

> There was nothing exclusive about Mazzini's nationalism: for him, the different national questions were essentially interdependent. Each nation had to discover its own special interests, aptitudes and functions in order to perform its particular 'mission' in the general cause of humanity. When all nations had been freed, a 'United States of Europe' would become possible and desirable. Mazzini was accepted as the prophet of nationalism not only in Italy but throughout Europe, and as far away as India.[90]

It was unfortunate but telling, then, that when Cavour realized Italian unity, Mazzini, as a republican, democrat, and advocate of a new republican Rome, was outraged that the nation had been unified under a king.

As elsewhere, the 1848 revolution in Germany was aimed at achieving political liberty and national unity. It was largely peaceful and stressed cooperation with other oppressed nations, thereby displaying little trace of the aggressive nationalism that appeared with Bismarck. By contrast, the German state that united 39 smaller states in 1871 was less a product of the desire for unity or popular sovereignty than a result of Bismarck's statecraft and the victories of the Prussian army over Austria in 1866 and France in 1871. As Kohn wrote, Bismarck 'was not, as Cavour was, a moderate liberal and a parliamentary constitutionalist but a conservative without any high regard for parliamentary institutions'.[91]

In Hungary, recognized in 1867 as a constituent part of a dual monarchy with Austria, the drive for cultural unity followed statehood – just the reverse of other nations where cultural unity was a given but statehood was not. It was symbolized by the semantic creativity found in the 1868 Hungarian law of nationalities: 'All citizens of Hungary form a single nation – the indivisible unitary Magyar nation – to which all citizens of the country, irrespective of nationality, belong.'[92] This ingenuity has been appropriated into the discourse of multiculturalism over a century later.

Why was it that in such a short period so many nations were able to attain statehood? For Anderson, many of the nationalisms that produced independent states in this period were modelled on American and French precedents. Therefore, they constituted 'reactionary, secondary modelling'.[93] Existing empires decided that they, too, might 'appear attractive in national drag' and adopted nationalist policies.[94] Thus, ' "Official nationalism" – willed merger of nation and dynastic empire ... developed *after*, and *in reaction to*, the popular national movements proliferating in Europe since the 1820s.'[95]

The tsarist empire was a case in point. In 1832 Count Sergei Uvarov proposed to Tsar Nicholas that the empire should be based on the three principles of autocracy, orthodoxy, and nationality. If the first two dated back to the time of the house of Riurik, the third was novel and suggested that minority populations ruled over by the tsar should now be russified. This policy was only fully adopted late in the nineteenth century, though it was applied selectively earlier on to certain recalcitrant people, like the Poles. Official nationalism in Russia marked the ascendance of an illiberal variant of nationalism.

Nonetheless, influential, liberal-minded theorists on nationalism in this period included John Stuart Mill, William Gladstone, and Ernest Renan. In his *Considerations on Representative Government* (Chapter XVI) published in 1861, Mill defined the nation not by virtue of its possession of national sentiment but by the fact that its members 'desire to be under the same government, and desire that it should be government by themselves or a portion of themselves exclusively'.[96] British prime minister Gladstone asserted that

a new law of nations is gradually taking hold of the mind ... , a law which recognizes independence, which frowns upon aggression, which favors the pacific, not the bloody settlement of disputes, which aims at permanent and not temporary adjustments; above all, which recognizes, as a tribunal of paramount authority, the general judgment of civilized mankind.[97]

Renan was celebrated for his view of the nation as 'un plebiscite de tous les jours' – a daily vote in support of the nation. In his lecture, 'Qu'est ce que c'est une nation?' delivered in 1882, he also cautioned that '[g]etting its history wrong is part of being a nation'.[98]

These liberal conceptions stood in stark contrast to the official nationalism beginning to emerge on the continent. The European state system was largely frozen in place between 1871 and 1914 and, outside the Balkans, the only change in the system was Norway's constitutional break with Sweden in 1905. Established powers were bent on protecting their acquired international rights and status from so-called subnational challenges.

The ascendance of economic and illiberal nationalisms

Hobsbawn inquired whether it was 'historically fortuitous that the classic era of free trade liberalism coincided with that "nation-making" which Bagehot saw as so central to his century?'[99] His own belief was that the nation-state performed specific functions in capitalist development. From the sixteenth to eighteenth centuries economic development had been based on territorial states that pursued mercantilist policies. Governments treated national economies as entities to be developed by state policy. But in mid-eighteenth-century France, the physiocrats, such as Quesnay (personal physician to Louis XV), began to question the assumptions of mercantilism. Their philosophy highlighted instead the role of the individual and of private property and, following the ideas of Voltaire and Rousseau, proposed universal general education in order to ensure propitious conditions for a new moral and economic order.

Economics was considered to be governed by its own set of natural laws, the most important being that of supply and demand. Mercantilism, with its authoritarian, statist character, seemed outdated and at odds with the new spirit of liberty and individualism. Most importantly, it had become a fetter on economic growth. Where the government refrained from regulating commercial activity and accepted *laissez-faire*, the new theory went, economic growth was promoted most efficiently.

The publication of Adam Smith's *The Wealth of Nations* in 1776 provided the most persuasive critique of the shaky mercantilist system and, conversely, advocacy of free market and free trade. Smith viewed political economy as based on the commonweal of the whole nation and on cooperation among citizens organized through a division of labor. Economics could not be limited to serving the interest of one particular social class. Smith argued that economic freedom was more productive than state regulation and that competition was preferable to monopoly. The economic interests of all nations were best served through a free exchange of commodities. Thus liberal economic views did not begrudge a nation its greater wealth, resources, or civilization and would not countenance wars on these grounds. Niebuhr appropriately called Smith a 'liberal imperialist' who believed that a just imperial structure could come to pass.[100]

The call for free market and free trade to determine economic relations produced a nationalist reaction. The French political economist Gustave de Molinari held that 'the fragmentation of humanity into nations is useful, inasmuch as it develops an extremely powerful principle of economic emulation.'[101] List was Germany's best exponent of the view that the national economy was to 'accomplish the economic development of the nation'.[102] The Canadian John Rae in 1834 wrote *The Sociological Theory of Capital* that anticipated the import-substitution policies of third world states in the twentieth century. Federalist Alexander Hamilton linked nation, state, and economy in the United States and justified strong centralizing national government.

After the civil war in the US and the French–Prussian war of 1870–71, a renewed wave of protectionism swept across Europe. A principal reason for this was the strategic consideration that vital goods should be produced domestically, not imported. But List unabashedly argued that German national interests were best served if the world economy, effectively located on Lombard Street in the City of London, was undermined. This led directly to the German tariff regime of 1879. It was part of a nationalist, protectionist reaction against the growth of global interdependence in the second half of the nineteenth century. Nationalism had begun to slip out of the hands of its liberal creators.

Nationalism became the dominant form of political discourse as European societies were transformed at this time through the spread of literacy, primary education, and mass-circulation newspapers. An illiberal variant of nationalism – one often identified as the source for nationalism's nefarious consequences – spread rapidly. By the 1870s and 1880s the competing nationalisms of European states fuelled a drive for colonial expansion. The 1881 Berlin Conference that carved up Africa into possessions of the rival European powers symbolized the rise of imperialist nationalism.

The character of nationalism had thus changed. Hobsbawm listed three differences between the Mazzinian phase of nationalism and the variant of nationalism from 1880 to 1914 that led to the First World War. First, the threshold principle was discarded. In the classical period of liberal nationalism, this unofficial principle came into practice whereby only viable nations (whatever this meant) were considered entitled to self-determination.[103] National movements were expected to strive for state unification or expansion rather than to produce a proliferation of new states. The ethnic heterogeneity of states formed as a result of such expansion was justified because small and backward nations had everything to gain by being annexed by greater states (as with Melos in ancient Greece). Absorption of smaller peoples by larger ones was viewed as progress. If the threshold principle seemed to contain injustice, the post-Mazzinian form of nationalism had even more adverse consequences. Intolerance towards minority groups increased when the creation of small but illiberal states was countenanced. The idea that any self-proclaimed nation, however 'unhistorical', was entitled to self-determination and even a national state, proved ill-conceived.

This becomes clear when we consider the second change in the character of nationalism discerned by Hobsbawm. The criteria for nationhood shifted from a historical basis to ethnicity and language in a country, in this way becoming more exclusivist and primordial. The notion of citizenship being grounded on a national idea, as in the US, was inappropriate for the Europe of that time. For Hobsbawm, a third change followed from this. National sentiments became more aggressive and marked a turn to the political right.

The way the term nationalism was used in the last decade of the nineteenth century was to describe aggressive, exclusivistic, right-wing movements. From originally being associated with the goal of political liberty and democratic progressive ideals, nationalism increasingly turned attention to past national glory and demanded social cohesion, order, and stability in society.

During the last decades of the nineteenth century the growing socialist movement was confronted with the 'national question'. The dilemma for socialists was that as a movement seeking to make workers of all countries aware of their exploitation at the hands of capitalists, the call for the political independence of entire nations, also being exploited and oppressed but by empires – tsarist, Ottoman, Habsburg – weakened the appeal of socialism. Here we may note with Hobsbawm that '[t]he combination of social and national demands, on the whole, proved very much more effective as a mobilizer of independence than the pure appeal of nationalism, whose appeal was limited to the discontented lower middle classes.'[104]

In addition to right-wing groups, nationalism now also had a strong appeal to much of the cultural intelligentsia. The various national bourgeoisie were not indifferent to the state-building project, as socialists averred, but became actively engaged in it. Furthermore, factoring in social grievances with national ones reinforced general disaffection with the status quo. Given these circumstances, it is not surprising that some of the most nationalistic leaders of the interwar period, such as Mussolini and Pilsudski, began their political apprenticeship as members of socialist parties.

Perhaps it misjudged the importance of nationalism and national movements, but the international socialist movement energetically opposed the war fever that swept across many European states in 1914 and that ensured rapid mobilization of armies once war became imminent. Nationalism was not the primary cause of the First World War, but it was a force that sustained the war long after its senselessness had become apparent.

Nationalism before and after the Second World War

English historian Hobsbawm took issue with the view that associated nationalism with the political right rather than with the left. He contended that defending national interests was, paradoxically, most effectively promoted by the left throughout much of the twentieth century. Especially in the interwar years and with the rise of national socialism in Germany and of the Falangists in Spain, 'antifascist nationalism', as Hobsbawm termed it, was a significant feature of the socialist parties. Though the majority of scholars would probably disagree with him, Hobsbawm polemicized how '[n]ationalism thus acquired a strong association with the left during the antifascist period.'[105] His tentative conclusion about the subsequent period is perhaps less contentious: 'It may be argued that from the 1930s to the 1970s the dominant discourse of national emancipation echoed the theories of the left.'[106]

The historical record strongly suggests that it was not the left that championed national self-determination in Europe after the First World War but the unlikely person of US President Woodrow Wilson. One of his Fourteen Points, announced in 1918, was the principle of national self-determination. Through his encouragement and inspiration, in place of the disintegrating Habsburg, Russian, and Ottoman empires, new states came into being such as Finland, Czechoslovakia, and Yugoslavia. Hungary was established as a separate, if much reduced, state unconnected to Austria, and Poland became independent after 125 years under partitioning powers.

While this was not Wilson's intention, the principle of self-determination was seized upon by nationalist movements outside Europe. Nationalist uprisings took place in Egypt in 1919 and spread across the Middle East. The Anglo-Afghan war broke out in 1919 and in short order uprisings occurred in Central Asia, India, Indochina, and the Dutch East Indies. Anti-colonial, nationalist, and religious agendas were often inseparable, as in Indonesia, and had been formulated several decades earlier. But the beginnings of a worldwide anti-colonial movement were unmistakably clear in the 1920s, though several decades were to pass before the first independent states successfully shook off their European colonial powers.

The interwar years represented the third period of nationalism identified by Carr. He saw few redeeming features about the form that nationalism took at this time. Signs of nationalism's preponderance over internationalism were already evident in the 1870s, but the expansion of political citizenship within each nation, the linking of economic with political power, and the increase in the number of nations after 1918 'explain the aggravation of the evils of nationalism in our third period.' They 'combined to produce the characteristic totalitarian symptoms of our third period.'[107] Indeed, nationalism became so closely identified with totalitarian systems that such bitter ideological rivals as Hitler and Stalin were cast as German and Great Russian ultra-nationalists respectively. Certainly the instigator of the Second World War, Hitler, was committed to an extreme nationalist agenda emphasizing the purity of the Aryan race, the underclass of Jews, Gypsies, and Slavs that had to be destroyed, and the need for expanded living space for German citizens. The Second World War was the product of an extreme variant of nationalism, but it was not shared by most of the participating states.

The most remarkable achievement of nationalism after the war was an end to colonialism. In the late 1940s hundreds of millions of people in South Asia became citizens of independent states instead of subjects of the British Crown. In a second wave freeing hundreds of millions from rule by European metropoles, many independent states in Africa came into being beginning in the early 1960s. Competing nationalisms still fuelled wars between states – Iran and Iraq in the 1980s was a particularly great human tragedy – and within states – Bosnia and Rwanda in the early 1990s reached near-genocidal proportions. At the turn of the millenium nationalist assertion by minorities unnerved established Western democracies, as in Britain, Canada, and Spain to mention the most notable cases.

At the same time the ideas of nation and nationalism seemed anachronistic during accelerated processes of globalization and trans-migration. Arjun Appadurai explained:

> One major fact that accounts for strains in the union of nation and state is that the nationalist genie, never perfectly contained in the bottle of the territorial state, is now itself diasporic. Carried in the repertoires of increasingly mobile populations of refugees, tourists, guest workers, transnational intellectuals, scientists and illegal aliens, it is increasingly unrestrained by ideas of spatial boundary and territorial sovereignty.[108]

Benedict Anderson seemed to move from the notion of 'imagined communities' to 'counterfeit communities' when he described the symbolism of the modern passport:

> these documents have high truth claims. But they are also counterfeit in the sense that they are less and less attestations of citizenship, let alone of loyalty to a protective nation-state, than of claims to participate in labor markets. Portugese and Bangladeshi passports, even when genuine, tell us little about loyalty or habitus, but they tell us a great deal about the relative likelihood of their holders being permitted to seek jobs in Milan or Copenhagen.[109]

In Western immigration societies, state nationalism seemed to be giving way to transnationality.

This overview of the historical development of nations and national identity has made clear how lengthy the nation formation process was, how the criteria determining national identity were numerous and inconsistent, and how nationalism was transformed in less than two centuries from a positive and functional to a negative and dysfunctional political force. The challenge to nationalism from within comes, in today's postmodern era, from fragmented identities. Nationalism may adapt by embracing a more individualist conception of the nation. Or it may galvanize a backlash against postmodernity's dilution of the traditional understanding of the nation. It retains its central position as a point of reference for other constructions of identity.

2
Nationalisms Conceptually

No one questions the importance of nationalism in giving life to individual nations, securing them homelands, and affecting much of international politics.[1] Investigating what the term actually means has generated an enormous body of scholarship over the past century. Defining nationalism is problematic for two general reasons. First, there is such a variety and large number of theories concerned with nationalism. Second, the concept is closely connected to other terms like nation, nationality, nation-state, national identity, national self-determination, and ethnicity. Scholars disagree not only about the meaning of nationalism but how it is related to these other terms.

This chapter approaches nationalism conceptually. It reviews different definitions, typologies, and schools of nationalism. The focus is on the most influential frameworks developed to study the phenomenon.

The concept of nation

The term nation has been understood in two main ways in modern times – cultural nation (*Kulturnation*) and political nation (*Staatsnation*). Cultural nation emphasizes the spirit of community based on objective characteristics such as common heritage and language, a distinct territory, shared religion, customs, and history. Individuals have little or no choice as to which cultural nation they adhere to: membership in it is determined by nature and history. Generally a cultural nation precedes the establishment of a state; the experience of Italy – precocious culturally, a latecomer politically – serves as a vivid example.

The transition to political nation occurs when a nation identifies political objectives and develops statist ideas.[2] A political nation is one based on shared political will, political values, citizenship, and loyalty and affection for the nation.[3] This is what the French historian Renan had in mind when, in his famous 1882 lecture '*Qu'est-ce qu'une nation?*' ('What is a nation?') he described it as a 'daily plebiscite'. The population of a territory must regard itself as a nation and, in addition, equate citizenship with nationality.[4]

A constructivist approach to the emergence of a nation stresses the centrality of people willing a nation to exist. At a minimum, a nation emerges 'when a significant number of people in a community consider themselves to form a nation, or behave as if they formed one'.[5] But greater proof of citizens' commitment may be required, so a stricter definition may be that '[a] nation is a socially mobilized body of individuals who believe themselves united by some set of characteristics that differentiate them (in their own minds) from outsiders and who strive to create or maintain their own state.'[6] The threshold for a political nation to exist is higher: there must be a general desire among its members to be politically independent or autonomous.[7] This quality of a nation distinguishes it from ethnic groups, such as 'hyphenate Americans' (e.g. Irish-Americans) in the United States and their counterparts in other countries. This political will 'separates states that are demographically diverse (the United States) from states that are nationally divided like Cyprus and Sri Lanka'.[8] Where the USA is ethnically diverse and calls itself multicultural while insisting on the existence of a single American nation, Cyprus (Greeks and Turks), Sri Lanka (Sinhalese and Tamils), and many countries in the world consist of two or more nations making it impossible to refer to one nation, one state (and therefore a nation-state).

The nation-making histories of France, England, and the USA illustrate how the political nation comes into being. Political developments in the eighteenth and nineteenth centuries transformed the nation into 'a community of politically aware citizens equal before the law irrespective of their social and economic status, ethnic origin and religious beliefs'.[9] In a political nation, nation and state seem to converge. A unified nation-state is founded upon common citizenship, a common judicial and administrative system, a central government, and the shared political value of popular sovereignty.[10]

Distinguishing between cultural and political nations has to be done circumspectly. For example, if one uses the cultural nation approach, then Alsatians and Silesians are part of the German cultural nation because of their culture, history, and language. If instead the political nation idea is used, then Alsatians must be regarded as French 'because of their desire to be citizens of the French state with which they have felt close ties since the Revolution of 1789 and the Napoleonic era, if not before'.[11] Silesians consider themselves 'autochtones' but nevertheless citizens of Poland or the Czech Republic.

The marker between the political and cultural nation is also obscured in situations where one political nation includes many cultural ones, not all of which willingly swear allegiance to the political nation. An overwhelming majority of states in the world today is multinational and incorporates more than one cultural nation. Nearly all former colonies in Africa and Asia, but also Western liberal democracies like Belgium, Canada, and Switzerland are multinational. Moreover, even in less contested historical examples of the political nation such as France, a lengthy process of cultural assimilation was promoted by the state by way of such policies as linguistic and judicial uniformity.[12] An ideological dimension exists as well: the French state claims that no national minorities live there despite the presence of Basques, Bretons, and Corsicans in the metropole country. Various European conventions that have tried to define what minorities are only reveal the complex and controversial nature of the subject.[13] In 1999 the French government adopted less than half of the 98 provisions of the European Charter on Regional and Minority Languages, effectively denying speakers of Alsatian, Breton, Corsican, Occitane, and Provençal *inter alia* rights to schooling or local radio and television programming in these languages. When a year later a government minister proposed an unprecedented expansion of political autonomy for Corsica, criticism came from all parts of the political spectrum.

Sometimes states come into existence before there is a political nation. In newer states found in the developing world and some former Soviet republics, '[n]ot only do groups claiming the status of nation seek states, but polities claiming the status of state also seek nations.'[14] States may proclaim the existence of nations in the hope that this will prove to be self-fulfilling. One historian thus wrote of 'invented nations' which had 'an assertive, self-worshiping, and aggrandizing nationalism'.[15] Were such invented nations peculiar to the third world? The answer is no: alongside indisputably ethnically-heterogeneous states like Brazil and Indonesia, countries like the USA and Israel could also be included. All of them required 'acts of mental invention of a mythic common past, usually glorious but sometimes persecuting, and suppression of the "sub-nations", units smaller than a nation'.[16]

The idea of nationality

Most scholars regard nationality as a recent development that evolved out of the French Revolution. But they disagree whether nationality is based primarily on political,[17] economic,[18] cultural,[19] or a combination of all factors.[20] Usually the state is regarded as the instrument enabling nationality to emerge. Kohn contended that

> statehood or nationhood (in the sense of common citizenship under one territorial government) is a constitutive element in the life of a nationality. The condition of statehood need not be present when a nationality originates; but in such a case (as with the Czechs in the late eighteenth century) it is always the memory of a past state and the aspiration toward statehood that characterizes nationalities in the period of nationalism.[21]

The great nineteenth-century sociologist Emile Durkheim, too, stressed the existence of a separate state as a crucial determinant of nationality, defined as 'a group [with common cultural attributes] whose members wish to live under the same laws and form a state'.[22]

Not all scholars agree that the state is needed for nationality to emerge. A nationality may simply see itself as an ethnic minority and desire nothing more than to obtain recognition and respect as an independent community. It need not 'seek to wield political power in its own separate state, but [only] strive for cultural and political autonomy within a broader state framework'.[23] There is a crucial psychological dimension to nationality, therefore, which distinguishes it from the nation. Nations and nationalities may share similar cultural attributes but 'in the former the specific "will to live" as a nation is lacking: this will must exist at one time or another if a national group is to become a nationality'.[24]

The psychological and emotional understanding of nationality owes much to the work of psychologists and psychoanalysts, including Sigmund Freud. In 1917 he introduced the notion of 'narcissism of minor differences' to highlight how husband and wife, parent and child, and neighboring town or nation become highly sensitized to the ways in which one differs from the other.[25] More recently psychiatrist and political psychologist Vamik Volkan developed this idea further: 'When the neighbor is our enemy and is tinged with our unwanted parts, we do not want to acknowledge any likeness to us. Therefore, we focus on minor differences-or create them-in order to stress dissimilarity and the existence of a gap between us.'[26] Representations of the other thus help define one's own nationality: 'At bottom, ethnicity and nationality are made up of those reservoirs that contain self- and object images . . . and their accompanying raw emotions.'[27]

Nationality, then, is 'the consciousness on the part of members of a group that they belong to that group and the gathering of a large number of different emotional dispositions round that group as their object or nucleus'.[28] As historian Arnold Toynbee concluded, nationality ultimately involves 'a subjective psychological feeling in a living people'.[29]

Closely related to nationality when it is treated as subjective and psychological feeling is patriotism, literally, love for one's fatherland.[30] During successive stages of social development, the concept of patriotism was 'extended in application from one's native locality to one's political country, from an immediate *place* to the *person* of a military or political leader, and thence to the *idea* of a state'.[31] In contemporary usage, '[w]henever the power of the nation is invoked – whether it be in the media, in scholarly texts, or in everyday conversation – we are more likely than not to find it couched as a *love of country*: an eroticized nationalism.'[32]

Patriotism's fusion with the idea of nationality did not occur until early modern times and the French embrace of the term *la patrie*. That changed the nature of patriotism from local sentiment and pride to loyalty towards one's nationality and national state.[33] Today, patriotism has an exclusively positive connotation, but in its exaggerated form it can lapse into chauvinism, an excessive and even obsessive kind of parochialism fixated on one's own nation.

The concept of the nation-state

A parsimonious definition of a nation-state is the congruence of the state – 'a legal concept describing a social group that occupies a defined territory and is organized under common political institutions and an effective government' – and the nation – 'a social group which shares a common ideology, common institutions and customs, and a sense of homogeneity'.[34] The nation-state 'is, in theory, the natural outgrowth of a nation's desire to have and maintain its own state and to govern itself independently'.[35] If the nation serves as the natural psychological home for a people, the state acts as its physical home. English sociologist Anthony Giddens has reiterated that nationalism accords psychological meaning in a detraditionalized world but it also plays a functional role in legitimizing the modern nation-state.[36] Many symbols represent the nation-state: the flag, the national anthem, and various state symbols – lions and dragons, eagles and cockerels, beavers and bears, thistles and daffodils, crosses and crescents, sun, moon, stars and, where there is a monarchy, crowns. Rhetorical pointing, or deixis, accompanies this symbolism: 'The deixis of homeland invokes the national "we" and places "us" within "our" homeland.'[37] Deixis acts, then, as a 'homeland-making language'.

The assumptions underlying the nation-state are that: 1) the world is 'naturally' divided into distinct nations based on identifiable objective and subjective attributes; and 2) states are the 'natural' political embodiments of nations. But in practice the nation-state is more a construct than a reflection of nature. For a start, as Walker Connor pointed out, '[a] nation may form a part of a state, may be coterminous with a state, or may extend beyond the borders of a single state.'[38] As long as a nation is coterminous with a state, we can call it a nation-state, although the number of such states is very small. Japan is a rare example of a preponderantly homogeneous state. Most states in the world incorporate several nations and should properly be termed 'multination-states'.

A second divergence from the ideal-type nation-state is that many nations overspill state borders. Many Serbs live outside Yugoslavia, a substantial number of Irish Catholics live in Northern Ireland and not the Republic, many Tutsis live beyond Rwanda, and many millions of South Asian Muslims live in India, not Pakistan. Perhaps the best example of what can be called a transnational group are the Kurds, who have no state of their own but form sizable minority populations in Turkey, Iraq, and Iran (not to mention Germany).

Finally, if the state is really the embodiment of the nation, as the concept of nation-state suggests, then we should expect the development of nations to precede the establishment of states. In many parts of the world, notably in Asia and Africa, state-building preceded nation-building. Colonization created states with artificial borders and did not take into account patterns of settlement of national groups, let alone ascertain what their political aspirations were. Two of the largest such creations were Nigeria and Indonesia, home to many diverse peoples. When political movements were organized within these colonies to bring about independence, they were anti-colonial rather than nationalist. These movements were more a function of colonial exploitation and dominance than an expression of the political will of the many nations taking part in them. Decolonization changed the relations of power between colonizers and colonized, but it did not change state boundaries. The result was the persistence of state structures encompassing different tribal, ethnic, and national groups which found little to bind them once independence was achieved. Thus the new independent states were born with a lack of internal cohesion, with civil discord and regime instability, and with cultural production not matching the nation-building objective.[39] The most recent round of decolonization came with the collapse of the Soviet Union. Especially in Central Asia, state borders had little in common with patterns of settlement of different groups. In sum, the term nation-state is almost an oxymoron.

The concept of national identity

Nationalism is often confounded with national identity. It is revealing that the main theme running through Anthony Smith's book *National Identity* is nationalism.[40] The two concepts are interrelated, though the author insists that they are not interchangeable: '*nationalism*, the ideology and movement, must be closely related to *national identity*, a multidimensional concept, and extended to include a specific language, sentiments, and symbolism'.[41] A more nuanced distinction between the two has been drawn by Ulf Hedetoft who began by asserting:

> Nationalism leaves the question of 'how' and 'why' someone might have acquired national identification open, and hence also the question of free will; whereas national identity is the postulate of an inexorable and inevitable common destiny, glued to citizens as a fact of nature, and normatively determining their loyalties and moral sentiments. National identity poses as fact and as explanation simultaneously.[42]

Hedetoft elaborates:

> Where nationalism – as a feature of mentality – is an attitude and possibly an emotion rooted in the merger between oneself and one's nation-state within the categories of allegiance, loyalty, and representation, ie, being

partial towards one's nation, seeing oneself as a representative of it, relating affirmatively to the national interest, possibly even feeling proud of one's nation, – there national identity goes further: it 'argues' for a deep, existential, naturalist bonding between citizens of a particular country along the lines of the 'ius sanguinis' (the right of blood) and within the firm circumference of a common cosmology of natural values; the formal elements of nationalism here assign national features to individuals as their personal characteristics and, thus, as a kind of preordained subjective personal destiny, morality, behaviour, and phenotypical traits.[43]

Another conceptualization of national identity stresses its tangible, material, ontological character. Political geographers highlight the importance of spatial identities to national ones: 'territory clarifies national identity by sharpening more ambiguous cultural and ethnic markers. Over time, as a group occupies and narrates a particular territory, a transformation occurs. Instead of the group defining the territory, the territory comes to define the group'.[44]

National identity is only one type of collective identity. Another is gender, which has an influence on national identity. Cynthia Enloe persuasively argued that 'nationalism has typically sprung from masculinized memory, masculinized humiliation and masculinized hope'.[45] Maja Korac added that '[n]otions of nation, people, state, and national history are male structured and defined. They imply a notion of patriarchal brotherhood and solidarity. Thus, thinking about ethnicity almost always takes place in a male-defined mould.'[46] The novelist Virginia Woolf made a more bombastic and perhaps pretentious claim: 'as a woman I have no country. As a woman I want no country. As a woman my country is the whole world'.[47]

Another collective identity is socio-economic, in particular, class. It has been discredited since the collapse of the Marxist project and, except for sociologists, receives little attention today.[48] Local and regional identities are also salient to national identity: 'Living somewhere means being exposed to the continuous stream of discourse produced by a local society *and* experiencing events which differ in kind from those happening elsewhere in the world.'[49] Territorial, religious, linguistic, and ethnic identities are also collective and shape national identity. Indeed, it may be best to speak of 'nested identities' shared by citizens in varying degrees.[50]

National identity is part fiction. As one specialist asserted, '[i]t is precisely because of the mythical or imaginary elements in national identity that it can be reshaped to meet new challenges and new needs.'[51] A novel by Julian Barnes, *England, England*, described how replicating and drawing excessively on the past can create a new and separate historical reality and, with it, identity. The book tells of the construction of the Project – a fantasy England on the Isle of Wight bringing together everything people used to think of as

England.[52] The effect is to produce a kitsch national identity, but an identity all the same. In 'Letters from London', Barnes had already noted how Margaret Thatcher had 'represented and successfully appealed to a strong and politically disregarded form of Englishness'. It was by appealing to the past that she was able successfully to abolish it.[53] A 'theme park' national identity must be distinguished from its reality, but in a commercialized world it is not as outrageous as it seems.

We can ask whether national identity can be natural at all:

> While undoubtedly the repository of distinctive collective experiences, it is finally an invention, involving the establishment of opposites and 'others' which are used as yardsticks for self-definition. National identity is a fluid entity, where categorization of 'self' or of 'other', inclusion and exclusion, is an arena of contest between competing groups and institutions within society.[54]

Many writers have remarked upon how in the 1990s a widespread perception existed, in Europe and beyond, of neglected or suppressed identities, with the centralized state invariably to blame. Not only in former communist states but also in Western Europe identities were being rediscovered or re-invented: 'a good many of the European ethno-nationalisms (for example, the Catalan, Basque, Breton, Scots, Welsh, and Flemish movements) were pre-war in origin, with cultural antecedents reaching back in some cases to the 1880s'.[55] National identity thus involves a process of self-definition, and one of the principal ways to carry this out is to use archaeological evidence. Until the nineteenth century, archaeology's role had been merely anecdotal but the rise of nationalism in Europe assigned to it a new task. 'If nationalist claims, especially claims to territory once occupied and now lost, were to be based on the antiquity and longevity of occupation, then only archaelogy could supply the proof.'[56] It could also provide evidence for myths of origin, ancestry, golden ages, and migration.

Anxiety about national identity can sometimes make the waging of war functional. Psychiatrist Vamik Volkan described how 'members of a large group may consider killing a threatening neighbor rather than endure the anxiety caused by losing their psychological borders and having holes in the canvas of their ethnic tent'. The problem is that a group in this position resembles the schizophrenic threatened with identity loss: 'He feels terror, regresses, loses his identity, and in his attempts to cure himself develops a new one. But the new identity is unrealistic.'[57] It is tempting to explain the cause of many wars through this political psychology paradigm; still, most wars are more about power than identity.

The question arises, therefore: 'what functions does national identity continue to serve that other types of identity either fail to cover, or address rather inadequately?'[58] Smith's answer includes: 1) 'to save people from personal oblivion and restore collective faith'; 2) 'to become part of a political "super-family" that will restore to each of its constituent families their birthright and their former noble status, where now each is deprived of power and held in contempt'; and, 3) a ceremonial and symbolic aspect that contributes to 'realizing the ideal of fraternity'.[59] Part of the symbolic nature of national identity involves high culture, and Smith cautions how '[w]e should not underrate the importance of aesthetic considerations – the feelings of beauty, variety, dignity and pathos aroused by the skilful disposition of forms, masses, sounds and rhythms with which the arts can evoke the distinctive "spirit" of the nation.'[60] From the Finland of Sibelius to the Gabon of its drummers, aestheticism brings a nation's identity to life.

Identity involves the rejection of what is regarded as low, repulsive, dirty, and contaminating.[61] Alterity, or the Other which one is not, is crucial to the construction of national identity. Not having an identity at all – not to be a nation – is the worst case scenario. For identity ultimately 'is also a normative concept, since having identity tends to be contrasted with not having succeeded in achieving it'.[62]

The principle of national self-determination

Part of being a nation is to have the distinct will to be one. Belgium, Canada, and Switzerland, to refer only to stable Western states that encompass more than one nation, claim that they constitute single nations – Belgians, Canadians, Swiss – regardless of their internal makeup. If the political will exists to create a single political nation which then becomes the focus of identity for the several cultural ones within it, then this claim is justified. The deixis of federalism in these three countries supports the construction of such a 'national nation' but, of course, the realities are quite different.

At times, one or more of the constituent nations will aspire for a separate state which would express and realize their political will. National self-determination is a principle that it is likely to invoke to legitimize this goal. Self-determination can serve as a test of the strength of the political will of a nation.[63] The principle confers a right to nations and their members 'to determine the sovereign state to which they would belong and the form of government under which they would live'.[64] It assumes that when nations are under alien rule, 'natural resentment' follows the denial of their fundamental group rights. Therefore 'each nation and no other entity has a right to constitute a separate state'.[65]

Often there can be unintended negative consequences from the exercise of the right to national self-determination. Thus,

> Considered normatively, ethnic mobilization may be seen as a defense (or countermobilization) against discrimination, marginalization, and anomie. But in fact it is regressive. It is the worst alternative to civic

and civil mobilization – the only real means of acquiring a tolerant society. The way in which particularist and discriminatory ethnic nationalism and ethnic countermobilization provoke one another produces anomie and irredentist orientations and feeds the potential for fragmentation and conflict.[66]

Sometimes genocidal actions result from the spiral of nationalisms, as occurred in Rwanda in 1994 and East Timor in 2000. In short, self-determination is usually a catalytic force: 'its power to create aspirations but also to cause upheaval, radicalize, and overcome rationality all demonstrate self-determination's ability to cause change. It alters borders, the shape and size of states; moves populations; and redistributes wealth – hence a state's power – and its relative position in the international system.'[67]

To be sure, national self-determination is fundamentally a noble concept. John Stuart Mill contended 'that the collective divisions of mankind are given unambiguously by nature and history' and lead to a need 'to accommodate self-determination to the nationality principle'.[68] The concept was embraced by US President Woodrow Wilson in his Fourteen Points outlining a blueprint for Europe after the First World War. Problems with *implementing* the idea led statesmen in Europe to a practical solution after the war which 'involved using the language of national self-determination but re-drawing the map of Europe so that it roughly reflected the nationality principle but without any fixed procedure and subject to considerations of practicality and political interest'.[69] After the Second World War, the right of self-determination was extended to the Third World but was confined to only 'the withdrawal of the European powers from their overseas possessions'.[70] This restricted use of the principle of self-determination was enthusiastically endorsed by many African and Asian states, most of which had used this idea to gain independence. But they were unwilling to extend the same right to national groups found within their borders.

Western states have long devised carefully-crafted autonomy and self-government arrangements for parts of their states, for example, for the Aland Islands (Finland), the Faroes and Greenland (Denmark), Puerto Rico (the USA) and most recently Nunavut (Canada).[71] In the 1990s acknowledging *de facto* states while not extending legal recognition was a new variation on the theme of national self-determination. In the former USSR, Abhazia broke from Georgia, Karabagh from Azerbaijan, Trans-Dniester from Moldova, Chechnya from Russia. In the Balkans Kosovo became effectively independent of Belgrade's control, as did Srpska Republika from Bosnia-Hercegovina. In Africa, countries like Angola, Liberia, Sierra Leone, Sudan, and former Zaire were for practical purposes partitioned states.[72] In Asia, Afghanistan, the Philippines, and Sri Lanka did not control important minority-settled regions of their countries. Arrangements for national self-determination were improvised, reflected military standoffs on the ground, and had no international legal basis. Still, *de facto* acknowledgment of nations' control over territories located in larger states became an increasingly viable alternative to the sovereignty/non-sovereignty dichotomy.

In sum, while the interpretation of the principle of self-determination continues to be based on the notion of nation, implementation of the idea has primarily involved political and practical considerations. The international system – the major international organizations, the most important state actors, and the international normative regime – is really the ultimate arbiter of when the principle should be applied. Accordingly, in their appeal to this system for recognition today's secessionists, unlike their predecessors of 30 years earlier, seek to find broader legitimacy for their cause – for example, a claim of genocide – than 'merely' the desire for national self-determination.

The meaning of nationalism

We come to the term nationalism, a word that people often use loosely but scholars employ in technical, even scholastic ways. What is or is not nationalism is the source of considerable disagreement. One historically-derived argument is that 'the only "authentic" nationalisms occur in countries in which the state "built the nation", in which the nationalist bourgeois counterelite that displaced the state-building nobility was culturally identical to its antagonist, and in which the major part of the population has not yet been socially mobilized'.[73] Yet today, it is precisely large-scale mobilization of a population that is considered a *sine qua non* of nationalism. Another apparent contradiction is between the assumption that nationalism can only emerge where a homeland has been defined by a people, and the assertion that nationalism precisely involves a project of 'mapping the homeland'.[74] Much of the time, whether a homeland emerges is decided in the interstices between these two events.

Nationalism has come to mean many things, then. It can refer to the historical process which establishes nationality, rather than tribe or empire, as the framework for political organization. It sometimes 'signifies both an intensification of the consciousness of nationality and a political philosophy of the national state'.[75] It can describe the activities of particular political parties, for example, 'Chinese nationalism' or 'Indian nationalism' symbolized by the Kuomintang or the Indian National Congress. Above all, nationalism can 'denote a condition of mind among members of a nationality . . . in which loyalty to the ideal or to the fact of one's national state is superior to all other loyalties and of which pride in one's nationality and belief in its intrinsic excellence and its "mission" are integral parts.'[76]

Nationalism may be more a mental than an emotional construct. Kohn averred that '[n]ationalism is first and foremost a state of mind, an act of consciousness.'[77] More commonly, it is treated as a sentiment which requires 'almost absolute devotion to and conformity with the will of the nation-state as this is expressed by the ruler or rulers (autocratic or democratic), and it demands the supremacy of the nation to which the nationalist belongs'.[78] The basis for such sentiment may have little to do with the actual attributes of nationality; instead, '[n]ationalism is what nationalists have made it [and the] fact is that myth and actuality and truth and error are inextricably intermixed in modern nationalism.'[79]

Other understandings of nationalism have emerged. It may be viewed as 'the convergence of territorial and political loyalty irrespective of competing foci of affiliation, such as kinship, profession, religion, economic interest, race, or even language'.[80] For Benedict Anderson, the term nation involved an imagined political community but nationalism referred to an artificial linguistic identity.[81] Nationalism may refer to particular types of economic policy, in particular development planning, that promote state autonomy from the global economy.[82] An unorthodox view, it seems particularly apposite in a world where resistance to globalization has been growing. In turn, Miroslav Hroch preferred the term 'national movement' to nationalism because it focused attention on empirically observable activity by specific individuals, above all, organizations, their members, and their leaders.[83]

For his part Anthony Smith equated nationalism with an ideology of solidarity that competes with such other ideologies as liberalism, socialism, and fascism.[84] It is 'first and foremost a political doctrine'.[85] The existence of a language community and a belief in common ancestry are insufficient grounds for the rise of nationalism. For Smith, a core nationalist doctrine contained a number of propositions: 1) humanity is divided naturally into nations; 2) each nation has its own character; 3) the source of all political power is the nation as a whole; 4) to achieve freedom and self-realization, men must identify with a nation; 5) nations can only realize their destiny when they have their own states; 6) loyalty to the nation-state overrides other loyalties; and 7) the primary condition of global freedom and harmony is the strengthening of the nation-state.[86] These propositions are contentious and can be attacked from differing perspectives. Postmodernists would not accept that individual identity is determined by membership in a nation. Advocates of multiculturalism would question whether a nation needs a state to flourish. Supporters of globalization would attack the notion that global stability and freedom are promoted by nationalism rather than free trade and interculturalism. Not surprisingly, therefore, the ideologues of nationalist doctrine as depicted by Smith have found little or no acceptance in the contemporary world.

The idea of nationalism as primarily a political principle was most forcefully expounded by the doyen of nationalism experts, Ernest Gellner. He stressed the contingent nature rather than universal necessity of nationalism: 'Nationalism as such is fated to prevail, but not any one particular nationalism.'[87] Gellner drew a distinction between nationalist *sentiment* –

'the feeling of anger aroused by the violation of the principle, or the feeling of satisfaction aroused by its fulfillment' – and a nationalist *movement* – the actualization of such sentiment.[88] This distinction helped explain why 'nationalism was at once inevitable *and* relatively weak, that is, that only a very few calls by nationalists for their own states have been successful'.[89] Nationalist passions are often forceful, nationalist movements less so.

The posited dependence of nationalism on a political movement and political system is taken for granted today but it was originally a revolutionary idea. One writer seeking to justify nationalism as an innovative force noted that '[a]t no other time had it ever been proposed that the identity of the governed must somehow coincide with the institutions of government.'[90] Even today, why nationalism should necessarily be linked to politics rather than just culture is a subject of discussion.

The debate on the meaning of nationalism is complex, far-reaching, and interminable. Part of the explanation for the disagreements about nationalism has been use of the term to mean an individual's loyalty to the state when, logically, it should be used to refer to one's loyalty to one's nation and homeland.[91] A parsimonious approach to nationalism is to hold that it is primarily about praxis. As such it signifies two things. One is that nationalism embodies an ideal resting on the existence of a cultural and political nation and it advances 'prescriptions for the realization of national aspirations and the national will'. The second is that it entails a political movement which aims at achieving 'the goals of the nation and . . . its national will'.[92] Because it is sentiment and ideal on the one hand, and movement and praxis on the other, and because it most often falls short of its objectives but occasionally succeeds, Gellner was justified in speaking of nationalisms in the plural.

Typologies of nationalism

We have been discussing nationalism without using qualifying adjectives. But the very title of this book indicates that adjectives – especially those signaling dichotomies – are inescapable when discussing the phenomenon. Isaiah Berlin wrote of 'two nationalisms' whose banal distinction was based on aggressive versus nonaggressive orientations.[93] Civic versus ethnic variants were the stock scholarly currency of the 1990s, and liberal as opposed to illiberal varieties have been highlighted for even longer. Indeed, as Michael Hechter observed, most typologies 'distinguish the liberal, culturally inclusive (Sleeping Beauty) nationalisms characteristic of Western Europe from the illiberal, culturally exclusive (Frankenstein's monster) nationalisms more often found elsewhere.'[94] Yet by invoking characters out of fables in order to dramatize difference Hechter's intention may be to alert us to the fact that we are dealing with false opposites. Let us begin our critical review of typologies of nationalism with this dichotomy.

Most modern states, including the vast majority of liberal ones, are founded upon a national principle. The overriding issue is how the national principle is recognized, that is, who is subsumed under it, who is excluded, and what consequences follow. The construction of home in an explicitly national way does not necessarily result in a transgression of individual rights (a cornerstone of liberalism), though there is a greater likelihood that it may impinge on group and minority rights. Nevertheless, by themselves the desire to promote a national culture, to protect a national language, and to instill a sense of community upon an otherwise fragmented people, do not preclude the building of a liberal home. Liberal nationalism, therefore, does not posit multiculturalism.

We can accept that liberal nationalists do better than illiberal nationalists in accommodating and respecting diverse beliefs, and thus in promoting tolerance and peace. The definition of liberal nationalism specifies a commitment to protecting individual rights and to tolerating differences. The question can be raised whether states embracing a liberal nationalism are fully committed to such universalistic norms as equal rights for all, tolerance and nondiscrimination, and government by the consent of all citizens. With racism, sexism, and other forms of discrimination still discernible, many Western democracies suffer from a 'liberal nationalism deficit' in this respect. Another problem is that there is nothing to prevent liberal nationalism from quickly becoming illiberal. The policy of the United States abroad and at home after the September 2001 attacks changed and became more aggressive and exclusionary. We should also remember that liberalism 'is at its weakest when it comes to constructing bonds of community.'[95] The relative absence of community solidarity can provide a breeding ground for ethnic discrimination, social marginalization, and other illiberal phenomena.

Illiberal nationalism is characterized by a commitment to the preeminence of one particular ethnic, religious, or linguistic group over others within the same society. That does not mean it is not a modern phenomenon; we encounter many examples of illiberal nationalists thriving in twenty-first century politics, as our case studies will show. Moreover, even illiberal nationalists can value personal autonomy and individual rights and freedoms, and can sustain a commitment to social justice both between and within nations. For political philosopher Yael Tamir, the ideal arrangement would be to forge a close synthesis of liberal and nationalist ideas, but she cautioned that in the twenty-first century 'Liberals, whom some had viewed as the great winners of the twentieth century, must come to terms with the need to "share this glory" with nationalism, and probably with religious fundamentalism too.'[96] This is easier said than done: liberalism may be seriously undermined whether it comes to terms or engages in combat with the intolerant forms of fundamentalism.

We can agree with Hechter, then, that 'normative differences between nationalist movements have been enormously important in history', but 'it is doubtful that they can be explained if the dimensions of nationalism are chosen on normative grounds.'[97] Accordingly it is preferable to view liberal and illiberal nationalisms as analytic categories that lend explanatory power to the study of modern politics. And other discrete factors have to be considered when discussing the forms that nationalism has taken.

Historians view nationalism as the product of centuries of development and frequently identify stages of evolution. One sixfold classification begins with 'humanitarian nationalism', which originated in the eighteenth-century Enlightenment era and exhibited 'tolerance and regard for the rights of other nationalities'.[98] The main representatives of this type were English statesman Henry St. John Bolingbroke, French philosopher Rousseau, and German philosopher von Herder. A second type was 'Jacobin nationalism' which followed the French Revolution and promoted the ideas of liberty, equality, and fraternity. Under the Jacobins nationalism first acquired many of its negative, dogmatic, extremist characteristics. A third type was 'traditional nationalism' propounding the view that it was better to place the fate of the nation in the hands of the aristocratic class rather than those of the masses. A leading traditional nationalist was philosopher Edmund Burke.

In the search for a nationalism that would not be excessively democratic (Jacobin) or aristocratic (traditional), 'liberal nationalism' emerged in England at the end of the eighteenth century and spread to other parts of Europe in the early nineteenth century. Its major characteristic was a synthesis of absolute state sovereignty and individual liberty, as British philosopher Jeremy Bentham sought to achieve. The fifth type, 'integral nationalism', developed later in the nineteenth century in hostility to both liberal and humanitarian types. Its defining features were a rejection of cooperation with other nations, promotion of militarism and imperialism, and the abrogation of personal liberties when they clashed with state objectives. Under integral nationalism, loyalty to the nation-state was 'elevated above all other loyalties, and all social, cultural, economic, and even religious considerations were subordinated to the ends of nationalism'.[99] In later years, integral nationalism came to characterize the politics of authoritarian states, fascist as well as communist. The last type was 'economic nationalism', which arose in the aftermath of the Industrial Revolution when nations sought to achieve economic self-sufficiency and growth, establish control of markets and raw materials, and compete successfully with other nations. Beginning in the nineteenth century, it was economic nationalism that combined with imperialism to launch a struggle among Western powers for colonial possessions.[100]

A different periodization of nationalism identified a first integrative stage (1815–71) when it helped 'to consolidate the states that most quickly outgrew their feudal divisions, and to unify others that had been long split into hostile factions' such as Germany and Italy.[101] The success of nationalism in bringing about the unification of Germany and Italy, however, led to the call by subject nationalities within Austro-Hungary and Ottoman Turkey for independence based on geographic cohesion, common language, customs, traditions, culture, history, and race. The stage was thus set for disruptive nationalism (1871–90). At the beginning of the twentieth century, aggressive nationalism (1900–45) took hold and became inseparable from aggressive imperialism.[102] This phase was punctuated by the world wars in which opposing national interests in Europe collided. Finally, contemporary nationalism (1945–54) was characterized by the demand for independence from colonial rule in Asia, Africa, and the Middle East. It was thus synonymous with the decolonization movement. We note how the first and fourth stages of nationalism evoked positive developments and the other two negative stages. Such a typology is more evenly balanced than those which sketch nationalism's linear development from constructive to destructive force.

Instead of historical periodization, another classificatory scheme for nationalism can be based on problems that a people wish to resolve. One such typology, developed after the First World War, categorized nationalism into oppression, irredentist, precaution, and prestige types.[103] Oppression nationalism signified the reaction of minority nationalities to systematic discrimination and oppression at the hands of the state or the dominant nationality – a dominant theme in that period. Irredentist nationalism involved the desire by a nationality for unification with co-nationals in an independent state. Precaution nationalism referred to a nation's 'identification of commercial expansion with the interests of national security and of general national well-being'.[104] In its extreme form, precaution nationalism was indistinguishable from imperialism. The last category, prestige nationalism, arose from the perception that outsiders had insufficient esteem for one's nation. Such nationalism was likely to emerge in situations where, from a particular nation's perspective, 'its glorious history of the past or its present and future possibilities entitle it to greater respect or consideration'.[105] Russia's quest today for international prestige furnishes a paradigmatic example of prestige nationalism.

A different framework highlights the salience of agency, that is, which group constructs nationalism. One analytical division is among 'established nationalism', 'mini-nationalism', and 'macro-nationalism' (also called 'pan-movements').[106] Established nationalism refers to the classic form of nationalism appearing in a nation having its own state. Mini-nationalism involves the attempt by a minority group in a parent state to secede from it; if it is successful in its efforts, mini-nationalism is transformed into conventional established nationalism. By contrast, 'when the nationalism of an established nation-state is expanded to a supranational form, there emerges a larger macro-nationalism'.[107] It encompasses 'politico-cultural movements promoting the solidarity of peoples united by common or kindred languages, group identification, traditions, or some other characteristic such as geographical proximity'.[108] Such movements attempt to include all those 'who by reason of geography, race, religion, or language, or by a combination of any or all of them, are included in the same group category'.[109] A common attribute of macro-nationalisms is the drive for domination: they seek to control all who are defined as forming part of the 'we-group'. Other common attributes include a common linguistic identity, messianic zeal (for example, pan-Slavism), territorial expansionism (pan-Germanism), religious zeal (pan-Islamism), racial unity (pan-Africanism), or anti-colonialism (pan-Asianism). This typology highlights how agency in nationalism can range from a community within a state to a broader movement beyond it.

A very simple classification based on the relationship between nation and state was provided by Kohn. Nationalism comprised two types: 1) as it evolved in the West – England, France, the Netherlands, Switzerland, the United States, the British dominions; and 2) as it developed elsewhere – in Central and Eastern Europe and Asia. In the Western world, the rise of nationalism was either 'preceded by the formation of the future national state, or, as in the case of the United States, coincided with it'.[110] It also reflected eighteenth century ideas of individual liberty and rational cosmopolitanism. On the other hand, in non-Western Europe and Asia, nationalism developed later in more backward social and political conditions and 'in protest against and in conflict with the existing state pattern – not primarily to transform it into a people's state, but to redraw the political boundaries in conformity with ethnographic demands'.[111] The past was revered by nationalists in order to construct the vision of an ideal fatherland of the future (Milosevic's Yugoslavia would serve as an example). Because Eastern nationalism did not enjoy the propitious social and political conditions that existed in the West, it became ridden with an inferiority complex and, according to Kohn, sought to overcome this by exaggerating the uniqueness of a nation's experience.

The distinction between Western and Eastern forms of nationalism has been taken up by scholars who emphasize differences in cultural rather than state development. The geographical breakdown is adjusted to reflect the shift to cultural criteria. Thus, in one view, Western nationalism is associated primarily with Western Europe and Eastern nationalism with Eastern Europe, Asia, Africa, and Latin America. The first type is characterized by the widespread belief that a nation is 'culturally equipped' to raise its status.[112] Eastern nationalism, on the other hand, arose among 'peoples recently drawn into civilization hitherto alien to them, and whose ancestral cultures are not adapted to success and excellence' by the cosmopolitan and dominant standards of Western nationalism.[113] Eastern nationalists stressed the need for a cultural transformation of their nations without at the same time losing their distinct national identities. Putting it differently, it entailed 'two rejections, both of them ambivalent: rejection of the alien intruder and dominator who is nevertheless to be imitated and surpassed by his own standards, and rejection of ancestral ways which are seen as obstacles to progress and yet also cherished as marks of identity'.[114] Eastern nationalism was therefore both emulative, in the sense that it accepted the value standards set by an alien culture, and hostile to the models it imitated. From this contradiction followed the disturbed, ambivalent, and illiberal nature of Eastern nationalism. Russia's nation building experience described in Chapter 1, centered on the notion of *ressentiment* of the West, is an illustration of Eastern nationalism.

Of course typologies that go beyond such a dichotomous view of the world will offer greater explanatory power. A few of these pay particular attention to the role played by minorities in a society in helping shape nationalisms. One such classification begins with 'original nationalism', which developed in Europe and sought 'to make the boundaries of the state and those of the nation coincide', and the 'Afro-Asian variety', which reflected incongruence in national and political boundaries (a legacy of colonialism) and was the product more of political will than nature.[115] But an original addition was the type of nationalism found among peoples in search of a home. This 'nationalism of the homeless' was attributable to 'Zionism and its imitator among American Negroes called the Black Muslim movement'.[116]

> Both the Jews in Europe and the Negroes in America belong to social minorities which have suffered various forms of discrimination . . . . But it takes the influence of nationalist theory to convince such sufferers, firstly, that they are a nation (for the Jews are in the first instance a religious community, the Negroes a racial category drawn from many sources) and, secondly, that the solution is to find a territorial home and establish a state. These two cases of homeless nationalism are spectacular because the European Zionist found his home in far-off Israel, and projects for an African home ranged from Canada to the partial application of the idea in Liberia.[117]

An intriguing approach, nationalism of the homeless can be more broadly interpreted to encompass the nationalism of the dispossessed. In their construction of home, some groups, invariably ethnically defined, believe that they have become strangers in their own societies, usually viewed as a product of immigration. While host society reactions to immigration can entail nationalism of such a negative kind, they can also be positive. Under one categorization, the latter means 'designating the nationalism of host societies that offer a measure of integration to immigrants and favor further modernization as *hegemonic nationalism* and the nationalism in societies in which opposition to immigrants and their integration is exhibited and accompanied by a fear of modernization as *corporate nationalism*'.[118] These are strange terms, but they do flush out the principal varieties of nationalism found in immigrant societies.

Let us consider a final, closely related typology that draws attention to the role of minorities in shaping nationalism. The first type is 'hegemony nationalism' involving the motivation of national groups to consolidate smaller collectivities into larger units (exemplified by the Italians' and Germans' drive for unification in the nineteenth century). The demand for secession or autonomy by a national group constitutes a second type called 'particularistic nationalism'. The next kind, nationalism of the minorities, can be found in almost every state where smaller groups seek to protect and promote their traditions, cultures, and languages. Lastly, 'marginal' or 'frontier' nationalism comprises the nationalistic sentiments of marginal peoples inhabiting regions bordering two states (such as found in Alsace-Lorraine, the Saar, and Silesia).[119] This type may increase in significance as regionalism becomes encouraged by the European Union.

Typologies tell us what the research agendas of scholars are. In the case of nationalism, these have been rich, at times original, and occasionally provocative. But because they comprise lists, typologies do not necessarily reveal what the main epistemological approaches to a subject are. The next section offers an overview of different schools that have emerged to study nationalism.

Schools of nationalism

In spite of widespread consensus on nationalism's importance, scholars differ over the etiology – the underlying causes – of nationalism. A long-dominant historical school, for example, draws upon the writings of European philosophers and invokes particular socio-economic conditions to account for nationalism's salience. Social scientists, by contrast, have distinguished two linkages between nationalism and modernization. Some restrict modernization's role to 'a prop in the background of the landscape, a general setting of various ideologies and movements'.[120] Instead they spotlight how modernization creates disintegrative tendencies in a society undergoing change. The other school makes a more 'direct connection between nationalism and "modernization"... believing this link contains the decisive clue to the problem'.[121] Industrialization and mass communication are singled out as being direct causes of nationalism. Let us explore these three major schools – they are far from exhaustive, of course – in more detail.

The historical school

Historians' explanations for the rise of nationalism are mainly diffusionist in character. They view nationalism 'as an ideology with specific roots in post-medieval Europe and trace its development from small beginnings to its present position as one of the dominant forces in the world'.[122] A second assumption, shared with the political psychology approach, is the security need people have to belong to a group. Economic historians have added economic conditions to the list of factors shaping nationalist feeling.[123]

Elie Kedourie was a leading representative of the historical school. He regarded nationalism as an idea that originated in Europe and was later embraced by peoples around the world. The French Revolution was a *caesura* in nationalism's rise because it rested on the belief that people possessed certain inalienable natural rights which society had to protect. But the historian asked 'how are we to assert that liberty, equality, and fraternity are the birthright of every individual, how at all indeed to lay down any rule of behavior which can withstand critical scrutiny; which does not, at length, dissolve into a perplexing haze of opinion and sensation?'[124]

Kedourie invoked Kant to find a way out. Kant had contended that '[m]orality is the outcome of obedience to a universal law which is to be found within ourselves, not in the world of appearances. For morality to be possible, it must be *independent* of the laws which govern appearances.'[125] This independence for Kant was freedom in the strictest, transcendental sense. Kant had no direct interest in nationalism but his thought had far-reaching political ramifications. Since man is free only when 'he obeys the laws of morality which he finds within himself, and not in the external world', Kant's doctrine made the individual 'in a way never envisaged by the French revolutionaries or their intellectual precursors, the very center, the arbiter, the sovereign of the universe'.[126] From this Kedourie drew the political implication that self-determination constituted the supreme good.

The revolution in European philosophy that preceded the French Revolution, therefore, contributed to the rise of nationalism. The simultaneous upheaval in eighteenth-century European social life also had a major impact. The dislocations of industrialization and urbanization revealed the weaknesses of the old system and stimulated a search for more innovative institutions fitting the new socio-economic conditions. The allure of novel political ideas was all the greater 'because society and state in eighteenth century Europe seemed cold and heartless'.[127]

The European nationalist idea, historians stress, inevitably spread worldwide. They pointed to the roles played by the rise of colonialism and the idea of 'imitation':

> In an age of increased communications through travel and the press, men experience a need to experiment with the ideas they encounter. Nationalism's widespread success is the outcome of the desire to imitate new ideas and ways. Nationalism – like democracy, science and monogamy – is an importation from the West. Once planted, the seeds of nationalism are carried back to fertilize lands which till then were blissfully unaware of its existence.[128]

And who transported this novel idea? Historians hold that educated elites in various parts of the world were primarily responsible for popularizing the nationalist idea imported from England and France in their respective lands.

A few historians single out an antecedent phase of nationalism grounded in its rural origins. The existence of a reactionary, nationalistic, rural population, it is sometimes argued, has been a necessary precondition for genocidal policies, whether carried out in Hitler's Germany,[129] Pol Pot's Cambodia,[130] or 1990s Rwanda.[131] Tom Nairn concluded that most 'ethnonationalist conflicts seem to go on recurring *in predominantly rural situations*'. He added: 'What the true story of "chauvinism" suggests is that modernization involves passage through something like a colossal mill-race, in which a multigenerational struggle between the (rural) past and the (urban-industrial) future is fought out'.[132] Perhaps this is an overly deterministic argument, but it reveals how the historical approach to nationalism is reticent to pin blame on ethnic entrepreneurs, demographic pressures, or institutional breakdowns and power vacuums for nationalism's persistence.

The disintegration school

Among writers treating modernization as providing merely 'backdrop' conditions for nationalism's emergence were Karl Marx and Emile Durkheim. For Marx, nationalism and religion were 'integral parts of the superstructure created by the dominant economic and political classes . . . to legitimize their rule'.[133] The victory of the proletariat, which for Marx would be the culmination of the process of modernization, was to erode nationalism as well as other social manifestations of class domination. The eclectic Marxian view of modernization was as a destroyer of nationalism. He envisaged what we might term a 'negation of negatives' that would usher in socialism: both class and nation – negative categories for him – would become obsolete structures following the triumph of international socialism. The world would subsequently consist of classless, nationless societies.

German sociologist Durkheim's writings about social change were less grandiose and prescriptive than Marx even though he shared the view that modernization's impact on nationalism was negative. Economic modernization created a division of labor that would transform a mechanically integrated society into an organically integrated one: in a mechanically integrated society, the national identity of its members (based on cultural and historical factors such as race, language, customs, origin, and descent) created and maintained social structure and unity. However, as society modernized, the division of labor replaced national identity as its organizing principle. When this happened, 'every citizen becomes dependent on every other citizen, because no person can be self-sufficient' and, hence, each person becomes 'a small piece in a huge puzzle that can only be completed when each performs his or her particular role'. In sum, functional bonds between people would integrate society organically and, with that, national identity would lose its importance.

How, then, did Durkheim explain the rise of nationalism in industrialized societies which were closer to his organic model? He responded that to meet the challenge of modernization, societies had to become cohesive or risk disintegration. This cohesive force could be created by reconstituting and modifying the 'collective norms of the "mechanical" type of society'.[134] This 'new' communitarian model – modifying the old *communitas* to fit the requirements of the modern age – is the crux of Durkheim's view of nationalism. It incorporates 'the notion of a single will or "soul", representing and expressing all the trends, customs and habits of a people'.[135] For Durkheim, nationalism was the logical corollary of modernization. It required remodeling society into a cohesive unit 'with a single focus of moral authority and systems of beliefs, yet this new "community" must be sufficiently flexible to allow some individual autonomy, and adaptive enough to cope with rapidly changing needs and circumstances'.[136]

Durkheim's followers clung closely to the view that the breakdown of traditional society caused by modernization was the cause of nationalism. Nationalism served as a bridge between a community's traditions and its modernization by creating new roles incorporating both the parochial and universal orientations of individuals.[137] In traditional societies modernization played a substitutive role for nationalism in maintaining order. People most adversely affected by the destruction of traditional society became attracted to collective movements like nationalism.[138] A study of India concurred that 'nationalism is a *sine qua non* of industrialization, because it provides people with an overriding, easily acquired, secular motivation for making painful changes'.[139]

The functionalist view of nationalism expounded by the Durkheim school was criticized for two principal reasons. First, it drew crude ethnocentric stereotypes of 'tradition' and 'modernity' that 'imputes teleological needs to societies undergoing transformation' and 'implies a retrospective determinism which makes analysis of actions and situations somewhat superfluous'.[140] Second, it mistakenly 'assumes that the motor of all structural change [in society] is continuous differentiation of roles and institutions to adapt to the environment'.[141]

Anthony Smith criticized what he termed the 'mass model of nationalism' that also adopted the disintegration perspective. The model ascribed the destruction of traditional elites and peoples' rising sense of insecurity to processes of modernization, democratization, and urbanization. Such dislocations and upheavals in tradition-bound third world societies created feelings of anxiety and helpless frustration. 'Into this psychological crisis step the ideologically extremist religious and political movements with their promise of immediate rewards and messianic activism.'[142] Nationalism became an important, though not exclusive, response 'of the new urban middle and lower-middle classes to the experience of physical disruption and cultural disorientation'.[143] A study of European societies took this argument further, contending that in societies experiencing urban anomie, elite permeability, and mass extremism, nationalism could be superseded by totalitarianism.[144]

Smith contended that the mass model of nationalism was 'largely irrelevant to an explanation of the *emergence* of nationalism. Where it is useful, is in its portrayal of those factors, notably urbanization, which act as vehicles for the rapid *diffusion* of nationalist slogans among "marginal" groups'.[145] Furthermore, not all nationalist movements had to be anti-democratic or extremist.

> In Persia, Argentina, Czechoslovakia and Nigeria and in French West Africa, nationalism, while attacking naturally the colonialist or imperial regimes, was a liberal, reformist and democratic force before the military interventions. Even where they curb civil liberties, no post-independence African movement aiming to integrate its population, would wish to subvert the established order – if only for fear of a rash of secessionist movements across the Continent. Political order and civil liberty do not always go together, and neither do extremism and a large-scale following (one need only contrast the Nasserist and Wafdist varieties of nationalism in Egypt for an equally common permutation).[146]

Also noteworthy were the cases of India and Israel where, in spite of the appeal of religious extremism, the nationalist movement was generally 'a self-critical, democratic and constitutional movement'.[147]

Paradoxically, in place of disintegration some political scientists writing in the 1950s and 1960s identified the contrary phenomenon – integration – as a variable intervening between modernization and nationalism. At the state level, integration involved a process of nation building which tried to bring different peoples together into free and equal association. At the international level, it referred to the strengthening of economic and political ties among states and the creation of regional organizations. The result was that by 'the late 1950s it was assumed that there was a dynamic towards assimilation, an incessant trend heralding a new era of progress and prosperity across the world'.[148] Such a hypothetical 'integration school', then, focuses on nationalist and even supranationalist outcomes and has persisted for several decades.

The modernization school

Theorists who assign a direct causal role for modernization in the rise of nationalism view this linkage in one of two distinct ways. Karl Deutsch's seminal work emphasized the crucial role played by the communications revolution – especially literacy and mass media – in the socio-political mobilization of the population in a modernizing society. By contrast, a theorist like Ernest Gellner stressed the part played by industrialization in the rise of nationalism.

The core proposition of Deutsch's theory was that mobilization produced by modernization's dislocating impact on society was the primary cause of nationalism.[149] Mobilization is a process which allows individuals, through intensive communication (especially through the mass media), to create a 'public'. The desire to form a nation stems from economic and psychological insecurity caused by the disruptions of modernization. To be sure, nation-building pressure was not constant and Deutsch compared nations to rising and falling tides, to a large extent depending on their current degree of political integration.[150]

Probably the most celebrated theory linking nationalism and modernization is Gellner's and not Deutsch's. Gellner's main objective was to refute the common claim of both liberals and Marxists that nationalism is either an epiphenomenon – an aberrant expression of a more fundamental group identity or loyalty, like to a social class – or an anachronism that would rapidly disappear with secularization and economic interdependence. Gellner asserted that modernization and industrialization actually *stimulated* the growth of nationalism rather than swept it away, as Marxism and liberalism anticipated.

Modernization, Gellner contended, required a remolding of a society into a standardized, homogeneous, centrally-sustained 'high cultural type' with which the entire population could identify.[151] This new society is the nation with its own particular language and culture. Reversing the logic of the disintegration school that believed nationalism was an *outgrowth* of modernization, Gellner contended that it was a necessary *condition* of modernization.

The author proposed a more general theory of nationalism that linked it to the global trend toward industrialism. Particular types of polity and culture, he contended, are better suited for launching industrial growth. The modern nation-state combines these forms whereas more traditional states could not maximize economic development until they changed their cultural life and state structure. Industrialization, therefore, requires 'the convergence of political and cultural units' – the core of the nationalist principle.[152] As Gellner saw it, then, 'nationalism is a theory of political legitimacy, which requires that ethnic boundaries should not cut across political ones, and . . . that ethnic boundaries within a given state . . . should not separate the power holders from the rest'.[153]

Gellner's theory revolutionized the study of nationalism but it nevertheless contains serious flaws. One of his students summarized the main indictments: 'At a substantive level, Gellner's theory was accused of being too modernist and too optimistic; at a more formal philosophical level, it was attacked again and again for having too instrumental a view of human motivation and for relying on functional argumentation.'[154] Reality has also disproved aspects of Gellner's theory. Contrary to what he thought nationalism entailed – the congruence of political and cultural units – today's ethno-political landscape is different. In an influential essay published in 1972, Walker Connor provided a counterfactual to Gellner's thesis by pointing out that '[o]f a total of 132 contemporary states, only 12 (9.1 percent) can be described as essentially homogeneous from an ethnic viewpoint.'[155] Since then states have, if anything, become even more multicultural, the few highly-publicized cases of ethnic cleansing being exceptional.

Another weakness in Gellner's theory is that although it offered insights into the development of nationalism in industrializing countries, it could not explain the rise of nationalism occurring elsewhere, whether in pre-industrial or advanced and post-industrial states:

> Many nationalisms are found in countries which are largely agrarian, non-industrialized, and non-centralized. A very important determinant of nationalism in the Third World is the legacy of colonialism, and the independence movements directed against 'White Rule'. Contemporary nationalisms have arisen in long-industrialized countries such as Britain, Belgium, and Spain, which Gellner might have called 'nation-states'. Something new seems to have happened there, outside Gellner's theory.[156]

Gellner's theory also did not shed much light on the factors that lead to the powerful emotional appeal of nationalism. As one critic asked:

> Why should people be prepared to die for what is in this [Gellner's] analysis an imperative of a rational economic and social system of industrialization? Nationalist behavior in its contemporary form is hardly explained in this theory. It deals instead with the reasons why industrializing states adopted a national form in order to prosper, and the nationalism which was associated with that.[157]

In short, Gellner's modernization approach helped explain nationalism in a specific historical period – the era of industrialization in Europe – and flushed out industrialization as a critical factor. Today the forces shaping nationalism are radically different. Thus, '[b]eing national is the condition of our times, even as the nation is buffeted by the subnational rise of local, regional, and ethnic claims, and the transnational threats of globalization, hegemonic American culture, migration, diasporization, and new forms of political community.'[158] The case studies that follow examine how such a new set of factors has given new shape and form to nationalism.

3
Home Writ Large: Nationalism and the Maintenance of Empire

What happens when homeland has been a large empire and must be reconfigured into a 'mere' multinational state or smaller imperium? How are identities reconstructed to reflect empires diminished in size? What part does nationalism play in providing meaningful new identities?

How new independent states have emerged out of the ruins of empire is well-documented. How the nationalism of subjugated peoples topples an empire is also a familiar, uncontentious proposition. But how an empire arises on the ashes of a preceding one and takes on new identity has received little attention, partly because this is generally viewed as a political and even logical impossibility.

A large nation can begin empire building even while it is caught up in the process of empire destroying. Russia since 1991 is a case in point. India after independence and partition in 1947 furnishes an earlier example. Both of these large nations shattered alien communist and colonial regimes respectively and replaced them with their own rule over vast territories inhabited by many different nations. Are Russia and India really empires today? From the perspective of Moscow and New Delhi, the answer is categorically no. But from the periphery, among Chechens or Muslim Kashmiris, the answer is just as clearly yes. For a dominant nation's rule can be a minority nation's subjugation and, conversely, one nation's subjugation may be another nation's empire.

Empires may have overseas possessions but they can also be land-based. Russia and India today encompass expansive territories and have heterogeneous populations. Empires may be ruled over using military force but they can also be controlled employing 'soft power', for example, economic resources. This is how contemporary Russia and India can be conceived of as empires.

A seminal study comparing the two countries was carried out by Paul Brass in 1991 in the midst of Soviet disintegration. While highlighting diversity in the USSR and India, the author hypothesized that language and culture were less important as factors strengthening centrifugalism than the congruity or non-congruity of nationality policy and systems of regional party and administrative control: 'the essential ingredients required to transform language – and other – cultural differences into political conflicts are struggles for political control between central and local elites and elite competition for jobs and other scarce resources'.[1]

The most influential factor that Brass found was a shift in the equilibrium between center and periphery. In both cases, 'in the Soviet Union under Gorbachev and India under Mrs Gandhi, *changes* in the existing balance in center–state relations precipitated crises of national unity'.[2] Furthermore, the existence of a dominant and privileged nation in the USSR – the Russians – and the absence of a single large ethnic group dispersed throughout India – there is only a wish among some Hindus, largely in northern India, to establish a Hindi-speaking dominant nation – made the political consequences of these changes different in each country.

The first case we consider is Russia. Alongside the nationalism of other peoples in the USSR, how did Russian nationalism help bring an end to the communist imperium? Russian nationalists debated whether the Russian homeland had to be as large and as authoritarian as the Soviet Union. But some of them also supported Russia's imperious behavior towards its national minorities and distant regions. The relationship between the Russian center and its periphery under Boris Yeltsin and Vladimir Putin, it can be argued, remains imperial. Home for them is Russia and its earlier territorial conquests.

The second case is India. In its long struggle for independence from British rule, Indian secular nationalists were unable to avoid a religiously-based partition of the subcontinent. Even after Pakistan was created as home for Indian Muslims, the reduced Indian state still displayed many characteristics of empire: a great diversity of nations including large Muslim minorities, core and peripheral nations, and coercive containment of the nationalisms of its parts – Assam, Kashmir, Punjab, and others. The trauma of losing part of home through partition was deep, but the effort to keep the home that remained from further disintegration led, it can be suggested, to imperial practices. How do the federal elites of these states use the construct of an imperial home to maintain subjects' loyalty?

The character of empires

One study of twentieth-century empires described the factors that shaped them: 'The course of modern empire has been determined by changes in the character of the international environment, in the domestic society of the metropole, and in the development of social change and the balance of collaboration in the peripheries.'[3] In this view, no single factor, including nationalism, can make or break empires.[4] An intriguing question is whether nationalism can *prevent* the establishment of empires. One view is that the quest by nations for modernity over the past two centuries hamstrung the construction of large empires. 'Whatever their official claims, medieval and earlier empires were actually limited in power and ambition. There was very little chance of the Chinese, Persian, Mogul, Habsburg or Ottoman polities attaining a literally "world empire." Modernization changed this: it became at least conceivable that Napoleon, the British Crown, German Aryanism or Soviet Communism could achieve just that.'[5]

Why did these powerful agencies fall short of becoming world empires? For one writer it was because many peoples rejected the imperial design and wished to achieve modernity on their own terms through their political and cultural independence. 'Nationalism was the effort by one "backward" culture and people after another to appropriate the powers and benefits of modernity for their own use' in the face of the 'imperial (arrogant, ethnocentric, homogenising and armed to the teeth) as well as gift-bearing' alternative.[6] The thesis that anti-imperial nation-builders have been invariably attracted to the modernist project is highly questionable. Furthermore, whether empires, such as the British or Soviet, had no interest in modernizing the societies they came to control is also disputable.

The study of empires has invariably been accompanied by analysis of their decline. Thus '[t]he theory of the constitution of Empire is also a theory of its decline, as European theorists of Empire have recognized for the last several thousand years. Already in Greco-Roman antiquity, Thucydides, Tacitus, and Polybius all recounted the sequence of rise and fall, as did later the Fathers of the Church and the theorists of early Christianity', especially Augustine.[7] The most acclaimed study of empire, Edward Gibbon's *Decline and Fall of the Roman Empire* written in the eighteenth century, made clear what an empire consists of: a core and a periphery. The core exercises highly centralized authority in the empire while the periphery is its subject. Even though elites may exist in both areas, one is dominant over the other: the central elite establishes a dictatorship over the regional. Another defining characteristic of empire is differentiation and inequality between core and periphery in virtually all spheres.[8]

Gibbon offered a complex explanation for the decay of Rome during its 1300-year history. The causes identified range from ecological degradation (poor urban planning, river flooding, erosion) to the invasions of other peoples (the barbarians of Germany and Scythia, the Saracens and Turks, the spiritual Christian sects). At home, the avarice and materialism of both the imperial nation, the Romans, and the peoples they ruled over weakened the social order. For Gibbon, however, 'the most potent and forcible cause of destruction [was] the domestic hostilities of the Romans themselves'.[9]

Two of the most influential twentieth-century theories setting out how empires were formed and imperialism was engendered were John Hobson's *Imperialism* published in 1902, and Lenin's *Imperialism: the Highest Stage of Capitalism* written in 1917. Hobson's analysis underscored how maintenance of the British Empire at the turn of the twentieth century already represented an increasingly costly alternative to domestic social reform and structural changes in the English economy.[10] In turn, the Bolshevik leader described how capitalist states were by nature so predatory that for the sake of capitalist expansion they would go to war against each other and destroy themselves.[11] Both Hobson and Lenin furnished examples of the metrocentric theory of empire where it was essential 'to look within the dominant metropoles and examine the internal drive to external expansion'.[12]

Indian scholar Nirad Chaudhuri concurred that '[t]here is no empire without a conglomeration of linguistically, racially, and culturally different nationalities and the hegemony of one of them over the rest.' But he succinctly captured another important relationship: 'nationalism and imperialism are the same political urge, the first being its defensive aspect and the second its assertive'. The two, he suggested, are often conflated. 'Nationalism becomes imperialism when a nation becomes so powerful that it seeks to bring other nations under its domination, but it does not cease to practise nationalism for that reason; it simply asserts the power of nationalism at its highest and most expansive.'[13] Homeland as empire is a nationalist proposition, then, as this chapter seeks to confirm.

An aspect of empire that has recently drawn some scholars' attention is whether it has proved cost-effective. An overlooked consideration in imperial decline, what this approach proposes is that an empire may not pay for itself. One scholar noted that 'the gains to metropolitan economies and societies as a whole from the conquest, settlement and retention of territory in other continents is more often asserted than investigated, let alone measured'.[14] Economic evidence supported early twentieth-century critics of the British imperial system who

> argued that the framework of imperial rule and institutions did little to ensure high rates of return on British funds invested abroad; that the Empire was not a particularly productive location for capital or manifestly popular with migrants leaving this country; and finally that holding on to alien territory and resources was not required to ensure access to markets or to supplies of food and raw materials imported from beyond the kingdom's borders.[15]

In the case of the Soviet Union, the 'empires are costly' thesis indicated how 'by the early 1980s dominance over Eastern Europe undermined rather than extended Soviet interests at home and, to some degree, abroad as well. Indeed, the domestic and the foreign goals of empire were at increasing variance'.[16]

Recent international relations studies related to empire have focused on the concepts of *world powers* and *world orders*. A much-acclaimed book published in the 1980s singled out 'imperial overstretch' as a cause of decline. A systematization of the 'empires are costly' school, the author used the term in a very specific way:

> all of the major shifts in the world's *military-power* balances have fol-
> lowed alterations in the *productive* balances; and further, . . . the rising
> and falling of the various empires and states in the international system
> has been confirmed by the outcomes of the major Great Power wars,
> where victory has always gone to the side with the greatest material
> resources.[17]

Since 1945 the world order has been centered on the United States (and up to 1991 the USSR).[18] Because it has served as a reluctant hegemon, one scholar has conceptualized the US as an 'empire by invitation'.[19]

If empire is still a meaningful concept, then, the US has to be the test case for analysis. From its founding, an idiosyncratic imperial idea was developed in the United States. 'From the standpoint of a Europe in crisis, the United States, Jefferson's "Empire of liberty," represented the renewal of the imperial idea.'[20] But at the turn of the twenty-first century a different conceptualization of empire and the US role in it may hold greater explanatory power. Today empire is still built on traditional means: 'enormous powers of oppression and destruction.' But according to a seminal work advancing the arrival of virtual empire, an empire expands precisely because of a lack of boundaries in a globalized international system. 'Spatial totality,' that is, rule over the entire civilized world, has become the defining feature of empire.[21] The US may not necessarily serve as an imperial center but it 'occupies a privileged position in the global segmentations and hierarchies of Empire.' That is because 'Imperial power is distributed in networks, through mobile and articulated mechanisms of control.'[22] We can suggest that the creation in late 2001 of a US government department concerned with homeland defense at the same time that the Bush administration declared a war on terrorism worldwide is clear evidence of the spatial totality of an American-organized postmodern empire.

Is this discussion of empires not anachronistic early in the twenty-first century? Not if we are to accept the thesis of one Russian studies specialist: 'Ironically, although imperialism may belong to the past, empire may belong to the future.'[23] Imperial emergence can occur 'via territorial expansion, regime change, elite formation, and societal transformation'.[24] By contrast, the emergence of empires through land acquisition, whether by war or purchase, is now improbable. The author contended that '[a]lthough the international sources of empire may have declined in importance, the internal sources are not only present, but, arguably, have assumed greater salience.'[25] The two principal internal sources are differentiation engendered by uneven modernization, and the replacement of democracy with dictatorship in multinational states.

Post-Soviet Russia may represent a combination of these two variants, as we discuss below, but it is not unique. For the problems associated with the processes of transforming empires into nations 'are found in many places: How is a national political identity forged in these cases? How was, or is, it possible to transform states and empires like Russia, China, Japan, Persia, Ottoman Turkey and Ethiopia into compact political communities and territorial nations?'[26] One view is that the 'movement towards the goal of the nation-state has been swifter where the dominant *ethnie* and its rulers have been able to divest themselves of their imperial heritage, usually by redrawing their borders'.[27] In Russia's case borders were redrawn but because it remained an empire it had still not become a nation-state with a problem-free national identity.

Let us examine the following proposition, then. The growth of nationalism in the periphery of reconfigured empires like Russia and India, when combined with a weak metropole elite and absence of legitimating ideology, can release a 'second round' of imperial disintegration with new breakaway movements tugging at the power of the center. The center's reaction to this is to attempt to reconstruct a home that remains an empire. In this task it faces a different series of challenges, as Fig. 3.1 outlines.

Russia

Russian nationalism and the imperial idea

Russian nationhood and national identity have been problematic in a way experienced by few other peoples. From its very beginnings in Kiev – the city

Russia	*India*
Globalization	Globalization
Deimperialized national identity	Colonially-constructed identity
Eurasianism	*Hindutva*
Regionalism	Faux secularism
Weak central authority	Centralization of power
Subnationalisms (Chechnya)	Subnationalisms (Kashmir)
Military weakness	Pakistan

Figure 3.1   Threats to empire in Russia and India

that today is capital of independent Ukraine – the Rus nation and the territories it inhabited were murky. As one prominent historian put it, '[t]he motifs of land, prince, and faith thus defined the essence and the boundaries of Rus from early times. It is important to note that the notion of the ''Russian people'' was absent, perhaps because of the tribal and ethnic diversity of Rus.'[28] A more ironic interpretation offered by a Russian historian was that as the Russian state expanded over time, the number of Russian people shrank.[29] Cases in point were the conquests, beginning in 1552, of the Tatar cities of Kazan and Astrakhan followed a century later by the annexation of much of Ukraine.

Another factor confounding Russian identity was the role of the West in defining it. In the late eighteenth century, much of the Russian nobility could not 'deny Europe's importance to the very sense of nationhood yet Russia's obvious cultural inferiority made the realization of equality a seemingly hopeless proposition'.[30] One academic has argued that throughout much of its history Russia was invariably cast as a nation striving to become like the West: 'Russia's specificity as Europe's Other does thus not reside along the spatial, but along the temporal dimension, as the country which is perpetually seen as being in some stage of transition to Europeanization.' It was constantly depicted as a pupil, a learner, a truant, sometimes gifted, sometimes pigheaded. Russia was always a 'not yet' or 'just'[31] At some point, 'the idea of apprenticeship had to give way to the idea of partnership'.[32] But this has clearly not happened at the turn of the third millennium.

In Chapter 1 we noted how the sense of *ressentiment*, combining admiration of with envy for the West, began to stake a permanent place in Russian national identity. Great eighteenth-century Westernizing leaders like Peter the Great and Catherine the Great were succeeded by xenophobic ones. The pattern continued into the following century, with the rules of Alexander I (who marched in triumph into Paris in 1815) and Alexander III ('the tsar liberator') squeezed in between anti-Western tsars. In this period Slavophile philosophers contended with Westernizers about Russia's future. If the latter stressed 'Europeanness', the first group held that '[t]he Russian road entailed a mixture of communalism, moral truth, authority and an interpretation of freedom which was somehow lost in the West.'[33] Twentieth-century Soviet history was also characterized by the cyclicity of Slavophile leaders (Stalin, Brezhnev, Chernenko) and Westernizers (Lenin, Khrushchev, Andropov, Gorbachev).

With its origins in Kiev and its ambivalence towards the West, Rus identity grappled with the fundamental question of whether it was European or not. There is irony in this debate:

The idea that Europe ends and Asia begins at the Urals was first presented by a Russian geographer. Having been charged by Peter the Great with the task of drawing up a new geography for his new empire, Vasiliy Tatishchev argued in the 1730s that instead of drawing the border along rivers, 'it would be much more appropriate and true to the natural configuration' to use the Urals – or the great belt – as the boundary.[34]

Identity was further complicated by Rus' diverse population. The supranational imperial notion of *rossianin* – a subject of the tsarist empire – was used to identify the increasing number of peoples ruled by Russia who were not *russkii* – ethnic Russians. All imperial institutions, together with the tsar himself, were described as *rossiiskii*, underscoring the supranational identity of Rus authority. When the Russian Orthodox Church broke from Western Christianity at the Council of Florence in 1439 and proclaimed Muscovy as the 'third Rome', it set itself up to be a supranational imperial institution inextricably tied to the Russian empire. Indeed, indistinct Russian national identity served an important purpose by advancing a quasi-universalist mission for the country. The much-criticized policy of russification of minority peoples in the nineteenth and twentieth centuries was in fact never very pronounced. In the nineteenth century 'the Russian government did not aim at eradicating nations and nationalities. It simply felt that their way of life should change in a process of natural evolution which their membership in the empire could speed up'.[35] As under the USSR, the national identities and nationalism of the minority peoples of the tsarist empire were stronger than that of the imperial nation itself, the Russians. By 1917, this pattern 'left the Russian nation, despite the wealth of its language, arts, and history, the ethnic group least prepared to develop a post-imperial identity'.[36] By the end of the twentieth century, Russian nationalists were complaining that 'the tragedy of Russia lay in the fact that small minorities had repeatedly imposed an alien ideology on the country, reducing the Russian people to mere bystanders and victims of their own history'.[37]

Finally, Russia's identity crisis was exacerbated by the historic crisis of the Russian state which had always served as an instrument of territorial expansion. One writer observed how Russia 'evolved as an empire-state rather than a nation-state, and the needs and rights of society have always been subordinated to the demands of the imperial state'. Just as important, 'the imperial state has been the product, as well as the cause of, much of Russian expansionary and militarist foreign policy'.[38] The Russian state, another specialist wrote, 'deliberately did not conceive itself to be a purely national instrument, in the West European tradition, but defined itself as the executor of a special supranational mission'.[39] That mission was loosely connected to variations of the 'Russian idea', whether defined in geopolitical, religious, or ideological terms. It followed that an ambivalent state identity engendered an uncertain national identity.

One imaginative attempt to capture contemporary Russian identity in an indirect way was through national self-images as representations of national identity:

Whereas identity in general provides an answer to the questions 'Who am I? Who am I not?,' and national identity like other collective identities addresses the questions 'Who are we? Who are we not?', the national self-image will provide, as it were, a Polaroid-like representation providing an answer to the questions 'What is our country? What is it not?'[40]

One study found major differences among regional politicians in their views on Russia's past (elements of pride and shame), its external dimension (mission in the world), and internal aspects (characteristics of the political system).

In the years following the USSR's disintegration, the position of Russia again seemed to be put more into question than that of other Soviet republics: 'Of all the nationalisms in the territories of the former Soviet Union, Russian nationalism has proved to be one of the weakest.'[41] The reasons for this involve

[s]ome basic patterns of Russia's historical development – such as (1) the immense power of the state and its arbitrary rule; (2) the hasty and ill-conceived Westernization, the result of which was an ever widening gulf between the higher and lower classes (almost 'two nations'); and (3) the lack of a strong middle class – combined to preclude the formation of civil society and *civic nation*, as opposed to *ethnonation*.[42]

We know that many nations rose against the USSR. But Russia's defiance under Yeltsin constituted a special case. Moscow had served as the cradle of communism, not its crucible. In the view of some specialists, communism had been an instrument 'enabling Russia to resist successfully that liquidation of colonialism carried out elsewhere in the world'.[43] But Yeltsin's peculiar brand of democracy after 1991 also seemed to be susceptible to the charge of balking at decolonization as both the newly-independent states neighboring it as well as the 'submerged' nations, or national minorities, within Russia still fell threatened by it. In short, 'just as in the case of the tsarist empire and the Soviet Union, modern Russia cannot behave simply as though it is the nation-state of the Russians. Whether that makes it imperialist is another question'.[44]

US statesman Dean Ascheson remarked in the 1950s that Britain had lost an empire but had not found a role. Russia without a newly-defined role is finding it difficult today to accept loss of empire. Not surprisingly, recourse to an imperial discourse is the easiest way out. That generates contradictory analyses from specialists. One stated emphatically that 'Russia is an empire. This assertion is as basic as the way that the famous historian Jules Michelet introduced his course on English history by declaring that "England is an island"'.[45] But others disagree and argue that

[t]he idea of the cost of the empire led to the slogan 'Russia out of the empire,' which became very popular in the early 1990s... in the new Russia, the Russian mind is no longer an imperial mind; on the contrary, the Russian population is largely, if not unanimously, convinced that the progress of the nation and the progress of the empire would be difficult to reconcile.[46]

How others view Russia is crucial in determining whether Russia is post-imperial or imperial still. There is a 'widespread perception throughout the region that, in spite of the collapse of the Soviet Union, the empire lives on'.[47] Furthermore 'perceptions of empire, a longing for empire, and a discourse of empire remain characteristic features of post-Soviet politics'.[48] Paradoxically, weakness and instability in some of the new independent states such as Belarus, Georgia, and Uzbekistan stimulate imperial ambitions: 'Failed state-building and the disorder that it engenders produces a kind of demand by the dominated themselves for external domination, giving rise to numerous opportunities for exercising legitimated domination',[49] thus engendering Russian power projection over non-Russian states. In addition, '[i]n the fractious realm of Russian domestic politics, one clear consensus among groups of all persuasions is that Russia should remain one of the world's "Great Powers"'.[50]

If Russia's imperial status has diminished greatly, its imperial identity seems to persist. Understanding contemporary forms of Russian nationalism is impossible without considering the impact of the collapse of the USSR. Walter Laqueur evoked the dramatic impact of this event – depicted almost exclusively in positive terms in the West – on the Russian psyche: 'Three centuries of Russian history were undone in a few days in August 1991 as the result of the weakness of the center.'[51] There could be no question, in his view, that the calamity of losing expansive Russian-ruled territories when the Soviet Union passed out of existence would evoke a backlash in Russian society:

The breakup of the Soviet Union is the central event bound to shape the course of Russian nationalism and of Russian politics, as far ahead as one can see. It could be compared with the impact of the Treaty of Versailles (1919) on postwar Germany and with the loss of North Africa for French politics in the 1950s and 1960s.[52]

Nostalgia for imperial status is at the core of many political movements in Russia today.

Another related reason for the persistence of imperial thought lies with the identity of Russia's other, the West. The relationship between these two identities is dialectical: 'Perhaps the most common element altering the national identity of a polity is the metamorphosis or the total disappearance of "the other." The collapse of the Habsburg empire, the disintegration of the USSR, and the withdrawal of European powers from their overseas possessions sharply redefined the "other" for scores of polities.'[53] But in the Russian case, the other has gained an even stronger identity over the past decade. Moreover, it has begrudged post-Soviet Russia recognition as a power to be reckoned with. It was especially important after Soviet collapse that Western powers should acknowledge Russia's unique role in the Eurasian land mass. The humbling of Russia's Soviet empire should have been followed by acclaim for the Russian Federation's continued status as a major power. Instead the West dramatized Russia's marginal status as NATO enlarged, Serbia was bombed, the G-7 kept Yeltsin on the outside, and the IMF compiled a school-like report card on Russia's economic behavior. It is not simply the strengthening of the other, but the other's perceived humiliating treatment of Russia, that has ensured that imperial identity has not vanished. Vladimir Putin's untroubled route to the presidency in 2000 is clear evidence of this.

An optimistic interpretation of *fin de l'empire* is that Russia is gradually learning about the folly of its imperial adventures:

> Three times in Russian history the loss of a war has brought about liberal political reforms within the country. The Crimean War of the 1850s led to the end of serfdom and to reforms in the legal structure, the army, and local self-government, as well as the weakening of censorship. After the Russo-Japanese war of 1904–1905, considerable limits were placed on the autocracy; civilian freedoms were strengthened and the beginnings of democratic rule were introduced. The Afghan war of the 1980s led to Gorbachev's perestroika. Each such reform brought the country nearer to the mainstream of social progress. And in each instance, reform struck a blow against the age-old Russian system of an all-powerful state.[54]

Lost wars affected Russia's domestic politics but they did not put an end to its imperial ambitions. The Crimean defeat did not stop tsarist Russia from going to war in the Pacific against Japan. That debacle became a footnote to Russia's twentieth-century history of expansion under communist tsars. The tragedy of Afghanistan has not discouraged post-Soviet Russia from undertaking a major military mission in the Pamirs. Putin's resolve to reverse the loss of the first Chechen war (1994–96) by launching the second war (1999–2000) casts doubt on whether any enduring lessons for empire are learned from military reversals.

One study summarized the debate about Russia's future as nation or empire this way: 'Some feel that Russia will not be able to retain its truncated integrity without at least a partial resurrection of the empire, while others believe that the demise of the empire has had a liberating effect on Russia that will allow it to become a normal nation pursuing its own national interest rather than imperial demands.'[55] As I have contended, the first approach seems to be the more influential: 'Although debates over Russia's national identity and interests have raged since the eighteenth century, the ideal of Russia as a superior civilization and a transcendent empire with a universal mission has remained. Indeed, a Russian national identity without this vision has yet to emerge.'[56] In addition, it is far from certain that even a thoroughly 'de-imperialized' Russia would usher in an era of peace for Russians and their neighbors.

Contemporary discourses on Russian identity

The crisis of Russian identity needs to be contextualized. It is interconnected with the more general postcommunist crisis of statehood. Many issues bearing on nationalities, like the status of minorities, are 'inseparable from the fundamental questions that the majority nation itself has to resolve concerning its own identity, its relation to the state, and the state's place in Europe and the wider international order'.[57] Especially given a weak state and weak central authority, Russian identity is in a profound existential crisis.

In the 1990s a variety of discourses on Russian identity appeared. In the evocative imagery of novelist Andrei Makine, the country was a pendulum pulled in two directions, swinging alternately between Europe and Asia. Two of his characters in Siberia grapple with this identity. As a pendulum Russia is 'nowhere at all', says one, 'neither one thing nor the other'. But his friend replies: 'to be neither one thing nor the other is also a destiny'.[58] Political leaders, historians, philosophers, and writers have formulated their versions of this existential drama. Let us review three of these.

The discourse of the Yeltsin administration was primarily statist and accepted that Russians' homeland (*otechestvo*) was now the Russian Federation. Provisions were made for the Russian diaspora living in the new independent states to become symbolically and legally part of the Russian nation. Accordingly,

> by offering extra-territorial citizenship to all those who have a connection – ethnic or historic – to the Russian homeland, Russia has attempted to redefine the nation while at the same time acknowledging the inviolability of the borderland states' sovereign spaces ... The [Yeltsin] regime has therefore attempted to create a Russian nation without restoring the homeland-empire.[59]

Two empire-restoring, irredentist discourses emerged alongside the statist one, one from the political right, the other from the left. The first underscored the need for reuniting historic Russian lands settled centuries ago by Russians, principally, Ukraine, Belarus, northern Kazakhstan, and the Narva region of Estonia. The second invoked the goal of a reconstituted Soviet fatherland (*sovetskaia rodina*): 'As the motherland of socialism, Russia is the advanced point of exemplarity.'[60] The mission of the Russian people was to unite with other peoples in a common socialist destiny. These various discourses on identity were grounded in differing visions of borders and borderlands.

Arguably the most debated variation of imperial identity in recent times has been Eurasianism. As one supporter of this idea has polemicized, at a symbolic level, 'The double-headed eagle of the Russian empire manifestly expressed the main geopolitical and geohistorical essence of the country: its inner Eurasian character.'[61] The idea highlights the inseparability of Russians' love of vast open spaces (*porstornost*) with communal consensus (*obshchennyi sobornost*). Through imperial restoration, both of these values can be realized. The Eurasian idea is relatively modern and originates in the works of Prince Nikolai Trubetskoi and geographer Pyotr Savitskii. They

> tried in the 1920s and 1930s to give a theoretical underpinning to the identity of Russia as a non-European state. They downplayed the significance of the Urals by drawing attention to the parallel zones of humidity and the corresponding vegetation zones which characterize Siberia and European Russia but not Western Europe. They tried to derive the character of Russian society from the perennial struggle between steppe and taiga.[62]

Eurasianism has an ethnographic dimension: 'Eurasia is not merely a huge continent, it contains in its center a super ethnos bearing the same name'.[63] It is part of a tripod that includes the Muslim world to the south and the Germano-Latin world to the west. The Eurasian idea asserts that

> [i]f Russia is to preserve its cultural heritage, it must maintain a culturally non-threatening union with the Turkic people or face a cultural annihilation inflicted by the West...Since, according to many statists, Russians cannot exist as Russians outside a Russian state, making a multinational Russian state across Eurasia is vital to the survival of Russians as a people.[64]

This point also holds true for the Russian Federation itself. As one scholar contended, its institutional framework cannot be anchored solely in Russian identity. The Western model of civic nation cannot replace the inter-ethnic links forming the core of a distinct Russian multicultural state.[65]

There is a bewildering political characteristic to Eurasianism. 'Unlike Western realists who emphasize nation-states as key players of international politics, Eurasianists argue in favor of empires as the key units of action.'[66] Unlike most other contemporary narratives of Russian identity, this one begins with the belief that a Eurasian Russia must be at least the size of the USSR and possibly even greater. Eurasianists are divided into two currents.

'Modernizers offer the restoration of the Soviet Union under the name of the Eurasian empire to maintain geopolitical balances and international stability.'[67] By contrast, in order to contain US imperialism, which poses the main threat to Russia, Europe, and Asia, '[e]xpansionists advocate a further imperial expansion of Russia beyond the borders of the former Soviet Union'.[68]

Eurasianists and neo-communists share a common cause and seem natural partners in a political coalition. Novelist-turned-political-activist Alexander Prokhanov was a key figure in the effort to forge a unified opposition to Yeltsin and worked closely with communist party head Gennadiy Zyuganov to establish a 'patriotic' front based loosely on Eurasian ideas. In Prokhanov's newspaper *Den* (renamed *Zavtra* in 1993), journalist Alexander Dugin established himself as the leading theoretician of neo-Eurasianism.[69] His vision of world history was of perpetual conflict between the order of Eurasianists and that of Atlanticists. 'The Germans and Russians have embodied the Indo-European ideal of rooted, spiritual, Aryan Eurasianism in more recent history; the Jews, British, and Americans, the rootless, materialistic, commercial Atlanticist idea.'[70] Enlisting both Islam and a spiritually-revived Europe as allies, 'Russia's long-term task is to unite the anti-Atlanticist, antimondialist forces of Eurasia in a new imperial alliance.... Dugin's envisioned continental imperial alliance will span the Eurasian landmass from Dublin to Vladivostok, with Moscow ("the third Rome") serving as the continental capital.'[71]

Such a model of Eurasianism flies in the face of admonitions for Russia to avoid the mistakes of the past. It also flies in the face of the views of much of the Russian public whose general cultural orientation is towards Europe.[72] A stigma is attached, especially by the better-educated, to the 'Asiatic' element in Russian society. No matter how appealing it may be as an ideological construct or strategic program, then, Eurasianism has much ground to cover in obtaining converts and becoming a popular movement.

Those opposed to empire rebuilding stress that Russia and the USSR have been victims of their vastness: 'the Soviet Union is so damned big that it has too many common homes for the comfort of its many neighbors'.[73] Nobel laureate Alexander Solzhenitsyn warned that Russia had to resist geopolitical imperatives and concentrate on reforming itself from within. 'Should we be struggling for warm seas far away, or ensuring that warmth rather than enmity flows between citizens?'[74] Russia had to 'free itself of great-power thinking and imperial delusions ... The time has come for an uncompromising choice between an empire ... and the spiritual and physical salvation of our own people'.[75] Solzhenitsyn thus rejected both Eurasian and pan-Slavic futures for Russia, preferring to concentrate on Russia's internal makeup: 'When we say "nationality," we do not mean blood but always a spirit, a consciousness.'[76] Yet, paradoxically, he ruled out the desirability of a multicultural Russia: 'Even after all the separations, our state will inevitably remain a multicultural one, despite the fact that this is not a goal we wish to pursue.'[77]

There is little agreement on the identity of contemporary Russia, then. To be sure, '[t]he common denominator of all nationalist discourse seems to be the attribution of a non-Western identity to Russia and the avowal of the unity of the Eurasian territory, an area which more or less corresponds with the pre-revolutionary empire'.[78] For Russia's political elite, the West unquestionably serves as alterity – what Russia is not. Some go further to impugn what the country should not be: 'Russian nationalists often describe the fate that awaits them with the advent of globalism as "genocide"'.[79] They fear that Russia could even become extinct if it accepted the premises of globalization. But the political establishment today affirms that Russia's salvation lies precisely in trying to become like the advanced West. Given that for much of the Russian population identity is based on language, Orthodoxy, and community, with the West not helping to define their Russia, it is not surprising that there has been so much havoc in the country.

Russian nationalists right and left

Russia's nationalist right consists of a potpourri of groups and leaders trying to influence those in power. One typology of Russian nationalism from perestroika onwards, identified 1) liberal nationalists who reject the authoritarian past but take pride in Russian culture; 2) centrist nationalists who are modern-day Slavophiles, cautious about Westernization but avoiding xenophobia; and 3) authoritarian nationalists who comprise the nationalist right and manipulate Leninism to achieve nationalist aims.[80] Such a typology does not take into account 'nationalist wildcards', for example, self-styled enlightened patriot Valerii Zorkin who introduced the oxymoronic idea of 'liberal imperialism'. Russia's past imperialism, he believed, involved a peaceful in-gathering of lands. For the future, '[t]he proponents of liberal imperialism reject the idea of reestablishing the USSR. Their desired goal is a new union of Russia, Ukraine, Belarus, and Kazakhstan on a voluntary basis'.[81]

Nationalist movements have generally been split internally into democratic and authoritarian factions. One of these, the loosely-organized monarchists, included both constitutional and autocratic forces, as well as those expressing tolerance towards minorities and others proposing an exclusionary notion of Russian citizenship. An extreme right-wing monarchist organization, *Zemshchina*, was both anti-democratic and opposed to rights for minorities and religions other than Russian Orthodoxy. It proposed the nineteenth-century Romanov slogan of 'Autocracy, Orthodoxy, Nationality' as the bedrock principle for the Russian Federation. This monarchist group was inspired in part by the absolutist and anti-Semitic Black Hundreds movement of the turn of the twentieth century.

Cossacks, too, can be viewed as a right-wing nationalist movement. Romanticized in Russian literature as horsemen of the steppe guarding Russia's borders and conquering new lands, they were made up of people of different ethnic backgrounds, especially Tatar, Turkic, and Ukrainian. Cossacks occasionally carried out the tsar's dirty work in the nineteenth century, harassing the Polish population living in Ukrainian lands and carrying out pogroms of Jews in the Pale of Settlement. Shortly after he became president, Yeltsin recognized their right to participate in Russian military activity, and Cossacks supported regular Russian army forces and helped destabilize their adversaries in the Caucasus, in particular in Chechnya and Abhazia.

The Orthodox church, revived at the end of the Soviet period, includes some nationalist groups. One historian explained the connection: 'Most clergymen feel more at home with the nationalists than with the liberals. The nationalists will not constantly remind them of their past collaboration with the Communist regime and demand purges in their leadership.'[82] Orthodox Patriarch Alexey sought to distance himself from right-wing nationalists such as Metropolitan Ioann of St. Petersburg who advocated anti-democratic, anti-Semitic, imperialist ideas that comprised *sobornost*, or spiritual unity. 'The geopolitical embodiment of Orthodox *sobornost* is empire, which Ioann defined as "great power statehood in the Christian sense", a great power covering vast territories and disparate peoples.'[83] In many respects Ioann, who died in 1995, represented a Christian adaptation of the *gosudarstvenniki* movement, those proponents of Russian state power who, like Alexander Rutskoi (Yeltsin's treacherous vice-president who led the parliamentary uprising against the president in October 1993), embraced the idea of *derzhava*, or great power, for Russia.

In March 1990 an obscure man established what seemed destined to be just another fringe political party, yet within a year he became the personification of Russian ultra-nationalism. In June 1991 Vladimir Zhirinovsky, founder of the Liberal Democratic Party of Russia (LDPR), received nearly six million votes – 'as many as all the people in Switzerland' – in Russia's first direct presidential election. He campaigned on an extremist platform characterized by vicious attacks on the Other – Germany, Japan, the Baltic states, the 'South' (Muslim lands), Jews. As a Western academic wrote of him, '[n]o politician in postcommunist Russia has more explicitly tied Russian survival and prosperity to territorial expansion than Vladimir Zhirinovsky. No politician has exploited *ressentiment* regarding the West as effectively as Zhirinovsky, and no other politician has managed to tap the Russian vice of neglecting personal responsibility and wallowing in envy of one's neighbor more skillfully than Zhirinovsky'.[84]

Zhirinovsky's popularity with voters peaked with the 1993 Duma elections. By the 1996 presidential election his nationalism was crowded out by that of other candidates, in particular Rutskoi, head of the *Derzhava* coalition; Alexander Lebed, former head of the Russian army in Moldova who placed a strong third behind Yeltsin and Zyuganov; and Yeltsin himself, who had become more nationalist as part of his maneuvering for reelection. In the Dumas elected in 1995 and 1999 Zyuganov's Communist Party of the Russian Federation (KPRF) won more seats than any other political grouping and therefore assured itself considerable legislative influence. With a restorationalist agenda, the KPRF continuously questioned Yeltsin's statist nationalism. It was sometimes supported by other nationalist parties (the LDPR in 1996, Fatherland-All Russia in 1999), transforming the Duma into the political tribune for the nationalist movement. In 1999 the Unity Bloc, hastily set up to support Putin's bid for the presidency, won just six seats less than the KPRF by campaigning on no specific nation building program. Whether the Russian legislature was less under the control of nationalist forces than before depended on whether Putin was to be viewed as a state builder like Yeltsin, or as a restorationalist.

Putin was appointed prime minister in August 1999, assumed the presidency in line with the constitutionally-delineated succession process when Yeltsin resigned at the end of December 1999, then won a simple majority (53.4 percent) in the first round of the presidential elections held in March 2000. His career path itself reflects lengthy service to empire. Putin became the third consecutive prime minister appointed by Yeltsin who came from the ranks of the KGB (Evgenii Primakov and Sergei Stepashin preceded him), the most secretive, repressive, and undemocratic institution in the former Soviet Union. His rise to power began with public revulsion with the bombings of Moscow apartment buildings in 1999, blamed on Chechen terrorists but with suggestions that the overhauled KGB that Putin headed (the Federal Security Service, or FSB) might have been involved. He quickly ordered the invasion of Chechnya which, for a time at least, was a popular war among Russians. The new president also recruited extensively from the security services in establishing his administration.[85]

In his speeches at home Putin has ambiguously referred to the greatness of the Russian state and the dictatorship of law. Whether suppressing the power of regional governors, enhancing presidential control over the media, more tightly regulating political parties, or approving increased surveillance of internet communications, the new president seems determined to associate himself with a stronger Russia. His foreign policy reflects a Eurasianist orientation illustrated by increased cooperation with China, Iran, and the Arab world. After the US had been blamed for the NATO attack on Serbia in 1999, for provoking the war in Chechnya that same year, and even for accidentally sinking the submarine Kursk in 2000, relations with the US improved after the first meeting between Putin and Bush in Slovenia in June 2001 and were further solidified by a shared struggle against Islamic fundamentalism after September 2001. But anti-Western outbursts distinguished the Putin presidency from that of his predecessor. In certain respects, therefore, it is possible to say that Russian nationalism had returned to the Kremlin.

Challenges from within the new Russian empire

We can identify two principal challenges facing the Russian state today. One involves the incongruence of homeland and peoples, in particular, non-Russian minorities living in the Russian Federation and large Russian diaspora populations residing in neighboring states. A second is secessionism in the ethnic republics of the Federation, above all in Chechnya. Both throw light on the question whether a revamped Russian empire has come into existence.

Multinational settings

In the 1980s many Russians came to believe that too many 'foreigners' were living in the USSR. Russian nationalists began to raise the issue of ethnic justice in the Soviet period when small or backward peoples seemed to be receiving more than their fair share of a dwindling pool of resources. They condemned the predatory behavior of many non-Russians: 'Why do Estonians and Latvians, Armenians and Georgians, enjoy higher standards of living than we do?' Average Russians felt that criminal activity also disproportionately favored the ethnic mafias. The ethnic *kto kovo* question – who was taking advantage of whom – became salient. One writer traced Soviet economic stagnation to 'the system of patronage inherent in the affirmative action programs which, in turn, led to the rise of regionally and/or ethnically based criminal networks that operated at the expense of the official economy'.[86] Perceptions of unequal competition, therefore, helped fuel the nationalist tide within Russia.

Russian nationalists also felt that many lands that were historically Russian, like the Crimea – indeed, most of Ukraine – the northern part of Kazakhstan, and much of the Caucasus, had been infiltrated and stolen by other nations. On the streets of Almaty (Kazakhstan), Kiev (Ukraine), Simferopol (Crimea), and Kazan (Tatarstan), a Russian backlash against the titular nationality became discernable. The 25–million-strong Russian 'beached diaspora',[87] stranded in Soviet republics that after 1991 became new states, felt that it had lost rights even if it lived in traditional Russian lands. A reactive nationalism emerged within a once dominant nation that sensed it was losing status, but interethnic relations alone did not explain the feeling of marginalization. 'The sources of a significant part of interethnic violence . . . are to be found in the *intragroup* politics of internal policing and boundary protection.'[88] Within the Russian diaspora, pressure could be brought to bear against anyone considering assimilation into, say, Estonian culture. Still, there could come a point at which identity shift began to cascade or 'tip'. In Latvia in the future, for example, Russians as a group might conceivably choose the local language for themselves and their children and thereby assimilate. This could be the result of rational economic choice or of Russian identity boundaries no longer being enforced or enforceable.

The option of Russians now living in the 'near abroad' returning 'home' to Russia was not as straightforward as it might seem. Even if they were guaranteed citizenship in the Federation, they still had to confront 'the cultural parameters of the 'otherness' of the 'other' Russia after their resettlement in Russia'.[89] As with other diaspora communities, then, in Russia too the assumption that the ancestral place of origin was still 'home' could represent an untenable ethnic view of the state.[90] Just as German unification revealed differences between citizens of Western and Eastern states, Russian diaspora incorporation into the Russian Federation was unlikely to be a smooth process.

Post-Soviet Russia showcased the preeminence of the titular nation. 'Today, for the first time in centuries, ethnic Russians represent a significant majority of the state they live in – 80 percent instead of 50 percent.'[91] For ethnonationalists like Solzhenitsyn whose views we described earlier, that high figure was still not enough. A multicultural Russia was undesirable; a purely Russian (*russkaya*) republic, designed for 'the preservation of the people', was.[92]

Ethnic republics

Strictly speaking, the Russian Federation is a multinational rather than multicultural state. This is evidenced in the establishment of 21 ethnically-defined homelands, or republics. Besides these republics are 68 territorially-delineated regions, many of them distrustful of centralizing Russian nationalism. The republics only account for 7 percent of the total population but span more than half the territory of the Federation. Their non-Russian population (which is still smaller than Russians) is concerned about the resurgence of Russian nationalism in the many forms that we have described. As early as the December 1993 referendum on adopting a new Russian constitution, differences between Russian administrative territories and the non-Russian republics emerged: while 60 percent of voters in the 'non-ethnic' regions voted for approval, it was supported by a minority (48 percent) in the ethnic republics. The extent of nationalism in the 21 republics varies from people to people. The Chechens fought two bitter wars in the 1990s to try to gain independence. By contrast, other titular nations (Chuvash, Dagestanis, Mari, and Mordovians) scored very low on a separatism index. Many reasons can be advanced for differences in the autonomy-seeking pattern of nations: histories, grievances, national character, leadership, ethnic homogeneity, wealth. The author of the index cited above offered an additional institutionalist perspective: 'it appears almost certain that the strength of national identity and the extent of links to nationalist movements depend in large measure on the ethnic institutions of the state'.[93]

At the beginning of the 1990s many minority peoples made concerted efforts to liberate themselves from rule by Moscow.[94] As the Soviet Union disintegrated, disturbances in Yakutia and the north Caucasus were among the first to demonstrate minorities' dissatisfaction at being ruled by the distant Kremlin. The seven million Tatars, scattered throughout Russia and now its largest minority group, also became restless. The center of the Russian Federation seemed as remote from Tatars and Yakuts as before. During 1990–91 most of the republics within Russia declared state sovereignty. These 'sovereignty games' were intended to consolidate local rulers' positions as well as to enhance the status of their republic within Russia. They also left open the possibility that these republics might be allowed to join the Commonwealth of Independent States (CIS) as separate states. In rare cases, sovereignty declarations were even intended for an international audience, as in the case of Tatarstan's assertion that it was the northernmost Islamic state in the world.[95] Chechnya alone took the sovereignty game literally and was attacked by Russia in December 1994.

The war in Chechnya reversed a trend of settling disputes over autonomy between the central government and the republics through peaceful means. In March 1992 Tatarstan, together with Chechnya, were the only two republics that refused to sign the Russian Federation treaty. However, after walking out of the Russian Constitutional Assembly in June 1993, Yeltsin and Tatarstan leader Mintimir Shaimiev signed an accord in February 1994 granting that nation considerable autonomy. Tatarstan secured sovereignty over its oil and other natural resources and obtained recognition for its self-proclaimed constitution and presidency, republican citizenship laws, and special rights for military service on the territory of Tatarstan. During the next months Russia concluded similar treaties with the republics of Bashkortostan and Kabardino-Balkaria (the latter next door to Chechnya).

The full-scale invasion of Chechnya showed that Yeltsin had abandoned his policy of encouraging minority nationalities to demand as much political autonomy from the center as they could manage. Chechen president Dzhokhar Dudayev's determination to hold Yeltsin to his word was a principal reason for the Russian invasion. The conflict gave the appearance of being a classic confrontation between the subnationalism of an upstart nation and the imperial nationalism of a humiliated great nation. Russian nationalism alone did not explain Yeltsin's decision to invade. Strategic considerations, national and economic interests, and his own power game were important factors as well.

There are four million Muslims in the north Caucasus and another fifteen million in the rest of the Russian Federation. Although most mosques and *medrese* ('seminaries') were shut down in the Soviet period and religious persecution pursued, Muslims of the north Caucasus continued to adhere to Islamic brotherhoods, or Sufism. The collapse of Soviet power provided an opportunity for the 're-Islamicization' of the region as people searched for a new identity. In the war with Russia, Islam became the fundamental ideology of the Chechen resistance. Rebels declared a *jihad* ('holy war') and attacked Russian positions shouting *Allahu akbar!* ('God is great'); and the cry was repeated as residents of Grozny greeted the victorious forces entering the city in August 1996. The Russians departed, for just over three years as events were to prove.

When Dudayev declared an Islamic state in 1991, it had little appeal to the Chechen population. This was partly because of some successes in the Soviet period in fashioning a secular, atheistic way of life here, and partly because Islam came late to Chechnya – in the nineteenth century, compared to southern Dagestan where it was introduced by the Arabs in the seventh century. Dudayev himself did not set out to politicize the Muslim faith and emphasized that 'Russia forced us into Islam'. Islam distinguished Chechens from the Russians, it had served as the ideological rival of Russian Marxism and now of Russian Orthodoxy, and it was embraced by Chechens because of the logic of resistance.

At the end of September 1999 prime minister Putin ordered a second invasion of Chechnya after apartment bombings in Moscow were blamed on Chechen terrorists. He was able to project the war as the start of Russia's return to great power status and most Russians, desperate for a political savior by then, gave him the benefit of the doubt. On New Year's Day 2000, when he took office from Yeltsin, Putin flew to Russian-occupied Chechnya to award medals to Russian commanders. There he reiterated Russia's goal: 'It is about putting an end to the breakup of the Russian Federation.' While that was his broader objective, the Chechen resistance was not destroyed and continued to plague Putin for a long time thereafter.

The attempted suppression of Chechnya was of a piece. The tough-talking president also began to rein in the powers of other ethnic republics and even of Russia's regions. If there was one message that he was sending out across the Russian Federation, it was that the games of sovereignty were over for good. Such a policy does not necessarily signify empire restoration, but it clearly is intended to put an end to further erosion of Russian Federation unity.

Russia's view of home

The odds are against Russia becoming a nation-state. It is more likely to resemble an empire, if in the guise of a multinational state. Moreover, as the threats of a Russia weakened by multinationalism, rebellious ethnic republics and recalcitrant regions recede, the probability of the adoption of an imperial agenda increases. Homeland as empire has seemed to be the way most Russians have viewed their history. Without empire, homeland becomes elusive. As one study concluded:

> Only to the extent to which the inhabitants actually see their country as their homeland, as their *patria*, as the unit to which they connect their own identity – only to that extent will the state be able to assume the nation-state mantle. That is why the most serious obstacle to Russian

nation-state consolidation is that so few of Russia's politicians contribute to it, whereas so many actively work against the entire project.[96]

India

Thesis–antithesis: the British empire and Indian nationalism

A historian at Cambridge University asserted that 'British rule in India became the most spectacular case of imperialism in modern times'.[97] This jewel in Queen Victoria's crown became, after London, the second center of British world power. 'By the later nineteenth century the Indian Empire covered a sub-continent of one and a half million square miles, inhabited in 1881 by some 256 million people. More than one-third of India was composed of native states, with a population of fifty-six millions. In the remainder, the British directly ruled almost two hundred million subjects.'[98] If Europe was Russia's Other, Britain was India's. But Britain colonized India where Europe did not impose itself on Russia.

Modern Indian nationalism emerged in the late nineteenth century and for the next fifty years struggled against British imperialism. It emerged victorious in 1947 when an independent – though partitioned – Indian state was proclaimed. The character of Indian nationalism was greatly shaped by British rule. As one Indian scholar noted, it 'emerged against the background of changes associated with British imperialism, notably as they impinged upon the political structure, economy and education of the country'.[99]

The absence of a national consciousness together with socio-political divisions were primary reasons for the relative ease with which the British seized power in India. The English East India Company had begun trading on the subcontinent in the seventeenth century when India was under the Mughals, but the Battle of Plassey fought in 1757 gave the Company, and England, effective control over the key Indian province of Bengal. The Raj, or India as it came to exist under British rule, comprised two types of political units. The first comprised the major bulk of territory ruled directly, first by the British East India Company, then after 1857 by the British Crown. However, numerous princely states existed, ruled by hereditary princes and monarchs who enjoyed substantial autonomy in return for loyalty to the British in India. The British East India Company succeeded in creating a national economy by linking landowners more directly to the state. This national economy 'became the material premise for the emergence of the Indian nation out of the amorphous mass of the Indian people'.[100]

The national economy was consolidated by the establishment of modern industries and the creation of a common currency. The British were primarily interested in industries that served their economic and military interests, such as jute, cotton, coal, and iron and steel. This led to the growth of modern industrial cities which became the arenas for modern India's socio-economic, political, and cultural life. Here new social forces combined to instil a spirit of national consciousness and nationalism. Industrialization also required modern forms of transportation and communication – railways, shipping, telephone and telegraph – thus further unifying the country.

Probably the best known reform implemented by the British in India was the political, administrative, and legal unification of the country. Replacing the old Indian legal system based on customary law, the British introduced common law which posited the legal equality of all citizens. A centralized bureaucracy was set up to take over the administrative powers of village and caste committees. A new education system patterned on that in England included new schools and colleges producing graduates to staff the vast administrative machinery and economic infrastructure of the country. The key administrative posts always remained in British hands but local help was needed, such as English-speaking administrative clerks, lawyers familiar with the English legal system, doctors trained in modern medicine, technicians to operate industrial plants, and teachers. The introduction of English education created a well-educated class of Indians called the *bhadrolok*, or gentlemen class. Its members became familiar with Western democratic political ideals and subsequently spearheaded the movement for India's freedom.

The power of the state was used to safeguard and enhance British interests in India. The colonizers used various strategies ranging from outright annexation of territory, collusion with local rulers in return for British protection, the creation of loyal social classes such as the *zamindars*, encouraging religious divisions in Indian society through the policy of divide-and-rule, and the use of brute force when necessary. Many sections of Indian society discovered the drawbacks of alien rule:

> The industrial bourgeoisie found in the absolute control of India by Britain an obstacle to carry through its program of unfettered industrial development. The educated classes found in the monopoly of key posts in the state machinery by the British an obstacle to their just ambition to secure jobs. The . . . peasantry, found in the new land and revenue systems introduced by Britain the basic cause of their progressive impoverishment. The proletariat found in the British rule a foreign undemocratic agency preventing it from developing class struggles for improving their conditions of life and labor and finally for ending the wage system itself under which they were exploited.[101]

These grievances formed the basis for the rise of anti-colonialism and of Indian nationalism. There was an underlying paradox in this. The ideas of national self-determination and liberal nationalism arose in the West. Indian nationalists viewed them as progressive but recognized that they originated in an alien culture and had to be adapted to India's culture. There was, thus, a double rejection: first, of the Western intruder though not of certain Western ideas and practices seen as progressive; and second, of one own's traditional culture, especially those beliefs, customs, and practices that were seen as obstacles to progress.

How were these two imperatives reconciled? Partha Chatterjee argued that Indian nationalists distinguished 'the world of social institutions and practices into two domains – the material and the spiritual'.[102] The material domain consisted of the 'outside' world of the national economy, politics and political institutions, and science and technology where the imperial power was to be confronted but where the superiority of certain Western ideas and achievements were to be replicated. The spiritual domain consisted of the 'essential' marks of cultural identity. 'The greater one's success in imitating Western skills in the material domain, therefore, the greater the need to preserve the distinctness of one's spiritual culture.'[103]

There were thus two components of Indian nationalism. First, at the material level, it involved political struggle against British imperialism, though not against Western political and economic ideas nor against Western discourses on modernity. Second, at the spiritual level, it involved the creation of a distinct modern Indian national culture which differed from both traditional Indian and Western cultures. This Indian national culture was both syncretist and exclusionary.

What part was played by the division of this culture into Hindu and Muslim communities? One specialist has contended that

> there is no reason to argue that antagonistic Hindu and Muslim nations existed before the nineteenth century. On the contrary, nationalist discourses emerged in India in the same period that thinkers in Europe tried to formulate them. Only then could Hindu and Muslim movements... start to transform a plethora of religious communities, which indeed were often antagonistic, into Hindu and Muslim nations.[104]

If the political manifestation of Indian nationalism was responsible for the end of British imperialism in India, then the spiritual dimension served to partition India at the time of independence.

Institutionalizing Indian nationalism

The Indian national movement started out as elitist, secular, non-confrontational, with limited goals. Over time it evolved into a mass movement that employed radical but generally non-violent means of political activity to achieve independence from British rule. It was accompanied by a concurrent increase in the strength of Muslim nationalism that, by the late 1930s, called for a separate state for the Indian Muslims. Facing this intractable double challenge, the ability and will of the British government to rule India declined over time.

The first nationalist uprising took place in 1857. Called the *Sepoy* (or Soldiers') Mutiny, cavalry units of the Bengali Army revolted against their British officers but were crushed within months. This represented the first nationalist spark 'in the way that the participants were imbued with the sense of a common nationhood and were fighting for their country and freedom'.[105] To be sure, nationalism as an *organized* political movement began with the formation of the Indian National Congress in 1885. From the outset, the Congress projected itself as a secular, all-India institution concerned with national policies and steering clear of issues that could give rise to religious or social conflict. The Congress strove for limited political and economic reforms that would give Indians greater say in the legislative councils, wider entry into the Indian Civil Service (ICS), and more equitable land taxes. Congress liberals wished 'to convince the British of the justness of the demands of the Indian people and of their democratic duty to meet them'.[106] When this strategy produced few tangible results, a group in the Congress called for more militant action.

The basis for a call for greater militancy was the belief in the spiritual greatness of India. Unlike the secular outlook of the liberals, the militants invoked indigenous symbols to identify closely with Hinduism. They claimed that India was the land of Hindus, that India's greatness came from the Hindu religion, especially the teachings of the *Bhagavad Gita* and the *Vedas*. For M.S. Golwalkar, an early guru of the Rashtriya Swayamsevak Sangh (RSS, or Association of National Volunteers), Hindus were the 'first thought-givers to the world'.[107] For the Hindu nationalist leader V.D. Savarkar writing in the 1920s, '[a] Hindu means a person who regards this land of Bharat Varsha, from the Indus to the Seas, as his Father-Land as well as his Holy-Land that is the cradle of his religion'.[108] Hinduness, or *Hindutva*, thus conflates religious and national identity and 'marked a qualitative change in Hindu nationalism, aspects of which had previously been combined in a loose ideology but which had now acquired a more systematic exposition'.[109] The RSS, a militant sectarian Hindu organization, was founded in 1925 to serve as an ideological training school for Hindu cadres. But it also became involved in violence against Muslim groups.

The militant Hindu faction of the Congress party called for a boycott of British products, the promotion of *Swadeshi* (economic self-reliance) and *Swaraj* (self-rule), and widespread political agitation (such as the anti-Partition agitation in Bengal after the province was partition by Lord Curzon in 1905). It engaged in bombings, assassination of government officials, and robberies to finance its activities.[110]

Predictably, the close identification of a part of the Congress party with Hinduism had a major impact on Hindu–Muslim relations and contributed to the growth of Muslim separatism. The Muslim community had mixed feelings about the Indian National Congress. On the one hand, the rise of

Indian nationalism provided India with an opportunity to regain the pride that had been lost when the British wrested power from the Mughals in the eighteenth century. On the other hand, 'the doctrine of nationalism and the general realization among the Muslims that the triumph of this ideology would reduce them to a state of permanent political subjugation by the more numerous Hindus' produced a sense of fear.[111] In 1906 those subscribing to this view decided to form the Indian Muslim League to promote their interests.

Religious polarization was embedded in the construction of visions of home on the subcontinent.

> From its very beginning in the nineteenth century nationalism in India has fed upon religious identifications. This is true not only for the two most important religious communities in India, Hindus and Muslims, but also for groups like the Sikhs and, in Sri Lanka, the Buddhists. In all these cases nation building is directly dependent on religious antagonism, between Hindus and Muslims, between Sikhs and Hindus, between Buddhists and Hindus.[112]

Some scholars reject this explanation for Muslim separatism. A few argue that Indian Muslims' attitude towards Indian nationalism was shaped by the teachings of their own religion, in particular, the supremacy of *umma*, the community of believers in Allah, over *watan*, the fatherland or territorial nation. Others suggest that the Indian Muslims' rejection of Indian nationalism was the result of deep-rooted cultural cleavage between the two communities which was reinforced under the Raj. Still other scholars question whether Indian Muslims formed a monolithic community.

The British government was the chief beneficiary of the split within the Congress Party and between Hindu and Muslim communities. It reneged on a promise of wider legislative powers for Indians contained in the draft constitutional reform bill introduced by Lord Morley in 1908. It fostered close relations with the Muslim League and negotiated directly with it to safeguard Muslim interests in India, for example, the 1909 Act that created a separate electorate for Muslims. To be sure, a short-lived rapprochement between Hindus and Muslims produced the Muslim League-Congress (Lucknow) Pact of 1916 which committed both movements to Indian self-government. But apart from a few Western-educated Muslim leaders like Mohammad Ali Jinnah, much of the Muslim religious elite remained hostile to the ideology of Indian nationalism.[113]

Gandhi, the national movement, and Muslim nationalism

A turning point in the history of the Indian national movement was the rise of Mahatma Gandhi to the Congress leadership in 1920. Until then the Congress had been controlled by Western-educated Indian elites who claimed to speak on behalf of the people. Under Gandhi's leadership, the Congress quickly became a mass movement with a more populist ideology and strategy. Gandhi had little faith in the approach taken by the Congress moderates but he abhorred the terrorism advocated by the extremists. His preference was for radical political action carried out non-violently. He reconciled this seeming contradiction through the novel technique of *satyagraha*, or truth force. In 1928 the Congress issued an ultimatum that if dominion status was not conceded by the British within a year, it would launch a civil disobedience campaign aimed at *purna swaraj*, or complete independence. When the British staled, Congress organized the Civil Disobedience Movement in 1930, stalted by Gandhi's historic Salt March to Dandi – a protest against the tax imposed by the British government on salt.

The Muslim League's reaction to Congress efforts to obtain independence was hostile. It viewed *purna swaraj* as a Hindu plot to oust the British from India and thereafter rule over Muslims. In 1920 Jinnah opposed *satyagraha* and resigned from the Congress, boosting the fortunes of the Muslim League. Only Muslim leaders who saw the British as a greater threat than the Hindu majority (as well as Muslims of the North-West Frontier Province) supported the Civil Disobedience Movement.

Under Labour Party leader Ramsay MacDonald, the British government took a small constitutional step forward and passed the Government of India Act of 1935. It proposed a federal constitution encompassing both British India and the princely states and contained provisions for minorities, such as separate electorates for Muslims in all the provinces.[114] It therefore reserved legislative seats for Anglo-Indians, Sikhs, landlords, Europeans, and Christians, and Muslims were guaranteed one-third representation in the central legislature.

The Government of India Act was condemned by both British Conservative Party leader Winston Churchill and the Indian National Congress. While Churchill, not without some foundation, saw the Act as 'the beginning of the dissolution of the Empire',[115] the Congress condemned it for providing parliamentary quotas for minorities, giving weight to princely states, and failing to bestow dominion status on India. In sum, the Act of 1935 fell considerably short of Gandhi's *purna swaraj*.

During deliberations over the Act of 1935, the Muslim League insisted on separate Muslim electorates within the framework of an undivided India.[116] But its dismal performance in the 1937 elections changed its political thinking. When, furthermore, the Congress reneged on its promise to include Muslims in ministerial posts, Jinnah accused it of trying to establish a 'Hindu Raj'. The inescapable conclusion was that a separate state had to be created for Indian Muslims. The idea was formally embraced by the Muslim League at its Lahore session in March 1940. Jinnah's justification for a future independent Pakistan was based on the concept of 'separate nation'. Indian

Muslims were now defined not merely as a separate but as a 'self-determining political community', a separate nation that was smaller but equal to the Hindu. This was the essence of the 'Two-Nation' theory under which Jinnah called for the creation of a separate Muslim nation, Pakistan.

The Two-Nation theory was originally developed by a Muslim poet and philosopher, Muhammad Iqbal, and a young Muslim student at Cambridge, Chaudhuri Rahmat Ali. In 1930 Iqbal, then President of the League, had contended that for Indian Muslims to achieve self-government and avoid Hindu discrimination, the provinces of Punjab, North-West Frontier, Sind, and Baluchistan should be merged into a single state. Rahmat Ali was unequivocal in advocating in 1933 the creation of a separate Muslim state in the north-west of India to be called Pakistan – 'the land of the pure'. He argued that the dominant culture in north-west India was Muslim. 'Hence, for Rahmat Ali, India contained two nations, namely Pakistan and Hindustan, and it was a violation of the principles of national self-determination to impose a single political system on them as the British had done'.[117]

Jinnah's contribution was to elaborate these principles into a political program. He declared:

> It is extremely difficult to appreciate why our Hindu friends fail to understand the real nature of Islam and Hinduism. They are not religions in the strict sense of the word, but are, in fact, different and distinct social orders, and it is a dream that Hindus and Muslims can ever evolve a common nationality and this misconception of one Indian nation has gone beyond its limits and is the cause of most of your troubles and will lead India to destruction if we fail to revise our notions in time.... The present *artificial unity* of India only dates back to the British conquest and is maintained by the British regime.[118]

The Lahore Resolution calling for a Muslim state changed the course of the Indian national movement. By creating a fault line in the British Indian empire it hastened its end. Furthermore, it meant that the successor Indian empire would be without what many Hindus believed was an integral part of India. It did not undermine the new Indian state but, rather, focused the minds of many of its political leaders on empire consolidation.

Hindu nationalism triumphant

One historian provided an eclectic interpretation of the relationship between British imperialism and Indian nationalism:

> If imperialism and nationalism have striven so tepidly against each other, part of the reason is that the aims for which they have worked have had much in common. Each, with its own type of incertitude, each with grave limitations on its power, has set about modernizing the societies under its

control; nationalism has sought to conserve the standing of some of those elites which imperialism had earlier raised up or confirmed; at various times both have worked to win the support of the same allies.[119]

Nationalist politics in India from 1940 to 1947 were marked by both the clash between imperialism and nationalism and increasing communal unrest caused by contending programs of the Muslim League and the Congress party. The Congress view of the Muslims was best articulated by Nehru:

> The Moslem nation in India – a nation within a nation, and not even compact, but vague, spread out, indeterminate. Politically, the idea is absurd; economically it is fantastic; it is hardly worth considering. To talk of a 'Moslem nation,' therefore, means that there is no nation at all but a religious bond.[120]

But religion could not serve as the basis for separate nationhood because, as Nehru further pointed out, '[a]lmost always it seems to stand for blind belief and reaction, dogma and bigotry, superstition and exploitation, and the preservation of vested interests'.[121] Perhaps this was just hyperbole, but such an apparently secular approach could lay the foundation for a new multi-religious, multicultural state.

When the Second World War broke out, the British government made an effort to obtain the support of all Indian political parties for the war. Prime minister Winston Churchill sent a member of his War Cabinet, Sir Stafford Cripps, to India in 1942 to work out a solution for India's future. The Cripps proposals – dominion status for India after the war, the right of an independent India to secede from the Commonwealth, the establishment of an elected constituent assembly to draft a constitution for independent India, and the right of individual provinces to secede from the Indian Union – proved unacceptable to both Congress and the Muslim League. The Congress insisted on the immediate formation of a national government while the League demanded acceptance of a future Pakistani state.

Following the British general election of July 1945, Churchill was replaced as prime minister by Clement Attlee, head of the Labour Party. Historically, this party had been more sympathetic towards the Indian national movement, and getting out of India was one of its major platforms. In March 1946 a Cabinet Mission was sent to India to try to resolve differences between the Congress and the Muslim League over the country's future. After considerable debate, it recommended a three-tier plan for the transfer of power. 'The plan proposed that at the top a Union of India would control executive and legislative powers for external affairs, defense, communication, and finance; at the bottom provinces would control everything not delegated to the Union; and in the middle would be groupings of provinces to handle regional affairs.'[122]

The Congress opposed the grouping of the Muslim-majority provinces which lent implicit support for the Muslim League's Pakistan objective. It also condemned the decentralization contained in the Plan since it feared a balkanization of India and wished to inherit the British empire intact. Despite these reservations, the Congress decided to participate in the Interim Government. The Muslim League also, 'while reiterating its desire for an independent Pakistan, agreed to cooperate in the constitution-making process because the Mission Plan had grouped the Muslim provinces together, thus forming the basis for Pakistan'.[123]

Friction between the Congress and the League over the Interim Government began immediately. Jinnah played on Muslim apprehensions about Hindu domination and reiterated his demand for an independent Pakistan. He exhorted 'Direct Action' if necessary to achieve it. Communal violence erupted on the day of Direct Action (August 16, 1946) and cost many lives, especially in Bengal. Frustrated by the failure to bring the two sides together, on February 20, 1947, Attlee declared in the House of Commons that 'His Majesty's Government wish to make it clear that it is their definite intention to take necessary steps to effect the transference of power to responsible Indian hands by a date not later than June 1948'.[124] The Government announced the appointment of Lord Louis Mountbatten as Viceroy of India to work out the plan that would transfer power to Indians.

Soon after coming to India, Mountbatten realized that the gulf between the Congress and the Muslim League was unbridgeable. By early 1947, key Congress leaders, including Nehru, were persuaded that partition of the country was inevitable. Rather than giving the British government a pretext to delay the transfer of power, Acharya Kripalani, the Congress President, notified the Viceroy on April 17, 1947 that '[t]he point has now been reached at which the Congress must reluctantly accept the fact that the Muslim League will never voluntarily come into a Union of India. Rather than have a battle we shall let them have their Pakistan, provided you will allow the Punjab and Bengal to be partitioned in a fair manner'.[125] On June 3, 1947, Viceroy Mountbatten formally announced the Partition Plan that would create two countries, India and Pakistan. The latter would comprise Sind, Baluchistan, and the North-West Frontier Province – all with Muslim majorities. Bengal and Punjab would be divided, with East Bengal and West Punjab (Muslim majorities) going to Pakistan. On July 18, 1947, the Partition Plan received Royal Assent and became the Indian Independence Act of 1947. Even as partition approached, however, Gandhi insisted: 'Both India and Pakistan are my country'.[126]

The issue of the political status of the Princely States locked the two new countries into conflict immediately after their independence. Technically, the Indian Independence Act, by providing for 'the termination of British Paramountcy gave the rulers of the Princely States [562 in total] the right to opt for either India or Pakistan or . . . to remain independent'.[127] Although the option of independence was offered to the Princely States, Mountbatten encouraged their rulers to opt for India or Pakistan not only for practical reasons but also to ensure a peaceful transfer of power.[128] The two principal factors determining this choice were the communal allegiance of the people and geographical contiguity. Except for Hyderabad, Junagadh, and Jammu and Kashmir, all the Princely States agreed to join India or Pakistan by August 1947. The three holdouts became independent.

At this point, the Indian government began imperial retrenchment. Hyderabad was a predominantly Hindu state located within the heartland of Hindu India. When its Muslim ruler delayed accession, the Indian army forcibly took Hyderabad in 1948. Junagadh was also a Hindu majority state with a Muslim ruler. The latter expressed a desire in September 1947 to join Pakistan and as a result 'the Indian army entered the country and assured the people of their right to express themselves about their future'.[129] They decided to join India, of course.

The princely state of Jammu and Kashmir proved less amenable to a quick solution. It was a predominantly Muslim state contiguous to Pakistan and Jinnah claimed it for himself. The Pakistani claim over Kashmir was strengthened by the existence of the All Jammu and Kashmir Muslim Conference, some of whose members 'felt that the best hope of Kashmiri Muslims lay...in or in close association with Pakistan'.[130] But the Hindu ruler of Kashmir, Maharaja Hari Singh, calculated that by refusing to join either India or Pakistan during the transfer of power he might emerge as the ruler of an independent Kashmir state. His plan was supported by some influential Hindus. In the Jammu region, however, the militant Hindu RSS demanded Kashmir's accession to India. The intractable ethnopolitical character of Jammu and Kashmir convinced Pakistani leaders that only force could resolve the impasse and an attack was launched on Kashmir in October 1947. Hari Singh asked India for help and Nehru agreed on condition that the Maharaja consent to Jammu and Kashmir accession to India. Hari Singh had no choice but to comply and as soon as the accession papers were signed Indian troops were airlifted into Kashmir. This first Indo-Pakistan war ended with UN intervention and resulted in a *de facto* partition of Kashmir, with Pakistan controlling about one-third of its original territory and India the remaining two-thirds. The unsatisfactory outcome to the 1947 war led to repeated attempts over subsequent decades by both sides to seize Kashmir. Indian nationalism, equated by Pakistan's leaders with imperialism, made Kashmir a *casus belli*.

The Indian empire and subnationalist challenges

The partition of British India and the creation of two states on the subcontinent in August 1947 – the Republic of India, the official successor state to British India, and the Islamic Republic of Pakistan – marked the end of the Indian nationalist struggle against British rule. The cost of independence was high: massive communal violence took place on the eve of partition, millions of refugees fled their homes as a result of partition, and bitterness between the two new countries grew. In a short time, each of these new states faced serious ethnonationalist and secessionist challenges of their own, often with the support of its rival. Here we consider only two of the centrifugal movements in India.

India specialists have pointed to the importance of the so-called Congress system (created after independence by Congress leader Nehru, prime minister from 1947 to 1964). It advanced four guidelines for dealing with ethnic conflicts:

> First, no secessionist movements were to be tolerated; where necessary they would be suppressed by force. Second, given the commitment to secularism 'no demand for political recognition of a religious group would be considered.' Third, no 'capricious concessions would be made to the political demands of any linguistic, regional or other culturally defined group.' Finally, 'no political concessions to cultural groups in conflict would be made unless they had demonstrable support from both sides.'[131]

Partly due to these strictures, the President's Rule, allowing the central government to take over the administration of a state, was invoked 65 times up to 1982. Yet political mobilization of ethnic groups has remained a central feature of Indian politics. Does struggle by national groups against Indian rule indicate that, viewed from the periphery, India is an empire inherited by Hindus from the British? Many groups have mobilized against central rule; in north-east India alone these include Assamese, Bodo, Naga, Kuki, Mizo, Manipuri, and Tripura insurgent groups. Here we focus on only two cases: the Sikhs and Kashmiri Muslims. For more than a decade 'Punjab festered and Kashmir went out of control'.[132] Let us begin with the more explosive case.

The Kashmiri Muslims

Before Indian independence, repression of Muslims had been a policy pursued by Kashmir's local ruler, the Hindu Maharaja Hari Singh. When Kashmir acceded to India in 1948, Kashmiri Muslims hoped that the central government in New Delhi would defend their rights as a minority. Initially they were reassured by the leadership of Sheikh Abdullah and his Kashmir National Conference. Sheikh Abdullah was a vigorous champion of the rights of the Kashmiri people and a key policy of his Kashmir National Conference government was to carry out radical land reform and give land back to the Muslim peasantry.[133]

Sheikh Abdullah's populist economic policy alienated the small but powerful Hindu Pandit community in Kashmir which historically had controlled the state. The group demanded Kashmir's complete integration into India. Faced with rising Hindu resentment and simultaneously increased Kashmiri nationalist rhetoric from Sheik Abdullah, the Indian government arrested him in 1953.[134] New Delhi allocated large sums of developmental assistance to Kashmir, but much was absorbed by corruption, waste, and bureaucracy. The economic backwardness of Kashmiri Muslims made it difficult for them to compete with the Hindu Pandit community. Surprisingly, however, Kashmiri Muslims remained loyal to India until the mid-1980s. This was the result of substantial political freedom granted them by New Delhi, but also manipulation of a geographically-peripheral and economically-backward people.

By the 1980s, demographic changes, modernization, and communications produced a better educated, more politically conscious generation in Kashmir.[135] However, economic development and employment opportunities had not expanded commensurately. Moreover, from the early 1980s on, the Congress government led by Indira Gandhi engaged in voter fraud and subversion of the electoral process to further its own interests. Frustrated Muslim youths resorted to violence against the state and the Hindu minority in Kashmir. The central government retaliated with repressive military actions. The spiralling violence alienated Kashmiri Muslims from the Indian state to a degree not experienced since independence. Militant groups engaged in terrorist acts, such as taking foreigners hostage, as a means of forcing the Indian government to grant political concessions.

Political independence became the objective of some Kashmiri leaders belonging to the Hurriyat Conference – an umbrella organization of various Kashmiri political groups. They were supported by the Pakistani government. In 1948 and 1965 Pakistan unsuccessfully fought wars to annex the region. Since the late 1980s, the Pakistani Inter Services Intelligence agency coordinated military training of and arms deliveries to more than 30,000 members of the fundamentalist Hizb-ul-Mujahideen party and the Jammu and Kashmir Liberation Front (JKLF). Some of these groups were provided with operating bases on the Pakistani side of the Line of Actual Control (LAC), which forms the *de facto* border between India and Pakistan in Kashmir.[136] Fully-trained Afghan mujahideens also infiltrated the region.[137] Diplomatically, Pakistan depicted Indian army action in Kashmir as human rights violations, calculating that 'foreign countries, unwilling so far to rake up Kashmir on the strength of outdated UN resolutions, might do so if the question of human rights is brought to the fore'.[138] The strategy was partially successful, for in May 1993 the Organization of Islamic Countries voted for sanctions against India.[139] In Britain, some Labour Party leaders called for self-determination for Kashmir under UN auspices.[140] In the US, the Clinton Administration criticized India for human rights violations in Kashmir.[141]

In order to finance their operations, some separatist groups in India, including the Kashmiri militants, have become involved in the South Asian narcotics trade. Afghanistan, Pakistan, and Myanmar have been the largest suppliers of heroin in the region, and it has been estimated that over 70 percent of this heroin is shipped to the West through India.[142] Kashmiri and Sikh separatist groups are said to act as couriers for the drug lords in return for cash to pay for arms.[143] Muslim militants in Kashmir also received assistance from the Taliban regime in Afghanistan until its ouster in 2001.

The first Assembly elections in Kashmir since fighting in the region began were held in 1996. Predictably the result was a pro-Indian majority, marking a further step in India's legitimization of Kashmiri incorporation into its empire. Sporadic clashes between Pakistani-supported guerrillas based in Indian-held territories and the Indian military occurred from 1999 onwards. After the US launched a war in October 2001 against Muslim extremists in Afghanistan, it seemed only a matter of time before Western-led military action would be taken against mujahideen in Kashmir or, at the least, India would be given the green light to attack Islamic militant groups in Kashmir and even Pakistan. The region became a last battleground over whether India consisted of two nations or one.

The Sikhs

A relatively small group, the Sikhs have gained a reputation for economic entrepreneurship, in large part engendered by the agricultural revolution that occurred in Punjab, their home state, in the late 1960s.[144] The green revolution brought prosperity to Punjab but it also increased the number of landless Sikh peasants whose small tracts were consolidated to promote large-scale, mechanized agriculture. Those dispossessed of their land flocked to urban centers where, lacking skills, they were forced to take menial jobs. Thus, the benefits of Punjab's prosperity went mostly to large farmers and gave rise to tensions between the rich and poor.[145]

By the 1980s the green revolution in Punjab had also created high unemployment among the educated Sikh youth. Prosperity had brought educational advancement not matched by a proportional increase in non-agricultural employment opportunities. The Indian government was reticent to locate heavy industries in Punjab because of its status as a high-risk border state with Pakistan. Feelings of discrimination and deprivation spreading among the Sikh youth intensified when they realized that the proportion of Sikhs in their traditional sector of employment, the armed forces, had declined. Although the absolute number of Sikhs in the armed forces continued to increase, their overall proportion decreased from 25 percent at the time of independence to 11 percent by the mid-1980s. The same was probably true of their other preferred professions, such as the bureaucracy and state police.[146]

Sikh political mobilization increased and acquired a separatist agenda because of the negative impact of Punjab's unbalanced economy on Sikh religion and culture. Sikhism is an offshoot of Hinduism and a major concern of the Sikh religious leaders has been the preservation of the Sikhs' unique religious and cultural identity and the establishment of communal boundaries with the Hindu community. Maintaining cultural homogeneity and a communal boundary with the Hindu community, however, became difficult during the period of prosperity.

Fearing cultural dilution and a loss of ethno-religious homogeneity, together with its concomitant political consequences on Punjab's electoral politics, militant Sikh religious leaders called for a separate Sikh state, Khalistan. A terrorist campaign in Punjab was launched 'to trigger an exodus of Hindus from the province. If such violence would prompt reprisals against Sikhs outside the Punjab, this in turn would only lead to Sikh emigration to the Punjab from other parts of India. By this process, the Punjab would become a Sikh state'.[147]

The call for a separate Sikh state also suited the Akali Dal, the Sikh political party, which was unable 'to enjoy absolute political preeminence in state politics, even though it is the party of the Sikhs in a Sikh majority state'.[148] One reason for this was that the Hindus in Punjab generally voted for the Congress Party, the political rival of the Akali Dal. Another was that not all Sikhs voted for the Akali Dal: most lower- and middle-caste Sikhs voted against it since it is a party dominated by large Jat landholders. These Sikhs preferred either the Congress Party or the two communist parties. In a sovereign Sikh state, however, the Akali Dal would enjoy absolute control. It therefore often encouraged the separatist demands of more radical Sikh groups.

In June 1984 the Indian army stormed the Sikhs' holiest shrine, the Golden Temple, leaving thousands dead. The action was taken to crush Sikh secessionist leaders who had supposedly used the temple as an organizational base. The tragedy was the culmination of a policy initiated by prime minister Indira Gandhi which 'systematically dismantled the elaborate framework for ethnic conflict management established by her father, Nehru'.[149] Shortly thereafter she was gunned down by her own Sikh bodyguards.

The Sikhs' position close to the center of Indian politics turns any secessionist threat they make into a serious challenge to India's political and territorial integrity. What is more, their relative prosperity offers Sikhs the prospects of post-independence economic viability. Support from the Sikh diaspora also raises their leverage within India. For example, Sikhs living in Canada were responsible for what before September 2001 was the worst act of air terrorism in history, the mid-air bombing of an Air India flight off the coast of Ireland in 1985. As this case shows, therefore, a Hindu state would not resolve the issue of sectarian Hindu separatism.

Secular pretensions, religious realities

This discussion of separatism in India suggests that New Delhi is in large part to blame for discontent within the 'empire'. The benefits of economic development have not always reached groups on the periphery due to nepotism, corruption, waste, and bureaucracy. Central government indifference to the fears of assimilation and of threats to minority cultures sparks discontent and nationalist assertion. If in the Russian Federation, strengthening the center is crucial to stemming centrifugal forces, the key in India seems to be not in more centralization of authority but in greater decentralization.

To what extent does India's secular nationalism hold the empire together? Some experts see the dichotomy between secular nationalism and religious communalism as artificial.[150] The Congress Party, the purported agent of secular nationalism, engages in political discourse that is not secular but that 'imagines a common ethnic culture of India in terms of religious pluralism. In this moderate view the different communities that populate the nation have to be represented in the state'.[151] In reality the notion of *Sarva Dharma Sambhava*, or equal treatment of all religions, puts religion squarely in the middle of political discourse on homeland. Since 80 percent of citizens are Hindu, the notion implicitly recognizes the hegemonic position of this religion.[152] Mahatma Gandhi's legacy can be interpreted to mean 'religious transnationality in "Hindu spiritualism" and in the Muslim *umma*'.[153] In practice, religions do not enjoy equal status and by force of numbers Hinduism has a place as special as that once constitutionally enjoyed by the Catholic church in Ireland.

Communal conflict between Hindus and Muslims has been a regular feature of Indian political life since independence. It transcends the intractable problem of Kashmir. But conflict is not spread evenly across the country; one study found that only 3.6 percent of deaths in communal violence between 1950 and 1995 occurred in rural India where the majority of Indians live. 'Hindu–Muslim violence turns out to be primarily an urban phenomenon' and is concentrated in eight cities where 46 percent of all deaths in Hindu-Muslim violence took place.[154] Religious differences are therefore salient in city-specific rather than state-specific contexts.

During Congress rule of India the state fostered the myth of religious ecumenism – not secularism – which is crucial to modern Indian nationalism:

> When conflict arises between groups with different ethnic and/or religious identities – that is, between subnationalities – the state is seen to represent a superior common interest and to stand above the conflicting parties, so that it is able to arbitrate. At the same time, the state must promote the idea of religious tolerance in a pluralist society, which it can only do by emphasizing the commonality of spiritual pursuits. Thus the state is not secular. Rather, it promotes a specific view of 'religion' as a universal characteristic of Indian ethnicity. The different religions are only refractions of one great Indian spirituality.[155]

The rise since the 1980s of the Bharatiya Janata Party (BJP), the political wing of the RSS, represents a backlash against the long-ruling Congress party's pseudo-secularism in favor of a confessional Hindu state. In the 1996 elections to parliament (the Lok Sabha) it emerged as the country's largest party, receiving over one-fifth of the vote; by comparison, in the first five national elections between 1951 and 1971, the BJP's predecessor, the Bharatiya Jana Sangh, never received more than ten percent support. If in 1984 it had two seats in parliament, in 2001 the BJP held 182.

Officially the BJP stresses *Hindutva*, that is, a Hindu nationalism that proclaims the need for an Indian identity centered on its historic culture and religion, not politics, and the need for the creation of a single community through assimilation of groups around a common set of Hindu symbols. As one academic summarized, '[t]he Hindu nationalists desire to transform Indian public culture into a sovereign, disciplined national culture rooted in what is claimed to be a superior ancient Hindu past, and to impose a corporatist and disciplined social and political organization upon society'.[156] To this end, the BJP ceased to be a party dominated by high-caste traders. It even began recruiting Muslims to its senior executive positions.[157] When after the 1999 elections it headed a 24-party government coalition, called the National Democratic Alliance, the BJP accepted a moratorium on bringing up sensitive communal issues. According to one scholar, '[t]he regional parties were uncomfortable with the perceived extremism of the Hindu nationalist party. In return for an electoral alliance and later support in government, they expected the BJP to moderate its policies'.[159] Several militant Hindu coalition affiliates were upset by the pragmatism of BJP prime minister A.B. Vajpayee, but his personal popularity allowed him to neutralize these as well as even Cabinet colleagues from his own party.

The BJP rise, like that of Putin's restorationalism in Russia, is connected to popular support for making the homeland strong. Growing Hindu nationalism and anti-Muslim sentiments were strengthened by the Muslim Kashmiri insurgency that began in 1989 and contributed to greater communal violence. In late 1992 a Hindu mob destroyed the historic Babri mosque at Ayodhya, which had been erected in 1528 by a Muslim general on the site of a temple that marked the supposed birthplace of Lord Ram, the most popular reincarnation of the divine. The BJP did not have a direct hand in the destruction but clearly gained from the communal conflict at the site. The party also launched an attack on other allegedly-nefarious influences on Hindu culture, such as Western fast-food and beverage companies. Its program is to set aside the secular fiction and openly base India's identity on *Hindutva*.

The late Bengali scholar and iconoclast Nirad Chaudhuri questioned whether there was anything called Hindu spirituality to begin with. He viewed Hinduism as simply a way of getting along in the world with the help of some metaphysics.[159] But not many in India would agree with him. Indian voters have recently demonstrated a contrary view. 'India's spiritual superiority and the universal mission of Hindu philosophy to be a "spiritual corrective" to a materialistic and overly rationalist western world remains a cornerstone in contemporary Hindu nationalism.'[160] It remains difficult to imagine how *Hindutva* can preserve the multinational Indian state any more effectively than secular nationalism, however spurious it has been.

At the beginning of this chapter we asked whether nationalism among peoples of the periphery could undermine reconfigured empires such as Russia and India. We have found significant differences between the two cases. A weak metropole elite lacking a legitimating ideology in Yeltsin's Russia produced an opportunity structure for separatist and regionalist forces. By contrast, in India, strong central government and a secular ideology led to similar problems. In both countries political forces have emerged seeking to manufacture a homeland that is an empire. An imperial home, seen as a solution by some in the political elite, is the obstacle to be overcome by certain counterelites and the national groups that support them.

4
Home Writ Small: Nationalisms of Separatist Movements

Even though they reflect opposing tendencies, both globalization and secessionism represent important phenomena in the contemporary world and have received considerable attention in recent scholarship.[1] In many respects, each phenomenon is a challenge to the long-prevalent centrality of sovereign states in the world system. From the perspective of the neoliberal advocate of a global world order, secessionism, subnationalism, state sovereignty, regional integration, and globalization are points on a political development continuum running from the past to the future. From the viewpoint of a separatist wanting self-determination for his or her nation, the normative order is reversed and globalization may be the most serious threat to a nation's cultural uniqueness and economic independence. Generally, evaluations of the processes of globalization and integration tend to be positive, those of nationalism and secessionism are usually negative.

To be sure, countervailing tendencies have arisen. With the increasing powers accumulated by the European Union, for example, national publics have come to doubt the national loyalty of their elites.[2] Efforts to brand such publics, whether in Denmark, England, or France, as reactionary or xenophobic have been counterproductive. Across the globe protests against globalization forums have grown in frequency and intensity. For one writer, 'the politics of national self-affirmation seems to be part of the same postmodern meltdown that brought the end of communism and of the Cold War. For despite homogenizing trends in a capitalism that is planetary in character, forms of cultural resistance are everywhere'. Examples are numerous: 'From Islamic fundamentalism to the ethnic nationalisms of the Balkans or Central Asia, from the debates over citizenship and immigration in Germany or France to the Zapatista rebellion in Mexico, identity politics are the flavor of the decade. And we in English Canada may be no more immune to its charms than are our counterparts in Quebec.'[3]

Political elites themselves are split over identity politics, specifically, whether the nation-state remains a tested formula for a politically cohesive structure or is now obsolete:

Some react by reasserting the cultural and mythical roots of their national identity. Others by withdrawing into smaller circles of 'local knowledge,' perhaps realising the relative artificiality of national identity if measured by the standard of cultural homogeneity, or trying to reinvent it by creating smaller, more manageable and culturally more close-knit nation-states. Regionalism and localism here transform into a new, late 20th century national movement ... A third category effect or negotiate hybrid identities for themselves across national boundaries, drawing on a diverse pool of cultural-ethnic potentials.[4]

One rational response to integration is, therefore, a return to traditional national identities; another is a turn to new forms of transnationalism.

The strength of nationalism in the close-knit nations of Europe can be exaggerated. For example, in elections to a new Scottish parliament in May 1999, the Labour Party obtained more votes and seats than the Scottish National Party (SNP). In the Basque country in this same period, a moderate nationalist party attracted more support than the militant Basque Homeland and Liberty (*Euskadi Ta Askatasuna*, or ETA). Further evidence of the fragility of European subnationalism comes from a 1999 survey carried out in the 18 French-speaking districts of Belgium, together with the Walloon district of Brussels. It found that 79 percent of respondents did not know the official name of their region, 'Wallonie.' In addition, nearly two-thirds (63 percent) could not identify its capital, Namur.[5]

These are trends occurring within Western democracies. Over the past decade their reaction to separatism in the world's authoritarian or unstable states has generally been harsh. Especially problematic for them was former Yugoslavia because it was at one and the same time European, postcommunist, and multinational. Western powers were torn between interventionist and non-interventionist options. One view was that

the break-up was best left to the Yugoslavs to resolve themselves, with the outside world confining itself to charitable relief. This was the policy adopted by Britain – with no hysterical cries of 'appeasement' or 'you're doing nothing' – during the Croatian war and the Krajina clearances, and in Rwanda, Angola, Liberia, Congo, Algeria, Chechnya and Azerbaijan. In Croatia, the hands-off policy did not prevent ethnic cleansing, which was as bloodthirsty as in Kosovo, but that war was short and the resulting partition has proved stable. Bosnia was the turning point that made the Balkans 'our business'. Yet military intervention was tardy and half-hearted and merely froze a ceasefire line. The Nato colony is now the most dependent statelet in the world, not remotely a secure and autonomous nation.[6]

When NATO ended its bombing campaign against Serbia in June 1999 following a pullout of Serb troops from Kosovo, the latter displaced Bosnia as the most dependent statelet (bantustan might be more accurate if less charitable) in Europe. Much excellent scholarship by both Balkan and international relations specialists has addressed the Yugoslav breakup and the Western response.[7] Fundamentally, the involvement of Western powers in former Yugoslavia marked what was termed 'the Athenian Problem: How can a democracy behave as a world power?'[8] In some ways the West's preoccupation with the Balkans has drawn attention away from Western democracies' response to their own separatist crises.

This chapter seeks answers to questions concerning democracies' abilities to accommodate separatist forces. Is the political violence associated with contemporary breakaway movements restricted to emergent, fragile, or quasi democracies, such as Indonesia (East Timor), Russia (the Chechens), Sri Lanka (the Tamils), and Turkey (the Kurds)? Conversely, why do separatist groups in established democracies like the Catalans in Spain, the Northern League in Italy, and Scotland in Great Britain not engage in violence but push their objectives within the framework of procedural democracy? Does the very nature of liberal democracy have a mellowing effect on nationalist assertion? In particular, do identities have to be reconfigured in order to meet the criteria set by liberalism?

To explore answers to these questions we compare two systems at different stages of democratic development. By studying South Africa, which only had its first free elections in 1994, we can observe whether there has been a shift, corresponding to the growth in democratic culture, from coercive to constitutional efforts to attain self-rule and even independence. The most fabled ethnic group in South Africa is the Zulu; we inquire whether black majority rule has had an effect both on their means of carrying out their national agenda and on the very objectives themselves. The second case is of a mature democracy: Quebec's bid for sovereignty from Canada. 'Canada is a test case for a liberal theory of secession not simply because it can set a model for the rest of the world but also because it is one of the purest cases of nationalist liberal secession.'[9] What happens to a nationalist movement unable to win independence through constitutional means? Does it wane in importance precisely because of unfavorable but democratic outcomes?

The essential comparability of these two cases is questionable. Cultural differences between southern Africa and North America, divergent historical paths, different applications of the Westminster model of democracy, the relative newness of the Canadian confederation contrasted with the longer history of contact among African peoples, and differing stages of social and economic development can help explain different means and pathways to sovereignty struggles. In this chapter the two cases are not the subject of direct comparison. Rather, we wish to learn how democracy, the explanatory variable, can affect nationalist movements in different settings.

South Africa

Secession in a new democracy

The majority of secessionist movements in the world today exists in the developing world. With its white minority government and relative prosperity, South Africa was not an archetypical country of the third world, but it did share many problems with other countries on the continent such as ethnic divisions and artificial borders. After the end of the apartheid regime, it also shared problems with countries elsewhere which began to democratize. Reconciling democratization with nation-building became an important challenge.

In his autobiography, South Africa's first black president, Nelson Mandela, described the effect on those accused of treason of a poem read in court about the great Zulu king Shaka: 'Suddenly there were no Xhosas or Zulus, no Indians or Africans, no rightists or leftists, no political or religious leaders; we were all nationalists'.[10] Mandela took this lesson to heart in the transition period and tried to limit racial and ethnic violence between black and white and between black and black. His major institutional adversary was the Inkatha Freedom Party (IFP) representing the wishes of many Zulus for a political homeland. An African specialist observed how 'it was naive for liberals, Marxists or other anti-racists to imagine that once white domination had been overthrown an ethnic Zulu nationalism would not seek to fill the power vacuum within its own area'.[11]

Are the Zulus' historical grievances, land claims, sense of oppression, and other moral claims justified? What conditions mitigate against the separation of the Zulu kingdom from the rest of South Africa? Has wide-scale political violence been avoided as democratic values in South African spread? Considering that Zulu King Goodwill Zwelethini's definition of the Zulu nation, given in a May 1991 speech, was 'Brothers born of warrior stock', has the Zulu quest for homeland not ruled out political militancy and even violence?

Inkatha is one of many nationalist movements having a separatist agenda operating in Africa and Asia today. The multitude of ethnic and communal groups living here combined with artificial state borders drawn by European colonial powers decades ago make this a natural phenomenon. 'After more than thirty years of independence ... the hegemonic status of the belief that African borders are immutable, and thereby excluded from calculations about how Africans can respond to the exigencies of their existence, appears to be breaking down.' As a result, 'Africa faces, among its other woes, the possibility of cascading patterns of fragmentation and attachment'.[12]

Unsettled states may be a charitable description for what one writer bluntly terms state collapse – a widespread phenomenon on the African continent. 'Current state collapse – in the Third World, but also in the former Soviet Union and in Eastern Europe – is not a matter of civilizational decay.... Nor is the process merely an organic characteristic of growth and decay, a life cycle in the rise and fall of nations.'[13] State collapse entails the loss of a multiplicity of functions:

> As the decisionmaking center of government, the state is paralyzed and inoperative: laws are not made, order is not preserved, and societal cohesion is not enhanced. As a symbol of identity, it has lost its power of conferring a name on its people and a meaning to their social action. As a territory, it is no longer assured security and provisionment by a central sovereign organization. As the authoritative political institution, it has lost its legitimacy, which is therefore up for grabs, and so has lost its right to command and conduct public affairs. As a system of socioeconomic organization, its functional balance of inputs and outputs is destroyed; it no longer receives supports from nor exercises controls over its people, and it no longer is even the target of demands, because its people know that it is incapable of providing supplies.[14]

State collapse, like unsettled states, may not simply be a byproduct of secessionism, then, but may actually serve as a factor producing a retreat into nationalist identities. The genocidal events in Rwanda between April and July 1994 underscored this. Hutu militias slaughtered up to 800,000 Tutsis, a minority group that had formed the traditional ruling class in the region. After July, Tutsis returned to power and over 100,000 Hutus were killed in reprisals. State collapse and struggle for power – not secessionism – caused genocide in Rwanda. Ethnic clashes between these and other groups spread subsequently to neighboring Burundi and the Democratic Republic of Congo where weak states also existed. To what extent did the collapse of the apartheid regime in South Africa lead to ethnic conflict?

The Zulu kingdom

For three and a half centuries South Africa was ruled by colonial powers and then by an apartheid regime. When the first historic democratic elections were held in 1994, South Africa represented one of the most inegalitarian societies in the world. The white population making up 13 percent of the country's inhabitants owned 86 percent of the land and over 90 percent of its wealth. By contrast, of the 30 million blacks, 50 percent were unemployed, living below the poverty line, illiterate or semi-literate, and under 20 years of age. One in ten had no home and was a squatter. In addition, South Africa is an ethnically-heterogeneous society. Of the largest black groups, about 8.5 million are Zulu speakers, 6.6 million are Xhosa, and

6.3 million are Sothos. The white population is made up of 5.8 million Afrikaners and 3.5 million English speakers.

Most of the recent scholarship on the country has justifiably been concerned with its transition from an apartheid to a democratic system and from white to black rule. But black South Africa has never been homogeneous in ethnic, political, or geographical terms. The first sign that many in the West had of divisions prevailing within black South Africa was the brutal black-on-black violence that flared up at the beginning of the 1990s as the apartheid system began to be dismantled. At the center of the conflict were the Zulus.[15]

During the European conquest of southern Africa, many indigenous groups succumbed without a fight. Some were rewarded with a measure of political independence, like the Sotho in Lesotho, the Swazis in Swaziland, and the Tswana in Botswana. The Zulu resistance cost more British soldiers' lives than did the entire conquest of India, but Zulus were not to be given independence.

Zulus share characteristics with other peoples in the region as well as having internal differences. The Zulu language is one of the nine main Bantu language groups in South Africa alongside Xhosa. Zulu society is made up of numerous lineage groups proceeding from separate ancestors, thereby resulting in hundreds of clans spread across both sides of the Tugela river. North of the river is what is known today as KwaZulu, the heartland of the Zulu kingdom and its most prestigious clans. South of the Tugela, in today's Natal, lived the inferior *kaffir* Zulus. The differences between the two were based not only on ascribed social status but on distinct political histories.

Before his death in 1828, King Shaka transformed the Zulus from a relatively unimportant tribe in southern Africa into the strongest native empire in African history. He took over the chieftaincy in 1816 and went on to defeat many of the more powerful neighboring peoples. Some literary critics 'suggest that Shaka is largely a textual invention, a malleable symbol available for any ideological distortion, from the early white settlers' self-serving monsterization to the Inkatha Freedom Party's nationalistic lionization'.[16] But political historians fully recognize Shaka's role as nation-maker.

At its zenith, the Zulu empire had more than two million subjects. An ever-expanding force of *impi*, the Zulu warrior class, was able to conquer new territories. But Shaka's bloody rule engendered conspiracies against him, and one led by his two half-brothers finally succeeded in 1828. Before dying, Shaka's prophetic last words were reputed to be: 'The whole land will be white with the light of the stars, and it will be overrun by swallows.'[17]

One historian summarized the situation in 1878:

> Fifty years after Shaka's death, his predictions had been fulfilled. The Zulu were surrounded. Across the Tugela, the *abelungu* [white intruders] had indeed descended 'like swallows', to cultivate and multiply. Half of Sha-

ka's empire had been a British colony called Natal for two decades. To the north, another breed of white colonist, the *amabuna* or the Boers, had also chipped away at the old kingdom.[18]

Shaka's successor, Dingane, confronted the Boers who were encroaching from the north. Admittedly 'Dingane had no intrinsic preference for Briton over Boer. The English had simply been associated in the Zulu mind with a limited presence and the Afrikaner with a larger, more intrusive one'.[19] But in 1838 he massacred a party of Afrikaners who had come to obtain his signature on a land transfer. This was followed by an *impi* attack on Durban, south of the Tugela in Natal. Boer revenge was quick in coming, and it was enduring. By the end of 1838 the Zulus were routed on the banks of the Ncome. One hundred and fifty years later, the apartheid regime, on its last legs, belatedly and bizarrely decided to commemorate the victory with a large memorial on the site. Indeed, the apartheid system itself was seen as just retribution for what the Zulus had done to the Boers long ago.

In 1843 a treaty turned Natal into a British colony while recognizing Zulu sovereignty north of the Tugela. This marked the start of a period of British expansion in South Africa. The colonists recruited cheap black labor to work the Natal sugar plantations and Cape diamond fields. Lord Carnarvon, who had just helped engineer a Canadian dominion out of British North American territories, was sent from the Colonial Office to South Africa. 'Since 1874, Carnarvon had pondered how the jumble of ethnic and political blocs that made up the subcontinent – British colonies, Boer republics, and Bantu kingdoms – could be neatly composed into a South African confederation.'[20] To construct such a dominion, the British annexed Transvaal and its capital, Pretoria, in 1877, claiming that they wished to save the Boer population there from a Zulu attack. The annexation was to lead to two Anglo-Boer wars several decades later.

As part of its new imperial policy, Britain next set out to demilitarize and incorporate Zululand into the confederation. Among the conditions stated in a British ultimatum delivered to the Zulu king in 1879 were that the army was to be demobilized, a British resident diplomat was to be installed in Zululand who would have final political authority, and missionaries were to have unimpeded rights to proselytization. When the king did not accept the conditions in the time provided, the British army – which included close to 10 000 Zulu-speaking levies conscripted in Natal – marched into Zululand. But the British were taken by surprise by the mobile, large *impi* – up to 25 000 warriors, larger than any put together by Shaka. In January 1879 at Isandlwana, the British were overrun and suffered heavy casualties. In another battle of that campaign, Louis Napoleon, French prince imperial who had been driven into exile in England following France's defeat at the hands of the Prussians in 1870 and who had volunteered to serve as a uniformed observer with the British forces in Africa, was cut down by Zulu warriors. In

London prime minister Disraeli was stricken by the bad news emanating from Zululand and commented laconically: 'A wonderful people, the Zulu. They beat our generals, they convert our bishops, and they write *finis* to a French dynasty'.[21] A year later, Disraeli was voted out of office, to be replaced by Liberal leader William Gladstone who exhorted, '[r]emember the rights of the savage'.

Zulu valor and mobility were to prove no match for European firearms. In 1879, at Ulundi, the Zulu force was finally crushed by British forces, the capital burnt, and the king taken away in chains. As with Kosovo Polje for the Serbs, the Alamo for Americans, and the Plains of Abraham for Quebecers, Zulus regard this lost battle as a defining moment in their national history.[22] For a time, the British colonizers were content with setting Zulu chieftains to fight each other. But in 1886 the Conservatives returned to power in London and in May of that year Zululand was formally transformed into a British colony. The political unification of the two territories took place in 1897 when Zululand was incorporated into the self- governing colony of Natal. Paradoxically, there were more converts to Christianity, the *amakholwa*, in the more industrialized Natal Zulu lands, and they were to become the future Zulu elite.

One historian mused '[h]ow different it would have been if, after the conquest, Britain had extended the same protective wing over Zululand that it did to three other large ethnic groups in the region' – the Tswana, Sotho, and Swazi.[23] As High Commission territories they were ruled directly, even benevolently, by London until granted their independence in the 1960s. The Zulus struggled harder for political autonomy but were repeatedly disappointed, as when the Union of South Africa was established in 1910 or when black majority rule came to the country in 1994.

The Zulu struggle continued intermittently throughout the twentieth century. Zulus on both sides of the Tugela rose up against a poll tax imposed by the British in 1906. The struggle was again uneven, with British forces slaughtering any Zulus suspected of taking part in the protests. When, four years later, the British government transferred control over the Union of South Africa to an all-white parliament, it was the English community in Natal that, ironically, opposed the Act of Union. Up until 1948, successive South African governments pursued a segregationist program, and the ideological revival of Zulu nationalism for a brief period in the 1920s made no inroads in changing this system. When a nationalist Afrikaner government took power in 1948, it went further and institutionalized the system of apartheid.

Transition to democracy and ethnic politics

It is irresistible to draw comparisons between the collapse of the communist regime in the USSR and that of white-ruled South Africa which occurred within two years of each other. The imperial analogy is an obvious point of comparison: 'The South African state formed in 1910 was a British empire in microcosm and, without apartheid, was always likely to show the same fissiparous tendencies of the Russian empire without communism'. The consequence in each case was that '[e]thnic politics, so long obscured or concealed, suddenly mattered a great deal'.[24]

The transition from apartheid to black majority rule in the 1990s inevitably involved a struggle for power among South Africa's major ethnic groups. Zulu leaders were concerned that, paradoxically, the transition process would deprive them of the limited autonomy that they had been given under apartheid. When President de Klerk made his overture for democratic reform, it was to the African National Congress (ANC) that he turned. ANC leaders refused to include a Zulu representative as part of their negotiating team. After the Afrikaners, then, the Zulus felt that they had most to lose from a transfer of power to the ANC.

The shift from white minority to black majority rule required many changes, above all, a constitutional one.[25] Political reform meant that 'tribal homelands' had to be dismantled. These, including the semi-autonomous kingdom of KwaZulu, had been set up under the 1953 Bantu Authorities Act to 'train' the Bantu for self-government while moving them away from white-populated areas and denying them citizenship. In 1955 future prime minister Hendrik Verwoerd announced that Zulus were to be given back their lands and would be ruled by their traditional chiefs. The white South African government was to provide three-quarters of the funding for a 'Zulustan'. But Nobel Prize laureate and great pan-African nationalist Albert Lutuli remarked: 'The modes of government proposed are a caricature. They are neither democratic nor African. The Act makes our chiefs into minor puppets of the Big Dictator'.[26]

An 'independent' KwaZulu was formally established in March 1972 and consisted of 44 pockets of land on both sides of the Tugela – a 'polka-dot state' in the words of Inkatha head Mangosuthu Buthelezi. It was a fraction of the size of Shaka's kingdom. But control over the homeland's substantial budget placed Inkatha leaders at the top of a large patronage system. Accordingly,

> [a]llegiance to the 'Zulu nation' – measured through membership of Inkatha – could determine access to resources. Inkatha claimed total representation of 'Zuluness' in the first years after its formation in 1975. It was also the sole party in the bantustan government. Those who sought to politicize and mobilize Zulu ethnicity also controlled pensions, land allocation and education; signed worker-seekers' permits; and approved bottle store licenses.[27]

Buthelezi's political objective was the recognition of a Zulu state as a unit in a new South African federation. Zulu king Goodwill also preferred a reconstituted, multi-racial Zulu state with constitutional ties to South Africa over outright independence. Just before the 1994 elections, he led large numbers of Zulus to Ulundi and made the case for Zulu self-determination.

Black majority rule in South Africa eliminated the homelands. In their stead, nine non-ethnically-determined regions were created. Zulu and other homeland rulers who had built up fiefdoms of power and patronage were marginalized. In order to ensure that the 1994 general elections brought all major groups into the political process, the outgoing white government of President F.W. de Klerk sought to avoid an election boycott by Inkatha. On April 25, a day before voting began, de Klerk handed over the KwaZulu homeland to King Goodwill as a trust to remain under his personal control. In return, the Zulus agreed to participate in the elections.

While relations between de Klerk and the Zulu king were cemented, South Africa's black political leaders were drawn into conflict. The most significant rupture was between the ANC led by Mandela and Inkatha headed by Buthelezi.[28] It is simplistic to see the ANC as a multi-ethnic movement and Inkatha as a Zulu one but it is also true that in the 1994 electoral campaign Inkatha invoked the great history of the Zulus while the ANC emphasized the future that all blacks in South Africa would build together.

ANC–Inkatha rivalry was transformed into violent clashes between black groups. Many black townships in Natal province (three-quarters of whose population of eight million are Zulus) were turned into war zones. Hundreds of blacks were killed and a state of emergency had to be imposed by de Klerk. Many of the violent protests were organized by Inkatha to promote a sovereign Zulu state – at a minimum, one that would be outside the control of the ANC. Buthelezi was depicted as a nationalist leader who 'stood belligerently in the way of what was being described as the New South Africa'. For one historian he 'was a mass of paradoxes, a Christian who honored African tradition and an avowed democrat who yet clearly distrusted the ballot. Urbane and charming, with connections in the boardrooms of Western corporations, he could, in a moment, turn from avuncularity to the language of tribal war'.[29] Not surprisingly, while some Africans regarded Buthelezi as an instrument of Western business interests others saw him as a nationalist.

Inkatha leaders did not see Mandela as the conquering hero portrayed in the West. At the time of his release from prison in February 1990 after serving 27 years, widespread violence was occurring across Natal. In order to quell the unrest, Mandela visited Durban shortly after his release and was welcomed by tens of thousands of Zulus. He had still not met personally with Buthelezi but agreed to make concessions to the Zulus: there would be formal recognition of KwaZulu and of its king in the new constitution. For his part, Buthelezi demanded that the constitution establish a federal system with strong powers for the provinces. But as one scholar observed, '[t]o recognize nationalism below the level of an inclusive Black nationalism is to run afoul of an important South African taboo'.[30] In fact, this specialist compared the binationalism in Canada between English- and French-speaking nations with a plan for binationalism in South Africa between white and black communities and was skeptical that it would work any better here.

Mandela agreed that elections would consist of two ballots: one for the constituent assembly and another for regional assemblies. He also accepted the right of Inkatha leaders to seek international mediation over the province's status. But this proved to be an insignificant promise since it was obvious that black South Africans would now be deciding their future on their own. One South African newspaper even praised Mandela for his duplicity on KwaZulu-Natal: 'It is almost reassuring to note among the blemishes on his track record the reneging on solemn promises made to the Inkatha Freedom Party before the previous elections to invite foreign mediation in the problem of endemic violence in KwaZulu-Natal.'[31]

Buthelezi, then chief minister of the KwaZulu black homeland, attacked Mandela and the ANC on a number of fronts. He accused them of seeking to re-subject the Zulus by stripping them of KwaZulu and of being pawns of the rival Xhosa tribe. Sensitive to such criticism, the ANC elected a Zulu as vice-president in 1992. What were the supposed differences between the two groups? Most importantly, they had separate political development paths. 'The Xhosa-speakers of the Cape were the most politically aware Africans in the country, having grown up within a relatively liberal environment in which a qualified franchise had long been available .... Zulu-speakers were conservative, even parochial, by comparison.'[32] At the time of the Union, there were already 12 000 black and mixed race registered voters in the Cape but only a handful in Natal. The implication is that Zulus lag behind Xhosa in democratic culture and it is the latter that must constitute the core group in the new democracy.

The two groups pursued different tactics under apartheid. The ANC waged an armed struggle against the apartheid government in the hope of making South Africa ungovernable. Inkatha concentrated its efforts on a negotiated solution. After the democratic transition Inkatha allied itself with opponents of change, ranging from the bantustan leader of Ciskei to representatives of the white Afrikaner right, including leaders of the Conservative party. This discredited Inkatha as much as did the ANC's acceptance of Soviet and Cuban backing and its inclusion of communist leaders within its ranks during the anti-apartheid struggle.

The results of the 1994 elections produced the expected victory for the ANC. Mandela was selected by the legislature to become the country's first black president. But Inkatha did not fare poorly: despite organizing its campaign at the last minute it gained 10.5 percent of the vote nationwide, winning 43 seats compared to 252 by the ANC and 82 by the Nationalists. This entitled it to three of 27 cabinet posts. Inkatha entered into a power-sharing agreement with the ANC and Buthelezi was appointed to the cabinet. But since Mandela had courted a few bantustan leaders and had effectively reached an unspoken alliance with the former ruling all-white National party, to coopt Buthelezi into government was no distinction for the Zulu nation.

In elections for the Natal-KwaZulu regional assembly, Inkatha defeated the ANC by a comfortable margin of 50 percent to 32 percent. The ANC later charged that there had been widespread voting irregularities but, notwithstanding that, an Inkatha–ANC regional coalition government was formed under the premiership of a moderate, Frank Mdlalose, Inkatha vice-president. Real power in the region remained in Buthelezi's hands.

Shortly after these elections Buthelezi withdrew from South Africa's Constitutional Assembly responsible for drafting a new constitution. He accused Mandela of failing to honor a promise to allow for international mediation of the question of federalism. He also was dissatisfied with the 1993 constitution which came into effect in April 1994. It proclaimed 11 official languages in South Africa, acknowledged the institution of traditional indigenous leaders, and recognized the principle of self-determination for all groups within the country. But in its commitment to an inclusive democracy, it extended no special status for Zulus.[33] While Zulus may have achieved absolute gains under the new legal framework, Buthelezi was unhappy that they had recorded no relative gains compared to other groups.

By 1995 the rift between Mandela and Buthelezi had widened. The South African president became more outspoken about the destructive influence on the country exerted by his Zulu coalition partner. In a speech given to the South African parliament in May 1995, Mandela claimed that more than 20 000 blacks had died in KwaZulu-Natal in the past ten years. A Human Rights Committee found that in the first 20 months after the April 1994 elections, 1500 people had been murdered in political violence in the province. Mandela held Buthelezi responsible for fomenting violence: 'Chief Buthelezi has made a public call to Zulus to rise against the central government and has said if we do not get the right to self-determination it is not worth being alive'.[34] He threatened to cut funding to KwaZulu-Natal if Inkatha continued to destabilize the new political system.

In May 1999, just prior to South Africa's second free national election, the quarrel between the two parties was again patched up. The ANC signed an accord with Inkatha to bring an end to conflict between their memberships. It was estimated that more than 12 000 people had been killed in clashes between rival supporters since 1985. The agreement established a code of conduct for the general election and even envisaged a joint election rally to be addressed by the two party leaders, the ANC's Thabo Mbeki, who had succeeded Mandela, and Chief Buthelezi. While it never took place, Buthelezi did praise the outgoing president in election rallies and, for the first time, each party was able to campaign in some of the strongholds of the other in KwaZulu-Natal. At 71, suffering from diabetes and mollified by his cabinet post, Buthelezi engaged less in the rhetoric of Zulu nationalism than that of party-based competition.

The ANC–IFP agreement defused tension that followed the discovery of a seven-ton Inkatha arms cache a few days earlier. It ensured that the electoral campaign was relatively free of the political violence that preceded the 1994 vote. Both parties still possessed large arsenals. Over 100 people were killed in KwaZulu during the election and political intimidation was a common occurrence in rural areas. For example, when the ANC took its campaign to Nongoma, an IFP bastion on the east coast, '[i]t was eventually forced to leave in a hurry by a fierce mob shouting abuse and stomping out the rhythmic war dance of a Zulu battalion'.[35]

Inkatha itself was being transformed in the process of South African democratization. Launched in the 1920s as a Zulu cultural organization, by the turn of the twenty-first century it sought to dispel its Zulu nationalist image and adopted a new logo: a family of elephants signifying 'unity in diversity'.[36] Its campaign program also stressed a pan-South African program and accused the ANC of having 'no answers for the future'. Buthelezi's electoral platform asserted that South Africa was 'deeply troubled. By unemployment. By crime. By poverty. By disease. By corruption. By a breakdown in the social fabric. By a lack of discipline. By a lack of respect for others. By indolence. In key respects, South Africa is not being governed properly and is becoming, and has at times already become, ungovernable.' In sum, 'life is getting rougher and tougher for all South Africans' and Buthelezi exhorted: 'If the government of the day can't cope, then it is time to change the government. It's time for a government that will make South Africa governable. It's time for the IFP.'[37] For its powerbase of KwaZulu-Natal, however, Inkatha again demanded wider autonomy and invoked the section of the constitution asserting the right of more territorial self-determination for ethnic communities.

In the 1999 elections, an overwhelming ANC victory nationwide was tempered by its one regional loss – in KwaZulu-Natal to Inkatha. The ANC won 66 percent of the national vote and was one seat short of a two-thirds legislative majority. Inkatha, which had placed second in 1994, obtained 8.6 percent of the vote, behind the 9.6 percent registered by the Democratic Party (formerly the Progressive Party which had been the lone parliamentary voice opposing apartheid). But in KwaZulu-Natal, the IFP edged out the ANC by 40.5 percent to 39.8 percent. Even though Inkatha had not matched its 1994 performance, as part of an effort to ensure cooperation between the two parties Buthelezi and two IFP colleagues were included in Mbeki's cabinet. There was even talk of merger between the parties.[38]

Setting aside Buthelezi's ambitions, it was the ethnic fault line that was largely responsible for the strife between the ANC and Inkatha. Even before the democratic breakthrough, a leading African specialist noted that Xhosa and Zulu 'occupy polar positions on some key questions of ethnic identity, ideology, organizational affiliation, leadership preferences, and strategic inclinations'. Not only that: 'one of these groups is significantly overrepresented and the other underrepresented in the leading extraparliamentary opposition organizations'.[39] Underrepresentation is a classic grievance of a breakaway group in any state, including one claiming to be democratic.

Competing visions in Zulu politics

Buthelezi rose to leadership in the 1960s, a descendant of a family of advisers to Zulu kings and a protégé of Lutuli, who had refused to compromise with the apartheid regime while rejecting the ANC's revolutionary militancy.[40] In 1975 he revived *Inkatha ya KwaZulu* ('Ring of the Zulu') as a cultural liberation movement. The name was soon changed to *Inkatha ye Nkululeko ye Sizwe* ('Ring of the Nation') to emulate the ANC's multi-ethnic image and soon it was able to recruit the Natal-based ANC leadership. Nevertheless

> Inkatha's dominant 'tradition' involves Zulu ethnicity (an ethnic populism) which depends in content, structures and agents on the apartheid system....The ethnic exclusivism of Buthelezi and other Inkatha leaders has led to a racially exclusive position....The 'traditions' used by Inkatha have served to both mobilize and control people.[41]

Inkatha came to be seen as a major beneficiary of the ban under apartheid on African nationalist parties. When Ulundi was selected as the site of the Zulu homeland capitol and legislature, it worked to the IFP's advantage: 'Within the heartland of KwaZulu, Buthelezi and Inkatha have "captured" monuments and historical sites to define territory, both physically and symbolically.'[42] Buthelezi's political base thus became Zululand, not Natal, despite his vision of building a Zulu state spanning both sides of the Tugela.

During the Soweto uprising of June 1976, Zulus in the township did not support the general strike intended to cripple the white-run economy. Reprisals against Zulus, cast as collaborators, followed. The absence of protests against apartheid in KwaZulu and Natal at this time also raised blacks' suspicions about Buthelezi's implicit cooperation with the racist regime. As a KwaZulu chief minister concerned with police and justice, it seemed he was too zealous in acting in the interests of the Pretoria government. Buthelezi's discourse remained nationalist, however, and he repeatedly invoked the golden age of the Zulu nation in the nineteenth century before it was subjugated by outsiders.

The Inkatha leader was also a world statesman even if deprived of a political homeland. He met with world leaders including president Richard Nixon and Pope Paul VI. He argued against sanctions and disinvestment because they would hurt blacks more than whites (in this camp he found himself with Ronald Reagan and Margaret Thatcher). At home he courted Afrikaners who, he alleged, were victims of British rule like the Zulus.

Not all Zulus supported Buthelezi's agenda for sovereignty and Inkatha was not the sole voice of the Zulu people, especially in Natal. Here, for example, although Zulus outnumbered other groups by three-to-one, ANC supporters outnumbered those of Inkatha by two-to-one. Many young Zulus living in the townships of Durban and rural areas around Pietermaritzburg preferred the United Democratic Front (UDF) – the legal nationwide front set up in 1983 by the outlawed ANC – to Inkatha. It should be noted, then, that '[t]he enemy, for Inkatha, involved not only political opponents but included "Zulus" who rejected the version of politicized ethnicity propounded by the Inkatha leadership and the Zulu king'.[43]

Zulu youths clashed with each other in political violence that cost tens of thousands of lives in the 1990s. Between 1990 and 1994 nearly 15 000 people were killed, two-thirds of them in KwaZulu and Natal, in bloody confrontations between ANC and UDF supporters on the one hand and Inkatha supporters on the other. South African police identified the ANC as the main subversive group in the apartheid state and did little to discourage Inkatha supporters from killing their political rivals. In turn, in their testimony in October 1997 to the Truth and Reconciliation Commission set up to investigate police abuse under apartheid, Inkatha leaders demanded an investigation into alleged hit squad activities during a bloody 'seven-day war' between rival Zulu groups in March 1990 that caused hundreds of deaths.

What was known as 'faction fighting' seemed almost endemic to the Zulu people dating from the civil war in the 1880s. Ethnic identity was clearly not the sole factor shaping political allegiances. Instead

> the clearest feature of the divisions between Zulu-speakers is still the fault line of the Tugela. Traditionalism remained strong in the old Zulu country, where little development took place and cattle and land remained the first and last arbiter of status. South of the Tugela, meanwhile, industry and development flourished around the centers of Durban and Pietermaritzburg.[44]

For this writer '[i]t is regionalism, and more specifically the immediate precolonial and colonial regionally-distinctive history, that has made a population "available" for ethnic mobilization and ethnic confirmation in Natal'.[45]

Another political axis differentiating Zulus was the traditionalist group around the royal court and Westernized converts. In some respects King Goodwill was a less compromising nationalist than Buthelezi. When the king was unable to gain recognition for the special status of the Zulu people, he announced that the Zulu homeland encompassed both Natal province, which he claimed had been stolen from the Zulus by the British, and disputed parts of the neighboring Transkei homeland. In March 1994 he even threatened to proclaim a sovereign Zulu state before the Zulu parliament. This hard bargaining paid off and when an accord had been reached with de Klerk's government on the status of KwaZulu the king backed away from the sovereignty declaration. A rapprochement between Mandela and King Goodwill followed. In 1995 the king even invited the new South African President to attend a sacred Zulu ceremony commemorating King Shaka.

Conclusions on Zulu separatism

Zulu demands for political autonomy have been a recurrent problem in South Africa's transition from apartheid. It has produced widespread violence, not least because Zulus were divided on a sovereignty program. Buthelezi's personal ambitions shaped the Zulu political agenda, and his erratic discourse and behavior – including a fistfight with rivals that was televised – discredited him further. With negligible outside support, in contrast to the near-universal sympathy Mandela enjoyed, Buthelezi became isolated. As with popular perceptions of Winnie Mandela's use of violence against ANC opponents when her husband was in prison, so perceptions of Buthelezi's occasional recourse to violence were of gangster tactics rather than politics.

From this we should not conclude that Zulus have given up the struggle for separation. Proud of their history, they have pushed for a special status within South Africa, and concessions made by de Klerk and Mandela have been a start in extending this status to them. Not all political differences between KwaZulu and Pretoria are ethnic and many can be resolved through the political process.[46] Channeling disputes into constitutional arenas can build confidence in the new system and carry over to issues that do involve ethnically-based differences. When compared to the phenomenon of collapsing states in parts of Africa and elsewhere, South Africa's efforts to construct nationhood are remarkable.

Canada

Quebec's struggle for sovereignty

The sources of Quebec nationalism can be found in many different spheres: ideological, economic, technocratic, social, cultural, linguistic, psychological, structural, developmental, elitist, continental, strategic, legal, and political.[47] As one of Quebec's leading political scientists has asked about the nature of Quebec nationalism, 'Could it simply be that even in the age of globalization and interdependence, nationalism remains somewhat of a mystery to us all?'[48]

Let us begin our examination of Quebec nationalism and its bid for sovereignty with a review of the historical grievances and territorial rights claims which for a long time have been central to the nationalist movement.

In 1534 Jacques Cartier landed in the Gaspe peninsula and claimed the land for the King of France. The first settlement was established by Champlain in 1608 but French colonization proceeded much more slowly than that of the British. At about the time of the battle on the Plains of Abraham in 1759, 65 000 French settlers lived among one million English colonists. The British victory over the French army at Quebec City was, in retrospect, almost irrepressible. Nevertheless myths about 'the Conquest' became etched in the minds of generations of *Canadiens*, an earlier term for what are today called Quebecers and the name of a nation that Quebec nationalists say no longer exists.[49]

The Constitutional Act of 1791 divided the British colony into two provinces, Upper (Ontario) and Lower (Quebec) Canada, each with a governor and legislative assembly. These post-conquest institutional arrangements were successful enough to have English and French forces join forces in beating back an American invasion in 1812. But rivalry began to increase between a dominant English merchant class in Lower Canada, based almost exclusively in Montreal, and the French population located primarily on farmlands. A French nationalist movement, 'Les Patriotes', staged a revolt in Montreal in 1837 but the rebellion was crushed by British forces and political oppression ensued.

In 1839 a newly-appointed British governor-general, Lord Durham, published his 'Report on the Affairs of British North America'. As ways to address the causes of the 1837 rebellion, he simultaneously put forward the idea of responsible government for Canada and forced assimilation of French speakers into English culture. He therefore recommended a legislative union of Upper and Lower Canada.[50] The political uncertainty that followed the Durham Report coupled with severe economic recession in Lower Canada persuaded half a million French Canadians to emigrate to the US between 1840 and 1900. Others moved to the Canadian west and established small French-speaking communities. The threat to the survival of French Canada was never as great as in the mid-nineteenth century.

While a small nationalist group demanded full independence for Lower Canada, liberal French Canadian leaders were persuaded to enter talks about creating a federal union. The renewed threat from the US – its abrogation of the Reciprocity Treaty in 1866, which had initially been signed in 1854 to promote free trade in natural resources between the two countries, and the Alaska purchase in 1867 from Russia – accelerated negotiations to form a Canadian union. With strong British prompting from Lord Carnarvon, a confederation agreement was concluded in Charlottetown, Prince Edward Island, and Canadian independence proclaimed on July 1, 1867. Lower Canada was renamed Quebec, much to the disgust of French nationalists whose argument was that '[t]he English reduced our territory to a small reservation along the river. The name Quebec is thus linked to a terrible humiliation inflicted on our ancestors.'[51]

For nearly a hundred years afterwards, French Canadian society remained largely rural. *Survivance* ('survival') was shaped by the interests of the Catholic Church which encouraged large families while controlling the provision of education, welfare, and social services. Whether the Church did so unwittingly or purposefully, Quebec historians concur that it served the interests of the British political and economic elite in the province.[52] A sense of economic backwardness and political inferiority to English Canada was increased by the Canadian government's decisions to support British war efforts, first against Calvinist Dutch settlers seeking greater autonomy in South Africa in 1899, then its entry into the First World War. French Canadian leaders argued that they could not identify with king and country when these were British. The interwar period produced the intellectual father of the Quebec sovereignty idea, Abbe Lionel Groulx, who developed the idea of an independent French-Canadian state.

The demographic character of Quebec was transformed by large-scale immigration from Europe after the Second World War. On arriving in Montreal – the almost-exclusive site of immigrant settlement in the province – most immigrants spoke no English or French and had to choose one of the languages of the host society. Then and now, too, many immigrants did not see Quebec as a distinct society within Canada. Between 1945 and 1972, when language legislation was passed making French the required language for most immigrants, most opted for English, aided and abetted by the indifference that francophone authorities displayed towards them.[53]

A so-called Quiet Revolution began in Quebec in 1960 when a progressive Liberal government under premier Jean Lesage came to power. It inaugurated far-ranging institutional and societal changes, beginning with the establishment of departments of education (previously this sector was controlled by a committee of the Catholic Church) and cultural affairs, as well as new bodies to oversee the provision of social services and economic development. The Lesage government also nationalized hydro-electricity, thereby assuring that Quebec would remain energy-rich for a long time and laying a foundation for future industrial development.

Other important changes affecting Quebec's hitherto inferior status within Canada were taking place at the federal level. The 1965 report of the Royal Commission on Bilingualism and Biculturalism recognized the threat that French Canadians felt to their culture and language. In 1968 Montreal native Pierre-Elliot Trudeau was elected prime minister and oversaw passage of the 1969 Official Languages Act which made French and English co-equal official languages. His utopian vision of a country built on two nations and functioning smoothly in two languages was never realized; on the contrary, it galvanized both French- and English-Canadian nationalists against the supposed artificiality of biculturalism and bilingualism. One criticism was that 'Trudeau's image was of French-speaking Canadians as individuals without the collective dimensions of identification with *la nation canadienne-francaise*'.[54]

One year after the Languages Act was passed, a terrorist cell called the Front de Liberation du Quebec (FLQ) kidnapped and killed a Quebec government minister seen as too sympathetic to Trudeau's ideas. The Canadian prime minister reacted to the October 1970 crisis with harsh measures. He invoked the War Measures Act, effectively establishing martial law; the Canadian army moved onto the streets of Montreal; many of Quebec's intellectual and cultural nationalists were interned; and the influence of the FLQ was inadvertently strengthened. Eventually, cell members were given safe passage to Cuba, to return to Quebec over a decade later as resistance heroes.

Quebec nationalism intensified in the aftermath of the October 1970 crisis. It had already received financial and moral support from the ruling Gaullist party in France and was offered continued assistance over the next two decades by a highly-placed Quebec lobby in ministerial circles in Paris that had not let go of a French imperial vision.[55] Quebec nationalists like Rene Levesque declined offers of financial assistance but the RCMP used the French connection as a pretext to steal the membership list of the fledgling Parti Quebecois (known as Pequistes or PQ) in 1973. The CIA had also become interested in Quebec nationalist leaders and as early as 1969 had questioned Jacques Parizeau, another future prime minister of the province. In order to stop the CIA from infiltrating the movement Parizeau agreed that he would keep the US consul in Montreal informed of developments.[56]

In November 1976 the PQ, running on a platform of making Quebec independent following a referendum victory, won the provincial elections. The charismatic Levesque became a premier Quebecers revered. He engineered economic expansion that transformed the province into a modern, secular, post-industrial society. He also made French language and culture secure through enactment of the Charter of the French language (called Bill 101). French became the language of work, commerce, signage, and education in the province, not a *joual* or *patois* confined to the home or the tavern. When, by a margin of 60 to 40 percent (52 to 48 percent among francophones) the first referendum on Quebec independence was defeated in 1980, Levesque contended that it was the linguistic and cultural security produced by the French language Charter that made Quebecers view the independence project as no longer so crucial.

The bases of Quebec nationalism

Traditional Quebec nationalism springs from the alleged injustices that French Canadians have suffered as a result of forming part of a confederation with English Canada. Like Abbe Groulx's approach, it is premised on an ethnic understanding of Quebec identity that engenders an ideology of nationalism.[57] A related cultural understanding of the nation depicts French

Canadians as the Latins of the North and forming a distinct 'Homo Quebe-censis'.[58] One of Quebec's foremost intellectuals framed Quebecers' identity in terms of a negotiation process between oneself and the other and between the individual and the collectivity.[59] A socio-economic explanation for the resurgence of Quebec nationalism in the 1970s was advanced by an FLQ theoretician in the well-known essay *White Niggers of America*.[60] Structural explanations highlighting how the 'rules-of-the-economic-game' have been stacked against French Canadians and produce, therefore, an overlapping ethnic and economic schism, have elaborated on this polemical approach.[61] Furthermore,

> Closely related to the division-of-labor explanation is the class interpreta-tion of Quebec nationalism, according to which Francophone elites cleverly manipulated the symbols and discourse of nationalism to con-solidate their own position within the Quebec class structure while acquiring more 'elbow room' vis-a-vis the dominant English-Canadian bourgeoisie.[62]

A technocratic offshoot of the class thesis is that the burgeoning well-educated francophone middle class has declared that it possesses the unique indispensable managerial competence to govern Quebec and it uses identity politics to assure ideological reproduction of its control.[63] Elite explanations for Quebec nationalism are usually predicated on the special role that the state plays in Quebec society. Indeed in 1999 Quebec prime minister Lucien Bouchard advanced a 'Quebec model' of political life in which the state was the central actor. Quebec nationalism and the Quebec state are seen as two sides of the same coin, struggling against the Canadian state and its weak nationalism.[64] Finally, to counter the etatist bias in many inquiries into Quebec nationalism, two writers have contended that the strength of civil society will determine whether Quebec consolidates into a nation or be-comes a mere Canadian region: 'The more autonomous, the more dynamic, the more activist Quebec society is, the more national its outlook'.[65]

Quebec nationalism clearly has many sources and one can exaggerate the importance of, say, economic or social factors while overlooking more holis-tic explanations. As one writer observed, '[s]alary differentials, job market segregation, dependency, and class structure tell us *something* about the Quebec story. But one has the feeling that these interpretations, even when combined, miss some of the mixture of "extraordinary" and "ordinary" that has characterized the Quebec saga through its various incarnations'.[66] While various forms of Quebec nationalism have their own rationale, '[w]hat is missing...is a more strategic perspective on the nation. For it to exist, the nation must make sense of itself in relation to its environment.'

Just as Quebec society has undergone radical change since the 1960s, so has its political environment. Any national identity is 'continuously reconstructed as external events and even the definition of what the "outside" really is are changed'.[67] The 'Rest of Canada' (ROC) plays a crucial role in defining what Quebec identity is. On the one hand, '[t]he program to construct a single Canadian nation threatens the distinctive identity and culture of Quebec.'[68] On the other, a postmodern understanding of Canadian identity may not threaten Quebec. In a best-selling book on this topic, John Ralston Saul combined banal, often repeated assertions about Canadian identity with provocative arguments about the country's cultural uniqueness: 'complexity is Canada's central characteristic'. It is 'a permanently incomplete experiment built on a triangular foundation to produce an American phenomenon versus the European republic to the south.'[69] Not only was the configuration of English, French, and first peoples in a political union unprecedented, then, Canada did not have the same exaggerated sense of borders and markers that characterize Europe and the US. From this it followed that a distinct Quebec identity was perfectly compatible with Canada's ongoing experiment in identity construction. To be sure, this benign view of Canadian identity has come under attack from Quebec nationalists. For example, one prominent party leader, Gilles Duceppe, made the clever if unconvincing argument that just as Quebec nationalism was embracing a civic, inclusive identity where there was a place for people of all backgrounds, Canada was turning French Canadians into a mere ethnic category.[70]

The two identities are dialectically related, then: 'As in the case of all identities, the Other is a critical factor, and now for Quebec the Other may be changing. The emergence of new possibilities in North American civilization is freeing Quebec from some aspects of its problematical links to English Canada'.[71] In short, though still significant the Quebec–Canada dyad no longer monopolizes Quebec nationalism. 'While Quebec's relationship with its privileged Other, Canada, remains a central element of the Quebec imaginary landscape, it has lost some of its exclusivity....The rest-of-Canada or, to use its traditional name, English Canada, now shares the limelight with Ottawa and the federal government as the main *definisseurs* of the Canadian "out there".'[72]

To complicate the construction of Quebec identity further, 'many of the central components of the Quebec identity have been given shape by making use of selected stereotypical views of "English Canadians".'[73] To take a prime example, one of the dominant perceptions Quebecers had of English Canada was its subordination to the commercial interests of the Canadian establishment – to Bay Street (the financial heart of Toronto). Yet the Free Trade Agreement concluded with the US in 1989 dispelled the notion that English Canadians sought at all cost to protect indigenous English Canadian commercial interests. The unstated policy of successive Pequiste governments – that an independent Quebec would prove a better friend of the US than the latently anti-American Canadian federal governments –

was effectively undermined. Significantly, then, '[t]he Quebec nationalist movement is one of the few around the world that has eschewed anti-American rhetoric'.[74] But as the Liberal government of Jean Chretien positioned itself closer to the US in 2000–2001, discussing the subjects in Cabinet of monetary union with the US, open borders, and a closer political union across North America, Quebec's Other was no longer so otherly.

Building a North American community is not necessarily inconsistent with Quebec nationalists' agenda. One scholar put it this way:

> Quebec has always seen itself as an original founder of the North American compact, along with the Americans and the Mexicans.... For the Quebecois, North America has been from the beginning a 'tale' of three experiments, that of New England, New France, and New Spain....They see themselves as cofounder and certainly as co-owner of the original American dream. English Canadians, for their part, are seen as second-class North Americans, principally because of their presumed incapacity to differentiate themselves from Americans and because they rejected the American Revolution (as did Quebec, to be sure).[75]

Moreover, when globalization is included as a factor shaping contemporary Quebec identity, we arrive at a portrait of Quebec nationalism that differs markedly from that offered by the conventional primordial, historical, or political paradigms. If the latter approaches convinced some observers that Quebec nationalism was illiberal, thereby disqualifying Quebecers from being Canadians,[76] the contemporary amalgam is quintessentially liberal. Kenneth McRoberts, an insightful English Canadian specialist on Quebec, reported that

> virtually all francophones are committed to the development of a modern, technologically advanced society that functions first and foremost in French. As the last few decades have so clearly shown, this is really possible only in Quebec. Accordingly, most francophones are going to share in a Quebec nationalism, whether they see the nation as drawing upon peoples of all origins or restricted to descendants of the inhabitants of New France.[77]

Indeed, even the leaders of ROC have sought to share in such Quebec nationalism. For example, on Quebec's national holiday (St. Jean-Baptiste on June 24) 'anglo' Canadians have competed with each other in praise of Quebecers. In 1999, then Reform party head Preston Manning sent Quebecers a telegram of congratulations while Progressive Conservative chief Joe Clark praised Quebec nationalism as being true to the original vision of European settlers. Quebec nationalism had become respectable – even chic – in English Canada.

Institutionalizing nationalism

With the exception of the period 1985 to 1994, when Robert Bourassa's Liberals formed the government, the PQ has held power in Quebec since 1976. Its general strategy has been to fuse Quebec nationalism with populism. The Pequiste leadership has obtained widespread support and political legitimacy by claiming that it represents the unarticulated feelings and values of the French-speakers. Until its second referendum defeat (discussed below), Pequiste populism was rooted in an exclusionary conception of Quebec na-tionhood, restricted not merely to French speakers but to those of ancient Quebec lineage. Accompanying this approach was a barely-concealed intoler-ance towards outgroups not forming part of this community: initially towards those of British stock (English, Scottish, Welsh, Irish), then towards 'neo-Canadiens' (Italians, Greeks, Portugese), and more recently towards non French-speaking visible minorities (South Asians, Arabs, English Caribbean). Until the PQ began in the late 1990s to rethink its strategy for winning a sover-eignty referendum, its populism was clannish, nativist, *volkist* in character.

In another respect, however, the Quebec sovereignty movement has not followed traditional populist lines. Whereas populist movements yearn for a simple, often rural, idealized, mythical past and reject modernity, Levesque and his successors have stressed the modernity of Quebec nationalism, above all, that Quebec society and its economy are well prepared cogni-tively, organizationally, and technologically to meet the challenges of twenty-first century statehood. While accurate at the time, no assertion can misrepresent contemporary Quebec nationalism more than one made in 1965 that Quebecers 'live in the past to a degree almost inconceivable to the English speaking North American'.[78]

The 1980 referendum loss was taken by some as a beacon that the Quebec sovereignty movement was fading. That was the conclusion reached by Trudeau, who seized the opportunity to patriate the Canadian constitution which was still based on British statutes. Yet an unintended consequence of Trudeau's success of concluding a new Canadian constitution in 1982 was to revive the Quebec sovereignty movement. Whether a deliberate act or not, Levesque was left out of the all-night negotiations involving Trudeau and the other nine provincial premiers that hammered out the new document. With patriation a *fait accompli*, Quebec refused to ratify the constitution (its position to this day) and charged English Canada with discrimination against it. 'Quebec argues that the province has been unjustly denied even the kind of constitutional recognition that in 1982 was accorded Aboriginal peoples, the multicultural associations of English Canada, women, and the other interests that left their mark on the Charter.'[79] The result has been a constitutional stalemate lasting two decades.

The so-called Meech Lake accord, agreed upon in April 1987 by new Canadian prime minister Brian Mulroney (like Trudeau, a Quebecer), new

Quebec prime minister Bourassa, and the nine other provincial premiers, came close to breaking the constitutional impasse. It provided for Quebec's accession to the Canadian constitution in return for recognition of Quebec as a distinct society, a constitutional veto for it, three Quebec appointments on the nine-person Supreme Court, Quebec's right to opt out of federal programs, and shared jurisdiction over immigration. But the amending formula for the Canadian constitution enacted by Trudeau required the unanimity of all ten provinces and, in 1990, first Manitoba and then New-foundland refused to approve the Meech Lake accord.

A sharp nationalist backlash in Quebec followed the collapse of the Meech Lake formula. A November 1990 poll reported that 62 percent of Quebec respondents and 75 percent of francophone ones now supported Quebec sovereignty.[80] A Quebec political scientist wrote alarmingly that '[t]he defeat of the Meech Lake accord marked the end of the system of compromise and accommodation between francophone and anglophone elites, upon which Canadian federalism had rested for more than a century'.[81] To stave off the resurgent movement, a new round of negotiations was held in August 1992 which produced what was designated the Charlottetown accord, in substance differing little from Meech Lake. In October 1992 a referendum on the proposal was held across Canada but failed to obtain majorities in six provinces. English-speaking provinces opposed the Charlottetown accord because it made too many concessions to Quebec, while the 56 percent of Quebecers who voted against it did so primarily because it did not go far enough in empowering Quebec. In the subsequent decade this deadlock was not broken even though a new Canadian prime minister, Jean Chretien (yet another Quebecer), passed a bill through parliament officially recognizing Quebec as unique. It had no constitutional status since provincial legislatures had not given their consent, but as one Quebec attorney caught up in the constitutional imbroglio observed, given the facts of Quebec's distinct language, culture, civil code, and institutions '[o]ther provinces would not be doing Quebec a favor by recognizing its specificity; they would be doing Canada a favor, for our majority francophone culture effectively permeates all of Canadian society'.[82]

At the time of the Meech Lake discussions, a federal politician from Quebec, Lucien Bouchard, broke ranks from the ruling Conservative cabinet and established a new federal party, the Bloc Quebecois (BQ) which was designed to promote Quebec sovereignty from within the Canadian parliament. In the House of Commons he justified his cause: 'Take a look at the Western world . . . . Ninety-five percent of its population lives in nation-states. And the fact is, Quebec is the only nation of more than seven million people in the Western world not to have attained political sovereignty.'[83] In the October 1993 federal elections, the Bloc recorded the best showing in Quebec, winning 54 of the 75 seats. Combined with a strong performance in western Canada by the new Reform Party, committed to securing greater powers for Canada's western provinces (it won 52 seats), 106 of 295 seats in the Canadian parliament were held by populist, anti-establishment, quasi-secessionist parties. Ironically, the sovereigntist BQ beat out Reform to become the official opposition party in Ottawa.

In turn, in Quebec elections held in September 1994, Parizeau led the PQ to victory, promising a swift referendum on sovereignty. In December 1994 his government introduced a draft bill – in reality a government document rather than *projet de loi* – on Quebec sovereignty:

> It is proposed that Quebec become a sovereign country through the democratic process. The accession to full sovereignty has been defined by the National Assembly as 'the accession of Quebec to a position of exclusive jurisdiction, through its democratic institutions, to make laws and levy taxes in its territory and to act on the international scene for the making of agreements and treaties of any kind with other independent States and participating in various international organizations'.[84]

Accordingly, on October 30, 1995, Quebecers went to the polls to say yes or no to a convoluted question: 'Do you agree that Quebec should become sovereign, after having made a formal offer to Canada for a new economic and political partnership, within the scope of the Bill respecting the future of Quebec and of the agreement signed on June 12, 1995?' The Bill in question, introduced in the Quebec legislature in September 1995, provided for drafting a new Quebec constitution and clarified the territory, citizenship, and currency status that a sovereign Quebec would invoke. The agreement cited in the referendum question was one concluded in June 1995, by the three major pro-sovereignty movements: the PQ, BQ, and the Action Democratique du Quebec, a small party represented in the Quebec National Assembly.

The referendum was suspenseful. After swings in each direction, at the end of ballot-counting 50.6 percent of voters had opposed the question and 49.4 percent had supported it. Of francophone voters, just over 60 percent opted for the sovereignty option, while the overwhelming majority of English speakers and members of Quebec's ethnic groups rejected it. Conceding defeat that night, Parizeau attributed the narrow loss to the influence of corporate money and Quebec's ethnic groups. The traditional ethnic construction of Quebec identity had become embarrassing for the PQ. Parizeau's tactlessness led to pressure for his resignation, and he soon gave up the prime ministership to BQ head Bouchard.

Bouchard's assumption of the PQ leadership marked the fifth party that he had been affiliated with in his political career, leading one commentator to describe him as a 'gypsy-nationalist'.[85] Even though the PQ was reelected for another term in 1998 (though it obtained a smaller share of the popular vote than the opposition Liberal party), Bouchard resigned as prime minister in

January 2001, frustrated that he had been unable to create the 'winning conditions' necessary for holding another referendum on independence. His support for globalization and a neoliberal program had adverse effects on many disadvantaged Quebecers. They were also not part of the nationalist mainstream in Quebec.[86]

Legal challenges to Quebec's right to secede

Studying secessionism in a democratic state entails an examination of legal and constitutional questions. The close referendum result prompted interested parties, including the government of Canada, to seek judicial clarification from high courts concerning the legality of separation. There were moral and political issues, of course, and questions of political philosophy that no court could clarify. For example, whether a referendum was an instrument of democracy was one of the subjects that was contested. Another was the question of authority. Those opposing secession invoked formal authorities, such as elected bodies and appointed courts. For secessionists, the notion of 'authentic authority' – one resting in the people – was paramount: 'Authentic authority is not rooted in one's role in an institutional structure but comes from an authentic source, either because that source is the ground of other authority or because it is the one most knowledgeable about an entire situation'.[87] As a result,

> [s]eparatism is not primarily about how government or its assignees exercise their authority. It is about who is to be accepted as the definitive group for selecting a government to decide our fundamental obligations and which groups should assign roles. Separatists subordinate the division of roles and responsibilities to recognition of a people as a primary source of authentic authority.[88]

Guy Bertrand, a former PQ lawyer turned federalist, was particularly active in challenging Quebec's constitutional right even to contemplate secession. In his petition to the Quebec Superior Court filed in September 1995, the day after Bill 1 had been introduced in the Quebec National Assembly ('An act respecting the future of Quebec'), he contended that the draft sovereignty bill tabled in the National Assembly by Parizeau in December 1994, together with the June 1995 agreement among three Quebec parties to support sovereignty, constituted 'an actual parliamentary and constitutional coup d'etat, a fraud upon the Canadian Constitution and an abuse of powers, resulting in a violation and a denial of his rights and freedoms and those of all Quebec taxpayers'.[89] By empowering the Quebec government to declare independence unilaterally following a successful referendum, the procedure set forth in the Canadian constitution would be bypassed. Superior Court Judge Robert Lesage ruled that even though Quebec had not ratified the 1982 constitution, it and the accompanying

Charter of Rights and Freedoms did apply to Quebec. The key legal precedent was the December 1982 decision of the Canadian Supreme Court:

> The Constitution Act, 1982 is now in force. Its legality is neither chal-
> lenged nor assailable. It contains a new procedure for amending the
> Constitution of Canada which entirely replaces the old one in its legal
> as well as in its conventional aspects. Even assuming therefore that there
> was a conventional requirement for the consent of Quebec under the old
> system, it would no longer have any object or force.[90]

Therefore for Quebec to obtain sovereignty, it would have to seek an
amendment to the Canadian constitution for its secession. The amending
formula, in turn, requires the consent of the House of Commons and Senate
and the consent of a minimum of seven provinces containing at least 50
percent of the Canadian population. For Justice Lesage, the procedure for
sovereignty mapped out by the Parizeau government repudiated the constitution of Canada and gave his government a mandate which was not
conferred upon it by the constitution. But he allowed that the public should
have the opportunity to express its opinion in a referendum. Thus, Parizeau
could seek the approval of 'authentic authority' through a popular referendum, but democratic means were not synonymous with constitutional
means. In a strictly legal sense, Bertrand was not far off the mark in claiming
that the Parizeau government was guilty of planning a constitutional coup
d'etat.

For their part, the Pequiste government defendants cited in Bertrand's
petition – the Quebec Attorney General and prime minister Parizeau –
declined the jurisdiction of the court and withdrew their attorneys. They
also refused to contest the next legal challenge to sovereignty, this time
brought to the Canadian Supreme Court in September 1996. In this case the
amicus curiae appointed by the Court to represent Quebec questioned the
Court's right of jurisdiction over the issue; further, it asked whether, given its
political character, the issue was justiciable at all. But the Supreme Court
held that it did have the constitutional right to answer the questions involved and that since it was addressing only aspects of the legal framework
for secession it could not 'usurp any democratic decision that the people of
Quebec may be called upon to make'. Accordingly, in 1996 three questions
were referred to the Supreme Court for adjudication:

> Question 1: Under the Constitution of Canada, can the National
> Assembly, legislature or government of Quebec effect the secession of
> Quebec from Canada unilaterally?
> Question 2: Does international law give the National Assembly, legis-
> lature or government of Quebec the right to effect the secession of
> Quebec from Canada unilaterally? In this regard, is there a right to

self-determination under international law that would give the National Assembly, legislature or government of Quebec the right to effect the secession of Quebec from Canada unilaterally?

Question 3: In the event of a conflict between domestic and international law on the right of the National Assembly, legislature or government of Quebec to effect the secession of Quebec from Canada unilaterally, which would take precedence in Canada?[91]

The Court's ruling was published in August 1998. The answer to the first question gave some satisfaction to each of the parties. A referendum victory for the sovereignty side could be the basis for separation: 'A clear majority vote in Quebec on a clear question in favor of secession would confer democratic legitimacy on the secession initiative which all of the other participants in Confederation would have to recognize'. On the other hand, Quebec separation could not be unilateral: 'Quebec could not, despite a clear referendum result, purport to invoke a right of self-determination to dictate the terms of a proposed secession to the other parties to the federation'.[92]

The Court showed particular ingenuity in balancing the exigencies of democracy and constitutionalism: 'The democratic vote, by however strong a majority, would have no legal effect on its own and could not push aside the principles of federalism and the rule of law, the rights of individuals and minorities, or the operation of democracy in the other provinces or in Canada as a whole.'[93] Specifically, '[t]he relationship between democracy and federalism means, for example, that in Canada there may be different and equally legitimate majorities in different provinces and territories and at the federal level. No one majority is more or less "legitimate" than the others as an expression of democratic opinion.'[94] Furthermore, 'Canadians have never accepted that ours is a system of simple majority rule',[95] for democracy and popular sovereignty include respect for constitutionalism and the rule of law as well as for voting majorities.

In short, 'Democratic rights under the Constitution cannot be divorced from constitutional obligations.' On the other hand, 'The other provinces and the federal government would have no basis to deny the right of the government of Quebec to pursue secession should a clear majority of the people of Quebec choose that goal, so long as in doing so, Quebec respects the rights of others.'[96]

In a carefully-researched answer to the second question concerning international law, the Supreme Court focused on the principle of the right of a people to self-determination. It recognized, of course, that 'the precise meaning of the term "people" remains somewhat uncertain', even though 'it is clear that "a people" may include only a portion of the population of an existing state'.[97] The Court did not consider whether Quebecers constituted a people but examined the hypothetical circumstances which would justify a people's right to unilateral secession.

It found that international law, 'by and large, leaves the creation of a new state to be determined by the domestic law of the existing state of which the seceding entity presently forms a part'.[98] Moreover, it 'expects that the right to self-determination will be exercised by peoples within the framework of existing sovereign states and consistently with the maintenance of the territorial integrity of those states'.[99] Put differently, 'the right to self-determination of a people is normally fulfilled through *internal* self-determination – a people's pursuit of its political, economic, social and cultural development within the framework of an existing state'.[100] The right to *external* self-determination, in practice, statehood, is accorded only to peoples of 'former colonies; where a people is oppressed, as for example under foreign military occupation; or where a definable group is denied meaningful access to government to pursue their political, economic, social and cultural development'.[101]

If the right to external self-determination only arises when a people is denied the right to internal self-development, Quebec did not meet the threshold since it did not have a colonized or oppressed people. The Court provided evidence why '[t]he population of Quebec cannot plausibly be said to be denied access to government'.[102] Specifically,

> For close to 40 of the last 50 years, the Prime Minister of Canada has been a Quebecer.... During the 8 years prior to June 1997, the Prime Minister and the Leader of the Official Opposition in the House of Commons were both Quebecers. At present, the Prime Minister of Canada, the Right Honorable Chief Justice and two other members of the Court, the Chief of Staff of the Canadian Armed Forces and the Canadian ambassador to the United States, not to mention the Deputy Secretary-General of the United Nations, are Quebecers.[103]

Summing up the argument, Quebec did not qualify under any of the three circumstances envisaged under international law for a people to exercise external self-determination. Since this answer to the second question submitted to the Supreme Court was consistent with the answer to the first question and therefore neither under international nor domestic law did Quebec have the right to unilateral secession, question 3, inquiring which body of law has precedence, became moot.

The Canadian Supreme Court's arguments about the right of secession in the country reveal how difficult it is for a would-be breakaway group to succeed in a Western democracy. The penultimate paragraph of the ruling was categorical:

> *A state whose government represents the whole of the people* or peoples resident within its territory, on a basis of equality and without discrimination, and respects the principles of self-determination in its internal

arrangements, is entitled to maintain its territorial integrity under inter-national law and to have that territorial integrity recognized by other states.[104]

This restates the 1995 UN General Assembly's 'Declaration on the Occasion of the Fiftieth Anniversary of the United Nations': the right of self-determination of all peoples

> shall not be construed as authorizing or encouraging any action that would dismember or impair, totally or in part, the territorial integrity or political unity of sovereign and independent States conducting themselves in compliance with the principle of equal rights and self-determination of peoples and thus *possessed of a Government representing the whole people* belonging to the territory without distinction of any kind'.[105]

It follows from this that a democracy *qua* democracy cannot be rent asunder. Two concessions only are offered to a democratic separatist move-ment within a democratic state. First, 'one of the legal norms which may be recognized by states in granting or withholding recognition of emergent states is the legitimacy of the process by which the *de facto* secession is, or was, being pursued'. Compliance with the legitimate obligations arising out of its earlier status and with procedural rules can 'weigh in favor of inter-national recognition'.[106] This normative approach was elaborated in the 1992 European Community's 'Declaration on the Guidelines on the Recog-nition of New States in Eastern Europe and in the Soviet Union'.[107]

Second, the 'effectivity' principle, that is, recognition of a factual political reality, can give hope to democratic secessionists. It 'proclaims that an illegal act may eventually acquire legal status if, as a matter of empirical fact, it is recognized on the international plane'. Squatters do sometimes acquire property rights, for example, and a change in factual circumstances may produce a change in legal status – even in international politics, as the widespread recognition of Jerusalem as Israel's capital illustrates. But it does not follow from this that 'subsequent condonation of an initially illegal act retroactively creates a legal right to engage in the act in the first place'.[108] Quebec's democratic separatists are warned, therefore, not to bank on the effectivity principle.

Reimagining Quebec

From this discussion we observe how democracies believe themselves legally and morally invulnerable to the claims of secessionists. As Unionists in the US argued in 1861, who would want to break away from a democracy if not for anti-democrats? In the case of twenty-first century Canada, the argu-ment runs deeper. Ranked highest from 1993 to 2000 in terms of quality of life by the UN World Development Program report (in 2001 it fell to second place behind Norway), it is incomprehensible that a group would want to reject such well-being. Furthermore if Canada were to break up, which advanced country in the world would not have groups with more serious grievances for leaving? It is this logic that reinforces the perception gap between a civilized, orderly 'us' – where separatism may be indulged because it is ultimately legally out of the question – and a chaotic, volatile 'them' – where anything may happen.

Is the most important fault line in Canada today still language and ethno-linguistic identity? Political understandings of the nation seem more important. 'For English Canadians, who are acutely aware of the diversity of the country, of the tenuous and indefinable nature of what holds it together, the question of unity is paramount. For any part of Canadian society to demonstrate that it prizes its part over the whole smacks of treason.'[109] Political identification more than ethno-linguistic identity is the central problematic in ROC–Quebec relations. Quebec's identity rests, to be sure, on its distinctive ethnic makeup, but it has been its increasing identification over the past three decades with a polity distinct from Canada – the Quebec state – that has made English Canada unable to accommodate it.

Quebec's Other is more than just English Canada, or even North America or globalization. Because of large-scale immigration – albeit on average less to Quebec than to English Canada – 'for the first time Quebecois are forced to deal *internally* with "others" and the "outside". For the first time, Quebecois are forced to come to terms with the very notion of nationality. The key questions have become, can one *become* a Quebecois? Can the Quebecois dream be *shared*?'[110]

At a party meeting in April 1999 designed to reinvigorate the sovereignist project for the new millennium, BQ leader Gilles Duceppe urged his party to adopt an open-ended definition of a Quebecer and set aside the traditional view stressing French ancestry, symbolized by the use of the French *Quebecois* rather than English Quebecer. His proposal was to regard as a Quebecer anyone who simply lives in Quebec. 'For the large majority of us, a Quebecer is someone who lives in Quebec, no matter how many generations it has been.' The reason for this shift was related to demographic changes: 'The new face of Quebec obliges us to redefine our project and place it in the new socio-demographic context that has developed.'[111] Or, put differently, 'in its secessionist rhetoric, Quebec must lay claim to a deepening of its diversity'.[112]

However, many Quebec nationalists hold that Quebecers are defined by primordial criteria such as ancestry and race. Under this model, *maitres chez nous* ('masters in our own house') effectively signifies the hegemony of *la vieille couche* ('the old stock'). Some members of the Bloc objected to a definition of the Quebec people as diverse because it discarded the centrality of French language and culture. One riding president argued that '[i]f we adopt the term in the document, we are denying ourselves, we are not a people, we are not a culture, we are nothing. We are denying Rene Levesque. We are denying our history behind us. We no longer exist.' Another asked whether under such an inclusionary definition eminent English-language novelist Mordecai Richler, a Montrealer hostile to francophone nationalism (he died in 2001), could be considered a Quebecer while racing driver Jacques Villeneuve, who lived in Europe, could not. These protests led to a modification of the definition of a Quebecer, reflected in the Bloc's policy document of September 1999 which asserted that '[t]he role of the French language as the cement in the construction of the Quebec identity is capital'.[113]

Moderate nationalists committed to redefining Quebecers in more civic terms advanced revisionist views of nationalist goals. The Bloc vice-president contended that Bill 101 was not designed to assimilate immigrants into Quebec's predominantly francophone society but simply to integrate them. He denied that an independent Quebec would adopt the American melting-pot approach to immigrants, but said it would not endorse Canada's multicultural-mosaic view either. Indeed, 'Quebec has been trying to define an immigration model that is different from the melting-pot approach of the United States, the multicultural mosaic of Canada, and the strict assimilation vision of France'. Quebec, then, does have flexibility in developing its own model of an immigration society: 'The fact that French and not ethnicity (although ethnicity continues to have an impact) or race is the core of Quebec identity makes that identity more permeable to outside influences and less rigid. One can learn and acquire a language; one cannot do so with race.'[114]

In August 2001 a commission headed by Gerald Larose issued a report addressing the relationship between Quebec civic identity and French as Quebec's one official language. It put forward a controversial proposal: Quebec should institute its own citizenship that would be founded on the principle of a French language common to all.[115] Using the discourse of multiculturalism against Canada, the Larose commission said that it was time to break with the federal tradition of dividing Canada into English and French-speaking populations. Instead a civic approach should be adopted in Quebec which would be characterized by inclusionary politics: non-French groups would be welcomed into Quebec society but they would have to adopt a common language – French – and take part in a common culture formed from diverse sources. One PQ cabinet minister stated that the government found the Larose commission proposal 'interesting' and 'seductive', and that it would further study whether other federal systems in the world had provisions for different orders of citizenship. The traditional federal critique of Quebec ethnocentrism was clearly blunted by this report, but it engendered a different type of criticism from federalist groups – that Quebec nationalists were using a back door approach to achieve the trappings of sovereignty that they could not obtain through electoral means.

Quebec nationalists' discovery of a multicultural society was not, of course, without strategic objectives. As the birth rate of French Quebecers remained low and the influx of immigrants continued to rise, those set on another referendum on independence were facing a 'demographic dead-line'. Somewhere around the year 2010 the proportion of French Quebecers living in the province would have fallen enough so that even their over-whelming support for independence would not cancel out the support of immigrant and ethnic groups for Canadian federalism. The conclusion had to be that ethnic groups should somehow be converted to French Quebec nationalism, clearly a difficult task.

One further obstacle was thrown into the path of the *independantiste* movement in March 2000. With the support of all parties except the Bloc, Canadian prime minister Chretien obtained passage in the House of Commons for the Clarity Act. It requires that the Canadian parliament decide in advance if the language of a referendum question is clear. This issue became important following the convoluted 1995 question on Quebec sovereignty which had apparently misled some voters to believe that they were voting on partnership with Canada rather than outright Quebec independence. The Clarity Act also stipulates that the Canadian parliament is to consider the referendum result and determine 'whether under the circumstances...there has been a clear expression of will by a clear majority of the population of that province that the province cease to be part of Canada'. No threshold is set, therefore, but 50 percent plus one support for independence would be unlikely to be seen as a 'clear majority'.

Federal Intergovernmental Affairs Minister Stephane Dion, who assumed the chief role in Chretien's government in attacking the logic of Quebec separatism, elaborated on why clarity was needed. Since the founding of the United Nations, 13 referenda leading to secession were held, excluding the case of colonies. Every one of them used the word 'independence' in the referendum question and in all 13 cases the majority in favor was over 70 percent of votes cast; the average was over 90 percent support. As Dion put it, '[t]hese referendums did not divide those populations on such a sensitive issue as secession. On the contrary, they officially confirmed an obvious consensus in favor of secession.'[116] In cases where the referendum majority was narrower, the effort to secede was thwarted. For example, in 1933 in Western Australia 'only' 66 percent voted for secession, in 1946 in the Faroe Islands just 51 percent supported separation from Denmark, and in 1998 in Nevis 62 percent voted for separation where a two-thirds majority was required.

There was relatively little backlash in Quebec to the adoption of the Clarity Act. PQ leaders insisted that Quebecers would decide their future democratically, without constraints from Canada. But there seemed to be tacit support by many in Quebec for setting the political rules of the independence game. Moreover, despite alarming stories about the decline of the

French language, the *Conseil de la langue francaise* overseeing language laws reported that 87 percent of public discourse in Quebec in 2000 was in French. More than anything, however, the weakness of the nationalist movement resided in its aging leadership and inability to connect with young Quebecers. The PQ continued to be steered by the Quiet Revolution generation: Bouchard's replacement in 2001 as PQ head and Quebec prime minister by Bernard Landry confirmed that the old generation was not about to give up power. The PQ establishment seemed reluctant to reach out, then, not only to the minorities of Quebec but even to young French Quebecers.

Conclusions on Quebec nationalism

How Quebec and ROC negotiate their futures has importance for many other countries. In 1991 *The Economist* wrote:

> 'The Canadian model' – whether of disintegration or of holding together in some new, post-modern version of the nation-state – is going to be an example to avoid or follow for all but a few federations, for all multicultural societies, especially immigrant ones, for countries whose borders reflect conquest more than geography, and for all states riven or driven by nationalism.[117]

Not unexpectedly, prime minister Chretien reported that on his visit to the United Nations just several days before the 1995 referendum was held, '[p]residents and prime ministers from some sixty countries had approached him to express their puzzlement that anyone would rip asunder such a successful country. A group of Islamic leaders had told him they were praying for Canada.'[118]

The 1995 referendum did not put an end to Quebec's sovereignty bid or Canada's unity crisis. As writer Lansing Lamont noted, '[n]ations, like stars, burn out. Amid the world's constellation of 180 or more countries, some, like Austria or Greece, supernovas in their day, have seen their once brilliant empires and cultures dim or go dark....Others, brief comets of glory or conquest, have flamed out.'[119] While '[m]ost people, Americans in particular, comfortably assume that Canadians are too decent, too passive a society to propel themselves into breakup', Lamont cautioned that '[m]aybe Canada is not meant to live. Maybe it isn't destined to live out its span as a nation'.[120] If Canada's breakup could occur and be politically justified by the seceding group, no state in the world would be immune to partition or dismemberment. That is why the discourses of liberalism and democracy are brought in to stigmatize would-be secessionists.

5
Uninational Homes: Right-Wing Nationalism

Reactionary forms of nationalism

There are forms of nationalism that are not centered on the project of transforming a homeland into a state. They focus instead on the task of transforming the homeland itself. Homeland is approached as the abode of a particular nation, the titular nation, and no one else. Such nationalism is reactionary, fundamentalist, and right-wing because it invokes a mythical nation residing in a mythical home untouched by migration of peoples – a process that is as old as human history. The type of nationalism that assigns homeland to the titular nation – the insiders – is, ironically, espoused today by outsiders, those located on the periphery of their societies. Such nationalism attacks the modern state principally because it does not provide for an exclusive religious or spiritual home. The radical right proposes a fundamentalist, primordial, purist, uninational version of the state in place of the modern secular, democratic, multicultural state. It therefore undertakes militant action and organizes movements in opposition to what is seen as a hegemonic state.

This chapter examines two cases of radical nationalism, in Germany and Israel, seeking to confiscate the idea of home from the state. Both can be considered right-wing nationalist movements even though some scholars have argued that nationalism is irrelevant to right-wing ideologies (including Nazism) or, at best, that the radical right embraces 'irrational nationalism'.[1] Both movements we look at are active not in authoritarian or developing states but in Western democracies that form part of Judaeo-Christian civilization. Extremist xenophobic nationalism in a Germany reunified in 1990 makes up our first case, Jewish fundamentalism as reaction to the surrender of Israel's historic territories to Arab neighbors in the mid-1990s represents the second. The two movements share little with each other except for an ideology that assigns a privileged position to their nation over others. Such a position, in their belief, is not reflected in state policies. They espouse what has been termed ideologies of order – religious and secular nationalist frameworks of thought that 'provide the authority that gives the social and political order its reason for being'.[2] But their conceptions of order are framed by their conceptions of who belongs in the homeland.

Conservative political parties, neo-Nazi organizations, and skinheads encompass the spectrum of the contemporary German right. Religious zealots, Zionist nationalists, and Jewish settlers constitute the Israeli right. Paradoxically, it was Germany's reunification that served as a contributing factor to the rise of the right, whereas it was Israel's ceding of territories to the Palestinians that sparked militant right-wing activity in that country. In each of the cases, moreover, the definition and status of the Other – foreign migrants to Germany, non-Jewish inhabitants of historic Jewish lands – were the catalysts for the rise of the nationalist right. In addition, spates of headline-making political violence credited these movements with greater influence and durability than they really possess.

At the outset we need to recognize that the political starting points for German and Israeli societies differ. Each has to demonstrate its inclusiveness and tolerance but the historical encumbrances of each are very different. Charles Maier has pointed to the connection between history and victimhood: 'The hunger for memory has brought about a change in the status of victimhood. Victims used to be pitiful; their very helplessness contributed to the segregation and depersonalization that helped seal their fate.'[3] Today, victimhood can serve as a moral advantage which, Maier warns, must be gauged carefully:

> if it behooves Germans to stress the anti-Jewish specificity of the Holocaust, it is sometimes important for Jews to do the opposite.... The obligations of memory thus remain asymmetrical. For Jews: to remember that although they seek legitimation of a public sorrow, their suffering was not exclusive. For Germans: to specify that the Holocaust was the Final Solution of the Jewish problem as its architects understood it. The appropriateness of each proposition depends upon who utters it.[4]

Objectivity depends, then, on who the subject is, a tricky condition to meet when comparing German civic and ethnic models and Israeli secular and religious conceptualizations.

Germany

Sources of right-wing extremism

A widely-held sociological explanation for the rise of fascist movements in the 1930s was that they constituted 'a revolt against modernity' and a manifestation of middle class extremism.[5] The more visible role played in

European politics from the 1980s onwards by right-wing nationalist groups can also be explained in terms of disenchantment with modern society and the backlash of the middle class to its economic decline. One scholar suc-cinctly noted: 'The *Modernisierungsverlierer*, those who feel threatened by technological innovation and the erosion of traditional qualifications, oc-cupational recognition and work processes, are the potential clientele of the extreme right today.'[6]

Postmodern culture exacerbates anomie. It 'fosters and reproduces the fragmentation of the economic and social spaces of postindustrial consumer society' and leads to 'new challenges to the individual's capability to adapt to rapidly changing circumstances'.[7] Individualization of life styles and life chances taking place in fragmented and differentiated postmodern society also entails individualization of risks. Making economic miscalculations can have high personal costs, can lead to alienation and marginalization of many individuals, and may contribute to the emergence of a permanent underclass of citizens. As the author of one important comparative study summarized, 'the resulting feelings of anxiety and social isolation, political exasperation and powerlessness, loss of purpose in life, and insecurity and abandonment have paved the way for radical right-wing populist parties'.[8]

When right-wing nationalist groups resurfaced in Germany, there was a natural tendency to advance not just conventional sociological explan-ations but also explanations grounded in modern German history and the German national character.[9] Especially when nationalist sentiment was expressed through violent means, German society was again confronted with the ascription of collective guilt. Conversely, part of the attraction of the right lay precisely in the desire by many Germans to emerge 'out of the shadow of Auschwitz'.

There is general agreement that growing nationalism in Germany has gone hand-in-hand with expanding immigration numbers. In the words of one journalist, '[d]emographic change had brought the country its largest ethnic minority ever, the Turks, and they were so much more foreign than the Jews had ever been'.[10] Over two million of the nearly eight million foreigners (nearly 10 percent of the population) who have settled in Ger-many are Turks. Most live in urban areas and are seen as a cause of high unemployment. In the 1990s Turks were joined by immigrants from the disintegrating Soviet bloc and refugees from the wars in the Balkans. Even though these were one-off short-term developments, some demographers projected that foreigners would account for 18 percent of the total popula-tion by 2010 and 30 percent by 2030.[11]

One intriguing study compared the politics of immigration in Germany, Britain, and the US.[12] The author found that 'Germany, with both a strong constitution celebrating human rights and the moral burdens of a negative history, is an extreme case of self-limited sovereignty, making it one of the most expansive immigrant-receiving countries in the world'. This is therefore the result of self-imposed moral norms rather than domestic client politics or external constraints. 'At the risk of stating a tautology, accepting unwanted immigration is inherent in the liberalness of liberal states'.[13] Such liberalism is all too frequently taken for granted by liberalism's own adherents. And it can engender illiberal opponents.

There is a close connection between nationalism and anti-immigration sentiments. One scholar contended that '[a]ttitudes to immigrants in the modern era are frequently articulated by nationalist movements or justified by reference to nationalist sentiments'.[14] Another was more blunt: 'Anti-immigrant movements are self-proclaimedly nationalistic. That is, they declare the interest of the nation the touchstone of their policy, and they define the interest of the nation as phenotypical and ethno-cultural continuity. "This is a Christian nation; and it should remain one" epitomizes their demand'.[15]

German nationhood has been pulled in different directions by immigration and citizenship policies grounded in an unusual combination of old laws and contemporaneous improvization which are largely inconsistent. The dynamics internal to immigrant groups may also be a source of conflict. Even Benedict Anderson, arguably the most eminent nationalities expert of recent years, described the 'radically unaccountable form of politics' of some migrant groups that involved transnational trafficking of drugs, arms, and money.[16] For the adherent of 'long-distance nationalism', Anderson bitingly noted, '[t]hat same metropole that marginalizes and stigmatizes him simultaneously enables him to play, in a flash, on the other side of the planet, national hero'.[17] In short, '[p]ortable nationality, read under the sign of "identity", is on the rapid rise as people everywhere are on the move'.[18] Formulating this theoretically, one conclusion is that '[e]thnicity has no existence apart from interethnic relations'.[19]

Within their host societies, immigrants have come to learn about, demand, and enjoy rights that were unavailable to preceding generations of newcomers to 'immigrant societies'. Writing about the US but applicable elsewhere too, Samuel Huntington noted how '[p]reviously immigrants felt discriminated against if they were not permitted to join the mainstream. Now it appears that some groups feel discriminated against if they are not allowed to remain apart from the mainstream'.[20] This has followed on from the more general phenomenon of 'multi-ethnic chic': 'The commodification of Otherness has been so successful because it is offered as a new delight, more intense, more satisfying than normal ways of doing and feeling. Within commodity culture, ethnicity becomes spice, seasoning that can liven up the dull dish that is mainstream white culture'.[21]

The result has been that in place of the immigrant groups of the past which wished to integrate into host societies, a new breed of diaspora groups has emerged which 'forge and sustain multiple social relations that link their societies of origin and settlement'.[22] These have 'recently experienced an unprecedented range of linguistic, religious, cultural, and even political choice'.[23] It has led one writer to speak of immigrant groups' 'postnational membership': the international normative regime on human rights – not the domestic laws of the host society – would govern citizenship rights.[24]

The reaction in host societies – Austria, France, Germany, and others – has been a turn to 'corporate nationalism' embodying anti-immigrant movements. 'Today, the increasing power and visibility of ethnic minorities and the accompanying social problems which growing migration is producing, have raised concerns over what has been described as "cultural pollution", "overforeignization", or "minorization"'.[25] More practical concerns deal with the economic costs of receiving immigrants, the fraudulence regularly occurring in refugee and asylum claims, and the lukewarm commitment of newcomers to their host societies.

Much has been made of the differences in the French and German models of citizenship.[26] In France, '[t]he republican values which are now most commonly associated with the revolutionary heritage include universalism, unitarism, secularism and assimilationism'.[27] This signified that, first, the rights of man proclaimed in August 1789 apply to all humanity and, second, France's unitary corporate nature has by definition to be inclusionary. Trapped in its own republican logic, to stem the tide of immigrants and, therefore, future French citizens, as early as 1974 France halted labor recruitment from non-European Community countries. The politics of immigration and citizenship took a different course in Germany and led not to the emergence of an electoral right, as in France, but to a more violent grassroots right.

Backlash against anti-nationalism

With the end of the Cold War and reunification in 1990, Germany shed the last vestiges of foreign domination. In September 1994 Allied troops formally handed over the defense of Berlin to German soldiers. Chancellor Helmut Kohl promised $10 billion to Russia to pay for the cost of withdrawing Soviet forces from east German territory and he also granted close to $5 billion in credit and aid to Poland, which was concerned about having a powerful German state on its western border. Although there were reunification skeptics in neighboring European states and even in Germany itself, such as Nobel laureate Gunter Grass,[28] no obstacles remained to the country assuming the role of a normal state in the European system.

Succeeding postwar generations of Germans had been taught to view their country's history and role in Europe critically. Forced to subject the past to an unsparing critique, young Germans were socialized into a value system making skepticism a virtue and national pride a vice. The only highly-circumscribed German patriotism that was encouraged was what Jurgen Habermas called *Verfassungspatriotismus* – loyalty to the 1949 constitution of the Federal Republic of Germany (FRG). This constricted and contingent nationalism offered reasons for optimism: 'United Germans are not necessarily nationalist Germans. Big Germany is not necessarily mighty Germany'.[29]

Inevitably, a consensus emerged among German conservatives that it was time to restore some of the country's traditional values. In the 1990s some writers pointed to the sterility and even absurdity of the values of Western liberalism in a post-socialist era. Interest began to grow in early twentieth-century intellectuals such as Carl Schmitt, Ernst Juenger, and Oswald Spengler who had little time for democracy and extolled the pagan sources of German culture. These conservative thinkers had helped inspire Nazi ideology.

The emergent German right thus questioned the conventional wisdom of the postwar era. Some fringe groups denied that the Holocaust had occurred. The leader of the German Youth Education Organization which tried to unify the young neo-Nazi movement refuted the existence of extermination camps for Jews during the Second World War. But reaction to the guilt Germany had to shoulder in the postwar era had a broader audience. Criticism was directed at Germany's special postwar path that required it to atone for wartime guilt by adopting a liberal political asylum policy. The small-sized army with limits on deployment, designed to make up for Hitler's military aggression, also came under fire. Mainstream right-wing cultural critics attacked the veniality of Western capitalism and consumerism. Other conservatives expressed dislike for long-serving chancellor Helmut Kohl's vision of a tightly integrated core of states within the European Union, and for making the Franco-German alliance its cornerstone. By the end of the 1990s Kohl, viewed as the last great European, and his Christian Democratic Union (CDU), in power for all but 13 years since the Federal Republic's establishment, were seen as incapable of generating change. His view of the 1991 Maastricht treaty that accorded EU institutions unprecedented, if still limited authority over foreign and defense policy, social and environmental questions, and monetary policy was that it was an insurance policy guaranteeing lasting German integration into Europe. This integrationist agenda was attacked by the radical right which saw it as hindering Germany's ambitions.

The nationalist right asserted that, whether it wanted to or not, Germany was destined to be a great power again. At the least, the country should model itself on the Second German Reich (the first was the Holy Roman Empire formed with the coronation of Otto I as secular ruler of Christendom in 962). Created by chancellor Otto von Bismarck in 1871, the Second Reich moderated its founder's previous nationalist and militarist sentiments. Bismark came to accept that imperial Germany should become a status quo power and not challenge the existing European balance-of-power system.

A few groups in Germany hold irredentist claims. One of their centers is Potsdam, the former Prussian capital in the heart of 'middle Germany'. This area encompasses the territory of former East Germany (the German Democratic Republic, or GDR) where the radical right has been particularly strong. For more extremist nationalist leaders for whom German homeland is more than today's FRG, the real eastern Germany subsumes the regions of East Prussia, Pomerania, and Silesia, conquered by Frederick the Great at the end of the eighteenth century but ceded to Poland in 1945 as part of the Yalta accords.

Conservative German thinkers have returned to the issue of national identity. Because an identity was stunted by Allied occupation and political division into two states, they assert, Germany has to reconstruct it by celebrating past glories and loosening ties with the West. They categorically reject a German identity based on war guilt and reparations. President Ronald Reagan's visit in May 1985 to the Bitburg military cemetery, where SS officers were among those buried, was seen as a prelude to forging a more complete identity. The visit lent support to those Germans who believed that they had also been victims of Hitler's policies. Part of an emerging German identity, as construed by the right, would lie in it, too, being regarded as *Opfer*, or victim, of history.

Becoming 'foreign' or reclaiming the German home?

Extreme right-wing violence in Germany peaked in the early 1990s when the country became the first destination for millions of citizens of former communist countries anxious to savor the West. In September 1991 a firebomb was thrown into a foreigners' dormitory in the state of Saxony. The following month a similar attack killed two Lebanese girls near Dusseldorf. In August 1992, to the cheers of a large crowd, right-wing extremists attacked a building for asylum seekers in Rostock, where 200 Romanian Gypsies were awaiting a decision on their status. Soon afterwards, extremists attacked refugee hostels in towns in Brandenburg. The most notorious case of anti-immigrant violence took place in November 1992 when a firebomb was set off in Molln, near Hamburg, killing a Turkish woman and two Turkish children. The number of criminal acts committed by extremists increased from 270 in 1990 to 2084 in 1992.[30] But that was not the end of the violence. In May 1993, a day after the Bundestag (the German parliament) passed a law tightening immigration laws, neo-Nazis set alight a three-story building in Solingen, near Cologne, leaving five Turks dead. The amount of right-wing violence declined after that but anti-immigrant sentiment was unabated.

Right-wing violence has been directed at not only immigrant groups but a wider set of targets. As one specialist observed,

[a]lthough concentrated against foreigners with darker skin hues, the aggression was by no means restricted to non-Germans or people of

color. Jews, leftists, Roma, the mentally handicapped, and homosexuals – the victims of Nazi persecution, and also of proto-fascist gangs in the GDR and West Germany – found themselves the victims of popular hatred once again in the united Germany'.[31]

The fact that so many different groups have been targeted has made the rise of the right in Germany very ominous. Politicians and the media made efforts to disassociate the radical right from German nationalism and reports usually referred to right-wing extremists or, on occasion, ultra-nationalists. It was rare to find mention of the rise of German nationalists, in contrast to Russia where right-wing extremism and Russian nationalism were equated. Yet the overriding political objective of Germany's right has been exclusionary nationalism – to make the country an *auslanderfrei Staat*, that is, a state (and homeland) free of foreigners. This objective brings to mind the *judenfrei* project of the Third Reich that was to do away with the Jews.

The constitution of the FRG, called the Basic Law, recognizes two categories of rights – general and reserved.[32] The first applies to all individuals living in the FRG and includes freedom of expression and conscience. The second is reserved for German citizens and includes freedom of association, peaceful assembly, and movement.[33] Citizenship has been important, therefore, not just in conferring voting privileges but in securing a larger package of rights taken for granted in many other Western countries.

Until May 1999, when a new citizenship law was passed, German citizenship was based on the principle of *jus sanguinis*, or bloodlines. It reflected the myth of the unity of a German *Volk*, or people. The Basic Law did not delineate how citizenship was granted, so the rules originated in the July 1913 imperial naturalization law that determined that German citizenship was transmitted by descent from parent to child. In most other Western states, the principle of *jus soli* is used, making place of birth the determining criterion. Germany's unusual approach was the result of the need to achieve national unity.

German regulations on citizenship were only of scholastic interest so long as few foreigners migrated to the country. By the mid-1950s the economic miracle required an expanded labor pool and the federal government signed its first employment contract with Italy in 1955 to recruit workers for agricultural and construction jobs. The erection of the Berlin Wall in 1961 and the subsequent cutoff of East German labor led to additional employment contracts negotiated with Greece, Spain, Turkey and, later, Portugal and Yugoslavia. By 1973 12 percent (some 2.5 million) of the total German work force were guest workers. By 1980 Germany had granted resident alien status to an additional one million people. In 1991 foreigners comprised 8 percent of the work force in a reunited Germany; one-quarter of these were European Community (EC) nationals.[34] Reunification worsened the status of minorities in the country because the federal government gave economic priority to developing East Germany.

Opinion polls showed that by the early 1980s about half of German citizens already had negative attitudes towards the presence of foreigners. The dislike of foreigners seemed a symptom of xenophobia, itself triggered by economic considerations. Xenophobia 'reflects the desire on the part of the population of the affluent West European societies to protect their islands of prosperity against an outside world marked by poverty, environmental destruction, interethnic violence, and growing desperation'.[35] As one of the most prosperous states in the world, Germany nevertheless decided to make it difficult for outsiders to share in the wealth.

Serious efforts to control the influx and presence of guest workers began when Kohl took office in 1982. He formulated an emergency program that encouraged unemployed foreign residents – whose unemployment rate was up to 5 percent higher than of Germans – to return 'home'. They were offered a lump sum of approximately DM 10 000 (close to $6000 at that time). But offering such a generous 'separation package' to guest workers only encouraged more foreigners to come, calculating that they would be in a 'no-lose' situation.

Throughout the 1980s many guest workers and their families decided to stay in Germany after their labor contracts had expired. They accordingly applied to become permanent residents. With a rapidly-expanding number of German-born, second-generation residents of foreign origin, the issue that faced the government was how to normalize the legal status of these resident aliens. For example, by 1990, 25 percent of all foreigners had been resident in Germany for over 20 years, and 60 percent for more than ten years. Two-thirds of Turks and three-quarters of Yugoslavs had lived in the country for more than ten years. At the end of 1998, 30 percent of the 7.3 million foreign nationals living in Germany had been there for 20 years and about a half for at least ten years. It seemed natural to offer such lengthy residents the opportunity to become FRG citizens.

An Aliens law passed in April made it somewhat easier for second- and third-generation residents to acquire German citizenship but it simultaneously tightened other provisions. It now required that applicants for residence rights make contributions into social insurance funds for a minimum of five years. And it continued to categorize immigrants into second- and third-class aliens: minorities from EC countries had rights, such as not needing work permits, not enjoyed by those coming from elsewhere. Different categories of residence permits were also introduced.

Up to 1998, when the Social Democrats (SPD) under Gerhard Schroeder took power in a coalition government with the Green party, chancellor Kohl's approach had been to treat naturalization as an exceptional process which might only occur under very strict conditions: a minimum of ten years of residence in the FRG (five years if married to a German citizen), mastery of German, residence in one's own dwelling, a demonstrated ability to support oneself and one's dependents economically and, generally, 'whether the applicant in his or her personal standing is a valuable addition to the population, but also, whether the naturalization of the applicant from a general political, economic, and cultural viewpoint is desirable'.[36] Given such rigorous criteria, it was not surprising that even as it took in the largest number of foreigners, Germany had one of Europe's lowest naturalization rates, 83 000 in 1997 or about three percent of resident aliens annually.[37]

Consequently,

> two conflicting political conceptions of citizenship coexisted within the postwar consensus in the Federal Republic: the traditional ethno-cultural concept of the German nation characterized by a common history, language, culture, and descent; and a civil concept based on individual rights of citizens modeled after enlightened 'Western' traditions.[38]

A move towards the civic approach took place with the passage of the 1999 citizenship law. The two principal departures from *jus sanguinis* were that: 1) children born in Germany to foreign nationals, one parent who had been residing legally in the country for at least eight years and had a residence permit for at least three years, would acquire German citizenship by birth; 2) foreign nationals legally resident in Germany for eight years who professed loyalty to Germany's democratic order, possessed a residence permit, were able to support themselves without the help of welfare benefits, had renounced their previous citizenship, did not have a criminal record, and possessed an adequate command of the German language could obtain German citizenship. The stated purpose of the law was 'guaranteeing and ensuring social and domestic peace in Germany'.[39]

Apart from formal rights, there are different ways of belonging and not belonging in Germany. In the case of Jews, for example,

> Though granting them legal rights, German citizenship does not guarantee their belonging to the native community. Poles, ethnic Germans, and East Germans, who are physically indistinguishable from West Germans, also feel strange in their adopted country. Due to differences in habitus, even the conception of filiation through descent can be undermined by time, space, and political ideology. Belonging must not only be understood in terms of objective criteria such as laws, statutes, and policy, but also in terms of subjective experiences of marginalization and discrimination.[40]

The prevailing ethnic understanding of the German nation convinced many immigrant groups, such as the Turks, to embrace a core non-German identity around which a separate community in Germany might be constructed. This community would then negotiate its recognition by the German state and would also expect recognition of dual citizenship, for example, as Turks and as Turks in Germany.[41] The 1999 Citizenship law excluded the possibility of dual citizenship or additional rights for foreign nationals. For example, under the 'requirement to opt', children acquiring German citizenship by the fact of being born in Germany had to decide before their 23rd birthday whether they wished to retain their German citizenship or some other. In exceptional cases where renunciation of foreign citizenship was impossible, the law would not countenance the type of 'negotiation' of recognition pressed for by some Turkish groups. 'A German who holds multiple citizenship cannot use his other citizenship to assert additional rights or evade his obligations'.[42] Thus Schroeder's citizenship reform was drafted to appease German sentiment at least as much as normalizing the status of foreign nationals.

Germany's efforts to manage the influx of foreigners was not limited to guest workers who had become permanent residents and in rare circumstances German citizens. As with other European countries, the FRG faced a wave of asylum seekers from foreign countries in the 1990s and after. The reason for the rise in the numbers of asylum seekers was obvious: 'Since international law does not recognize unemployment amd misery to be relevant reasons for seeking asylum, many would-be immigrant workers were forced to seek entrance into Western Europe as political refugees'.[43] The Basic Law guarantees the right to asylum for all persons persecuted on political grounds but applicants had to demonstrate that their fear of persecution in their home state was well-founded and was based on their religious or political beliefs or other personal attributes.

Whereas in 1983 the number of asylum seekers entering Germany was only about 20 000, by 1993 it was almost half a million, representing 60 percent of all asylum seekers in Europe. In May 1993 the Bundestag passed legislation amending the asylum law. It now denied asylum to persons coming to Germany from an EC country or any other state adhering to international conventions on human rights. For the year 2000, the figures for asylum seekers had fallen to under 80 000 applicants accounting for about 25 percent of claims in Europe. The German government continued to provide them with subsidies and free housing. Only the most extremist forces opposed this policy for those clearly in fear of their lives in their own countries, for example, the 75 000 asylum seekers in 1991 that were refugees from the wars in Yugoslavia. But some asylum seekers sought to exploit the existence of not fully democratic systems at home to better their personal economic conditions abroad.

Under 10 percent of applicants received asylum in the peak years of the early 1990s. But rejection of the asylum claim did not require that the applicant leave the country. Evidence suggested that only about 20 percent of rejected applicants returned home, another 20 percent dropped from official view, presumably remaining illegally in Germany, while the remainder filed appeals.[44] The indeterminate status of many asylum seekers provided further grist for the mill of the xenophobic forces organizing on the German right.

Apart from guest workers and asylum seekers, Germany was also subjected to large in-migration of 'foreign-born Germans'. Throughout the 1980s the number of 'ethnic Germans' entering the FRG had grown, but it increased dramatically after the collapse of the Soviet bloc in 1989. Article 116 of the Basic Law gives citizens of other countries who can demonstrate German ancestry full citizenship rights in the FRG. No one disputed that the *Ubersiedler*, or refugees from the GDR, were German. But there was skepticism whether the *Aussiedler*, those claiming German ancestry and coming from countries such as Czechoslovakia, Poland, and Russia, were German at all. The *Aussiedler* were seen by many Germans as just another group of foreigners coming to the country for economic motives and wishing to take advantage of the country's generous social system. In 1991 about 150 000 people from the collapsing Soviet Union claimed German ancestry and settled in Germany. Another 40 000 Germans holding Polish citizenship decided to leave the new democratic system in Poland for life in Germany. Hostility to the sudden influx of purported 'ethnic Germans' was not confined to neo-Nazis. Many otherwise liberal-minded Germans objected to ethnic Germans being given a fast track to citizenship over longtime residents. For example, in 1995 and 1996, only 77 000 Turks were naturalized while 2.1 million Turks were still deemed foreigners. By contrast, 410 000 ex-Soviet citizens (most invoking German ancestry) were naturalized while 175 000 remained foreigners.[45]

One final category of foreigners arriving in Germany was made up of illegal immigrants who worked on the black market. After the Cold War, Germany dropped visa requirements for citizens from many of the former Warsaw Pact countries. Instead of having to queue for hours, sometimes days, in front of consulates to obtain visas to travel to Germany, Czechs, Hungarians, Poles, Romanians, and Slovaks were now able to cross into Germany with only their passports. Many of these people brought cheap goods with them to sell at Berlin bazaars, then returned home with hi-tech goods for profitable re-sale. Others simply went underground and worked illegally in Germany as waiters, agricultural laborers, and prostitutes. The stereotype of the disreputable foreigner living illegally in Germany exacerbated the sense of *Auslanderfeindlichkeit*, or animosity towards foreigners, and provided additional structural conditions for the rise of the right.

Many Germans were bewildered by the paradox that so few foreign residents could become naturalized yet the country had porous borders and provided generous social services for foreigners. German fears of losing their homeland to foreigners were regularly aroused by prognoses of think tanks that claimed that up to 25 million people in Russia and Eastern Europe wanted to work in the West and that the majority identified Germany, with its strong economy and slack immigration laws, as the preferred host country. In response Chancellor Kohl's government imposed limits on the number of self-professed ethnic Germans accepted from other countries.

The party of government until 1998, the CDU, and the longtime opposition party, the SPD, each wrestled with the *Auslander* question. Both tapped into the anti-foreigner rhetoric emanating from specialist one-issue parties on the far right.

Political parties of the right

Across Europe right-wing parties flourished in the 1990s.[46] Until the 1990s, the peak of popular support for the right in Germany had come in the 1964 federal elections when the National Democratic Party (*Nationaldemokratische Partei Deutschland* or NPD) captured 4 percent of the vote – below the 5 percent threshold needed to secure parliamentary representation. The explicit goal of that party was to bring the German right out of Auschwitz's shadow and give it a new identity unconnected with the Nazi past. The NPD also sought to exploit an issue still very much alive at that time: a return to Germany's pre-war borders that would give it possession of Alsace-Lorraine (from France), Silesia and Pomerania (from Poland), East Prussia (from Russia), the Sudetenland (from the Czech Republic), and Austria.

The salience of irredentism waned over the next two decades and attention turned to the more pressing issue troubling the electorate, the influx of foreigners. The far right was first to be converted to the *Auslanderfeindlichkeit* theme but establishment conservative parties followed: 'In 1980, the National Democratic Party (NPD) launched a "Stop the foreigners" campaign in the North Rhine-Westphalia elections. Similarly, the authors of the far-right Heidelberg Manifesto of 1982 developed this theme. Ever sensitive to the issues that attract right-wing support, the CDU/CSU quickly followed suit'.[47]

Electoral support for right-wing parties exceeded 10 percent by the 1990s. Two of them were banned in 1992 for extremist activities – the German Alternative led by a neo-Nazi, and the Nationalist Front, self-styled neo-Nazi shock troops. Chancellor Kohl understood that the issues raised by the right had an appeal to voters and he began to seek restrictions on immigration and illegal foreigners resident in Germany, as we have seen. The CDU wished to protect its nationalist flank by stealing some of the rhetoric from the far right. In 1993 Kohl appointed a hardline interior minister to crack down on both neo-Nazis and illegal immigrants. He won reelection in 1994 and avoided the embarrassment that the French political elite suffered when in the first round of the 1995 presidential elections three right-wing candidates polled a combined 20 percent of the vote. By 1996, even the SPD under its then leader, Oskar Lafontaine, played the anti-immigrant card and demanded constitutional changes to restrict in-migration.

What one writer termed the German dilemma involved the basic dissonance between immigration and citizenship requirements: 'while the completion of nation-state building makes it possible to conceive a political (rather than ethnocultural) grounding of German citizenship, the current economic situation and the political conflicts over the kind and degrees of inclusion of foreigners prevent Germany from devising an appropriate immigration policy'.[48] Kohl, and Schroeder after him, were hard pressed to unravel the dilemma.

Almost all parties wanted to make political capital from rising anti-foreigner sentiments. Immigrant groups were blamed for growing unemployment and underemployment, lower living standards, abuse of the welfare system that resulted in higher taxation, an increase in crime and, less often, a threat to national and cultural identity. On unemployment's connection to racism, the European Community issued a report in 1991 that concluded how xenophobia was rooted in 'the fear and insecurity of the individual facing the future', in turn spawned by rising unemployment and poverty.[49] Regarding the emotive issue of crime, perceptions of immigrant groups as more often engaged in illegal activities were to some degree substantiated. While in 1991 foreigners represented 8 percent of the German population, they were charged with over one-quarter of all crimes. Setting aside offenses associated with immigrant status (working without a permit, entering Germany illegally, violating residence requirements), foreigners accounted for 31 percent of all murder and homicide cases and 36 percent of all rape cases.[50]

Apart from the immigration issue, the rise of right-wing parties was tied to the de-alignment of traditional electoral loyalties and a widespread sense of *Parteienverdrossenheit*, or disaffection with parties, that had first emerged in the 1980s. In addition, the ideological orientation of the established conservative parties may have inspired far-right groups. Not altogether convincingly, one author linked Thatcherism to the emergence of a broader right-wing movement:

> Like Thatcherism, the radical Right have appealed to the knowledge accumulated by ordinary people, a popular pragmatism that put the family, respectability, hard work, 'practicality', and order first. Like Thatcherism, they have offered an exclusionary ideology as a compensation for the anxieties inevitably created by the new insecurities generated by the globalization of the market place.[51]

The radical right was also able to gain mileage from the wars fought in the Balkans in the 1990s to gain greater support. The general message that it propagated was of the supposed danger of creating 'multiracial' states such as Yugoslavia. In addition, hatred of Muslims linked German rightists with Serb nationalists and there was support for the Serb campaigns in Bosnia and Kosovo. The NPD and other right-wing movements also advanced the argument that Germany had a special role to play in the Balkans and it was prevented from doing so by US intervention. At the same time, the NPD condemned the inclusion of German soldiers in NATO operations, termed wars of aggression, in the Balkans. The German right's sympathy for Serbian dictator Slobodan Milosevic's ethnic cleansing produced more virulent anti-Americanism when the US bombed Serbia in 1999 and brought Milosevic before the War Crimes Tribunal in the Hague the following year.[52]

In the end, however, it was the spread of anti-foreigner sentiment that reanimated the radical right in Germany. The *Republikaner Partei* (REP), started up in 1983 by a former SS-man, became the third right-wing extremist party to be formed in the FRG following the *Sozialistische Reichspartei* (SRP) in 1951 and the NPD. The REP's best electoral showing was winning 7 percent of the German vote to the European parliamentary elections in 1989. In examining the REP, two German academics commented: 'The question is whether it serves as a safety valve for discontented voters who wish to "let off steam" and express their disappointment in the established parties, or whether it is supported for ideological reasons'.[53] Other right-wing parties also made inroads and a total of five were represented in municipal and state governments and in the European Parliament. Ten militant right-wing organizations also were formed, four of which were banned.

The nationalist right had become part of both populist and electoral politics, but could it carry on in both arenas simultaneously? One student of German affairs cautioned that the right was likely to be driven back from the political center stage into the ghetto of neo-Nazi violence:

> As long as social norms and taboos about the past and racism remain in sharp relief in German society there will be a difficult-to-reconcile tension between those on the far right who would pursue their agenda within the constraints of electoral democracy and those who find such efforts themselves in conflict with far right principles.[54]

By the start of the new century, the far right was faltering in both arenas.

Shock troops of the right

The strength of right-wing radicalism cannot be measured exclusively in terms of electoral results. Neither can it simply be ascribed to skinheads and soccer hooligans, even if soccer matches have become an outlet for racist violence. Right-wing supporters range from anomic groups of young people in depressed East German cities, where unemployment reaches 40 percent, to ambitious political leaders in Berlin. The right is organizationally and ideologically diverse. Police estimate there are about 64 000 rightists in Germany, of whom 6000 are militant extremists and 2000 hard-core neo-Nazis. They are organized into thousands of action groups in various cities. Their activities have ranged from arson of homes where foreigners live to the publication of leaflets that listed the names and addresses of liberal opponents targeted for 'final elimination'.

At least 100 right-wing publications exist. The largest of these, with a circulation of 100 000, is the weekly *Deutsch National-Zeitung*. A youth newspaper, *Junge Freiheit* ('Young Freedom') honors the German military tradition and seeks to rehabilitate the intellectuals of the 1920s and 1930s discredited by their association with Nazism.

Surprisingly, German neo-Nazi groups receive much of their logistical support from their counterparts in other countries including the US. As the production of neo-Nazi propaganda is banned under the Basic Law, American organizations like the National Socialist German Workers' Party – Overseas Organization (NSDAP – AO) print Nazi materials and smuggle them into Germany. Both Denmark and Austria have become centers for neo-Nazi publications and organizational activities. The Internet has provided these groups with greater reach; the neo-Nazi Thule computer discussion group was one of the most popular.

Most incidents of what the Federal Office for the Protection of the Constitution terms 'right-wing extremist and xenophobic crimes involving violence' were committed by the young: 70 percent of perpetrators are under 20. With a sometimes impassive police force and a consenting majority, fascist youth exploited conditions to carry out violence. Many young people consider themselves to be skinheads rather than right-wing militants but the impact is often the same. Skinhead rock groups like *Stoerkraft* ('Disruptive Force') inflame hatred with lyrics such as:

> Our heads are shaved, our fists are as hard as steel,
> Our hearts beat true for the Fatherland,
> We are the force, the force that makes Germany clean.[55]

The defining characteristic of violent right-wing groups is that they consist largely of young people, not old Nazis. Unlike left-wing groups whose members are generally well educated, right-wing youth tend to be school dropouts, unemployed, or in deadend jobs. As in US inner cities, they join street gangs for their unique cultures, comradeship, and kicks.[56]

A common belief since 1989 has been that citizens of former East Germany have provided the far right with its strongest support. In 1993 Kohl's candidate for the German presidency, Steffen Heitmann, was forced to withdraw from the race for, among other reasons, asserting that Germany should not be permanently shamed by its past. Heitmann had also stressed the need to consider the views of Germans who felt adversely affected by the arrival of so many foreigners. These remarks were deemed controversial but what sealed his fate was that Heitmann came from the eastern state of Saxony. For many West Germans, he was voicing the 'redneck' right-wing sentiments held by most of the 'Ossi', or East German population.

In the GDR, Germans had been largely sheltered from the presence of large numbers of foreigners. When they were admitted, it was under stringent conditions: nearly all of the nearly 200 000 foreigners in 1989 were on fixed-term contracts. The largest number, 60 000, came from Vietnam, while 50 000 came from neighboring Poland. The labor contracts of third world women workers – whether from Vietnam, Mozambique, or Cuba – even expressly forbade them to have children while in the GDR.[57]

For many East Germans the discovery after unification of the multiethnic character of West Germany was unsettling. About one-quarter of young East Germans professed to have right-wing views and some even praised communist leader Erich Honecker for having preserved an island of 17-million pure-race Germans displaying Aryan consciousness. In October 1989 it had been the chant of 'We are the people' in Leipzig, in the former GDR, that put German reunification into overdrive. But the chant soon changed to 'We are one people' indicating how short a step it was to the one fatherland concept and to *Heimat*, the deep cultural identity with the fatherland.

The headway recorded by the extreme right in the east was the byproduct of an authoritarian state that had inculcated order, discipline, unqualified respect for authority, athleticism, conformity, and patriotism. 'The Skinhead phenomenon constituted neither the blind expression of frustration nor the protest of an economically deprived group. Rather, the youth movement represented an active, albeit extreme extension of the authoritarian, petty bourgeois mindset that the state had nurtured'.[58]

Furthermore, as we have seen, fascist views were hardly the monopoly of East German youth. 'The western German establishment's attempt to blame the new eastern federal states for the racist violence conceals its own cynical complicity in the aggression toward foreign nationals in the new states. Unification transformed German racism and the activities of the two Germanies' ultra-rights into a single all-German problem'.[59]

Conclusions on the German radical right

From the 1990s the common slogan of right-wingers in East and West Germany – and, indeed, among similar groups across Western Europe – became 'foreigners out'. European homelands were for Europeans, right-wing nationalists proclaimed. They took heart from the backlash against Muslims that followed the terrorist attacks on the US. A fringe form of nationalism based on a restrictive notion of home and belongingness was becoming respectable and, indeed, had become transnational. It was no longer possible to say that nationalist extremists were confined to the periphery of Europe – the Balkans, Eastern Europe, Russia. They had become part of the EU political landscape and an embarrassment to moralizing Western democracies.

It was no surprise, then, that in 2000 the EU was quick to impose diplomatic sanctions on a member state, Austria, when 27 percent of voters backed a right-wing politician, Joerg Haider, head of the Freedom Party, who joined a coalition government. The impact was that Austrians turned away from the right and sanctions were lifted by the end of the year. Germany is arguably the key actor in Europe, however, and reining in the right is a task that the EU is likely to leave to its own political leadership. Most Germans today agree that '[t]he new Germany may have to give up the Romantic notion of *Heimat* literally grounded in a genealogically rooted common past and a country (the remnants of the old Nazi *Blut und Boden* [blood and soil] concept) that is used to confirm a present fixed in a particular place'.[60] Despite what the radical right claims, this is not the same as giving up a German home.

Israel

Right-wing fundamentalism

On November 4, 1995, Israelis, long accustomed to political violence in their state, were traumatized by the news that a young Jewish fundamentalist, Yigal Amir, had shot and killed prime minister Yitzhak Rabin after a large peace rally in Tel Aviv. Also shocking was that a small number of Israelis, including a few Orthodox rabbis, condoned the assassination of Rabin, who they accused of selling out the traditional lands of Israel and the principles of Zionism by signing a peace-for-land deal with the Palestinians in Oslo in September 1993. The striking observation of one political scientist gives an uneasy sense of this tragedy: 'What is ironic is that the State of Israel is presently the only country where people are killed because they are Jews'.[61]

Until Rabin's assassination, the most notorious act of Jewish violence sparked by the agreement with the Palestinians had occurred in February 1994. A respected Jewish doctor and devout Orthodox Jew, Baruch Gold- stein, went on a killing spree against Muslims praying at the Tomb of the Patriarchs mosque in Hebron. A New York-born Jewish settler, Goldstein had been an ardent supporter of an extremist group, *Kach*. Twenty-nine Arabs were killed and over 100 wounded before Goldstein was beaten to death. Examining these events, an expert on the Israeli right observed: 'The shocking and senseless atrocities committed by Israelis in 1994 and 1995 did not take place in a vacuum. They were the peak of intense Jewish– Muslim and Jewish–Jewish confrontations in territories captured and occu- pied by Israel in 1967'.[62] He added that

> both events show how domestic terrorist interaction between Muslim and Jewish religious extremists can damage – and potentially destroy – the peace process.... Though they represent a minority, religious extre- mists on both sides are heavily armed and enjoy strong support in their communities. Each side is convinced that God's command is to free the country from the infidels of the other side.'[63]

Nationalist violence in Israel has many sources. Four types stand out in the confrontation between Israel and its Arab neighbors: 1) violence generated by the conflict between the Israeli right and left over the country's borders and the desirability of peace with the Arabs; 2) violence originating in the perception of a socio-ethnic gap between well-to-do Ashkenazi and poor Sephardi Jews; 3) violence resulting from the political gap between Israeli Jews and Israel's second-class Arab citizens; and, 4) violence caused by the conflict between ultra-Orthodox and secular Jews.[64] Each of the sources raises the philosophic questions of who make up the people of Israel and what does their homeland encompass. A group's resort to violence in advancing its conception of the Israeli nation and homeland has been a constant feature of Israeli politics since the state's founding. Reactionary nationalism involves the rejection of a strictly political, etatist, democratic construction of Israel, as by many ultra-Orthodox Jews, and the adoption instead of a Halakhic, theocratic notion of Israel.

Zionism, nationalism, fundamentalism

Zionism is a world-view that has generated much controversy.[65] To its enemies it is a supremacist ideology deserving the universal condemnation it received in United Nations resolution 3379, passed in 1975, that equated it with racism. This resolution was only repealed in 1991 when the Soviet-led voting bloc in the UN crumbled. To its followers, by contrast, Zionism proposes an inspirational belief system that after two millennia still exhorts followers to consolidate the biblical Jewish homeland, gives them spiritual enlightenment and faith and, for some adherents, embraces non-Jews in a wider community. Zionism has engendered secular as well as religious movements and it has been invoked both by left-wing political groups that constitute Labour Zionism and by right-wing groups. Here we examine the nationalist, fundamentalist movements that claim to be Zionist.

One writer has captured the contradictory tendencies in Zionism that recall some of the features of the ancient Israelites described in Chapter 1:

> Zionism has always been torn by an inner dialectical struggle between the universal and the particular, between humanism and nationalism. On the one hand, the Jew was to rise out of the dank ghetto into the fresh fields of enlightment and effect a dramatic return to the stage of universal history. But he was to do so through an embodiment of particularistic national aspirations. He was to assert a universal belonging, the Jew as part of the unity of mankind, through an emphasis on the particularity of Jewish nationalism.[66]

The emergence of the Hebrew people and their transformation into a community displaying a universalist idea is the subject of the Pentateuch. The covenant struck between God and the Jews was the symbol of a covenant to be forged between God and all humanity. But a narrower interpretation of the covenant was that it situated Jewish nationalism on a higher plane than that of other nations. Modern Zionism was founded on this view. One scholar asserted that 'Zionism, like all nationalisms, never considered it its vocation to defend the rights of people or to establish equality among nations'.[67]

Modern Zionism evolved in the late nineteenth century in both Western and Eastern Europe. It was developed by Theodore Herzl, a Budapest-born playwright, who organized the first Zionist Congress – in effect, the first Jewish parliament in modern history – in Basel in September 1897.[68] He directed that the energies of the world's scattered Jewish communities should be turned to reestablishing a Jewish homeland in Palestine – 'a land without people for people without a land'. What made Herzl's conception modern was its secular thrust: 'The secularization of Judaism was a necessary precondition for political Zionism, as its adherents were no longer satisfied with waiting for the messiah to come'.[69] The binding force of Zionism was to be the Jewish nation rather than the authority of the Torah. As a result, political Zionism was criticized by fundamentalists for turning the Torah into a mere religious guidebook and a matter of private conscience.

If Herzl was the father of the Western variant of Zionism, the East European form emerged in what is now Poland and its influence on the state of Israel was significant since so many of Israel's first leaders originated from there. A journalist described the reciprocal influence of Polish and Jewish thought:

> The Polish–Jewish relationship was always an uncomfortable but intimate symbiosis, and both peoples borrowed each other's ideas. From the splendour of Jewish history, the Poles drew their sense of a nation specially chosen by God to demonstrate his purposes through suffering and resurrection, a sense expressed in the Messianic notion of Poland as the collective reincarnation of Christ. From modern Polish nationalism, however, and especially from the anti-Jewish politician Roman Dmowski, the first Zionists of Russian Poland learned the doctrine of 'national egoism', the absolute moral primacy of the national interest, which is all too clearly expressed in the ethic of the Israeli state today.[70]

In some ways, then, Zionist ideas emerging in Eastern Europe were bound to be more nationalistic than those in the West. Still, what Zionists held in common was the perception of the abnormal status of the Jews as a diaspora people and of the need for their own state. The unique status of Jews as a minority living in many countries helped inspire the religious fundamentalist movement: 'fundamentalists interpret what they consider the wildly irrational opprobrium heaped upon Israel by the world community as yet more evidence of the Jewish people's special, divine destiny'. By attracting outrage and persecution, Israel was returning to its role given in Numbers (23:9): 'a people that dwells alone and that shall not be reckoned among the nations'.[71] This stress on a unique sorrowful destiny produced different historiographies. Writing in the late 1950s, Ya'acov Talmon noted how

> The older historians were impressed by the uniqueness of the history of a people dwelling apart. The newer ones are likely to be struck by the paradox that it is precisely in the uniqueness of a clannish, marginal community dispersed around the world that the secret of the universal significance of Jewish history lies.[72]

The state of Israel embodied such contrasting historical beliefs. It inculcated deep national pride while imparting respect for universalist humanist values that transcended national boundaries, as Jewish theologian Martin Buber championed.[73] Israel's history as an independent state reflected such dualism. After 1967 'Nationalist Israel pushed for annexation of the territories, humanist Israel for their return'.[74] The rise of the Likud ('Unity') coalition and of messianic religious fervor in the 1970s reflected national particularism. By contrast the ethos of Labour Zionism, Mapaam, and the 'Peace Now' movement was more internationalist in orientation.

The formative years of modern Zionism shaped the development of a Jewish state. The British government made a promise in the November 1917 declaration of foreign secretary Arthur Balfour to create a Jewish homeland in the Middle East out of the ruins of the collapsing Ottoman empire. The evolution of the Jewish national idea 'added a new focal point between the Jews and their adversaries'.[75]

Zeev Jabotinsk, founder of the revisionist wing of Zionism in the interwar years, exerted a decisive influence on the development of Jewish nationalism. Although sharing a secularist outlook, he insisted that the goal of Jewish nationalism should be the return to all of Biblical Israel including both east and west banks of the Jordan. He protested against the separation of Transjordan (the east bank) from the Palestine mandate (or future Jewish homeland) implemented by British administrative fiat in 1921.

As we noted, Zionism always contained a mix of secular and religious fundamentalism. But it did not follow that religious fundamentalists were the most ardent supporters of Jewish nationalism. Ultra-Orthodox fundamentalist Jews, the Haredim, largely kept out of politics before and after the establishment of Israel, preferring to search for inner spiritual life. The reason was that 'Orthodoxy's fundamental objection to Zionism was theological. It followed from the Zionists' intention to reverse the course of Jewish history and remake the Jewish people – in effect, to redeem them – through mere human agency'.[76]

Constructing Israel historically and conceptually

The state of Israel came into existence as an affirmation of Jewish nationalism rather than of liberal democracy. Like other nations' struggles for independence it was accompanied by political violence. In recent years a systematic reexamination and questioning has been under way by Israeli scholars of the country's earlier historiography, and many founding myths have been destroyed.[77] Other historical facts are beyond dispute.

The most extreme of the extremist groups fighting for independence in the 1940s was Lehi. Its founder Avraham Stern, who was killed by the British army in 1942, had asserted that '[f]orce always forged the destiny of nations' and that '[t]he destiny of the land of Israel has always been determined by the sword, not diplomacy'.[78] Virtually the entire Zionist movement, from Menachem Begin, commander of the right-wing Irgun from 1943 to 1948, to founder of the Israeli state David Ben-Gurion, repudiated the violence of Lehi.[79]

Former right-wing Israeli prime minister Yitzhak Shamir had served as a member of Lehi's inner leadership. He vilified the *Realpolitik* of Ben-Gurion, who had established the Mapai party (forerunner of the Labour party), as the building of a 'Jerusalem National Old-Aged Home'. Lehi's most despicable act was the assassination in 1948 of Count Folke Bernadotte, a Swedish diplomat appointed by the UN to mediate the Arab–Israeli dispute.[80] Shamir denied involvement in the killing but upheld the principled use of terror in creating an Israeli state.[81] After independence Shamir worked in the Mossad (the Israeli intelligence service) until 1970 and became prime minister in 1983.

Violent methods to attain independence were not the monopoly of Lehi. Irgun, the military wing of revisionist Zionism, also used force to drive Britain – ruling under a League of Nations mandate – and the Arabs out of Palestine. Another future prime minister received his apprenticeship in a right-wing organization that made use of terror tactics. In 1946 Begin ordered the bombing of the King David Hotel which served as British military command headquarters. The bomb killed 91 people and was pivotal in persuading the British to leave Palestine. Then in April 1948, a month before the declaration of Israeli independence, Irgun attacked the Arab village of Deir Yassin, near Jerusalem, killing 200 civilians and sparking off an exodus of Arabs. Such action would be described today as ethnic cleansing and indeed Irgun became a pariah in the Zionist movement of the time.[82] But the wider lesson of the War of Independence for the Israeli state was that '[n]ational construction was a process whereby priority was given to political and economic power.... To Ben-Gurion and the other founders, Tzahal (the Israel Defense Force) was more than an army. It also, and to no less a degree, had the function of building a state'.[83] From the beginning, a functionalist rather than spiritual approach informed the Israeli state-building project.

Responding to the hostility of surrounding Arab states, Israel began a nuclear weapons program in the mid-1950s with help from France. The rationale was that the Arabs could afford to lose many wars but Israel only one. The country did not sign either the original nuclear non-proliferation treaty or its extension in 1995. The 1956 Suez crisis, precipitated by the pan-Arabism of Egyptian president Gamal 'Abd al Nasser who had decided to nationalize the Suez Canal, led to British and French military intervention in, together with an Israeli attack on, Egypt. The intervention was cut short by strong US opposition, contributing further to Israel's sense of having to become self-reliant. In June 1967 a preemptive attack by Israel on its increasingly-bellicose Arab neighbors led to the capture of new lands including the Sinai (which was part of Egypt), the West Bank (part of Jordan), and the Golan Heights (part of Syria). The Six Day War, as it became known, represented the apogee of Israeli nationalism. But its consequences served to divide domestic politics as never before and led to political polarization out of which right-wing extremist groups emerged.

Support for right-wing movements increased after the 1967 war, the offshoot of a triumphalist climate. Egypt's surprise 1973 attack on Israel during Yom Kippur awoke Israelis to the continued security threat to the country. During the next 15 years the terrorism of the Palestine Liberation Organization (PLO), worsening economic and social conditions, the military misadventure in Lebanon, and the breakout of the Intifada (or Palestinian rebellion) in December 1987 drove many Israelis to join right-wing movements. The liberalization of the law of return in 1970 to allow not just Jews but those with Jewish roots and connections (for example, children and grandchildren of Jews, non-Jewish spouses) changed Israel's own demographics. The amended law paved the way for the massive emigration of Russian and East European Jews – one million between 1992 and 1995, by some estimates. The country faced a severe unemployment problem and at least half a million highly-educated native Israelis were underemployed. The expanding ranks of the economically-disadvantaged proved fertile ground for recruitment into right-wing organizations.

The imperative of state-building by a people without a homeland for two millennia and in a region dominated by Muslims is self-evident. If French philosopher Jean-Paul Sartre was right, then anti-Semitism defines the Jew.[84] Jewish fundamentalism emerged out of this context. The fundamentalist movement was shaped by the tension caused by Jewish occupation of Arab lands and mutual hostility between Jews and Arabs. Fundamentalism undermined the consensus on what Jewish nationalism signified and what the State of Israel encompassed:

> Its objectives are to ensure Jewish rule over the 'whole Land of Israel,' substitute its radical and apocalyptic vision of Jewish destiny for the

pragmatic Zionism that Israel's founders had made the 'common sense' of the society they created, and advance the world-historic process of redemption in which the Jewish people and the State of Israel play central roles.[85]

A consensus may never have existed on what the territorial scope of Israel should be. Religious fundamentalists look to biblical descriptions of the Promised Land whereas nonreligious leaders of fundamentalism envisaged a Jewish state extending from the Nile to the Euphrates. Right-wing nationalists did agree that land is essential to nationhood. Jewish identity is grounded in historic lands such as Jerusalem, they asserted, and indeed, this city is at the heart of Jewish national self-definition. The Orthodox counterargument is that Jewish identity depends primarily on the worship of God, not of land.

Divisions within Jewry are multifold. For one political scientist, '[u]p to modern times the identity of a Jew was shaped by three factors: profound faith, birth into an "organic" community involving lineage and strong social control; and the hostility of the surrounding society'.[86] Language is not a determinant: today less than 5 percent of Jews worldwide speak Yiddish, while Ladino is spoken only by Sephardim. As a result, the 'linguistic "promiscuity" of Jews contributed to confusion of identity'.[87]

For one Israeli specialist, Jewish cultural worlds could be divided into: 1) Judaism – the theocratic mentality of religious Jews; 2) Jewishness – the ethnocentrism of diaspora Jews; and, 3) Israeliness – the local nationalism of Hebrew-speaking Gentiles that is neither Judaism nor Jewishness.[88] Fundamentalists see at least two threats posed by these multiple Jewish identities. One is that Jewishness – the ethnocentrism of ardent diasporists – can engender the reality depicted in Philip Roth's novel *Operation Shylock* in which the protagonist exhorts: 'The time has come to return to the Europe that was for centuries, and remains to this day, the most authentic Jewish homeland there has ever been, the birthplace of rabbinic Judaism, Hasidic Judaism, Jewish secularism, socialism – on and on. The birthplace, of course, of Zionism too'.[89] Put differently, '[t]he idea that Israeliness exists but differs from Jewishness is a frightening anathema for many Jews, and for Zionists in particular. The reason is simple: Zionism is the idea that all the Jews in the world constitute one nation whose homeland is Zion (the biblical name for Palestine)'.[90]

The second threat for fundamentalists is that even if a secular, inclusive Israel is more democratic, it nevertheless represents a form of post-Zionism since it is no longer centered on Judaism. The *Kach* movement discussed below was particularly concerned with the dangers posed by a fully-democratic Israel. Fundamentalists gave higher priority to a national than a state identity:

Israeli nation-building was a project designed to establish an ethnona-tional–territorial identity, based on a reconstructed 'imagined' Jewish past and unity. Israeli state-building is a complementary project intended to establish territorial and institutional infrastructures for 'reviving' the nation, affecting all state residents, including the marginalized Arab minority'.[91]

Isaiah Berlin remarked that Jews had much history but little geography.[92] Not surprisingly, therefore, the more radical the vision of Jewish destiny and the larger the vision of what greater Israel should consist of, the more nationalist the group. Israeli rightists have laid claim to lands that contain holy places, above all Jerusalem's Old City. Here the Al Aqsa mosque stands on a plateau that Muslims call Haram al Sharif but Jews revere as the Temple Mount, the ancient ground on which a temple was built by Solomon (and Herod). Riots here in 1990 left dozens of Arabs dead and led to revenge killings of Jews. A visit by right-wing political leader Ariel Sharon to the Temple Mount in September 2000 sparked a renewed Palestinian Intifida. But five months later, riding the wave of an Israeli backlash he won a one-sided victory in the election for prime minister. Making good on his promise to end Arab terrorism through military means Sharon plunged Israel into a brutal conflict with the Palestinians that resulted in renewed occupation of lands transferred to the Palestinian Authority a few years earlier. The 'little geography' that Israel possesses has been jealously guarded and skillfully exploited by the fundamentalist movement.

Right-wing organizations

While other movements exist, let us focus on three principal right-wing organizations that espouse Jewish nationalism, fundamentalism, or both. These are the *Tehiya* (Renaissance) party, *Gush Emunim* (Block of the Faith-ful), and the *Kach* party. All were inspired by the Israeli victory in the Six Day War.

The *Tehiya* represents the constructive right and advocates non-violence and respect for law and institutions while promoting the concept of a greater Israel, annexation of occupied territories, and a return to traditional Zion-ism.[93] *Tehiya* was formed in 1979 as a reaction to what was perceived as a land betrayal by prime minister Begin in the Camp David accords with Egyptian president Anwar Sadat in that year. Begin had agreed to return the Sinai peninsula to Egypt in return for a peace agreement. *Tehiya* viewed the accord not just as a political mistake but as 'a sign of national weakness, weariness, and inability to face the real challenges' of the modern world.[94] Accordingly, *Tehiya* took on the mission of 'movement of national revival' and 'rejuven-ation of Zionism'. It insisted that Israel should never give up an inch of its conquered territories, that Palestinian autonomy should be throttled, and that Jewish settlements should be increased in the occupied territories.[95]

In 1986 one of *Tehiya*'s leaders made the provocative assertion that half a million Arab refugees in the West Bank and Gaza Strip should be resettled in Arab countries; conversely, Jews living in Arab states should be repatriated. The *Tehiya* party platform adopted in 1987 reiterated the call for resettling Arab refugees but agreed that other Arabs resident in Israel could stay. A minority in *Tehiya* even considered granting Arabs living in Israel a form of citizenship, but stringent criteria would be set: the Arabs' declaration of loyalty to Israel as a Zionist state, national service in the Israel Defense Forces (IDF), and proficiency in Hebrew. For most Arabs these were not real options.

In 1984 *Tehiya*, with five seats in the 120–member Knesset, briefly became the third largest party in Israel. It formed a political alliance with *Tzomet*, or the Movement for Zionist Renewal. More nationalist than *Tehiya*, *Tzomet* lumped together Begin's 'treason' with that of pacifist leftist groups urging Israeli withdrawal from Lebanon. Israel's political objectives in invading its northern neighbor in 1982 had always been murky, but *Tzomet* praised the militarism and austerity that the war entailed. One well-known *Tehiya* leader was Geula Cohen, a fighter in the independence struggle. She made clear that '[m]y goal is not peace. I came here to build a homeland. I'm not giving up pieces of my homeland for peace'.[96]

A second major right-wing movement is *Gush Emunim*, less a political party than a community sharing a religious fundamentalist view of the world. It is based largely on some 130 Jewish settlements in the West Bank and the biblical areas of Judea and Samaria. Its philosophical founder was Rabbi Moshe Levinger who had established the first settlement in Hebron in 1968. The movement subscribes to the view that the Jewish people live in 'an age of redemption'. After centuries of persecution, the salvation promised to Israel is at hand. The spoils of the Six Day War and the reunification of Jerusalem are seen as signs of this redemption. Related to this, *Gush Emunim* holds that the entire land of Israel is holy and that the Jewish people alone are entitled to all of it. The 'land is inseparable spiritually' from the people.[97]

Gush Emunim urges a return to the pioneering spirit of original Zionism. At the same time, unlike other fundamentalist groups, it extends respect for the secular state, regarded as the legitimating institutional force undergirding the concept of greater Israel. Most *Gush Emunim* followers do not have any stated ethnic or racist agendas although they do regard the organization as 'an essential part of the collective identity of the nation'.[98]

The *Kach* party constitutes the 'destructive right' in Israel and does not renounce violence. Indeed, Rabin's assassin reputedly belonged to 'Eyal', an offshoot of *Kach*. Not surprisingly, therefore, offshoots of *Kach* like *Kahane Chai* ('Kahane Lives') were immediately outlawed following Rabin's assassination and appear on the US list of terrorist organizations.

Like many fundamentalists, *Kach* members regard democratic government and law as expendable and subscribe to the substitution of 'authentically Jewish' forms of government for Western democracy. 'Whether religious or nonreligious, Jewish fundamentalists contrast the materialism and shallowness of the Christian West with the discipline, historicity, and spiritual depth of Judaism. Democracy and equality, regardless of race, religion, or ethnic background, may be appropriate values for Europe and America, but they do not apply to Israel'.[99]

Levinger, *Gush Emunim*'s founder, had elaborated on the unsuitability of democracy for the Jews: 'If in Europe and the United States a moral and democratic mission requires equality of rights for all, it is clear and obvious that in Israel what must determine rights to vote and to be elected to public office must be identification with and participation in the struggle of the people of Israel to accomplish its mission'.[100] *Kach* founder Rabbi Meir Kahane put it more starkly: 'I'm a Jew, not a democrat.'

Kahane's youngest son, Benjamin, who became leader of *Kahane Chai*, voiced similar anti-democratic sentiments. In a collection of essays published in 1995 in honor of Goldstein under the title *Baruch Hagever* ('Baruch, the Man') that earned notoriety for its extremist views, he wrote:

> The moment of truth has arrived. One possibility is to follow the path of Judaism, the entire Jewish idea, to reject the fear of the Gentile, Western democracy and the idea of co-existence with the Arabs. This way is the condition for the existence of a Jewish state. The other option is the acceptance of the yoke of democracy and the giving up of the dream of a Jewish state. There is no third way.[101]

Meir Kahane began his political career in the US in the late 1960s as founder of the Jewish Defense League and the American Jewish Vigilante Organization.[102] Under investigation by US authorities for his involvement in violent organizations, Kahane emigrated to Israel in 1971 and in 1984 was elected to the Knesset. In the following year, the *Kach* party gained 22 percent of the vote in municipal elections in Kiryat Arba near Hebron, the largest Jewish settlement on the West Bank where Jews had been killed in Arab terrorist attacks. But Kahane's party was banned in 1988 for its racist and undemocratic practices.

In contrast to other right-wing groups' almost exclusive focus on the Arabs, Kahane saw the establishment of modern Israel as a punishment for Gentiles who had persecuted Jews for centuries. For him the 'very definition of Jewish freedom implies the ability to humiliate the Gentiles'.[103] But Kahane did not overlook the Arabs, who he referred to as dogs, and he advocated Jewish terrorism to counter Arab terrorism and the use of random violence against Arab populations suspected of assisting the PLO. He was the most outspoken advocate of the wholesale expulsion of the Arabs from Israeli-settled lands. Kahane was assassinated in New York City in 1990 by an Egyptian-born US resident apparently acting on his own.

Kahane's name became prominent again in February 1994 when one of his followers, Goldstein, opened fire at Muslims in the Hebron mosque. Unlike Goldstein, however, who was a doctor, most of Kahane's supporters in Israel are economically disadvantaged Jews. Apart from Kahane, another American adopted by the Israeli right as a symbol of Jewish nationalism is Jonathan Pollard, convicted of spying for Israel and sentenced in 1985 to a long jail term.

The right's grip on power

Likud's victory in the 1977 general elections allowed Begin to become the country's first non-Labour prime minister. The established Jewish elites, mostly Ashkenazim (Jews of Central European ancestry), lost influence. Though Begin was of Polish background, Likud came to power on the votes of the hitherto-disadvantaged Sephardim (Jews of Middle Eastern and African ancestry) who now represented the majority of the Israeli population. Open conflict between the two groups had erupted twice in the past, in the 1959 Wadi Salib disturbances near Haifa and the 1971–72 Black Panther riots led by Sephardim youth. The rivalry between them increased in the 1981 elections but was put aside until 1997 when Sephardi leaders in the Shas party were prosecuted on corruption charges. This produced a Sephardic backlash in the 1999 elections that transformed Shas into the Knesset's third-largest party.

In the first six years of Begin's administration, Jewish settlements on the West Bank increased from the ten that had been established between 1967 and 1976, to 62. The number of settlers rose from a few thousand to nearly 50 000, and the government pumped $1 billion into settlements in the West Bank and Gaza Strip.

As the right gained ascendancy in Israeli politics, a left- wing peace movement arose. Already in 1975 *Oz VeShalom* ('Strength and Peace') was founded as a religious Zionist peace movement opposed to the exclusionary world view of right- wing groups. It viewed the 1979 Israeli-Egyptian peace treaty as the first step in reconciling Jews and Arabs. The peace movement grew in strength in 1982 in the wake of the massacre of Palestinians at the Sabra and Shatila refugee camps near Bierut. The Israeli army had stood aside and allowed Israel's Christian militia allies to rampage through the camps. Likud's decision to invade Lebanon proved a fiasco in other ways. Begin agonized over the toll the invasion took in Israeli lives and soon resigned as prime minister, to be replaced by Shamir.

Right-wing Jewish groups were galvanized against both the peace movement and Palestinians' political rights.[104] The PLO was stigmatized as a terrorist organization. Israeli control over the West Bank and Gaza, where two million Palestinians lived, was tightened. Mutual hatred and demonization followed. In 1987 the Intifada broke out when Palestinians rose up against Israeli military authority, first in the refugee camps of the Gaza strip, then in the occupied territories of the West Bank. As one Israeli specialist wrote, '[t]he persistence of the Intifada (it lasted until 1993) caused Israelis to realize that the Likud's ideology of "Greater Israel" entailed the permanent burden of controlling a murderously hostile population'.[105] The Intifada took a psychological toll on the Israeli public and the security forces. More and more Israelis wanted extrication from the Palestinian imbroglio even if it meant giving up the West Bank and Gaza.

Rabin and the right

In 1992 the Labour Party led by Rabin returned to power after 15 years. War fatigue shared by Israelis and Arabs in large part explained the end of Likud coalition rule. Taking advantage of its initial period of grace, the new Labour government quickly entered into negotiations with Palestinian leader Yasser Arafat in Norway in 1993. In September 1993 Rabin agreed to a plan to grant autonomy to the PLO. His administration reversed the logic of the fundamentalists and was guided by the idea that '[t]he loss of the Jewish character of the state was juxtaposed to the equally undesirable option of the loss of the democratic nature of Israel'.[106] Right-wing groups rejected both the land-for-peace option and giving priority to democracy rather than Jewishness. They intensified civil disobedience and even resorted to violence, punctuated by the 1994 Hebron mosque massacre.

The peace process went forward and culminated in accords signed between Israel and the PLO in Washington in 1993. One commentator eloquently explained the fast pace of Israeli peace initiatives: 'The monumental self-reliance that Zionism introduced into Jewish life sufficed to secure survival, but it did not suffice to secure normality'.[107] Not every day could be lived as Masada – the defense and suicide of Jews defending a mountain fortress in the Judean desert against the Roman legions in 73 AD.

The provisional solution devised by Rabin's government was based on the formula 'separation without statehood'. Gaza and Jericho were to be returned to the Palestinian administration but no independent Palestinian state was envisaged for the immediate future. Some critics of the plan commented how Palestine was to become a bantustan.[108] For the agreement to work much depended on the ability of the PLO to combat terrorism launched by Islamic fundamentalist organizations like Hamas and Islamic Jihad. Conversely, Israel had to manage the disaffection of Jewish settlers forced off the territories that were being handed back to the Palestinians. Many of these settlers turned to more extremist organizations to defend their interests. When neither rabbinical bodies nor the Yesha Council – the major settler organization – could halt the peace process, a new radical right movement *Zo Artzenu* ('This is Our Land') was established in 1995 to engage in civil disobedience and, generally, to question the legitimacy of the Rabin government.

Under Rabin, Israeli public opinion was characterized by political realism. A majority regarded Palestinian statehood as inevitable: in early 1995

64 percent of respondents believed that this would be the consequence of the peace process.[109] This seeming inevitability of a Palestinian state was the catalyst for the right-wing terrorism carried out by Jewish settlers in the occupied territories. Rabin sought to defuse this fear by stressing that he himself was opposed to a Palestinian state. He referred to the 1993 Knesset Law Committee resolution asserting that if the Palestinian self-rule authority in the occupied territories declared itself a state after Israel's withdrawal, the peace agreement would be null and void. Still, as architect of the peace process, Rabin's assurances were not taken seriously by right-wing nationalists.

The opposition to an independent Palestine was cemented in Zionism and the armed struggle against Palestinian organizations, some of which were terrorist. The arguments of right-wing nationalists against granting Palestinian autonomy were primarily historical. The Palestinian claim to being a distinct people, Israeli nationalists argued, was largely spurious since they are indistinguishable from their fellow Arabs and possess no separate religion or language. Their only claim to uniqueness was in professing to have a national homeland – Western Palestine – made up of the state of Israel, Judea, Samaria, and Gaza. For many Israelis it was no coincidence that this alleged historic Palestinian homeland was precisely where the Jewish people were authorized by the British mandate of 1922 to create their homeland. When this territory became Transjordan in that year, Palestinians did not claim it as a homeland. Similarly, in the years after the Second World War when Egypt occupied the Gaza Strip and Jordan controlled the West Bank, Palestinians did not make claims on these Arab-held territories. Only at the founding congress of the PLO held in Jerusalem in 1964 was the goal of the liberation of all Palestine, including areas under Jordanian sovereignty, expressed.[110]

The 1991 Gulf War increased the urgency of achieving stability in the Middle East. Saddam Hussein stated that Iraqi withdrawal from Kuwait was contingent on Israeli withdrawal from the occupied territories. The Iraqis were driven out of Kuwait but in his speech announcing the ceasefire with Iraq president George Bush referred to the need to implement United Nations resolution 242 requiring an Israeli pullout from lands occupied in June 1967. The spread of religious fundamentalism in the Islamic world and in Israel added impetus to Israeli and Palestinian moderates to reach an agreement.

The Labour government under Rabin and his successor, Shimon Peres, searched for a comprehensive peace formula going beyond the Palestinian question. So as to normalize the status of Arabs living in Israel, Rabin put forward a bill called the 'Basic Law: Human Rights', which would eliminate all distinctions between Jewish and Arab citizens and bring into question the very idea of Israel as a Jewish state. The bill expanded the rights of Arab residents who were now allowed to purchase land anywhere in Israel, send their children to Jewish schools, receive the material benefits granted to Jews emigrating to Israel, and have Arabic, already an official language of the state, placed on an equal footing with Hebrew as a language of education. Such a change in the understanding of citizenship would revolutionize the Jewish state. For right-wing critics, the bill effectively nullified the law of return allowing Jews from all over the world to obtain Israeli citizenship automatically.[111]

But it was the agreement with the PLO that was most momentous:

> The 1993 Oslo peace accords between the Palestinian national movement and the Labour government were meant to bring to an end the historical process started by the young Polish and Russian Jews who at the turn of the century settled in Palestine with the intention of gaining a country for their people.

The inevitable establishment of a Palestinian state undermined the very notion of a chosen people: 'The Jews were no longer officially regarded as the sole legitimate owners of the Promised Land'.[112]

Opposition to the Rabin government strengthened when the prime minister drew up plans for the removal of a handful of Jewish families from Tel Rumeida, a hill in central Hebron. They were seen as at risk, surrounded by 30 000 hostile Palestinians. But 'Tel Rumeida expressed the ultimate ultranationalist defiance, epitomizing the claim of the Jewish right to settle all of Eretz Israel'.[113] Resistance to evacuation was bolstered by several Halakhic rulings issued by prominent Orthodox rabbis claiming that the evacuation-of- settlers order was illegal. Rabin decided to back away from a confrontation but his retreat was risky: 'Small and large rabbinical gatherings, protesting the peace process and expressing intense delegitimation vis-à-vis the government, continued'.[114] Another ruling by a rabbinical council came in summer 1995, when implementation had begun of phase II of the Oslo accords requiring an Israeli pullout from seven major West Bank cities. It judged withdrawal from military bases in Judea and Samaria as illegal. Moreover, soldiers were justified in disobeying the orders of their commanding officers – an extraordinary edict in a country dependent for its survival on a unified military.

The radicalization of Israel's ultranationalists was discernible in their discourse. In May 1993 graffiti over a motorway near Tel Aviv ironically observed: 'Once all the world was against us, now it's the government as well'.[115] In the wake of a series of suicide bombings in February 1995 by Hamas and Islamic Jihad members that killed 87 Israeli civilians, the heads of Yesha's Rabbinical Council began to examine whether the Labour government, and Rabin and Peres in particular, were responsible for Jewish deaths. If they were, the Halakha principle of *din rodef* might apply: a person about to commit a murder can be justly killed in order to save Jewish life. While no rabbinical authority ever agreed to issue a ruling that the prime minister was guilty under *din rodef*, the culture of Halakhic defiance inspired Rabin's assassin in his planning and subsequent legal defense. The establishment right did not condemn the fundamentalist right. One month before his assassination, placards of Rabin dressed in a SS uniform were waved at a large rally held in Jerusalem by anti-Labour groups. Neither opposition leader Benyamin Netanyahu nor any other speaker criticized this culture of hatred.

Referring to the assassination, one writer lamented: 'Israel was the first democratic state – and from the end of the Second World War until now the only one – in which a political murder achieved its goal'.[116] In May 1996 Labour candidate Peres was defeated in Israel's first direct election of a prime minister. The winner was the Likud coalition's Netanyahu, by less than 30 000 votes. The difference was accounted for by the army's vote: Netanyahu had served in the IDF and was involved in the 1976 Entebbe, Uganda, airport rescue of Israeli hostages; Peres had never served in the army. The outgoing prime minister interpreted the close result this way: 'the Jews won but the Israelis lost'.[117]

Netanyahu's three-year reign marked a return to a 'Greater Israel' conception found in Zionist nationalism and the refutation of liberal nationalism. Fundamentalist violence fell as he acceded to the demands of settler groups and ultra-Orthodox alike. Even though he had not received a mandate to freeze the Oslo accords, that is exactly what Netanyahu did. He missed a series of deadlines for returning captured lands to the Palestinians.

From the first months of his administration, when he was implicated in an influence-peddling scheme, to his last months, when several cabinet ministers resigned in an atmosphere of continuing scandal, Netanyahu's political problems dogged him more than the split in Israeli society between those urging peace and Jewish fundamentalists determined not to surrender historic lands. Under pressure, in fall 1998 Netanyahu signed the US-brokered Wye River accord which required Israel to relinquish 13 percent of its West Bank territories to Palestinian control. But by the end of the year he froze the pact after giving up only 2 percent of the land. His many about-turns alienated even his supporters and in early 1999 he lost his majority in the Knesset and was forced to call early elections.

Netanyahu's opponent in May 1999 was Ehud Barak, a much-decorated former army commander. Even though he had introduced a clause in the Labour party program supporting Palestinian statehood, Barak could not be labeled as being soft on Israel's national security. He won the prime ministership by a comfortable margin (56 percent to 44 percent) though within the Jewish population he barely edged out Netanyahu (51.5 percent to 48.5 percent). The biggest winner in the Knesset was the religious Shas party, strongly aligned with the Sephardic community: its Knesset strength increased from four in 1984 to ten in 1996 to 17 in 1999. Led by charismatic but scandal-plagued Aryeh Deri, Shas held a religious conception of the

Jewish state while accepting the peace process. It therefore joined Barak's coalition government.

How could Israelis' choose a secular-oriented prime minister but a reinvigorated religious party? For one academic the answer lay in the so-called national liberal voter bloc: 'In times of crisis with the Arabs the national liberal becomes intensely nationalistic and may vote for a rightist party; but in calmer periods he favors an urban, Westernized Israel, anti-clerical if not wholly antireligious'.[118] In 1999, the primordial instinct of national liberals was subordinated to the 'futurist' attitude stressing how Israel must become just another normal state and well-ordered nation.

Barak seemed intent on playing a historic role and bringing the Israeli–Arab conflict to closure. He withdrew Israeli security forces from Lebanon, initiated peace overtures to Syria, and met regularly with Palestinian Authority chairman Arafat. However, since the founding of the state the persistent dilemma for Israeli leaders has been that peace with the Arabs was likely to disturb peace among Israelis. Sharon demonstrated this point by walking to the Temple Mount in September 2000. The counter-terrorism and assassination campaigns he launched against Palestinians beginning in 2001 seemed only to make stark the seemingly irreconcilable conceptions of Israel, its people, and its lands.

Conclusions on the Israeli right

Like its German counterpart, the Israeli radical right imagines a homeland exclusively for the pure and the good. A corollary of its strict understanding of who an Israeli is is a sweeping conception of the Other. Israeli belongingness is emphasized in any number of rituals, but the distinctive quality of the fundamentalist right is that at times it is prepared to use intimidation of and violence against the Other. One writer has suggested that '[w]hen nationalism dies, religious fundamentalism often fills the void, as both Arabs and Israelis are now discovering'.[119] To the extent that secular nationalism has declined in Israel, this proposition is probably acurate.

There are enormous differences between racial and religious constructions of home. For a start, the source of authority has different legitimacy. Jewish fundamentalists can invoke ancient texts to explain why Israel is home to their people. Setting aside myth-making, the Aryan claim to German lands can only go back a few centuries. Where Aryan ideology associated with the German right has set out to subordinate or destroy alien races, neither Judaism nor political Zionism aims at any such thing. The proponents of German and Israeli fundamentalism also differ in their abilities to elaborate systematic visions of their homes and their futures. Finally, a single spiritual home is never likely to be as exclusionary and intolerant as a single racial one. The first involves an inner struggle of faith and belief; the second is anchored in irreversible primordialism. To be sure, as a comparative study of religious fundamentalism concluded, these movements adopt violent means not because of some inexplicable aberration but because it follows from the absolutist structure of their belief systems.[120] There is nothing reassuring about fundamentalism's choice of means.

Right-wing nationalisms are out of place in societies of increasing diversity. The most effective method of disarming them is by recognizing that all peoples with history have homelands.

6
Transnational Homes: Pan-Nationalisms

Transnationalism is a phenomenon widely recognized as putting into question the modern sovereign state. The massive global population migrations of the late twentieth century have changed the 'national' character of many states, especially in advanced economies. If most of the countries in the world were already multicultural before these population movements gathered steam, they are even more so now. Recognition of the benefits of diversified societies has caused the reverse process, ethnic cleansing by a state, to be vigorously denounced. Today's international norms do not tolerate it.

At first glance the phenomenon of transnationalism appears to undermine ethnic nationalism in a particular state. Another view, however, is that it can actually widen the reach of particular nationalisms. Thus,

> the nationalist genie, never perfectly contained in the bottle of the territorial state, is now itself diasporic. Carried in the repertoires of increasingly mobile populations of refugees, tourists, guest workers, transnational intellectuals, scientists and illegal aliens, it is increasingly unrestrained by ideas of spatial boundary and territorial sovereignty.[1]

If transnationalism can serve as a carrier of state nationalism, can it also help transmit pan-nationalisms, that is, ideologies that propagate political or religious identities that extend beyond state boundaries? This chapter examines the influence and reach of pan-nationalisms, sometimes termed macro-nationalisms (see chapter 2). One important objective shared by several pan-national movements today is to counter the global hegemony of the Western world and especially the United States. From the West's perspective, 'good' forms of globalization, regionalism, and integration are exemplified by such institutions and processes as the World Trade Organization and the European Union, which showcase Western models of modernity and development for the rest of the world. Pan-nationalisms are stigmatized as a 'bad' kind because they urge solidarity and action by poorer countries against the wealthier world. Ostensibly, in attempting to construct national, religious, and political identity across state boundaries, such transnational understanding of home is in keeping with contemporary norms. But pan-nationalisms run foul of the world's major powers in their insistence that the societies they seek to construct should be impermeable to what are viewed as nefarious outside influences, such as those emanating from the West. A transnational terrorist organization like Al-Qaeda ('the Base'), calling itself 'The World Islamic Front for Jihad', has become the most notorious pan-nationalist movement.

The two case studies in this chapter are of Islamic fundamentalism and Latin American *anti-yanquismo*. Each tries to unify peoples from different nations and living in many states around a core ideology. While Islam has long served as a powerful force binding peoples from the Arab, Asian, and African worlds into one community, the resurgence of Islamic fundamentalism in the past two decades has transformed it into a global force. Perceived to be a monolithic phenomenon opposed to the modern secular state, to Western liberal ideology, and especially to the hegemonic role played in world politics by the US, Islamic fundamentalism can be viewed as the most widespread pan-nationalism seeking to unite an otherwise divided third world.

The second case considers the special role of the United States as a perceived obstacle to the cultural and economic development of other states in the Western hemisphere. To some degree anti-Americanism had always constituted a type of pan-nationalist consensus in Latin America, but it became a political force following the 1959 Cuban revolution. It was solidified at the 1967 Trilateral Conference convened in Havana to condemn Western imperialism. *Anti-yanquismo*, with its paradigm of humiliating economic dependency on the West, became a largely inchoate ideology of the weak in the Western hemisphere. Whether it really became established as a pan-nationalism is a question we consider below.

The Islamic *Umma*

(Mis)understanding the Islamic world

In the view of one specialist, the rise of religious fundamentalism in the Islamic world as well as in Israel was spurred by 'the perception that secular institutions have failed to perform. In many parts of the world the secular state has not lived up to its own promises of political freedom, economic prosperity, and social justice'.[2] Religious nationalism came to the rescue of the nation-state. The latent assumption in Western liberal thought that secular nationalism was in competition with religion and superior to it gave Islamic leaders grounds to attack what Iran's Ayatollah Ruhollah Khomeini called *gharbzadegi*, or 'West-intoxication'. For many in the West, mixing religion and politics could lead to fanaticism and extremism; cases in point included Iran, Libya, Algeria, and Afghanistan. Moreover, '[a] merger of the absolutism of nationalism with the absolutism of religion might create a rule so vaunted and potent that it could destroy itself and its neighbors as well'.[3] But in most Islamic states neither religion nor politics has an absolutist character.

Islam aspires to be an organic religion where the idea of the separation of church and state is notional at best. The precept *al-islam din wa dawla* ('Islam is both religion and state') prevails. Accordingly, 'in Islam, political institutions are designed to defend and promote Islam, not the state. Moreover, such institutions are intended to establish and uphold an Islamic system based on the *Shariah* [immutable religious law]. Furthermore, the primary loyalty of Muslim citizens is to the *umma* [community of Islam], rather than the state, and to the *Shariah*, rather than the ruler'.[4]

The Qur'an is considered the word of God. In the hands of religious and political leaders it can serve, too, as a pan-nationalist movement. The injunction to Muslims of different nations is to get to know one another (*Qur'an* 49:13). Early in the twentieth century the idea of *Al-Jami'ah al-Islamiyyah*, or Islamic Commonwealth, was developed and efforts to forge Islamic patriotism followed.[5] To be sure, intercultural contacts among Muslim peoples more frequently occur at a normative than a political level and for one writer Islam therefore 'represents a prominent non-statist, non-national identity discourse which today claims widespread – in fact, one would almost be justified in saying truly "global" – validity as an ethical construct'.[6] The *umma* exists at this metaphysical level but it is far from a reality in global Islamic politics.

Popular Western perceptions of Islam are of a medieval-like, harsh, and illiberal religion. Pictures of Afghani women in burkas under the Taliban regime have reinforced this image in the West. Even respected scholars have tried to explain the supposedly reactionary nature of Islam. 'Since 1945, most intellectuals, writers and journalists in the democratic Western world have supported democratic, progressive and liberal causes and purposes.... They present a stark contrast to Arab and Islamic intellectuals and writers who have either consistently supported totalitarian movements or who have failed to oppose them effectively'.[7]

Even though Muslim scholars do not strictly interrogate the Qur'an, which is the word of God, it provides a register of political ideas that inform them. The strictest register is found in Saudi Arabia, though it has spread elsewhere. Thus '[o]ne of the chief obstacles to critical thinking in Islam during recent years has been the fact that Islamicist discourse is usually constructed around a set of claims represented as non- or even anti-Western in nature. To critique this discourse, therefore, would be to betray and weaken its anti-Western potential'.[8] Even this explanation requires circumspection. Reform-minded president Khatami of Iran hosted Islamic conferences in

1997 and 1998 that specifically focused on such contentious issues as political and ideological pluralism within Islamic societies. Islamic intellectuals do not, therefore, speak with one uncritical voice.

Another perspective prevalent among Western specialists of Islam that troubles Islamic intellectuals is the Orientalist perspective: it is timeless culture posing an obstacle to modernity. How has the *umma* reacted to this? One French scholar summarized:

> The Muslim responses to the 'Orientalist' discourse are often stereotypical and can be sorted into three categories: (1) the nostalgia argument ('it was Islam that brought civilization to the West'); (2) rejection of the hypothesis ('in what way are Western values superior?'), combined with a denunciation of Western doubletalk, which applies its strict requirements only to others; (3) the apologia for Islam ('everything is in the Qur'an and the Sunna, and Islam is the best religion').[9]

If it is true that the West has painted Islam as a fearful and anachronistic religion practiced by millions of zealots and thousands of fanatical terrorists, so the West has some fearful and ambiguous connotations to many Muslims. Fatima Mernissi asserted that '*[g]harb*, the Arabic word for the West, is also the place of darkness and the incomprehensible, always frightening. *Gharb* is the territory of the strange, the foreign (*gharib*)'.[10] This is an exaggeration: the root word *ghurub* denotes where the sun sets, not necessarily frightening nor foreign.[11] It is nevertheless true that Islam, as a result of apprehension, has created a picture of the West that ranges from blundering to satanic, just as the West, for similar reasons, has found it difficult to accept a benign image of Islam.

Historical reasons account for this unquestionable clash of civilizations. Writing in 1957, Palestinian author Walid Khalidi cited as the single most important source

> the great battle between Christian Europe and the world of Islam which began in the 7th century and ended only with the stemming of the Ottoman tide in eastern Europe in the 18th century. All the fears, animosities and suspicions of these times are reflected, sometimes explicitly and sometimes by implication, in the contemporary Western writings . . ., both prose and verse, lay and ecclesiastical. They therefore form part of the literary heritage of every educated European.[12]

The resonance of this historical clash has faded since Khalidi wrote of it, albeit to be replaced by other Western fears about Islam. More recently, Edward Said also undertook to expose the bias against Islam found in much of Western writing. He reported how Islam 'has licensed not only patent inaccuracy but also expressions of unrestrained ethnocentrism, cultural and even racial hatred, deep yet paradoxically free-floating hostility'. He added caustically that 'always it is supposed that the "Islam" being talked about is some real and stable object out there where "our" oil supplies happen to be found'.[13] Particularly striking is the way the Islamic world has consistently been contrasted unfavorably with Israel. 'Israel has appeared as a bastion of Western civilization hewn (with much approbation and self-congratulation) out of the Islamic wilderness. Secondly, Israel's security in American eyes has become conveniently interchangeable with fending off Islam, perpetuating Western hegemony, and demonstrating the virtues of modernization'.[14] Islam is invariably depicted in conflict with everything that is normal, Western, 'ours'.

Ernest Gellner's work on nationalism, which we considered in Chapter 2, has remained very influential in framing analysis of the subject. His mis-conceptualization of Islam was therefore all the more striking and perni-cious. He spoke of an Islamic society – not societies – because he regarded it as a faith imposing 'essential' constraints on the conduct and thought of its adherents. The exceptionalism Gellner attributed to it placed him in the same 'clash-of-civilizations' school as Huntington. Gellner wrote: 'To say that secularization prevails in Islam is not contentious. It is simply false. Islam is as strong now as it was a century ago. In some ways, it is probably much stronger'.[15] He supported a posited dichotomy of 'Mecca or mechan-ization'[16] even though the world had supplied many counterfactuals. For example, another writer stressed that

in the event of modernization, the presence of Islam does not demand the rise of fundamentalism, nor provide an impervious shield to secular-ization. The politics of industrializing Indonesia and Malaysia demon-strate that disparate Muslim communities do not necessarily merge into homogeneous nations of Islam. In Southeast Asia the challenge of iden-tifying emerging nations is better served by an ethnic guide than a spiritual one.[17]

But its supposed slowdown of the modernization process was part of a larger problem that Gellner had with Islam. The rejoinder can be that 'Gellner's claim that "fundamentalism" is the essence of a monolithic Muslim society runs counter to the highly diverse political and religious currents which suffuse Muslim societies and Muslim-majority polities'.[18] The alleged exceptionalism of Islam also did not stand up to scrutiny: 'as a system of belief Islam may be no more secularizable than Roman Catholi-cism or Christian fundamentalism, but Muslims, and Muslim societies, are secularizable, and the process is well advanced'.[19] Another scholar weighed in against Gellner's thesis found in *Conditions of Liberty: Civil Society and its Rivals* of the primacy of religion in Muslim states which thereby was said to delay modernization: 'While Islam has proved to be more resistant to the forces of secularization than other global religions, Gellner's model fails to account adequately for the particularist elements of a single culture among others of the same faith in determining a national culture'.[20] It seems all too typical, then, that a scholar so insightful about European identities should be so off base in comprehending Islam.

Finally, Peter Mansfield has offered an explanation for the Western bias against Islam and the Arabs specifically:

> The unique position of the Jews in Western Christian and post-Christian society, their persecution and Western guilt feelings of responsibility have all been reflected in attitudes towards the Arabs.... With very few exceptions, New York liberal intellectuals, European social democrats, left-wing writers, journalists and university dons have found that their pro-Zionism has made them hostile and unsympathetic towards the Arabs.[21]

Mansfield's study was published in 1976, shortly after the 1973 war between Israel and Egypt, which appeared to have resulted in an Israeli victory but was whittled down by the US-brokered Camp David accords of 1978. His analysis no longer holds true: the one-sided bias favoring Israel has eroded over the past two decades. But the cultural bias against Arabs, and Islam generally, is a separate issue.

The polycentrism of Islam

Muslims form a majority of the population in close to 50 countries in the world. Though usually identified with Arab states in the Middle East and North Africa, Islam is dominant in Asian countries like Bangladesh, India, Indonesia, and Pakistan. In addition, one-third of Africa's population is Muslim. There are also about 12 million Muslims living in Western Europe, including over 2 million in each of France, Germany and Britain. In general

> We find Islam divided into three geographic and cultural tendencies: the Sunni Arab Middle East, the Sunni Indian subcontinent, and Irano-Arab Shiism; Turkey, isolated from the Arab world, has its own organizations. These groups are as distinct politically as they are geographically, which is why it is more appropriate to speak of an Islamist sphere of influence than of an international union.[22]

From the 1970s Islam has reemerged as a global religious and political force. It has attracted converts among the world's disadvantaged groups, from Malaysians to African Americans. To be sure, Islam's influence may be self-limiting: 'unlike Marxism, Islam cannot reach beyond its cultural sphere: the age of converting entire peoples is past'.[23] There are political rather than religious reasons for the special appeal of Islam to the wretched of the earth. Mernissi wrote:

Seen today as the culture most capable of channeling popular frustrations, Islam gives the faithful enormous expectations of social solidarity. The sacred, after long being utilized to pacify the masses and keep them quiet, is today taking its revenge on those who have manipulated it. It has become, as at the time of its birth, a force for the destabilization of privilege, whether regional or global.[24]

But Islam is adhered to by very divergent groups. In many countries both incumbent leaders and the political opposition use Islam to legitimate their political programs. Over the years Islamic countries such as Egypt, Pakistan, Saudi Arabia, and Tunisia have been reliable allies of the West. Others like Iran, Iraq, Libya, and Syria have been its bitter enemies. One stereotype of Arab Muslims is as fabulously-wealthy oil-rich sheiks. But most Arabs are extremely poor, whether living in the Sudan, Jordan, or Oman. There is also a relatively weak connection between attitudes to the West and level of modernization. Before the 1991 Gulf war the most industrialized state in the Arab world was Saddam Hussein's Iraq. By contrast, traditional rule based on the past and the sacred 'groups together regimes as different as the kingdom of Saudi Arabia, the Iranian regime of Imam Khomeini or his caliph (successor), the military regime of Zia al-Haq in Pakistan, and the Sudanese regime that terrorizes its people in the name of the *sharia*'.[25] In short, groups from different and even conflicting backgrounds embrace the same Islamic faith.

Islamic resurgence has included a return to fundamentalism, witnessed in the case of Iran after the 1979 revolution and Afghanistan under the Taliban government from 1996 to 2001. It also has engendered a new class of modern Islamic leaders, as in Turkey, post-Zia Pakistan, and Malaysia, who are highly-educated, committed to economic growth, and place Islam in the mainstream of their societies. If Osama Bin Laden's Al-Qaeda and Islamic groups in Lebanon, Algeria, Nigeria and Indonesia have bitterly opposed democracy, other political leaders have embraced this system: 'The Islamization of democracy has been based upon a modern reinterpretation of traditional Islamic concepts of political deliberation or consultation (*shura*), community consensus (*ijma*), and personal interpretation (*ijtihad*) or reinterpretation to support notions of parliamentary democracy, representative elections, and religious reform'.[26]

Islam can hardly be approached, then, as a universalist political force. 'The contemporary Islamic revival is polycentric, heterogeneous, and multifaceted because of a number of factors. First, all four types of Islamic Revivalists (Fundamentalists, Traditionalists, Modernists, and Pragmatists) are very active simultaneously, and each group believes that it is working for the greater good of the *umma*'.[27]

Another reason is that like their Western counterparts, leaders of Islamic states put pursuit of national interest above other objectives. As an Arab scholar observed two decades ago: 'The institutions and policies of even the most fervently "Islamic" states cannot be explained without taking into account geographical position, economic needs, and the interests of dynasties and rulers'.[28] Only a few, such as Khomeini's Iran, Mohammed Omar's Afghanistan or Saddam's Iraq, have been prepared to commit national suicide to further broader objectives. Disunity in the Islamic world is no surprise to political scientists: 'in this age of nation-states, the twin ideals of nationalism and national interest are motivating the present leaders of most Muslim countries far more than the utopian ideal of an integrated and unified Islamic empire, or even the more attainable vision of a unified Islamic block'.[29] Nationalism has gnawed away at many state and international structures and has served less as a force for integration (as in the nineteenth century) than for disintegration. Consequently, 'nationalism...has further divided the Muslim world as a whole, and the leadership has pursued national interests at the expense of the *umma*. In the interests of realpolitik, Muslim nations have ignored fellow Muslims in distress, whether starving in Ethiopia and Somalia, or bearing Israeli assaults in southern Lebanon'.[30]

Neither anti-Americanism nor pro-Westernism, neither developmentalism nor traditionalism, have proved to be programs with a catch-all appeal for Islamic states. Islam is not a political monolith opposed to Western civilization. To the contrary, 'Monolithic Islam has been a recurrent Western myth which has never been borne out by the reality of Muslim history'.[31] If Islam has been inaccurately depicted as a cross-national monolith, so has the West in many Islamic societies: 'It is obvious that the powerful, monolithic West that haunts our Arab imagination is more fiction than fact.... Torn by ethnic and regional rivalries, it is disintegrating before our eyes'.[32]

The seeds of Islamic polycentrism were evident in the early twentieth-century efforts in Asia to overthrow colonial rule. Struggles for independence were not fueled by pan-Islamic ideology even though, as Indonesian novelist Pramoedya Ananta Toer narrated in his 'Buru Quartet', Islam was never far below the surface.[33] On obtaining independence such new states were led by Western-educated elites modeled on Western political and economic institutions and committed to the alluring Western ideology of modernization. At this juncture there was little strength to political Islam – 'using religion to control the government and imposing Islamic values on public space'.[34]

Since Islam is closely associated with the Arab world, has pan-Arabism emerged to embody an imagined *umma*? From its beginnings early in the twentieth century, pan-Arabism was as much a response to contact with the affluent West as it was a reaction, around 1914, to Young Turk nationalism or an ideological development of Islamic modernism.[35] Pan-Arab nationalism proved to be a shooting star, brilliant for the period that Gamal Abdel Nasser ruled Egypt but fading after his death in 1970. Nasser had been acutely aware how 'the most powerful political motivation in the present-day Arab world is the desire to redeem the century of humiliation at the hands of the West'.[36] His nationalization in 1956 of the Western-owned Suez canal gave him the credentials to lead the Arab world. Ultimately it became apparent that pan-Arabism was a thinly-disguised form of secular, primarily Egyptian, nationalism. Indeed, as one theorist has contended, any pan-nationalism will only succeed if 1) 'one state achieves leadership over others', or 2) 'popular movements which accept the pan-nationalist position . . . can impose it on particular states from below'.[37] Nasser's death marked the end of Egypt's role as disseminator of pan-Arabism. By contrast, in the 1990s fundamentalism sought to promote pan-Islam from below. In either case, Arab 'states have resisted all the "pan . . . ism" crises: pan-Arabism and pan-Islamism. Arab nationalists have secularized the notion of the *umma*'.[38] It is of little consequence, then, that Arabic is the sole official language of 17 independent Arab states since 'there is still a very real pan-Arab identity which is, for the foreseeable future, politically unrealizable'.[39]

Islam's radical leaders

In part for this very reason, the sustained effort to form an *umma* was undertaken in a non-Arab Middle East state. The accession to power in Iran of Ayatollah Khomeini in 1979 had been an implausible scenario: the likelihood that an aging fundamentalist cleric living in exile could topple the authoritarian US-backed regime of Shah Pahlavi and lead a national chant of *Marg bar Amerika* ('Death to America') seemed remote. But Khomeini rallied much of Iran around his message of anti-imperialism, an end to repression, and the building of a just society based on the teachings of the Qur'an. One explanation of his motives was that '[t]he empowerment granted by religious violence is especially appealing to those who have not had power before'.[40]

Islam represented not just a political alternative to the Shah's pro-Western regime but a theological imperative too. This was clearly formulated in the messianic constitution adopted after the revolution:

> The preamble to the constitution refers to the 'ideological mission' of the army and the Revolutionary Guard to 'extend the sovereignty of God's law throughout the world'. The constitution commits the government to strive for the political, cultural, and economic unity of the Islamic world. Khomeini often spoke of Islam as a potent weapon for the overthow of tyrants and for ridding the Islamic world of Israel, the great powers, and other alien influences.[41]

The revolutionary Iranian leadership adopted a universalist mission for itself. Evidence of this was the exhortation for the faithful making the pilgrimage to Mecca to stage an 'Islamic uprising' against the corrupt Saudi regime. Pro-Iranian groups in Lebanon proselytized on behalf of the founding of an Islamic state. Iran lent support to the mujahedeen fighting Soviet forces in Afghanistan, but was linked to terrorist acts against Americans from Berlin to Bierut, too. It seemed also to be involved in stirring Islamic unrest in distant Malaysia and the Philippines. Radical Islamic leaders in Iran were, therefore, 'committed to the pursuit of the vague but powerfully emotive slogans of the Iranian upheaval, such as "Neither East nor West", the export of the Islamic revolution, support for liberation movements abroad, support for the world's disinherited, and confrontation with the imperialist powers'.[42]

Due to the consolidation of his revolution and the ability to embarrass the US, the 'Great Satan', during the hostage crisis, Khomeini succeeded in reawakening radical elements in various parts of the Islamic world.[43] Earlier Libya's Muammar Qaddafi had tried to do the same. A decade before the Iranian revolution, the young army officer seized power and put forward a blueprint for the restoration of Arab and Muslim greatness.[44] Qaddafi's efforts did not appeal to the Islamic world for a variety of reasons. Very young and radical, leading a state distant from the lands of Mohammed, mixing politics and theology more than other Muslim rulers, and advocating an innovative but revisionist brand of Islam that had no resonance in fundamentalist circles, he was always unlikely to achieve leadership of the Muslim world. Paradoxically, when he turned to African unity in the late 1990s he enjoyed more success. The creation of the African Union to replace the Organization of African Unity in 2001 was largely his achievement.

It took the Iranian revolution to demonstrate how Islam 'is religion and state, governance and politics, economics and social organization, education and morals, worship and holy war'.[45] The revolution was the high point of state- based Islamic anti-Westernism, but

> [t]owards the end of the 1980s, the failure of the Islamist revolutionary idea brought about the drift of a revolutionary, political, Third World type of Islamism, incarnated in the Iranian revolution, toward a puritanical, preaching, populist, conservative neofundamentalism, financed until recently by Saudi Arabia but violently anti-Western, particularly since the end of the East-West confrontation has ceased to cast communism as a foil.[46]

The Algerian Islamic Salvation Front (FIS) was one example; Saudi sheik Osama bin Ladin, who the US accused of masterminding the terrorist attacks of September 11 2001, was another.

A bungled effort to use pan-Islam for political purposes was made by Iraqi leader Saddam Hussein in 1991. He justified the invasion of Kuwait in terms of artificial, colonially-drawn borders. 'Kuwait Incorporated' seemed more a

London-based financial house than a country or nation. But his call for oil-producing states to comply with OPEC-set production quotas was based on a pan-Islamic logic. He called for Islamic solidarity in the face of the massive airlift of Western forces into the Persian Gulf region in 1990 and 1991. Few Islamic leaders offered Saddam support, though millions of Muslims throughout the world sympathized with his cause. Islamic leaders were more aware of Saddam's duplicity than were average Muslims, for '[p]erhaps nothing seemed more incongruous than that Saddam Hussein, the head of a secularist regime who had ruthlessly suppressed Islamic movements at home and abroad, would cloak himself in the mantle of Islam and call for a jihad'.[47]

Whereas individual political leaders, many with unquestionable personal charisma like Nasser, Khomeini, and Qaddafi, had been unable to convert their prestige into broader transnational Islamic movements, some pan-Islamic institution-building has taken place over the past three decades. Shortly after the 1967 Six Day War, foreign ministers of Muslim countries met in Morocco. In March 1970, they founded the Organization of the Islamic Conference (OIC) which had several important objectives. The OIC was to promote Islamic solidarity and coordinate struggle against vestiges of colonialism and imperialism. Other goals were to assist Palestinians in securing a homeland and to protect Islamic holy sites. In 1975, under the auspices of the OIC, an Islamic Development Bank was formed. Conforming with Islamic law, it makes interest-free loans to poorer Islamic states. By 1995 the OIC had 54 member states and 20 other affiliated groups. Nevertheless, the organization was hamstrung in achieving political unity. 'The OIC's chronic inability to enforce the collective will over the objections of specific member nations represents the subordination of international Islamic law to Western international law in the Muslim world'. Specifically, '[t]he law of individual states – whether secular or religious – takes precedence over *shariah* law at the subsystemic and systemic levels. Submission of member nations to OIC rulings based on the *Shariah*, no matter if there is overwhelming support of most members, is wholly voluntary'.[48]

The resurgence of Islamic radicalism and even its recourse to terrorism have been the result of the failed efforts of Islamic states successfully to imitate outside models of development. In part, Islamic resurgence represents a turn inward toward Qur'anic teaching for answers to contemporary problems. In part it is a reaction to setbacks:

a sense that existing political, economic, and social systems had failed; a disenchantment with, and at times a rejection of, the West; a quest for identity and greater authenticity; and the conviction that Islam provides a self-sufficient ideology for state and society, a valid alternative to secular nationalism, socialism, and capitalism.[49]

(Ab)uses of the Other

It has been the West that Islam has used as its Other, its foil, to develop its own identity. As we encountered in the case of Russia, the West can be both uncritically admired and universally envied. 'It is a given that the West, which flaunts before us the dream of one world, bears responsibility for the future of humanity. Its responsibility is heavy because it holds a quasi-monopoly on decision making in matters of science and technology. It alone decides if satellites will be used to educate Arabs or to drop bombs on them'.[50] The sense of inferiority that invidious comparisons drawn with the West inevitably engender produces a backlash. Not to be overlooked, of course, are the centuries of European colonial dominance in the Middle East, North Africa, and elsewhere which 'left a legacy of both admiration of Western power, science, and technology and resentment of Western dominance, penetration, and exploitation'.[51] The attitude of a fundamentalist regime towards the leader of the Western world illustrated the schizophrenia: 'Iranians crave America's attention, be it strong approval, disapproval, or, most confusing, both at the same time'.[52] This was clearly seen in the Iran–US soccer match at the 1998 World Cup, which meant more to Iranians than Americans.

In its turn, the West has skillfully used the Arab world and Islam to construct its Other. While Western states are legitimate and democratic, the majority of Asian countries is depicted as searching for political legitimacy or, more recently, is regarded as 'democratically challenged'. Western writers often see this as congenital and seek to find 'biological, cultural, and/or religious causes for this disability'.[53] But as Nobel Prize laureate in economics, Amartya Sen, set out, '[t]here is clearly a tendency in America and Europe to assume, if only implicitly, the primacy of political freedom and democracy as a fundamental and ancient feature of Western culture – one not to be easily found in Asia'.[54] Sen found that many Asian historical leaders did value freedom and tolerance, such as Ashoka, emperor of a vast Indian empire in the third century BC, and Mughal ruler Akbar who reigned from 1556 to 1605. He found no support for the hypothesis that a grand dichotomy of values existed between the West and Asia.[55]

So we have to return to historical factors for helping explain the clash between the two civilizations. 'Both Christianity and Islam claimed a universal mission; each was a transnational community based upon common belief and a vocation to be an example to the nations of the world, the vehicle for the spread and triumph of God's kingdom'.[56] The Crusades that lasted from the eleventh to thirteenth centuries in and around the Holy Land have been viewed by some Muslim scholars as a historic precedent foreshadowing centuries of aggression of the Christian West on the Muslim world. Consequently,

[i]f there is an Islamic threat, there has also been a Western threat – of political and religiocultural imperialism, a political occupation accompanied by cultural invasion. As a result, many in the Muslim world, like

their counterparts in the West, opt for easy anti-imperialist slogans and demonization. At its worst, both sides have engaged in a process of 'mutual satanization'.[57]

Misunderstandings and recriminations do not belong to history. It has been argued in the West that the Islamic world never fully experienced the age of enlightenment and humanism. 'Humanistic ideas – freedom of thought, the sovereignty of the individual, the right to freedom of action, tolerance – were propagated in the West through secular schools. With a few rare exceptions (notably Turkey), the modern Muslim state has never called itself secular, and has never committed itself to teaching individual initiative'.[58] It is claimed that leaders of the anti-colonial struggle and the post-colonial ruling elite have had no interest in rehabilitating reason and liberty in Islamic societies. Indeed, '[t]he nationalist governments that supplanted them [the colonial powers] were just as brutal and just as hostile to the flowering of the scientific spirit and individual initiative'.[59]

It is ironic, then, to consider how the postcolonial governments in Islamic states have been the targets of radical Islamic groups as well as of secular progressive ones. Indeed, Osama bin Laden and his Al-Qaeda organization may arguably have been more bent on installing fundamentalist regimes in Islamic states than on destroying the US. Al-Qaeda originated in a pan-Islamic religious movement called Salafi that viewed the Islam practiced by most Muslim today as polluted, especially by the 'polytheism' that was produced when Islamic governments accepted laws fabricated by men. Salafi followers are a diverse group, disagreeing in particular on methods to adopt, but they concur on the desirability of a return to the pristine Islamic belief system that characterized the time of the Prophet. Salafi offshoots include the conservative Wahhabi orientation in Saudi Arabia, the Muslim Brotherhood in Egypt, and Al-Qaeda.

Salafi goals explain why 'idol-worshipping' Islamic regimes are the target of fundamentalist wrath perhaps as much as America. But those involved in this Islamic schism are not the only ones who take this view. An article in *Foreign Affairs*, a foreign policy journal sometimes viewed as a semi-official organ of the US government, made clear that bin Laden was trying to ensnare the US in an Islamic civil war:

Polarizing the Islamic world between the *umma* and the regimes allied with the United States would help achieve bin Laden's primary goal: furthering the cause of Islamic revolution within the Muslim world itself, in the Arab lands especially and in Saudi Arabia above all. He had no intention of defeating America. War with the United States was not a goal in and of itself but rather an instrument designed to help his brand of extremist Islam survive and flourish among the believers. Americans, in short, have been drawn into somebody else's civil war.[60]

In his 'Declaration of War' issued in August 1996, bin Laden called on Muslims to unify in the struggle against the 'Crusader-Zionist' enemy occupying Islamic holy lands. As he concluded, 'O you horses [soldiers] of Allah, ride and march on. This is the time of hardship, so be tough. And know that your gathering and your cooperation to liberate the sanctities of Islam is the right step toward unifying the word of the Umma under the banner of "No God but Allah"'.[61] The declaration called for the overthrow of the Saudi government and of other Islamic governments that cooperated with the US. The appeal to Islamic militants residing in many different states to take up arms explains why fundamentalism itself became organizationally polycentric.

Radical Islamic groups in various regions have developed constituencies that oppose the imperialist West. These have included the Muslim Brotherhood in Egypt, the Jamaat-i-Islami (Islamic Society) and Harakat ul-Mujahideen (HUM) originating in Pakistan and Kashmir, joined in the 1980s by AMAL (Lebanese Resistance Battalions), Hamas, Hizbullah (Party of God), and Islamic Jihad, all active in Israeli-occupied territories and in Lebanon. Prior to the US war on terrorism, para-military Islamic organizations had sprung up to fight not just in Israel but also in Afghanistan, Bosnia, Chechnya, Tajikistan, and Kashmir. But other groups had prepared the ground earlier for the revival of Islam. Thus '[t]he Brotherhood charged that faith in the West was misplaced. Western democracy had not merely failed to check but contributed to authoritarianism (the manipulation of the masses by modern elites), economic exploitation, corruption, and social injustice'.[62] This was particularly unfortunate since the West acted at cross purposes with many Muslim movements. As Said convincingly argued, '[t]he irony is that Western views of Islam on the whole prefer to associate "Islam" with what many Muslims themselves are opposed to in the current scene: punishment, autocracy, medieval modes of logic, theocracy'.[63]

But there was one overriding factor that contributed to the resurgence of radical Islam – the dominant US role in world politics and its use of dominance to vilify Islam even before 11 September 2001. US support for repressive regimes (the Shah's Iran, Zia's Pakistan) and for feudal monarchies (Kuwait, Saudi Arabia) intensified anti-Americanism, leading to the self-fulfilling prophecy of Islamic hostility to the West. 'American ignorance of and hostility toward Islam and the Middle East, often critiqued as a "Christian Crusader" mentality influenced by Orientalism and Zionism, were blamed for misguided US political–military policies: support for the "un-Islamic" Shah of Iran, massive military and economic funding of Israel, and the backing of an unrepresentative Christian-controlled government in Lebanon'.[64] US diplomatic clout in putting together a coalition against Iraq in 1991 and its military might in quickly defeating the Arab state stood in contrast to the plodding reaction to halt Serb atrocities against Bosnia's and Kosovo's Muslims. The resurgence of Islam began in a world where American hegemony had not been fully established, and one of the main goals in US foreign policy today is to establish its dominance precisely so as to roll back Islamic fundamentalism in the name of war on terrorism.

Islam has been hamstrung by its own lack of solidarity. Part of the reason for this is that, as we have suggested, Islam is a monotheistic but not monolithic religion. Another part rests in its self-defeating objectives. One writer has argued, not completely persuasively, that

> [t]here is no Islamist 'culture', and the *kulturkampf* of the Islamists against a culture that is an obstacle to pure devotion paves the way for the universal culture: that of Americanization . . . . The rejection of Western culture is thus on the order of a curse, a cry, an accusation; but it also has an element of fascination. Neofundamentalist society does not represent hatred of the other, but rather hatred of oneself and of one's desires.[65]

This type of psychological explanation can lead to facile conclusions unhelpful in understanding the discourse of the Other.

Conclusions on Islam as transnational community

Just as nationalism has dismantled empires, destabilized sovereign states, and hindered regional integration, so too it has proven to be an obstacle to the creation of a transnational Islamic community. Purist Islamic thinkers have pointed out how '[t]he moral basis of the modern national state, consisting as it does of secular, utilitarian principles, and narrow ethnic and national loyalties, is the antithesis of the true Islamic state; this latter state rises above such narrow loyalties, addresses itself to humanity as a whole, and recognizes only God as sovereign'.[66] Yet ethnicization of the Islamic world is a political fact. While it is sometimes depicted by the West as an integrated pan-nationalist movement, we have found little evidence of a successful construction of a common home.

Latin America

Identity and anti-Americanism

The identities of some nations are more dependent than others on what they are not. Their nationalism is often expressed as alterity to the perceived character of some greater nation in whose shadow they live. Many examples can be found in the contemporary world. Austrian self-identity is regularly formulated as not being German; indeed, a witticism has it, that the biggest difference between the two is language. A more recent effort to construct identity by employing alterity – what the nation is not – was undertaken, not very successfully, in Belarus; nationalist intellectuals argue how the history, language, and culture of the new state differs from Russian, but not all Belarusans are convinced.

Writers describing Canadian identity usually stress the ways it differs from American identity. One Canadian writer observed how '[o]ne primal definition of Canadianism has to be that we are among the few peoples in the world who, given a chance to be Americans, have chosen not to'.[67] Canadian novelist Robertson Davies was more emphatic: 'Americans are precisely what we are not and what we don't want to be'.[68] Following US independence, north of the border '[f]rom 1783 to the 1880s anti-Americanism was an olio of antirepublican prejudice, class consciousness, personal ambition, sanctimony about British moral superiority, envy over American energy and success, and loyalist justification for survival as losers in the War of Independence'.[69] Over the next two centuries, class-based politics and vested economic interests shaped anti-American sentiments above the forty-ninth parallel even if 'Canadian anti-Americanism has rarely been overtly xenophobic'.[70] As we see below, the other neighbor of the US, Mexico, developed an ambivalent anti-Americanism based on American territorial conquests and its own weaknesses.

Anti-Americanism is not only about identity politics. For two international relations experts the phenomenon represented an 'undifferentiated attack on the foreign policy, society, culture and values of the United States'.[71] Anti-Americanism could be issue-oriented (for example, policy disagreements), ideological (usually Marxist), instrumental (used by elites to mobilize support), or revolutionary (overthrow of a pro-American government by the political opposition). Paul Hollander believed it was more visceral than goal- or issue-oriented: it is 'a particular mind-set, an attitude of distaste, aversion or intense hostility the roots of which may be found in matters unrelated to the actual qualities or attributes of American society or the foreign policies of the United States'.[72] Third world variants also included hostility to US institutions, policies, values, economics, culture, national character, people, behavior, and dress.[73] A British academic clarified what anti-Americanism was not: it 'should not be confused with opposition to particular US policies or administrations'.[74] Instead the primitive or instinctive variant was based on envy and resentment: 'Anti-Americanism may be defined as straightforward opposition, ranging from distaste to animus, to the cultural and political values of the United States'.[75] Communist-rooted anti-Americanism also existed for a long time but '[a]s the ideology of Communism dies, anti-Americanism becomes simply destructive, critical, and bitter, and such negativism becomes an ideology in itself'.[76] A second British scholar identified both a conservative cultural elite and radical political circles as the carriers of anti-Americanism, thereby constituting an unholy alliance of 'snobbery and socialism'.[77] A study of Chilean *pensadores* on the right pointed out how they were 'aggressively opposed to American culture which they see as "lacking culture, grace, beauty, as well as widespread appreciation of aesthetic and spiritual values" '.[78] But intellectuals often have different outlooks compared to political and business elites. For example, '[a]lthough Canadian intellectuals and artists remain largely opposed to Americanization, the elites in society no longer resist it'.[79] In the era of globalization and free trade regimes, much the same is now true for Latin America.

Continental nationalism in Latin America

Defining the nationalism of a state or group of states in terms of opposition to a more powerful country is one way to understand 'Latin Americanism.' Clearly having a different history, culture, and language from the US and Canada, in the first half of the nineteenth century Latin America still shared many values with the former British colonies. American relations with the new independent states of Latin America were fashioned by 'the fusion of the benign nationalism inherited from England with the mystique of the Western Hemisphere idea – the idea that the peoples of the New World form a coherent, kindred group set apart by Nature and their nature from the wicked warring peoples of the Old World'.[80] This was the philosophical reasoning underpinning the Monroe Doctrine adopted in 1823 that opposed European intervention in the Americas.

From the Latin American perspective, in the mid-nineteenth century nationalism in most of the independent states was still influenced by a form of continentalism, or pan-Latin Americanism. Despite the failure of South American liberator Simon Bolivar and many of the generation of 1810 – the *proceres* – to achieve the political unification of Latin America, the notion of *la patria grande* continued to serve as a mythical identity and home for many peoples of Latin America. The imitation of divisive European nationalisms at the expense of a unifying *Americas* nationalism aborted Bolivar's project.[81]

Some historians claim that the fragmentation of Latin America was the result of the self-interest of colonial and postcolonial elites rather than of separate identities or national differences. In this view

> the independence movement was perverted from its true purpose by selfish oligarchs and military leaders, who perpetuated the injustices and localisms of the old regime under the guise of a fragmented nationalism borrowed from Europe. To make matters still worse, in Spanish America the configuration of the new states slavishly followed that of the political subdivisions of the colonial period, and differed from it mainly in that nationalism further widened the artificial and frustrating gap between one subdivision and another.[82]

The result was that the map of Latin America – like those of Africa and Asia – was regarded as a vestige of colonialism, thereby obscuring the role played by self-interested oligarchs.

Growing Latin American disunity in the early nineteenth century coincided with a period of American expansionism, and the main victim of these countervailing tendencies was Mexico. As a result of the US–Mexican war and internal instability within Mexico between 1836 and 1848, the country lost half of its territory. Had the civil war not broken out in the US, further American expansion into Spanish America seemed probable. This period demonstrated

> the strength of the expansionist forces in the United States and the weakness of the Latin American republics. This variance remained a constant in the international relations of the continent and hence a constant in the development of Latin American nationalism. The fear of the *coloso del norte* was real enough and well founded. It was further strengthened by the continued and growing penetration of Latin American countries by American venture capital, which often used piratical means to its ends.[83]

By the turn of the twentieth century, the half-developed sense of continentalism waned. The Spanish–American war and US military intervention in Cuba highlighted the contrasting political visions of the US and states in the Caribbean basin. While welcoming Cuba's independence from Spain, many Latin American nationalists foresaw, correctly, that the US would step in to take over the hegemonic role formerly played by Iberia. Panama's secession from Colombia in 1903 with US backing furnished another example of American intervention in the region. During President Theodore Roosevelt's administration in particular, the Monroe doctrine asserting the US right to police the Western hemisphere was given new vigor.

The beginnings of anti-Americanism

In the shadow of American power, literati in Latin America articulated both a continental nationalism and 'Yankeephobia'. Cuban poet Jose Marti – revered both by the Castro regime and anti-communist Miami exiles – denounced the evils of American society in a book describing his travels in the US.[84] Representing a form of pan-Hispanism that emerged at the end of the nineteenth century, the Uruguayan writer Jose Enrique Robo published a widely-read book, *Ariel*, which extolled Latin America as the inheritor of the great Mediterranean civilizations of Greece and Rome (personified by Ariel, a character from Shakespeare's *The Tempest*, who was moral and spiritual) while denouncing the US as uncivilized and imperial (the greedy and vulgar Caliban). In Argentina, literary nationalism reached its apogee with the publication of Ricardo Rojas' *The Nationalist Restoration* in 1909. The symbolist poet Ruben Dario, who lived mainly in Paris, also extolled Latin American civilization while castigating Roosevelt's meddling. These critiques of the US formed part of a longer-term trend of Latin American writers attacking the US. From the 1950s on, 'the Colombian novelist Gabriel Garcia Marquez, the Chilean poet Pablo Neruda, the Uruguayan writer Eduardo Galeano, Mexico's Carlos Fuentes, and Guatemala's Miguel Angel Asturias, followed in the tradition of Rodo, blaming Yankee imperialism for Latin America's problems'.[85]

Once again, the US evoked admiration, envy, and dread in the Other. One writer explained this phenomenon in the following way: 'Latin American nationalism appears to be a by-product of the encounter with Western capitalism'. In particular, 'Latin American nationalism, whether continental or individual, found an easily recognizable target, the materialistic Yankee, who in his pursuit of earthly happiness seemed to be the opposite of the Latin American ideal'.[86]

In the first decades of the twentieth century, celebrations of the centenary of independence in many Latin American states such as Argentina, Chile, Colombia, Mexico, and Venezuela, fueled the emergence of state nationalism and the corresponding decline of pan-Americanism. Political developments in the interwar period reinforced the sense of Latin Americans' separateness from British-colonized North America.

> It was brought home to them, as never before, that, though in varying degrees, all the Latin American countries were relatively weak, relatively poor, and both Latin (which set them off from the United States) and American (which set them off from Europe). The lesson was learned in a series of concrete situations, extending from the long controversy with the United States over intervention and the disaster of the depression decade after 1929 to the United States's preoccupation after World War II with Europe and Asia, which provoked a common Latin American complaint of neglect.[87]

In place of hemisphere-wide pan-Americanism, then, emerged a pan-Latin Americanism that specifically excluded the US. The rise of left-wing movements underscored how Latin America and the US were ideologically irreconcilable. By the 1930s communist parties had been organized in many Latin American countries and strongly influenced by the Comintern – the Kremlin-controlled Communist International – they made anti-imperialism, which became equated with anti-Americanism, part of their program. But as elsewhere, communists were not averse to using nationalism to promote their interests, and this served to divide further not just the individual states but the Communist movement in Latin America.[88]

For a time, Franklin Roosevelt's Good Neighbor policy kept the anti-imperialist forces off balance. But large US investments in the region needed to be protected and recourse to military intervention was commonplace. In the short term such intervention proved effective in safeguarding US interests, but over the longer term it contributed to ingraining in much of the

Latin American population resentment towards the self-ascribed *caudillo* role the US played.[89] A vicious circle followed. Large sums of money were poured into third world states 'with the aim of stopping communism, promoting United States trade, and above all, developing a cadre of native allies whose express raison d'etre seemed to be the transformation of backward countries into mini-America'. Inevitably, however, 'the initial investments required additional sums and increased military support to keep them going. And this in turn produced the interventions all over Asia and Latin America which regularly pitted the United States against almost every brand of native nationalism'.[90]

After the Second World War the US retreated into isolationism. When it did engage in international politics, as through the Truman Doctrine aimed at containing communism, it was largely in the European and Asian theaters. Reacting to US disinterest in and complacency about 200-million strong Latin America, Argentinian populist leader Juan Peron issued his 'Declaration of Economic Independence' in 1947 underscoring how this Southern Cone state wished to control its own destiny. As part of his social revolution, Peron intended to deprive the *vendepatria* oligarchy – members of the local ruling class who had enriched themselves by selling economic control of Argentina to foreigners – of their power while providing greater social benefits to the lower classes, generally more anti-American than the upper classes. Peron's economic nationalism was disowned by his successors but its uniqueness lay in being advanced by a populist, quasi-fascist movement unconnected to the traditional left.

Peron's authoritarian regime also put forward a distinctive foreign policy program, grandiosely termed the 'Third Position'. It envisaged the alignment of Latin American states in an independent bloc promoting the interests of this region. This bloc would be independent from both West and East. Given geopolitical realities, the call for Latin America to distance itself equally from the US and the USSR was transparently anti-American. It criticized long-standing American involvement in the region while recognizing that Russia never had much connection to these countries. Not surprisingly, Peron's Third Position had little real impact other than contributing to furthering anti-Americanism as part of the nationalist discourse of the region.

By the 1950s, both leftist and conservative groups subscribed to forms of Latin American nationalism, and both took aim at the pervasive economic influence exerted by the US. The critique of US economic colonialism peaked in the 1970s when some Latin American social scientists developed dependency theory. It blamed US capital for creating a cycle of poverty, need for foreign investment, and consequent economic dependency of Latin American states on the US. A succinct summary of the theory was that '[b]ut for North American development, there would have been no Latin American underdevelopment; that but for Latin American underdevelopment, there would have been no North American development.'[91] President Kennedy's response in 1961 to economic grievances advanced by Latin America was to organize the Alliance for Progress, a pale version of the Marshall plan for European reconstruction developed after the Second World War. After that the US provided little other institutional support to the region.

Pan-Latin American nationalism was particularly important in integrating the many political particularisms of the region: developmentalism and anti-imperialism, industrialism and agrarianism, syndicalism and populism, democracy and *personalismo*, Hispanism and Indianism. Many of these features making up Latin American uniqueness are the consequence of its encounter with Western capital and with the world's superpower.[92]

The rise and decline of anti-Americanism

When a nationalist ideology includes tenets with which a number of nations can identify, it has the potential to become pan-nationalism. An example is a set of ideas such as anti-Americanism and economic emancipation from Western capitalism that can arouse *la conciencia americana* and sense of Latin American community. For many Latin American leaders, from Peron to Castro, from the Sandinistas in Nicaragua to Hugo Chavez in Venezuela, patriotism entails opposition to US economic and political policies. National consciousness includes affirming Iberic identities but also Indianism, exemplified by Tupac Amaru in the Peruvian jungle and the Zapatistas in southern Mexico.

Efforts at transnational institution-building reflect the spirit of continental nationalism. In 1960 the Organization of American States (OAS) issued its Declaration of San Jose condemning outside (that is, non-US) interference in Latin American affairs. The Latin American Free Trade Area (LAFTA) and several regional organizations (Mercosur, the Andean Pact, the Central American Free Trade Association) were further attempts to spur Latin Americanism. The 1994 Partnership for Development and Prosperity signed by 34 Western Hemisphere leaders also marked a step towards closer integration and away from the *dependencia* paradigm.

A caesura in the rise of Latin American nationalism was the Cuban revolution of 1959. Its many dimensions – Marxist, populist, *caudillaje* (strongman rule), *anti-gringo*, nationalist – had something to appeal to most disaffected groups in Latin America. The entrenched elites of Latin America were threatened by the broad appeal of the Cuban revolution and the activist anti-imperialist foreign policy that Castro pursued in the 1960s. In his early years in power he demonstrated that it was possible to be a communist dictator and remain popular. One way he accomplished this was by playing the *anti-gringo* card to which the Kennedy administration, through its bungling of the Bay of Pigs invasion by anti-Castro exiles, proved an inadvertent accessory. More than any other revolution, Castro's was inextricably linked to the hegemonic role that the US had been playing in Latin

America. His radical nationalism was a singular success on a continent without any:

> such nationalism represents a violent reaction, or 'lashing back,' against collective humiliation, exploitation, and mistreatment by a smaller or weaker country against this powerful, overbearing nation at whose hands the humiliations were suffered. American military interventions (as in Cuba, the Dominican Republic, Grenada, Guatemala, Mexico, Nicaragua, and Panama), economic dominance, and, of late, cultural penetration provide the background against which these sentiments developed.[93]

As in the case of Islam, the Other was critical to forging a people's nationalism: 'it is hard to separate this variety of anti-Americanism from nationalism and nationalistic self-assertion'. Ironically, then, the US was indispensable to keeping Castro in power for four decades.

But the weight of anti-Americanism in shaping nationalist discourse has not been as great since the era of the *guerrillos* of the 1970s nor outside of Cuba. To be sure an anti-American current has persisted in Mexico, for example: 'Even the modern Mexican middle classes continue to harbor deep feelings of resentment and even anger at the United States. Their penchant for American lifestyles and products should not be mistaken for an ebbing of traditional suspicion and hostility towards the United States.'[94] But as Jorge Castaneda observed over a decade ago, a 'modernizing nationalism' allowed Mexican nationalists to recruit popular support for economic reform and democratization precisely because reform programs were implemented without US pressure or intervention.[95] The most effective way that Washington has to disarm anti-Americans is, then, to stay out of other countries' politics.

As a counterpoint to the revolutionary anti-Americanism of the Fidelistas and Sandinistas, let us examine the discourse of the Zapatista Front leaders in Chiapas, Mexico, from the 1990s on. Did *anti-yanquismo* still constitute a central platform in the populist, nationalist rhetoric of an insurgency group that emerged after the Cold War?

The uprising of the indigenous people, predominantly of Mayan descent, was timed to coincide with the formal start of the North Atlantic Free Trade Agreement (NAFTA), on January 1, 1994. Aware that their small farms could not compete with the highly-mechanized farming of Canada and the US, the Zapatista Army for National Liberation (EZLN) organized a revolt against the federal government. At the World Economic Forum held in Davos, Switzerland, in early 1994, then president Carlos Salinas de Gortari made light of the Chiapas uprising. It was 'a local problem in a region of extreme poverty where there is a large indigenous population'. He claimed that it had not been an indigenous uprising but organized by a well-trained armed group with a radical ideology. Salinas viewed the insurgency through the same prism as the US.

As the conflict festered, a letter was sent by Chase Manhattan Bank to newly-elected Mexican president Ernesto Zedillo urging him to put an end to the insurgency. With billions of dollars of investments in Mexico, the bank was concerned about the Zapatistas: 'While Chiapas, in our opinion, does not pose a fundamental threat to the Mexican political stability, it is perceived to be so by many in the investment community. The government will have to eliminate the Zapatistas to demonstrate their effective control of the national territory and of security policy'.[96] A few weeks later, in February 1995, Zedillo ordered the army to attack Zapatista-held villages in the southern state. The Clinton administration expressed understanding for Zedillo's actions. Under NAFTA Mexico had greater economic importance to the US just as Mexico became more dependent on its northern neighbor for financial stability.[97]

It is clear that '[a]nti-Americanism in Mexico has become incorporated into the political culture, turned into a major source of legitimacy of the political system and a key component of national pride and identity'.[98] But it has more symbolic than practical effects. Because they represented indigenous people the Zapatistas were not even prepared to play the 'Mexican' card of anti-American symbolism and rhetoric. Led by the publicity-savvy 'subcommandante Marcos', they also refrained from articulating separatist demands. Instead they highlighted the 400 years of oppression suffered by the Indian population at the hands of colonialists and they now demanded 'to govern themselves within the borders of their own communities'.[99] In short, they asked for more political autonomy from the center. By not engaging in the radical discourse used by many leftist movements (like the Sandinistas in the 1980s), the EZLN obtained the support of the local Catholic church as well as of liberal groups in the US and Western Europe sympathetic to the plight of the indigeneous peoples of the Americas.

The Zapatista case illustrates that if *anti-yanquismo* was a mobilizing force in parts of Latin America in the 1960s, it was recognized as counterproductive from the 1990s. Identity politics provided a more effective platform for advancing the interests of oppressed groups than ideological sloganeering. The Zapatistas' arrival in Mexico City in March 2001 differed radically from Castro's entry into Havana in 1959 or the Sandinistas' appearance in Managua in 1979. Incumbent officials greeted them and parliament opened the door to them.

To be sure, the American flag was still occasionally burned in Bolivia and Colombia, most often in reaction to cutoffs in US aid or US refusal to certify that a country's counternarcotics campaign was satisfactory. The presence of US Drug Enforcement Agency teams in Colombia and Peru contributed further to the perception that US interventionism had assumed new forms and adopted new pretexts but remained committed to protecting its economic interests at all costs. On the other hand, the US flag was raised in places unimaginable two decades earlier. In Nicaragua the Sandinistas flew it beside their own banner in election rallies in 2001.

Anti-Americanism has been put on hold, then, but it has not completely disappeared: 'Although talk of dependency is no longer fashionable, resentment in Latin America about the stance and style of the United States lurks not far below the surface'.[100] Can *anti-yanquismo* still galvanize nationalism in Latin America?[101] Surprisingly little academic research has been carried out on the topic.[102] A number of the studies carried out made no pretense of being objective. On the left, Noam Chomsky charged that American cover-ups of its clandestine military actions in Central America taken alone fueled anti-American sentiments and led to the growth of guerrilla groups in El Salvador, Guatemala, and Nicaragua.[103] But in the 1990s the Clinton administration's promotion of democracy in Latin and particularly Central America removed the sting from the anti-American forces.

By contrast, conservative writing identifying reasons for anti-Americanism often portrays it as a gratuitous attack by the powerless on an easy scapegoat. In the 1980s, when the Reagan administration was providing support for counter-insurgency movements in El Salvador (with its shadowy death squads) and Nicaragua (the Contras), three largely polemical studies sought to dismiss the importance of rising anti-Americanism. One alleged that '[t]he objective of the Third World ideology is to accuse and, if possible, destroy the developed societies, not to develop the backward societies'.[104] Another cited the importance Americans attach to being 'trusted and respected' rather than 'liked' for the unpopularity of the US in Europe and elsewhere.[105] A third contended that 'Latin America has paid dearly for those decades lost to excessive nationalism, "dependency", and flirtation with socialism and the nonaligned movement'.[106] A turn away from anti-Americanism would promote economic growth: 'Recognition that Latin America's problems are rooted in the Latin American mind, not in the evil designs of foreign devils, is a crucial first step toward fundamental change'.[107] As in the case of Islam, then, it was supposedly the problematic nature of Latin American culture, specifically its *anti-gringo* thread, that explained its underdevelopment and lack of modernization. Finally, in a comparative study of anti-Americanism that encompassed the mass media and universities in the US, as well as Canadian, Mexican, and Western European variants, Hollander stressed how politically convenient it was for many groups to attack Goliath.[108] Little consideration was given to American actions that could evoke an anti-American backlash.

Conclusions on anti-Americanism

From this analysis of Latin America as well as of the Islamic *umma*, it becomes clear that nationalism organized around a transnational program that attacks the global hegemon has had limited success. Such pan-nationalism seems unable to bridge the gap between individual nation states and the collective interests of a group of states. It may be because pan-nationalism is not *sensu stricto* a nationalism, embraced by one nation, that it has made few inroads. But political factors should be considered too. In a one-superpower world, anti-Americanism is a high-risk approach for any country to adopt. As one illustration, in the months preceding the 1991 Gulf War the US went about constructing a multinational anti-Iraqi coalition and threatened to terminate aid and credit lines to any state in the Gulf region which sided with Saddam. When Yemen refused to be bullied, it was punished with the loss of billions of dollars of investment. Symptomatic of the dilemma in which weak states found themselves was the headline in an influential American newspaper in 1995: 'Yankee Come Back: American Money Makes the Whole World Sing'.[109] A second example is Pakistani President Pervez Musharraf's acquiescence in October 2001 to US demands for the withdrawal of his political and military support for the Taliban regime in Afghanistan. No popular anti-American backlash followed in Pakistan that was capable of overthrowing Musharraf.

Today movements exhorting anti-Americanism and anti-Westernism seem more counterproductive than constructive. Ultra-nationalism in unstable states and banal nationalism in secure ones are commonplace and there is little wiggle room for unified pan-nationalist movements to insert themselves. Only capital has had success in building a transnational home. Both the state system and globalization processes, then, mitigate against the emergence of pan movements. The first pays homage to the independence of the individual state while the second structures the state's dependence on international capital. As a result any supranationalist movement faces insurmountable obstacles.

7
Nationalisms, Homes, and Hostilities

Westerncentricity

In *The Spectre of Comparisons*, Benedict Anderson recalls being asked in 1963 by a European diplomat to translate a speech given by Indonesian president Sukarno. Unexpectedly, in the middle of his speech, Sukarno began to discuss Adolf Hitler, describing him as a clever, idealistic, and patriotic leader. Anderson reported he felt vertigo as he listened to the account: 'For the first time in my young life I had been invited to see my Europe as through an inverted telescope'.[1] Characteristics that evoked opprobrium in one civilization could elicit praise in another.

It is unclear whether Sukarno wished merely to provoke Western diplomats and cause them to reflect on ethnocentrism, as Anderson subsequently did. His clinical assessment of Hitler reminded Anderson of his own school-teachers who spoke dispassionately of the deeds of Nero, Genghis Khan, and Pizarro. The inverted telescope was in use again. We can ask, then, whether the way nationalisms, especially of faraway and poorly-known peoples, have been presented to Western publics is not also an example of the use of the inverted telescope?

Intercultural breakdowns are commonplace in politics and can sometimes lead to tragic consequences. Sensing imminent conflict, Lieutenant-General Romeo Dallaire, the Canadian commander of UN peacekeeping forces in Rwanda, pleaded with his superiors at the United Nations to dispatch several hundred UN troops and disperse them to strategic locations in the country. He was certain that this preventive measure – a real-life example of the 'ethnic early warning systems' that attracted scholarly interest and grant-writing – could stem the outbreak of ethnic violence. Dallaire received a reply from the office of UN Secretary General Boutros Boutros-Ghali to do nothing. The US was not interested in increased intervention in Central Africa and the UN secretariat went along. Three months after Dallaire's first warning, mass killings began in Rwanda that led to over a million deaths. Blame for the slaughter was placed squarely on the murderous ethnonationalisms rampant among many African groups. The Canadian lieutenant-general returned home and was hospitalized with psychosis arising from the barbarism he had witnessed.

The Balkans have for some time been defined in the West as an ethnic powderkeg. For several years after the conflict in Bosnia, Western alliance leaders warned of the dangers of a new war in Kosovo. Serb nationalism was incurable, they charged, and would precipitate a conflict. War in Kosovo turned out to be a self-fulfilling prophecy. This time the West was determined to act. Preparations were made not for humanitarian assistance to the Kosovar Albanians but for a bombing campaign against Serbia. No people, including the Kosovars, want their territory to serve as the battlefield for international conflict. During the Cold War, many West Germans demonstrated against militarization of the country because they were concerned that a conventional or even theater nuclear war could devastate it. Canadians protested against American nuclear bases and weapons-testing in their country, fearing that in a strategic nuclear exchange Canada would become the battlefield. In 1999 Kosovo became the battlefield. It became the one theater for the Serb army where it could retaliate for NATO bombs. Thousands of Albanians were killed. The West blamed Serb nationalism, not NATO's war-fighting strategy, for those deaths.

Michael Ignatieff has forcefully argued how '[i]n a postimperial age, we have forsworn imperial methods, but traces of imperial arrogance remain'.[2] We recall from chapter 3 that while the era of empires may be over, that of imperialism is not. Writing before the Kosovo campaign, the author pointed to how

> [t]he liberal interventions of the early 1990s were all avowedly and self-consciously postimperial. Yet they were haunted by Conradian continuities and ironies. When Conrad symbolized imperial impotence in the image of the gunboat in *Heart of Darkness*, moored off the African shore, lobbing useless shells into the unanswering jungle, the contemporary imagination leaps to the image of NATO warplanes lobbing shells into abandoned Serbian artillery dugouts in 1994.[3]

And in 1999 in Kosovo and, with a change in adversaries, in 2001 in Afghanistan.

The West's 'imperial arrogance' has been perceptible in its approach to non-Western nationalisms. English social theorist Anthony Giddens, a leading ideologue of globalization, praises the global processes that put people in contact with those who think and live differently. Those who feel enriched by cultural complexity are the cosmopolitans; those who are threatened are the fundamentalists who take refuge in purified ethnic and religious identities. For Giddens, twenty-first-century conflict will occur on the axis cosmopolitan tolerance/fundamentalist intolerance.[4] From here it is a short step to deriding on moral grounds separatist movements that have surfaced in the developing world, whether of the Zulus, Sikhs, Kashmiris, Kurds, or Saharoui people. That has not stopped Western powers since 1991 from creating a network of bantustans in their own backyards, using the remnants of the former communist world as their raw material.

The G–7 group of industrialized states (G–8 when Russia is included) has masterminded globalization policy and constructed a world of nearly-free trade across international borders. But for Canadian and French concerns about the culture industry, it also nearly succeeded in pushing through a multilateral agreement on investment (MAI) in 1998 which would have given multinational corporations immunity from many domestic laws passed in individual countries, for example, dealing with environmental protection.

Let us take a closer look at the G–7 members: Britain, Canada, France, Germany, Italy, Japan, and the US. The first five states grapple with ethnic and regional schisms, some caused by mass immigration, others that come with the territory (Scotland and Northern Ireland in the UK, Quebec in Canada). Facing centrifugal problems at home, they denounce separatism and nationalism and instead advocate globalization policy abroad. The overriding political interests of G–7 members, therefore, explain their commitment to globalization and condemnation of all but their own banal nationalisms. And we do not even take up the matter of their economic interests.

The security interests of the developed countries have been tethered to the supposed indivisibility of human interests, even though this is never formally stated. For Ignatieff, '[t]he Conradian irony is that this interdependence was more apparent to the Kurtz figures of the nineteenth century than it is to the postimperial politicians and businessmen of the late twentieth century'. Does the security calculus alone explain why the West acted twice to halt Serb nationalism but did not even contemplate intervention to prevent human tragedies elsewhere, as belatedly in Rwanda and East Timor? Unfortunately, a well-concealed, perhaps unconscious racism was at work in shaping the West's foreign policy: 'Our moral engagements with faraway places are notoriously selective and partial. We are more likely to help people who look like us than people who don't; more likely to help people whose history or whose plight we can understand than people whose situation we cannot fathom'.[5]

Great powers have always acted in their own interests and only the ideology used to disguise self-interest has been fine-tuned to reflect the different spirits of the age. Today that ideology embraces a self-serving, culturally-defined set of values that includes liberalism, democracy, universalism, and civic nationalism. It is a Western-centric ideology. Efforts by countries to develop a different mix of values to reflect their cultural traditions are disparaged. Even within Western philosophical discourse, the attempt to promote a communitarian variant of liberalism that would stress group more than individual rights has been an uphill and largely unsuccessful struggle. Neoliberalism, with its fixation on individual economic free-dom and utilitarianism, has blocked the expansion of such a communitar-ian philosophy. In its turn, whether democracy actually exists or is being promoted in a country has generally been answered by the response to a second question: is a country pro-Western and 'open for business', or is it neutral and protectionist?

We must be clear about one thing. 'Denationalizing' political discourses have not been directly superimposed or forced upon empires like Russia and India by the great Western powers. Instead, through a variety of incentives they are steered in a direction that may for them be anti-historical, anti-traditional, not particularly democratic, and even self-destructive.[6] As Ali Mazrui put it, 'Western liberal democracy has enabled societies to enjoy openness, government accountability, popular participation, and high eco-nomic productivity, but Western pluralism has also been a breeding ground for racism, fascism, exploitation, and genocide'. He added: 'At bottom, democracy is a system for selecting one's rulers; humane governance is a system for treating citizens'.[7]

The link between home and hostility

In Chapter 2 we considered the differences between liberal and illiberal nationalisms. The principal characteristics of the first, we recall, are the protection of individual rights and toleration of differences. Like Mazrui, we questioned whether Western democracies that embrace a liberal nation-alism actually pursue policies incorporating universalist norms such as non-discrimination and equal rights for all. Some of these states are also weak in cementing community, thereby creating an opportunity structure for ethnic discrimination and social marginalization. By contrast, illiberal nationalism is unambiguously committed to the primacy and even hegemony of one ethnic, religious, or linguistic group over others. When nationalism is de-rided as a pathology, it is invariably its illiberal form that is being invoked.

Given these characteristics and caveats, how are these two types of liber-alism connected to constructions of home? Figure 7.1 presents a notional framework linking nationalisms to the kinds of home we have considered in our case studies. Each cell in the matrix identifies the defining features of a particular home that has adopted a liberal or illiberal nationalist ideology. We have added the multicultural state to our typology of homes – empire, breakaway state, uninational home, transnational community – to provide a further test of our theory that most types of homes can be envisaged as more or less liberal or illiberal constructs.

The Russian and Indian empires of today are markedly different from their Soviet and British predecessors, but the difference lies less in the fact that imperial rule has been abandoned and more in the fact that the nationalism underpinning the reconfigured empires is more liberal.

Types of Nationalism

Constructions of Home	Liberal	Illiberal
Multicultural state	Empowerment of minorities. No single dominant nation.	Faux multiculturalism. Dominant patronizing nation.
Empire	Respect for rights of minority nations. Consociational arrangements.	Core-periphery basis. Exploitation or neglect of periphery.
Breakaway state	Constitutional democracy. Minority representation.	Ethnocracy. Assimilationist pressures on minorities.
Uninational, or *Volkstaat* (*jus sanguinis* principle)	Economic democracy. Minorities as stake-holders and prospective citizens.	Xenophobia and racism. Second-class citizenship for minorities.
Transnational ideological/religious community	Common good of the wretched of the earth. Developmental project.	Fanaticism, bigotry, irrationality, and millenarianism.

Figure 7.1   Constructions of home and types of nationalism

In the 1990s Russia was prodded to adopt a procedural democracy, non-imperial identity, and *laissez-faire* economic system which left the country adrift. All forms of Russian nationalism other than folkloric were stigmatized: imperialist, Slavophile, Eurasian, ethnically essentialist, regionalist. The backlash to the increasing indeterminacy of Russian identity was the widespread support given to Putin with his KGB aura and tough talk after 2000.

We have seen that for most of its history the Russian home has been an imperial one. Since 1991 the construction of a 'mere' multinational home has not excited many Russians. The war in Chechnya demonstrated that the broad understanding of the Russian home was still popular and could evoke aggressive, prestige nationalism aimed at raising other countries' esteem for Russia. To stigmatize the imperial idea seems, therefore, to be counterproductive since Russia's sense of security depends on it. Instead, institutionalizing the right of minority nations through consociational arrangements allows Russia to develop into an empire of a liberal nationalist character.

A second case of Western powers' framing the discourse of nationalism is India. Seeking to fulfill Western expectations of it, the country has pursued an ostensibly liberal secular nationalism which has resulted in increasing disaffection with it among Hindus and non-Hindus alike. Its contrived character has led to a backlash evidenced in both separatist movements (Assamese, Kashmiri, Sikh) and national politics (the rise of the Hindu nationalist BJP party).

The spurious nature of Indian *faux* secularism gave way in the late 1990s to a more articulated Hinduism represented by the BJP government. If liberal secularism had been invoked, paradoxically, to enforce the political unity of the state, often with the use of force, the recognition of the dominant Hindu identity of the Indian state has helped facilitate alliances across regional political actors and has to some degree weakened the core-periphery hierarchy. The country's successful nuclear tests in May 1998 were naturally viewed as a demonstration of both Indian imperial ambitions and Hindu nationalism, coming three months after the BJP won parliamentary elections. Their greater impact may, however, have been to stimulate pride among Hindus and non-Hindus alike in the Indian home.

In this book we have encountered three cases of the organization of movements supporting ethnic definitions of nation and home: in Quebec, KwaZulu, and Germany. Ethnonationalist groups opposed the ideology of multiculturalism that was advocated by central authorities in these three cases. But the differences among them were far greater than the similarities. In Quebec the definition of a Quebecer was progressively broadened by a political party (the PQ) wishing to stay in power. Quebec itself soon borrowed the discourse of multiculturalism in painting its vision of home. In KwaZulu, the closest encounter we have had with a possible nationalism of the homeless, Inkatha prudently moved from ethnic to symbolic politics as South Africa came under the popular rule of Mandela and his multiethnic coalition. The nationalism of the ideologues of would-be breakaway states became increasingly liberal.

By contrast, in Germany nationalists operated outside of mainstream politics. They behaved as populists without having the populace behind them. The radical right here promulgated a racially pure home and the logic of such politics led to a recourse to violence. It has also led to its marginalization. A uninational home or *Volkstaat* would have greater appeal if it was construed in terms of liberal nationalism: an economic democracy in which ethnic and religious differences are not salient to economic success; and the political recognition of minorities as stake-holders in the system and prospective citizens is given, exemplified by the 1999 citizenship law.

Fundamentalists raise fundamental questions about the nature of being and belonging. When they ask who it is that is a Quebecer, a Zulu, or a German, the political establishment in these democracies provide elusive multiculturalizing responses that are difficult to counter. When these same questions are raised in states institutionally linked with a religion, however, responses cannot be evasive. Who is an Israeli or a Muslim cannot be answered by invoking an amorphous, homogenizing, multiculturalizing, secularizing state in which the Israeli or Muslim lives. In many cases reference to such a state only polarizes the conflict. The spiritual home that Jewish fundamentalists seek to build in Israel is by definition an exclusive home. When their project is challenged, they adopt aggressive nationalism. Much the same applies to waning Islamic fundamentalist movements in Afghanistan, Algeria, and Iran.

By contrast, when Islam is understood transnationally, it no longer follows that illiberal nationalism must emerge. Pursuing the common good of the hitherto disadvantaged and promising development can make a posited transnational home liberal. Perhaps the greatest frustration for illiberal religious fundamentalist groups is that they are convinced that history is on their side. In a postmodern world that conviction is more of a liability than asset.

It goes without saying that some of the fundamentalist groups examined here part with their nations' own traditions when they become terrorist organizations, sometimes in the mistaken belief that since violence forged the nation in the first place it can continue to be employed. Sikh and Zulu nationalists have emphasized their warrior past. German identity was shaped by the military Junker class. Jews revolted repeatedly against Egyptian, Roman, and Babylonian domination. Having an insurrectionary tradition has nothing in common, however, with battering co-ethnics because they do not belong to the same political movement, striking out against any and all newcomers, and assassinating co-nationals because they do not share a narrow religious definition of homeland. When fundamentalism uses violent means to try and reverse a nation's transformation brought on by modernization, it effectively negates that nation's set of cumulative traditions and is not fundamentalist at all.

We have found that pan-nationalisms are especially weak and not a threat to state stability. Whether it is Islamism or anti-Westernism, movements based on pan-ideologies are vulnerable to divide-and-rule tactics of adversaries and also cannot surmount the interests of the state. For example, an anti-American movement confronts the prisoner's dilemma of deciding at what point defection from a wider ideological bloc (such as anti-unilateralism) pays off more than continuing membership in it. No matter how principled and liberal they are, how committed to rectificatory justice they may be, how populist they have become and how much they constitute a nationalism of the dispossessed, in recent times pan-nationalist movements have been overwhelmed by the vitality of the processes of globalization.

Illiberal nationalisms originate in both broad and narrow constructions of home, then. The home that imperial Russian nationalists, especially Eurasianists, wish to build involves an ethnically broad home. The home longed for by the German radical right is a racially narrow home. The transnational space posited by anti-Western movements is nationally broad. The abode of the Jewish spiritual nation is religiously delimited. It is not whether home is conceived narrowly or broadly, then, that breeds radical politics. Instead, it is when radical, dogmatic, uncompromising, illiberal politics characterize the political establishment that constructions of home become bitterly divisive. As Michael Hechter has argued, radical nationalism arises from the imposition of direct rule in culturally heterogeneous societies. Instituting indirect rule and providing for more regional autonomy, thereby both recognizing and empowering multiple homes in a state, are the most effective means of containing nationalist violence.[8]

The multicultural threat

The most discussed nationalist threat to state stability is secessionism. When it occurs in Western democracies, it is cast as an ethnic group's ingratitude and disloyalty to a nurturing mother state. When secessionism arises in poorer countries, it is caricatured as opportunistic, vengeful, even barbarian. Yet it takes a leap of the imagination to accept that long-standing separatisms – in Catalonia, Kurdistan, Scotland, Tamil Eelam – should be represented first and foremost as a threat to state stability and only then as an expression of the national will of historic peoples. A contrasting representation occurs of recently-created states which had little prior history of separatism: Belarus, Bosnia, Macedonia, Moldova, Slovakia, Tajikistan, *inter alia*. Their accession to statehood has been depicted as an entirely 'natural' awakening of long-suppressed nations. Clearly it is not secessionism *qua* secessionism that is the threat. It becomes threatening when it does not serve the interests of dominant powers. Even then it can be fended off by the modern state equipped with its imposing arsenal of military, moral, economic, and ideological weapons.

Improbably, the type of nationalism posing the greatest threat to political stability today may be civic nationalism. The primary reason for this is that more than any other kind of nationalism it mascarades as *faux* cosmopolitanism and multiculturalism while denying or minimizing the discreet dramas in a nation's history. It is projected as the exemplary liberal nationalism of the most prosperous, developed, democratic, and tolerant of the world's states. Herein lies its perfidy, since that has not always been the practice of these states. It is more concerned with performance – recognizing diversity – than substance – empowering minorities. Not surprisingly then, as Michael Lind pointed out, '[t]he problem with civic patriotism is simple: it doesn't exist and never has.'[9] Another problem is that in its interventions to defend mythic multiculturalism in places like Bosnia and Afghanistan, Western policy has been narcissistic: 'We intervened not only to save others, but to save ourselves, or rather an image of ourselves as defenders of universal decencies'. This policy towards the Other also did not inform policy at home: 'it was ironic, of course, that a Western Europe that had shown no qualms about ghettoizing its own Muslim *gastarbeiter* minorities suddenly discovered in Muslim–Christian coexistence in Bosnia the very image of its own multicultural illusions'.[10] Indeed, the rise of fundamentalism and terrorism can be understood in part as backlash against the hollowness of the multicultural message.

Civic nationalism contains an inherent incongruity. As one literary critic observed, '[t]he dehumanizing universalism that congratulates itself – sometimes sincerely, sometimes not – on its own humane intentions even as it conceals a parochial and imperialist particularism comes to despise and persecute the more realizably tolerant possibilities of openly particularist brotherhoods'.[11] In the world of practical politics, this has signified that nationally-constructed particularism is out, depoliticized and defanged cultural particularism is in. Idiot identities are created, encouraged, and rewarded by the multiculturalizing state. Rediscovery of what is home is scorned and castigated as an intolerant brotherhood-building project. Dehumanizing multiculturalism is itself intolerant and short-sighted: 'Poststructuralist critics, who routinely praise boundary crossing and mongrel identities ... condemn nationalism and the dogmatism of the *Heim*. The one question they rarely pose is why individuals should not be happy with their homes or not keep their traditions'.[12]

Spurious civic nationalism is the main bestowal of Western ideological millenialism even if in practice it is *arriviste nationalisme*. To be sure, it is anchored in grassroots politics where multifarious groups scramble and seek recognition for their specific identities. What today are characterized as claims for recognition of identity were what structural-functionalists a generation ago termed the processes of interest articulation and aggregation. The politics of identity are today's interest group politics.[13]

Multiculturalizing nationalism is likely to have a limited life expectancy since it rests not on a recognizable identity but on feel-good sentiment. It does not defend differences, Julia Christeva cautioned, so much as obliterates them in a 'polyphonic community'.[14] Moreover such nationalism is exclusionary because it precludes diverse paths to recognizing diversity. It is the false consciousness of the age and a product of chiliastic thinking. It aspires to a clean break with the preceding two thousand years of history and its defining attributes – home, religion, nation, sovereignty. It transforms the modern state into an exclusively agnostic, secular, materialist home devoid of psychological meaning. That is why historically-derived nationalisms are so threatening to it: they frequently invoke non-materialist, spiritual, genuinely-communitarian values. Not surprisingly, '[t]he spread of cultural nationalism today represents a concentration on an ethnic self facing an inscrutable globality, the attempt of ethnicity to find havens of security in a heartless immensity'.[15]

There are more serious grounds for the indictment of this kind of nationalism than discursive duplicity. In the end, it has contributed little to the nurturing of the identities and interests of disadvantaged peoples. The economically oppressed in the developing world, hardly able to meet their basic needs, let alone afford passage to a Western state to be a refugee, have been ill-served by the substitution of identity politics for class politics. Kenneth Minogue's concept of the nationalism of the homeless is only too typical of this: his concern is with the culturally homeless, not with people with no homes or roofs over their head or food to give to their children.[16]

What is the alternative to the cynicism and smugness of civic nationalism? The answer is clear: a functional liberal nationalism based on a consensual construction of home, which usually overlaps with the realm of a state. It is a territorial nationalism that encompasses diversity and is not negated by it, one that is simultaneously historical and contemporaneous. Such a functional nationalism is located in the *juste-milieu* between cultural and political nation. Cultural primordialism and essentiality cannot be maintained under the conditions of modernity. At the same time, the idea of a mythical political nation exercising a general will and speaking with one political voice despite its cultural diversity runs the risk of being as undemocratic as Jean-Jacques Rousseau's posited state. Such a political nation is at best facile and at worst fictitious.

Identity politics and multicultural discourses have deflected concern with the really fundamental issues of politics: the distribution of wealth and power. The mantra *e pluribus unum* is used, paradoxically, to justify the political *status quo*. In referring to the leading ideologue of third world assertion, one writer admired how '[n]o one was more aware than [Frantz] Fanon of the attendant risks of projecting a fetishistic denial of difference onto a conveniently abstracted "collective will"'.[17]

The functional liberal nationalism of a people is likely to be centered on ethnicity but it will not be an ethnocentric nationalism. For it insists on inclusion, not isolation or separation. This distinction is clearer when we recognize the difference between belonging and being. A liberal nationalism that stresses the belonging of all its inhabitants to a territorial home while promoting the being of its titular nation offers an integrating, cohering ideology. It blends and bonds rather than breaks national identity. The matter of becoming, in the sense of assimilation or acculturation into a receiving society, is a choice left to the individual. For example, being Danish differs from belonging to Denmark. But there should be no normative aspect to this assertion. Furthermore, becoming Danish should be a possibility open to all citizens of the country. To disregard these distinctions as a matter of principle while making them salient in all the banal aspects of social life, as multicultural societies often do, is an objectionable kind of 'national liberalism'.

Appreciating the history of one's own nation can be the cognitive key to appreciating the history of the nations of Others. It can lead to empowerment and, after that, it is could be only a short step to begin to redress the imbalances and inequities that exist among nations.

Notes

Introduction

1 C.L.R. James, *Beyond a Boundary*. New York: Pantheon Books, 1963, p. 220.
2 Ulf Hedetoft, 'The Nation-state Meets the World: National Identities in the Context of Transnationality and Cultural Globalization', *European Journal of Social Theory*, 2(1), 1999, p.74.
3 Svetlana Boym, *Common Places: Mythologies of Everyday Life in Russia*. Cambridge, MA: Harvard University Press, 1994, p.287.
4 Ethnonationalism was the subject of my book with Rajat Ganguly, *Understanding Ethnic Conflict: the International Dimension*. New York: Longman, 2002. The concept is not analysed here.
5 Rogers Brubaker, 'Myths and Misconceptions in the Study of Nationalism', in John A. Hall, *The State of the Nation: Ernest Gellner and the Theory of Nationalism*. Cambridge: Cambridge University Press, 1998, p.300. The posited antagonism between nations and states informs Ted Gurr's empiricist study *Peoples Versus States: Minorities at Risk in the New Century*. Washington, DC: United States Institute of Peace, 2000.
6 Brubaker, 'Myths and Misconceptions', p.301.
7 Gregory Jusdanis, *The Necessary Nation*. Princeton, NJ: Princeton University Press, 2001, p.18.
8 Ulf Hedetoft, 'Discourses and Images of Belonging'. Paper prepared for the Conference on Diasporas and Belonging, Aalborg University, September 2000, p.1.
9 Hedetoft, 'Discourses and Images of Belonging', p.12.
10 Artemis Leontis, *Topographies of Hellenism: Mapping the Homeland*. Ithaca, NY: Cornell University Press, 1995, p.3.
11 In terms of both cases and conceptualization, this book builds on two earlier empirically-grounded studies: Milton J. Esman, *Ethnic Politics*. Ithaca, NY: Cornell University Press, 1994; John Hutchinson, *Modern Nationalism*. London: Fontana Press, 1994.
12 The more optimistic view of imagining home is found in a volume to which I have contributed: Ulf Hedetoft and Mette Hjort (eds), *The Postnational Self: Belonging and Identity*. Minneapolis, MN: University of Minnesota Press, 2002.
13 Michael Billig, *Banal Nationalism*. London: Sage, 1995.
14 Hans Kohn, *The Idea of Nationalism: a Study of its Origins and Background*. New York: Collier Books, 1944 and 1969.
15 Patrik Hall, *The Social Construction of Nationalism: Sweden as an Example*. Lund, Sweden: Lund University Press, 1998, pp.23–4. A similar argument is made by Partha Chatterjee, *Nationalist Thought and the Colonial World: a Derivative Discourse?* Minneapolis, MN: University of Minnesota Press, 1986 and 1995, Chapter 1.

1 Nations and Nationalisms Historically

1 Adrian Hastings, *The Construction of Nationhood: Ethnicity, Religion, and Nationalism*. Cambridge: Cambridge University Press, 1997, p.17.

2 Ian Buruma, *Anglomania: a European Love Affair*. New York: Random House, 1999.
3 Hastings, *The Construction of Nationhood*, p.51.
4 Liah Greenfeld, *Nationalism: Five Roads to Modernity*. Cambridge, MA: Harvard University Press, 1992, p.6.
5 Ernst B. Haas, *Nationalism, Liberalism, and Progress: The Rise and Decline of Nationalism*. Ithaca, NY: Cornell University Press, 1997, p.62.
6 Said Bouamana, 'The Paradox of the European Social and Political Ties: "Nationalitarian" Citizenship and Identity Ambiguity', in Marco Martinello (ed.), *Migration, Citizenship and Ethno-National Identities in the European Union*. Aldershot: Avebury, 1995, p.57.
7 Patrik Hall, *The Social Construction of Nationalism: Sweden as an Example*. Lund, Sweden: Lund University Press, 1998, p.25. His references are to Greenfeld, *Nationalism*; Hans Kohn, *The Idea of Nationalism: a Study in its Origins and Background*. New York: Collier Books, 1944 and 1969; Conor Cruise O'Brien, 'Nationalism and the French Revolution', in Geoffrey Best (ed.), *The Permanent Revolution*. London: Fontana, 1988; Elie Kedourie, *Nationalism*. London: Hutchinson, 1960 and 1985; Ernest Gellner, *Nations and Nationalism*. Oxford: Blackwell, 1983; and Eric Hobsbawm, *Nations and Nationalism Since 1780: Programme, Myth, Reality*. Cambridge: Cambridge University Press, 1990.
8 Paul James, *Nation Formation: Towards a Theory of Abstract Community*. London: Sage, 1996, p.xii. The theorists explored in this book include Benedict Anderson, Ernest Gellner, Anthony Giddens, Tom Nairn, Anthony Smith, and three classic writers: Emile Durkheim, Karl Marx, and Max Weber. Ernst Haas advances a fivefold typology of historical paths to the nation-state in his *Nationalism, Liberalism, and Progress: the Rise and Decline of Nationalism*. Ithaca, NY: Cornell University Press, 1997, pp. 34–7.
9 Kohn, *The Idea of Nationalism*, p.6.
10 Hastings, *The Construction of Nationhood*, p.22.
11 Kohn, *The Idea of Nationalism*, p.27. Part of this account is based on Kohn's seminal work.
12 Kohn, *The Idea of Nationalism*, p.27.
13 Doron Mendels, *The Rise and Fall of Jewish Nationalism: Jewish and Christian Ethnicity in Ancient Palestine*. Grand Rapids, MI: William Eerdmans Publishing, 1992, p.22.
14 Ernest Renan, 'Qu'est-ce qu'une nation?', in John Hutchinson and Anthony D. Smith (eds), *Nationalism*. New York: Oxford University Press, 1994, p.17.
15 For a political scientist's interpretation of Israel's discovery of identity under Moses, see Aaron Wildavsky, *The Nursing Father: Moses as Political Leader*. University, AL: University of Alabama Press, 1984. On Joseph's role, see Aaron Wildavsky, *Assimilation Versus Separation: Joseph the Administrator and the Politics of Religion in Biblical Israel*. New Brunswick, NJ: Transaction Publishers, 1993.
16 Kohn, *The Idea of Nationalism*, p.47.
17 See especially Paul's letters to the Romans, 1–4.
18 Aristotle, *Politics*, Book VII, vi.
19 Kohn, *The Idea of Nationalism*, p.36.
20 Cited by Frederick Hertz, *Nationality in History and Politics: a Study of the Psychology and Sociology of National Sentiment and Character*. New York: Oxford University Press, 1944, p.286.
21 Greenfeld writes not of sentiment but *ressentiment*, 'a psychological state resulting from suppressed feelings of envy and hatred (existential envy) and the impossibility of satisfying these feelings.' As with our distinction between national

sentiment and nationalism, so too Greenfeld claims that *ressentiment* does not generate nationalism in and of itself. *Nationalism*, pp.15, 496, n.14.

22 Hagen Schulze, *States, Nations and Nationalism*. Oxford: Blackwell, 1998, p.4.
23 Kohn, *The Idea of Nationalism*, p.79.
24 Philip K. Hitti, *The Arabs: a Short History*. Washington, DC: Regnery Publishing, 1996, pp. 92–3.
25 *The Koran Interpreted*. Trans. by A.J. Arberry. New York: Touchstone Books, 1996.
26 Cited by Hertz, *Nationality in History and Politics*, p.115.
27 Edward Hallett Carr, *Nationalism and After*. London: Macmillan, 1945, p.2.
28 Florian Znaniecki, *Modern Nationalities: a Sociological Study*. Westport, CT: Greenwood Press, 1973, p.83.
29 Reinhold Niebuhr, *The Structure of Nations and Empires*. New York: Charles Scribner's Sons, 1959, p.146.
30 C.M.D. Crowder, *Unity, Heresy and Reform, 1378–1460: the Conciliar Response to the Great Schism*. New York: St. Martin's Press – now Palgrave Macmillan, 1977, p.118.
31 Crowder, *Unity, Hersey and Reform*, p.120.
32 Hertz, *Nationality in History and Politics*, p.21.
33 Study Group of Members of the Royal Institute of International Affairs, *Nationalism*. London: Oxford University Press, 1939, p.7.
34 Greenfeld, *Nationalism*, p.9, Fig. 2.
35 Hertz, *Nationality in History and Politics*, p.153.
36 Niebuhr, *The Structure of Nations and Empires*, p.139.
37 On this, see Mikulas Teich and Roy Porter, *The National Question in Europe in Historical Context*. New York: Cambridge University Press, 1993.
38 Hugh Seton-Watson, *Nations and States: an Enquiry into the Origins of Nations and the Politics of Nationalism*. Boulder, CO: Westview Press, 1977, p.10.
39 Adrian Lyttelton, 'The National Question in Italy', in Teich and Porter, *The National Question in Europe in Historical Context*, p.92.
40 Schulze, *States, Nations and Nationalism*, p.33.
41 Schulze, *States, Nations and Nationalism*, p.15.
42 Greenfeld, *Nationalism*, p.95.
43 Cited by Hertz, *Nationality in History and Politics*, p.314.
44 Schulze, *States, Nations and Nationalism*, p.133.
45 Cited by Hertz, *Nationality in History and Politics*, p.347.
46 Hertz, *Nationality in History and Politics*, p.352.
47 On List and Marx, see Roman Szporluk, *Marxism and Nationalism*. Cambridge, MA: Harvard University Press, 1991.
48 Hagen Schulze, *The Course of German Nationalism: from Frederick the Great to Bismarck, 1763–1867*. Cambridge: Cambridge University Press, 1991, p.98.
49 Schulze, *The Course of German Nationalism*, p.76.
50 Greenfeld, *Nationalism*, Chapter 1.
51 Hertz, *Nationality in History and Politics*, p.83.
52 Kohn, *The Idea of Nationalism*, p.178.
53 Cited by Kohn, *The Idea of Nationalism*, p.171.
54 Kohn, *The Idea of Nationalism*, p.183.
55 Cited by Hertz, *Nationality in History and Politics*, p.44.
56 Greenfeld, *Nationalism*, p.191.
57 Greenfeld, *Nationalism*, p.220.
58 Greenfeld, *Nationalism*, p.250.
59 Greenfeld, *Nationalism*, p.261.

60 Greenfeld, *Nationalism*, p.254.
61 Svetlana Boym, *Common Places: Mythologies of Everyday Life in Russia*. Cambridge, MA: Harvard University Press, 1994, p.228.
62 Kohn, *The Idea of Nationalism*, p.263.
63 Mark Juergensmeyer, 'The Limits of Globalization in the 21st Century: Nationalism, Regionalism and Violence', Aalborg: Center for International Studies, Aalborg University, Discussion Paper No. 1/97, p.7.
64 David Miller, *On Nationality*. Oxford: Clarendon Press, 1995, p.63.
65 Alfred Cobban, *The Nation State and National Self-Determination*. London: Collins, 1969, p.30.
66 Grotius' major work was *De Jure Belli et Pacis* ('On the Law of War and Peace') written in 1625.
67 Benedict Anderson, *Imagined Communities*. New York: Verso Books, 1993, p.19.
68 Anthony D. Smith, *National Identity*. Reno, NV: University of Nevada Press, 1991, pp.59–60.
69 Anderson, *Imagined Communities*, p.36.
70 Anderson, *Imagined Communities*, p.41.
71 Anderson, *Imagined Communities*, pp.44–5.
72 Anderson, *Imagined Communities*, p.46.
73 Eugene Weber, *Peasants into Frenchmen: the Modernization of Rural France 1870–1914*. Stanford, CA: Stanford University Press, 1976, pp.67–8, 498–501.
74 Tony Crowley, *Language in History: Theories and Texts*. Routledge: London, 1996, p.197. The reference is to Seamus Heaney, 'The Interesting Case of John Alphonsus Mulrennan', *Planet*, 41 (1978), pp.34–40.
75 Ian Buruma, 'The Road to Babel', *New York Review of Books*, XLVIII, no.9 (31 May 2001), p.26.
76 Cited by Kohn, *The Idea of Nationalism*, p.276.
77 Cited by Kohn, *The Idea of Nationalism*, p.310.
78 Michael Howard, *The Lessons of History*. New York: Oxford University Press, 1991, p.40.
79 For example, George Novack, *Genocide against the Indians*. New York: Pathfinder Press, 1970.
80 For an interesting discussion of the consequences, see Alfred O. Hero, *Louisiana and Quebec: Bilateral Relations and Comparative Sociopolitical Evolution, 1673–1993*. Lanham, MD: University Press of America, 1995.
81 Jean-Jacques Rousseau, 'Political Writings'. Cited by Cobban, *The Nation State and National Self-Determination*, p.32.
82 Rousseau, 'Political Writings', p.30.
83 Cited by Eric J. Hobsbawm, *Nations and Nationalism Since 1780: Program, Myth, Reality*. New York: Cambridge University Press, 1993, p.19.
84 Andrea Stuart, 'Not Tonight, Josephine, I've Got a Novel to Write', *The Independent* (1 February 2001). This is a review of Andy Martin, *Napoleon the Novelist*. Cambridge: Polity Press, 2001.
85 Carr, *Nationalism and After*, p.6.
86 Hans Kohn, *Prophets and Peoples: Studies in Nineteenth Century Nationalisms*. London: Collier Books, 1949 and 1969, p.15.
87 Quoted in Study Group of Members of the Royal Institute of International Affairs, *Nationalism*, p.19.
88 Hobsbawm, *Nations and Nationalism Since 1780*, p.23.
89 John Breuilly, *Nationalism and the State*. Chicago: University of Chicago Press, 1994, Chapters 4–5.

90 Lyttleton, 'The National Question in Italy', p.83.
91 Hans Kohn, *Nationalism and Realism: 1852–1879*. Princeton, NJ: Van Nostrand, 1968, p.32.
92 Cited by Cobban, *The Nation State and National Self-Determination*, p.37.
93 Anderson, *Imagined Communities*, p.87.
94 Anderson, *Imagined Communities*, p.86.
95 Anderson, *Imagined Communities*, p.86.
96 Cited by Hobsbawm, *Nations and Nationalism Since 1780*, p.19.
97 William Gladstone, 'Europe: a Family of Nations', in Bruno Leone (ed.), *Nationalism*. St. Paul, MN: Greenhaven Press, 1986, pp.28–9.
98 Renan, 'Qu'est-ce qu'une nation?' pp.7–8. Cited by Hobsbawm, *Nations and Nationalism Since 1780*, p.12.
99 *ibid.*, p.25.
100 Niebuhr, *The Structure of Nations and Empires*, p.196.
101 Cited by Hobsbawm, *Nations and Nationalism Since 1780*, p.28.
102 Hobsbawm, *Nations and Nationalism Since 1780*, p.30.
103 Hobsbawm, *Nations and Nationalism Since 1780*, p.32.
104 Hobsbawm, *Nations and Nationalism Since 1780*, p.125.
105 Hobsbawm, *Nations and Nationalism Since 1780*, p.148.
106 Hobsbawm, *Nations and Nationalism Since 1780*, p.150.
107 Carr, *Nationalism and After*, pp.25–6.
108 Arjun Appadurai, *Modernity at Large: Cultural Dimensions of Globalization*. Minneapolis, MN: University of Minnesota Press, 1996, p.160.
109 Benedict Anderson, 'Exodus', *Critical Enquiry*, vol. 20 (Winter 1994), pp.323–4.

2 Nationalisms Conceptually

1 Until not long ago there were few studies of the connection between nationalism and international relations. Among recent books are Lars-Erik Cederman, *Emergent Actors in World Politics: How States and Nations Develop and Dissolve*. Princeton, NJ: Princeton University Press, 1997; David Carment and Patrick James (eds), *Wars in the Midst of Peace: the International Politics of Ethnic Conflict*. Pittsburgh, PA: University of Pittsburgh Press, 1997; David A. Lake and Donald Rothchild (eds), *The International Spread of Ethnic Conflict: Fear, Diffusion, and Escalation*. Princeton, NJ: Princeton University Press, 1998; Ray Taras and Rajat Ganguly, *Understanding Ethnic Conflict: the International Dimension*. New York: Longman, 2002. This book does not, therefore, consider the international relations–nationalism connection.
2 Peter Alter, *Nationalism*. London: Edward Arnold, 1989, p.14.
3 Such holistic definitions of the nation have been provided by Ernest Barker, *National Character and the Factors in Its Formation*. London, 1927, p.17; and James G. Kellas, *The Politics of Nationalism and Ethnicity*. London: Macmillan – now Palgrave Macmillan, 1991, pp.2–3.
4 See Alter, *Nationalism*, p.14. See also Norman D. Palmer and Howard C. Perkins, *International Relations: the World Community in Transition*. New Delhi: CBS Publishers, 1985, p.19.
5 Hugh Seton-Watson, *Nations and States: an Enquiry into the Origins of Nations and the Politics of Nationalism*. Boulder, CO: Westview Press, 1977, p.5.
6 Ernst B. Haas, *Nationalism, Liberalism, and Progress: the Rise and Decline of Nationalism*. Ithaca, NY: Cornell University Press, 1997, p.23.

7 John T. Rourke, *International Politics on the World Stage*. Guilford, CT: Dushkin, 1991, pp.140–1.
8 *ibid.*, p.141.
9 Alter, *Nationalism*, p.15.
10 *ibid.*
11 *ibid.*, p.16.
12 *ibid.*
13 See Patrick Thornberry, 'International and European Standards on Minority Rights', in Hugh Miall (ed.), *Minority Rights in Europe: Prospects for a Transnational Regime*. London: Royal Institute of International Affairs, 1994, p.19.
14 Mark R. Beissinger, 'The Persisting Ambiguity of Empire', in *Post-Soviet Affairs*, 11, no.2, 1995, p.156.
15 Peter Loewenberg, *Fantasy and Reality in History*. New York: Oxford University Press, 1995, p.196.
16 Loewenberg, *Fantasy and Reality in History*, p.198.
17 Elie Kedourie, *Nationalism*. London: Hutchinson, 1960.
18 Dudley Seers, *The Political Economy of Nationalism*. New York: Oxford University Press, 1983.
19 Carlton J. H. Hayes, *Essays on Nationalism*. New York: Macmillan, 1926, p.5.
20 Louis L. Snyder, *The Meaning of Nationalism*. New Brunswick, NJ: Rutgers University Press, 1954, p.61.
21 Hans Kohn, *The Idea of Nationalism: a Study in its Origins and Background*. New York: Macmillan, 1951, p.15.
22 Durkheim, quoted by Snyder in *The Meaning of Nationalism*, p.67. A similar approach is taken by Louis Wirth, 'Types of Nationalism', *American Journal of Sociology*, XLI, May 1936, p.723.
23 Alter, *Nationalism*, p.18. This view is shared by Harold J. Laski, *A Grammar of Politics*. London and New Haven, 1925, p.221.
24 Snyder, *The Meaning of Nationalism*, pp.67–8.
25 Sigmund Freud, *The Taboo of Virginity*, 1917 in *Standard Edition* 11, pp.191–208. Application of the theory to international affairs was developed in his *Civilization and its Discontents*, 1930, in *Standard Edition*, 21, pp.59–145.
26 Vamik D. Volkan, *The Need to Have Enemies and Allies: from Clinical Practice to International Relationships*. Northvale, NJ: Jason Aronson, 1988, p.105.
27 Volkan, *The Need to Have Enemies and Allies*, p.91.
28 Morris Ginsberg, *The Psychology of Society*. New York, 1921, p.97. Quoted by Snyder, *The Meaning of Nationalism*, p.70.
29 Arnold J. Toynbee, *Nationality and War*. London, 1915, p.13.
30 Hayes, *Essays on Nationalism*, p.24.
31 *ibid.*, p.24. Emphasis in original.
32 'Introduction', Andrew Parker, Mary Russo, Doris Sommer, and Patricia Yaeger (eds), *Nationalisms and Sexualities*. New York: Routledge, 1992, p.1.
33 Hayes, *Essays on Nationalism*, p.29.
34 Jack C. Plano and Roy Olton, *The International Relations Dictionary*. New York: ABC-CLIO, 1969. Cited by Walker Connor in 'Nation-Building or Nation-Destroying?' *World Politics*. 24, 3 (April 1972), pp.333–4.
35 Rourke, *International Politics on the World Stage*, p.142.
36 See Anthony Giddens, *Runaway World: How Globalization is Reshaping Our Lives*. London: Routledge, 2000.

37 Michael Billig, *Banal Nationalism*. London: Sage, 1997, p.106.

38 Plano and Olton, *The International Relations Dictionary*. Cited by Connor in 'Nation-Building or Nation-Destroying?', pp.333–4.

39 See Homi Bhabha, *Nation and Narration*. London: Routledge, 1990.

40 Anthony D. Smith, *National Identity*. London: Penguin Books, 1991. For another view, see Gyorgy Csepeli, *National Identity in Contemporary Hungary*. New York: East European Monographs, 1997.

41 Smith, *National Identity*, p.vii.

42 Ulf Hedetoft, *Signs of Nations: Studies in the Political Semiotics of Self and Other in Contemporary European Nationalism*. Aldershot: Dartmouth, 1995, p.26.

43 Hedetoft, *Signs of Nations*, pp.25–6.

44 Guntram H. Herb, 'National Identity and Territory', in Herb and David H. Kaplan (eds), *Nested Identities: Nationalism, Territory, and Scale*. Lanham, MD: Rowman and Littlefield, 1999, p.17.

45 Cynthia Enloe, *Bananas, Beaches and Bases: Making Feminist Sense of International Politics*. Berkeley, CA: University of California Press, 1990, p.44. See also her *Ethnic Conflict and Political Development*. Boston: Little, Brown, 1973.

46 Maja Korac, 'Understanding Ethnic-National Identity in Times of War and Social Change', in Robert B. Pynsent (ed.), *The Literature of Nationalism: Essays on East European Identity*. London: Macmillan, 1996, p.238.

47 Virgina Woolf, *Three Guineas*. London: Hogarth Press, 1986, p.125.

48 See Zygmunt Bauman, *Memories of Class: the Pre-History and After-Life of Class*. London: Routledge and Kegan Paul, 1982.

49 Gertjan Dijkink, *National Identity and Geopolitical Visions: Maps of Pride and Pain*. London: Routledge, 1996, p. 2.

50 Herb and Kaplan, *Nested Identities*.

51 David Miller, 'In Defense of Nationality', *Journal of Applied Philosophy*, 10, no.1 (1993), p.7. See also his *On Nationality*. Oxford: Clarendon Press, 1995.

52 Julian Barnes, *England, England*. New York: Knopf, 1998.

53 Cited by Michael Wood, 'Tight Little Island', in *New York Review of Books*, XLVI, no.11 (June 24, 1999), p. 58.

54 Martin Evans, 'Languages of Racism Within Contemporary Europe', in Brian Jenkins and Spyros A. Sofos (eds), *Nation and Identity in Contemporary Europe*. London: Routledge, 1996, p.34.

55 Smith, *National Identity*, p.125.

56 Margarita Diaz-Andreu and Timothy Champion, 'Nationalism and Archaeology in Europe: an Introduction', in Diaz-Andreu and Champion (eds), *Nationalism and Archaeology in Europe*. Boulder, CO: Westview Press, 1996, p.19.

57 Vamik Volkan, *Blood Lines: From Ethnic Pride to Ethnic Terrorism*. New York: Farrar, Straus and Giroux, 1997, p.115.

58 Smith, *National Identity*, p.160.

59 Smith, *National Identity*, pp.161–2.

60 Smith, *National Identity*, p.162.

61 Peter Stallybrass and Allon White, *The Politics and Poetics of Transgression*. London: Methuen, 1986, p.8.

62 John Rex, 'Ethnic Identity and the Nation State: the Political Sociology of Multi-Cultural Societies', in *Social Identities*, 1, no.1 (1995), p.22.

63 Kedourie, *Nationalism*, p.81.

64 Carlton J. H. Hayes, *The Historical Evolution of Modern Nationalism*. New York: R.R. Smith, 1931, pp.10–11.

65 James Mayall, *Nationalism and International Society.* Cambridge: Cambridge University Press, 1990, pp. 40–1.

66 Jurgen Fijalkowski, 'Conditions of Ethnic Mobilization: the German Case', in John Rex and Beatrice Drury (eds), *Ethnic Mobilization in a Multi-Cultural Europe.* Aldershot: Avebury, 1994, p.133.

67 Wolfgang Danspeckgruber, 'A Final Assessment', in Danspeckgruber (ed.), *The Self-Determination of Peoples: Community, Nation, and State in an Interdependent World.* Boulder, CO: Lynne Rienner, 2002, p.335. See Appendix C in his book for a detailed list of self-determination conflicts since 1990.

68 Mayall, *Nationalism and International Society,* p. 51.

69 *ibid.,* p.54.

70 *ibid.,* p.55.

71 Ruth Lapidoth, *Autonomy: Flexible Solutions to Ethnic Conflicts.* Washington, DC: United States Institute of Peace Press, 1997.

72 See I. William Zartman (ed.), *Collapsed States: the Disintegration and Restoration of Legitimate Authority.* Boulder, CO: Lynne Riener, 1995.

73 Haas, *Nationalism, Liberalism, and Progress,* pp. 34–5.

74 Artemis Leontis, *Topographies of Hellenism: Mapping the Homeland.* Ithaca, NY: Cornell University Press, 1995.

75 Hayes, *Essays on Nationalism,* pp.5–6.

76 *ibid.*

77 Kohn, *The Idea of Nationalism,* p.8.

78 Boyd C. Shafer, *Nationalism: Myth and Reality.* New York: Harcourt, Brace and World, 1955, p.10. See also his *Faces of Nationalism.* New York: Harcourt, Brace, Jovanovich, 1972.

79 Shafer, *Nationalism: Myth and Reality,* p.7.

80 Ernst B. Haas, 'What Is Nationalism And Why Should We Study It?' *International Organization,* 40, 3, (Summer 1986), p.709.

81 Benedict Anderson, *Imagined Communities: Reflections on the Origin and Spread of Nationalism.* London: Verso Editions & NLB, 1983.

82 Seers, *The Political Economy of Nationalism.*

83 Miroslav Hroch, *Social Preconditions of National Revival in Europe: a Comparative Analysis of Patriotic Groups among the Smaller European Nations.* Cambridge: Cambridge University Press, 1985.

84 Anthony D. Smith, *Nationalism in the Twentieth Century.* New York: New York University Press, 1979.

85 Anthony D. Smith, *Theories of Nationalism.* New York: Holmes and Meier, 1983, p.19. Emphasis in original.

86 *ibid.,* p.21.

87 Ernest Gellner, *Nations and Nationalism.* Ithaca, NY: Cornell University Press, 1983, p.47.

88 Gellner, *Nations and Nationalism,* p.11.

89 John A. Hall, 'Introduction', to Hall (ed.), *The State of the Nation: Ernest Gellner and the Theory of Nationalism.* Cambridge: Cambridge University Press, 1999, p. 11.

90 Gregory Jusdanis, *The Necessary Nation.* Princeton, NJ: Princeton University Press, 2001, p.18.

91 Connor, 'Nation-Building or Nation-Destroying?', pp. 333–4.

92 Smith, *National Identity,* pp.72–82. See further Stephen I. Griffiths, *Nationalism and Ethnic Conflict: Threats to European Security.* New York: Oxford University Press, 1993, p.13.

93   Nathan Gardels, 'Two Concepts of Nationalism: an Interview with Isaiah Berlin', *New York Review of Books* (21 November 1991).

94   Michael Hechter, *Containing Nationalism*. New York: Oxford University Press, 2001, p.15.

95   Donald Horowitz, *Ethnic Groups in Conflict*. Berkeley, California: University of California Press, 1985, p.87.

96   Yael Tamir, *Liberal Nationalism*. Princeton, NJ: Princeton University Press, 1993, p.3.

97   Hechter, *Containing Nationalism*, p.15.

98   Snyder, *The Meaning of Nationalism*, p.115. Snyder provides a synopsis of the categories developed by Carlton J. H. Hayes in his *Essays on Nationalism* and *The Historical Evolution of Modern Nationalism*.

99   *ibid.*, p.117.

100 A similar classification of the types of nationalism based on the stages in its development was provided by Quincy Wright. For Wright, nationalism can be classified into five different types – medieval, monarchical, revolutionary, liberal, and totalitarian nationalism. For details, see Quincy Wright, *A Study of War*. 2nd edn. Chicago: University of Chicago Press, 1965, pp.1004–9.

101 Snyder, *The Meaning of Nationalism*, p.114.

102 *ibid.*

103 Max Sylvius Handman, 'The Sentiment of Nationalism', *Political Science Quarterly*. 36, (1921), pp. 107–14.

104 Snyder, *The Meaning of Nationalism*, p.123.

105 *ibid.*

106 Louis L. Snyder, *Macro-Nationalisms: a History of the Pan-Movements*. Westport, CT: Greenwood Press, 1984, pp. 3–4.

107 *ibid.*, p.4.

108 *ibid.*

109 *ibid.*

110 Kohn, *The Idea of Nationalism*, p.329.

111 *ibid.*

112 Partha Chatterjee, *Nationalist Thought and the Colonial World: a Derivative Discourse?*. London: Zed Books, 1986, p.1. This is his reading of the approach expounded by John Plamenatz in 'Two Types of Nationalism', in Eugene Kamenka (ed.), *Nationalism*. Canberra: Australian National University Press, 1973, pp.22–37.

113 Plamenatz, 'Two Types of Nationalism', pp. 33–4.

114 Plamenatz, 'Two Types of Nationalism,' p.34.

115 K.R. Minogue, *Nationalism*. London: B.T. Batsford, 1967, p.12.

116 *ibid.*

117 *ibid.*

118 Gershon Shafir, *Immigrants and Nationalists: Ethnic Conflict and Accommodation in Catalonia, the Basque Country, Latvia, and Estonia*. Albany, NY: SUNY Press, 1995, p.18. Emphasis in the original.

119 Wirth, 'Types of Nationalism'.

120 Smith, *Theories of Nationalism*, p.87.

121 *ibid.*

122 Smith, *Theories of Nationalism*, p.27.

123 Such views can be found in Eric Hobsbawm, 'Some Reflections on Nationalism', in T. J. Nossiter, A. H. Hanson, and Stein Rokkan, (eds), *Imagination and Precision in the Social Sciences: Essays in Memory of Peter Nettl*. London: Faber & Faber, 1972, pp.385–406.

124 Kedourie, *Nationalism*, p.21.
125 *ibid.*, p.22. Emphasis added.
126 *ibid.*, pp.23–5.
127 Smith, *Theories of Nationalism*, p.33.
128 *ibid.*, p.28.
129 Emmanuel Todd, *Le fou et le proletaire*. Paris: Laffont, 1979. The author identifies the rural familial structure of the German population as part of the explanation for the rise of Nazism.
130 Ben Kiernan, *The Pol Pot Regime: Race, Power and Genocide Under the Khmer Rouge, 1975–79*. New Haven, CT: Yale University Press, 1996.
131 Gerard Prunier, *The Rwandan Crisis 1959–1994: History of a Genocide*. New York: Columbia University Press, 1995.
132 Tom Nairn, 'The Curse of Rurality: Limits of Modernization', in John Hall (ed.), *The State of the Nation: Ernest Gellner and the Theory of Nationalism*. Cambridge: Cambridge University Press, 1998, pp.107, 120.
133 Saul Newman, 'Does Modernization Breed Ethnic Political Conflict?' *World Politics*, 43, no.3 (April 1991), p.453.
134 Smith, *Theories of Nationalism*, p.46. The subsequent account draws from Smith's analysis.
135 *ibid.*
136 *ibid.*, p.47.
137 S.N. Eisenstadt, *Modernization: Protest and Change*. Englewood Cliffs, NJ: Prentice-Hall, 1966.
138 Neil J. Smelser, *Sociology*. New York: Prentice-Hall, 1994.
139 K. Davis, 'Social and Demographic Aspects of Economic Development in India', in S. Kuznets, W.E. Moore, and J.J. Spengler (eds), *Economic Growth: Brazil, India, Japan*. Durham, NC: Duke University Press, 1955. Quoted by Smith, *Theories of Nationalism*, p.44.
140 Smith, *Theories of Nationalism*, p.50.
141 *ibid.*
142 *ibid.*, pp.57–8.
143 *ibid.*, p.58.
144 William Kornhauser, *The Politics of Mass Society*. Glencoe, IL: Free Press, 1959.
145 Smith, *Theories of Nationalism*, p.60. Emphasis in original.
146 *ibid.*, p.61.
147 *ibid.*
148 Alexis Heraclides, *The Self-determination of Minorities in International Politics*. London: Frank Cass, 1991, p.3.
149 See Karl W. Deutsch, *Nationalism and Social Communication*. Cambridge, MA: MIT Press, 1953.
150 Karl W. Deutsch, *Tides Among Nations*. New York: Free Press, 1979.
151 Ernest Gellner, *Thought and Change*. Chicago: University of Chicago Press, 1965 and 1978, p.55.
152 Gellner, *Nations and Nationalism*, p.39.
153 *ibid.*, p.1. Cited by Haas in 'What is Nationalism and Why Should We Study It?', p.721.
154 Hall, 'Introduction', in Hall (ed.), *The State of the Nation*, p.3.
155 Connor, 'Nation-Building or Nation-Destroying?' p.320.
156 *ibid.*, p.44.
157 Kellas, *The Politics of Nationalism and Ethnicity*, p.43.

158 Geoff Eley and Grigor Suny, 'Introduction: From the Moment of Social History to the Work of Cultural Representation', in Eley and Suny (eds), *Becoming National: a Reader*. New York: Oxford University Press, 1996, p.32.

3 Home Writ Large: Nationalism and the Maintenance of Empire

1 Paul Brass, *Ethnicity and Nationalism: Theory and Comparison*. Newbury Park, CA: Sage Publications, 1991, p.327.
2 Brass, *Ethnicity and Nationalism*, p.323, emphasis added.
3 Michael W. Doyle, *Empires*. Ithaca, NY: Cornell University Press, 1986, p.353.
4 See Bernard Semmel, *The Liberal Ideal and the Demons of Empire: Theories of Imperialism from Adam Smith to Lenin*. Baltimore, MD: Johns Hopkins University Press, 1993.
5 Tom Nairn, *Faces of Nationalism: Janus Revisited*. London: Verso, 1997, p.71.
6 Nairn, *Faces of Nationalism*, p.71.
7 Michael Hardt, Antonio Negri, *Empire*. Cambridge, MA: Harvard University Press, 2000, p.370.
8 A more nuanced approach illustrated with graphs can be found in Barry Buzan and Richard Little, *International Systems in World History: Remaking the Study of International Relations*. New York: Oxford University Press, 2000, pp.176–82.
9 Edward Gibbon, *The History of the Decline and Fall of the Roman Empire*, Vol. III. David Womersley (ed.), New York: Allen Lane, 1994, Chapter LXXI, p.1073.
10 J.A. Hobson, *Imperialism*. Ann Arbor MI: Ann Arbor Paperback edn, 1967 (first published 1902).
11 Vladimir Lenin, *Imperialism: the Highest Stage of Capitalism*.
12 Doyle, *Empires*, p.123.
13 Nirad C. Chaudhuri, *Three Horsemen of the New Apocalypse*. Delhi: Oxford University Press, 1999, pp.56–7.
14 Patrick K. O'Brien, 'The Imperial Component in the Decline of the British Economy before 1914', in Kenichi Ohmae (ed.), *The Rise and Decline of the Nation State: the Rise of Regional Economies*. London: Blackwell, 1990, p.42.
15 O'Brien, p.42.
16 Valerie Bunce, 'The Empire Strikes Back: The Evolution of the Eastern Bloc from a Soviet Asset to a Soviet Liability', *International Organization*, 39 (1985), p. 41.
17 Paul Kennedy, *The Rise and Fall of the Great Powers: Economic Change and Military Conflict from 1500 to 2000*. New York: Random House, 1987, p.439. Another noteworthy study is Samuel E. Finer, *History of Government: Empires, Monarchies and the Modern State*, vol. III. Oxford: Oxford University Press, 1997.
18 For a stimulating discussion see Torbjorn Knutsen, *The Rise and Fall of World Orders*. Manchester: Manchester University Press, 1999, Chs. 7–9.
19 Geir Lundestad, 'Empire by Invitation? The United States and Western Europe, 1945–1952', *Journal of Peace Research*, 23, no.3 (1986), pp.263–77. See also his *The American 'Empire'*. New York: Oxford University Press, 1990.
20 Hardt, Negri, *Empire*, p.381.
21 *ibid.*, pp.xiv–xv.
22 *ibid.*, p.384.
23 Alexander Motyl, 'Thinking About Empire', in Karen Barkey and Mark ron Hagen (eds), *After Empire: Multiethnic Societies and Nation-building: the Soviet*

Union and the Russian, Ottoman and Hapsburg Empires. Boulder, CO: Westview Press, 1997, p.28.

24 Motyl, p.24.

25 Motyl, p.25.

26 Anthony Smith, *National Identity*, Reno, NV: University of Nevada Press, 1994, p.101.

27 Smith, *National Identity*, p.102.

28 Geoffrey Hosking, 'The Russian National Myth Repudiated', in Hosking and George Schopflin (eds), *Myths and Nationhood*. New York: Routledge, 1997, p.200.

29 The statement was by Vasilii Kliuchevskii, cited by Ilya Prizel, *National Identity and Foreign Policy: Nationalism and Leadership in Poland, Russia, and Ukraine*. Cambridge: Cambridge University Press, 1998, p.154.

30 Pierre R. Hart, 'The West', in Nicholas Rzhevsky (ed.), *The Cambridge Companion to Modern Russian Culture*. Cambridge: Cambridge University Press, 1998, p.91.

31 Iver B. Neumann, 'Constructing Europe: Russia as Europe's Other', in Ulf Hedetoft (ed.), *Political Symbols, Symbolic Politics: European Identities in Transformation*. Aldershot: Ashgate, 1998, p.259. See also his *Uses of the Other: 'The East' in European Identity Formation*. Minneapolis, MN: University of Minnesota Press, 1998.

32 Iver B. Neumann, *Russia and the Idea of Europe: a Study in Identity and International Relations*. London: Routledge, 1996, p.200.

33 Paul Flenley, 'From Soviet to Russian Identity: the Origins of Contemporary Russian Nationalism and National Identity', in Brian Jenkins and Spyros A. Sofos (eds), *Nation and Identity in Contemporary Europe*. London: Routledge, 1996, pp.225–6.

34 Neumann, *Russia and the Idea of Europe*, p.12.

35 Mark Raeff, 'Patterns of Russian Imperial Policy Toward the Nationalities', in Edward Allworth (ed.), *Soviet Nationality Problems*. New York: Columbia University Press, 1971, p.37.

36 Prizel, *National Identity and Foreign Policy*, p.177.

37 Prizel, *National Identity and Foreign Policy*, p.204.

38 Astrid S. Tuminez, *Russian Nationalism Since 1856: Ideology and the Making of Foreign Policy*. Lanham, MD: Rowman and Littlefield, 2000, p.12.

39 Zbigniew Brzezinski, *The Grand Chessboard: American Primacy and its Geostrategic Imperatives*. New York: Basic Books, 1997, p.97.

40 Bo Petersson, *National Self-Images and Regional Identities in Russia*. Aldershot: Ashgate, 2001, p.6.

41 Georgiy I. Mirsky, *On Ruins of Empire: Ethnicity and Nationalism in the Former Soviet Union*. Westport, CT: Greenwood Press, 1997, p.163.

42 Mirsky, *On Ruins of Empire*, p.172.

43 Walter Kolarz, 'Colonialism: Theory and Practice', in George Gretton (ed.), *Communism and Colonialism: Essays by Walter Kolarz*. London: Macmillan, 1964, p.23.

44 Quoted by Flenley, p.245.

45 Andre Liebich, *Les minorites nationales en Europe centrale et orientale*. Geneva: Georg editeur, 1997, p.129.

46 Helene Carrere d'Encausse, *The Nationality Question in the Soviet Union and Russia*. Oslo, Norway: Scandinavian University Press, 1995, p.54.

47 Mark R. Beissinger, 'The Persisting Ambiguity of Empire', in *Post-Soviet Affairs*, II, no.2, (1995), p.149. See also William Odom and Robert Dujarric, *Commonwealth or Empire? Russia, Central Asia and the Transcaucasus*. Indianapolis, IN: Hudson Insti-

tute, 1995; Uri Ra'anan and Kate Martin, *Russia: a Return to Imperialism?* New York: St. Martin's Press – now Palgrave Macmillan, 1995.

48 Beissinger, p.163.
49 Beissinger, p.177.
50 P. O'Prey, 'Keeping the Peace in the Borderlands of Russia', in William J. Durch (ed.), *UN Peacekeeping, American Policy, and the Uncivil Wars of the 1990s.* New York: St. Martin's Press – now Palgrave Macmillan, 1996, p.411.
51 Walter Laqueur, *Black Hundred: The Rise of the Extreme Right in Russia*, New York: Harper and Row, 1993, p.x.
52 *ibid.*, p.276.
53 Prizel, *National Identity and Foreign Policy*, p.33.
54 Sergei Kovalev, 'Russia After Chechnya', *New York Review of Books* XLIV, no.12 (July 17, 1997), p.30.
55 Prizel, *National Identity and Foreign Policy*, p.10.
56 Prizel, *National Identity and Foreign Policy*, p.155.
57 Judy Batt, 'The Politics of Minority Rights in Post-communist Europe', in Finn Laursen and Soren Riishoj (eds), *The EU and Central Europe: Status and Prospects.* Esbjerg, Denmark: South Jutland University Press, 1996, p.48.
58 Andrei Makine, *Once Upon the River Love*, New York: Arcade Publishing, 1998, p. 146.
59 Graham Smith, Vivien Law, Andrew Wilson, Annette Bohr, and Edward Allworth, *Nation-building in the Post-Soviet borderlands: the Politics of National Identities.* Cambridge: Cambridge University Press, 1998, p.13.
60 Smith *et al.*, *Nation-building in the Post-Soviet borderlands*, p.11.
61 Sh. Sultanov, 'Dukh yevraziitsa,' *Nash sovremennik*, no. 7 (1992), p.143. Quoted by Vera Tolz, 'Values and the Construction of a National Identity,' in Stephen White, Alex Pravda, and Zvi Gitelman (eds.), *Developments in Russian Politics.* 5th edn. Houndmills, Basingstoke: Palgrave, 2001, p.283.
62 Gertjan Dijkink, *National Identity and Geopolitical Visions: Maps of Pride and Pain.* London: Routledge, 1996, p.102.
63 Lev N. Gumilev, *Ot rusi k rossii: ocherki etnicheskoi istorii.* Moscow: Ekoproc, 1992, p.297. Quoted by Prizel, *National Identity and Foreign Policy*, p.230.
64 Prizel, *National Identity and Foreign Policy*, p.230.
65 Wanda Dressler (ed.), *Le second printemps des nations.* Brussels: Emile Bruylant, 1999, p.375.
66 Andrei P. Tsygankov, 'Hard-line Eurasianism and Russia's Contending Geopolitical Perspectives', *East European Quarterly*, XXXII, no.3 (Fall 1998), p.318.
67 Tsygankov, 'Hard-line Eurasianism', p.322.
68 Tsygankov, 'Hard-line Eurasianism', p.323. For all the differences between modernizers and expansionists, see Table 1, p.330.
69 Aleksandr Dugin, *Konservativnaya revolutsia.* Moscow: AKIRN, 1994.
70 Quoted in Wayne Allensworth, *The Russian Question: Nationalism, Modernization, and Post-Communist Russia.* Lanham, MD: Rowman and Littlefield, 1998, p.250.
71 Quoted in Allensworth, *The Russian Question*, pp.250–1.
72 See David Kerr, 'The New Eurasianism: the Rise of Geopolitics in Russia's Foreign Policy', *Europe–Asia Studies*, 47, no.8 (December 1995), pp.977–88.
73 Martin Walker, *Manchester Guardian Weekly*, (14 February 1988). Quoted in Dijkink, p.98.
74 Quoted in Dijkink, p.101.

75 Alexander Solzhenitsyn, *Rebuilding Russia*. New York: Farrar, Straus, and Giroux, 1991, p.10.
76 Alexander Solzhenitsyn, 'Russkiy vopros v kontse dwadstatovo veka', *Novy mir*, 7 (July 1994), p.174.
77 Solzhenitsyn, *Rebuilding Russia*, p.19.
78 Dijkink, p.102.
79 Allensworth, *The Russian Question*, p.330.
80 John Dunlop, 'The Contemporary Russian Nationalist Spectrum', *Radio Liberty Research Bulletin*. 19 December 1988, pp.1–10. This typology is based on his descriptive analysis.
81 Leokadia Drobizheva, 'Russian Ethnonationalism', in Drobizheva, Rose Gottemoeller, Catherine McArdle Kelleher, and Lee Walker (eds), *Ethnic Conflict in the Post-Soviet World: Case Studies and Analysis*. Armonk, NY: M.E. Sharpe, 1996, p.142. See V. Zorkin, 'Proshchanie s mifami', *Nash sovremennik*, no.4 (1994).
82 Laqueur, p.243.
83 Allensworth, *The Russian Question*, p.132.
84 Allensworth, *The Russian Question*, p.191.
85 See Amy Knight, 'The Enduring Legacy of the KGB in Russian Politics', in *Problems of Post-Communism*, 47, no.4 (July/August 2000), pp.3–15.
86 Kurt Nesby Hansen, 'Continuity within Soviet Nationality Policy: Prospects for Change in the Post-Soviet Era', in Miron Rezun (ed.), *Nationalism and the Breakup of an Empire: Russia and its Periphery*. Westport, CT: Praeger, 1992, p.15.
87 David D. Laitin, *Identity in Formation: the Russian-Speaking Populations in the Near Abroad*. Ithaca, NY: Cornell University Press, 1998, p.29.
88 Laitin, *Identity in Formation*, p.34, emphasis added.
89 Hilary Pilkington, *Migration, Displacement and Identity in Post-Soviet Russia*. London: Routledge, 1998, p.195.
90 Bhiku Parekh, 'Three theories of immigration', in S. Spencer (ed.), *Strangers and Citizens: a Positive Approach to Migrants and Refugees*. London: IPPR/Rivers Oram Press, 1994, p.101.
91 Andre Liebich, *Les minorites nationales en Europe centrale et orientale*, p.130.
92 Alexander Solzhenitsyn, *The Russian Question at the End of the Twentieth Century*. New York: Farrar, Straus, and Giroux, 1995, p.108.
93 Dmitry Gorenburg, 'Nationalism for the Masses: Popular Support for Nationalism in Russia's Ethnic Republics', in *Europe–Asia Studies*, 53, no.1 (January 2001), p.103. The index is reported on p.100 (Table 15).
94 See Peter J. Stavrakis and Joan DeBardeleden (eds), *Beyond the Monolith: the Emergence of Regionalism in Post-Soviet Russia*. Baltimore, MD: Johns Hopkins University Press, 1998.
95 See John W. Slocum, 'Sovereignty Games in the Russian Federation'. Paper prepared for the ISA-West Annual Meeting, 20 October 1995, University of Colorado, Boulder.
96 Pal Kolsto, *Political Construction Sites: Nation-Building in Russia and the Post-Soviet States*. Boulder, CO: Westview Press, 2000, p.227.
97 Anil Seal, *The Emergence of Indian Nationalism: Competition and Collaboration in the Later Nineteenth Century*. Cambridge: Cambridge University Press, 1971, p.1.
98 Seal, *The Emergence of Indian Nationalism*, p.25.
99 A.R. Desai, *Social Background of Indian Nationalism*. 4th edn. Bombay: Popular Prakashan, 1966, p.44. For a more recent history, see G. Aloysius, *Nationalism Without a Nation in India*. New Delhi: Oxford University Press, 1999.

100 Desai, p.49.
101 Desai, pp.307–8.
102 Partha Chatterjee, *The Nation and Its Fragments: Colonial and Postcolonial Histories*. Princeton, NJ: Princeton University Press, 1993, p.6.
103 *ibid.*
104 Peter van der Veer, *Religious Nationalism: Hindus and Muslims in India*. Berkeley, CA: University of California Press, 1994, p.201.
105 Jim Masselos, *Indian Nationalism: an History*. New Delhi: Sterling Publishers, 1991, p.24.
106 Desai, *Social Background of Indian Nationalism*, p.322.
107 M.S. Golwalkar, *Bunch of Thoughts*. Bagalore: Jagarana Prakashana, 1966, p.2.
108 V.D. Savarkar, *Hindutva*. Poona: S. R. Date, 1942, p.1. For a study of turn-of-the-century Hinduism, see John Zavos, *The Emergence of Hindu Nationalism in India*. New York: Oxford University Press, 2000.
109 Christophe Jaffrelot, *The Hindu Nationalist Movement in India*. New York: Columbia University Press, 1996, p.32.
110 Desai, *Social Background of Indian Nationalism*, pp.335–42.
111 R. Suntharalingam, *Indian Nationalism*. New Delhi: Vikas, 1983, p.187.
112 Van der Veer, *Religious Nationalism*, p.2.
113 Suntharalingam, *Indian Nationalism*, pp.232–3.
114 Suntharalingam, *Indian Nationalism*, p.377.
115 Masselos, *Indian Nationalism*, p.185.
116 *ibid.*, p.380.
117 Suntharalingam, *Indian Nationalism*, p.381.
118 Quoted in Sumit Ganguly, *The Origins of War in South Asia: Indo-Pakistani Conflicts Since 1947*. Boulder, CO: Westview Press, 1994, pp.20–1.
119 Seal, *The Emergence of Indian Nationalism*, p.351.
120 Jawaharlal Nehru, *Toward Freedom: the Autobiography of Jawaharlal Nehru*. New York: The John Day Company, 1941, p.292.
121 Nehru, *Toward Freedom*, p.240.
122 Ganguly, *The Origins of War in South Asia*, p.23.
123 *ibid.*, p.24.
124 Quoted in Manmath Nath Das, *Partition and Independence of India: Inside Story of the Mountbatten Days*. New Delhi: Vision Books, 1982, p.13.
125 Quoted in Das, *Partition and Independence of India*, p.88.
126 Quoted in Sunil Khilnani, *The Idea of* India. New York: Farrar Straus Giroux, p.165.
127 Alastair Lamb, *The Kashmir Problem: a Historical Survey*. New York: Frederick A. Praeger, 1966, p.35.
128 See K. Sarwar Hasan (ed.), *Documents on the Foreign Relations of Pakistan: the Kashmir Question*. Karachi: Pakistan Institute of International Affairs, 1966, pp.11–16.
129 Josef Korbel, *Danger in Kashmir*. Princeton, NJ: Princeton University Press, revised edition, 1966, p.49.
130 Lamb, *The Kashmir Problem*, p.33.
131 Gurharpal Singh, 'Ethnic Conflict in India: a Case Study of Punjab', in John McGarry and Brendan O'Leary (eds), *The Politics of Ethnic Conflict Regulation*. London: Routledge, 1993, p.86. See also Paul Brass, 'The Punjab Crisis and the Unity of India', in A. Kholi (ed.), *India's Democracy*. Princeton: Princeton University Press, 1987.

132 Maya Chadda, *Ethnicity, Security, and Separatism in India*. New York: Columbia University Press, 1997, p.217.
133 R.N. Kaul, *Sheikh Mohammad Abdullah: a Political Phoenix*. New Delhi: Sterling Publishers, 1985, p.24.
134 Ashutosh Varshney, 'Three Compromised Nationalisms: why Kashmir has been a problem', in Raju G.C. Thomas (ed.), *Perspectives on Kashmir: the Roots of Conflict in South Asia*. Boulder, CO: Westview Press, 1992.
135 Sumit Ganguly, 'Ethno-religious Conflict in South Asia', *Survival*, 35, no.2 (1993), p.92.
136 For details of the Indo-Pakistan confrontation over Kashmir, see Sumit Ganguly, *The Crisis in Kashmir: Portents of War, Hopes of Peace*. Cambridge: Cambridge University Press, 1999; also his 'Avoiding War in Kashmir', *Foreign Affairs*, 69, no.5 (Winter 1990–91), pp.57–73. See also William E. Burrows and Robert Windrem (eds), *Critical Mass: the Dangerous Race for Superweapons in a Fragmenting World*. New York: Simon and Schuster, 1994, pp.81–8 and 349–77.
137 P.S. Suryanarayana, 'Afghan Support to Pak. in the Event of War', in *The Hindu*, International edition (15 October 1994), p.3.
138 Inder Malhotra, 'One False Step', *Sunday* (16–22 June 1991), p.18.
139 N.V. Subramanian, 'Coping With Change', *Sunday* (6–12 June 1993), p.10.
140 Malhotra, 'One False Step', p.18.
141 'The Breaking Point', *Sunday* (3–9 May 1992), p.15.
142 See David Pugliese, 'Private Armies Threaten Established Borders', *Defense News* (4 April 1994), p.12, and Walter Jayawardhana, 'Guns For Drugs', *Sunday* (4–10 November 1990), p.84.
143 For details, see Bertil Lintner, 'The Indo-Burmese Frontier: A Legacy of Violence', *Jane's Intelligence Review*, 6, no.1 (1 January 1994).
144 See Rajiv Kapur, *Sikh Separatism: the Politics of Faith*. London: Allen and Unwin, 1984.
145 Pravin J. Patel, 'Violent Protest in India: the Punjab Movement', in *Journal of International Affairs*, 40 (1987), p.279.
146 Rajiv A. Kapur, '"Khalistan": India's Punjab Problem', in *Third World Quarterly*, 9 (1987), p. 1214.
147 Kapur, '"Khalistan": India's Punjab Problem', p.1216.
148 Patel, 'Violent Protest in India', p.278.
149 Singh, 'Ethnic Conflict in India', p.87.
150 See Sugata Bose and Ayesha Jalal (eds), *Nationalism, Democracy, and Development: State and Politics in India*. New Delhi: Oxford University Press, 1999.
151 Van der Veer, *Religious Nationalism*, p.23.
152 See A. Vanaik, *The Painful Transition: Bourgeois Democracy in India*. London: Verso, 1990.
153 Van der Veer, *Religious Nationalism*, p.202.
154 Ashutosh Varshney, 'Ethnic Conflict and Civil Society: India and Beyond', in *World Politics*, 53, no.3 (April 2001), p.371. The cities are Ahmedabad, Aligarh, Baroda, Bombay, Calcutta, Delhi, Hyderabad, and Meerut. They account for only 18% of the Indian urban population. Calcutta and Delhi drop out of the list if only post-1970 data are examined. See Table 1, p.372.
155 Van der Veer, *Religious Nationalism*, p.23.
156 Thomas Blom Hansen, *The Saffron Wave: Democracy and Hindu Nationalism in India*. Princeton, NJ: Princeton University Press, 1999, p.4.

157   See B. Graham, *Hindu Nationalism and Indian Politics: the Origins and Development of the Bharatiya Janata Party.* New Delhi: Cambridge University Press, 1990.

158   Andrew Wyatt, 'Two Steps Forward, One Step Back: the BJP and the General and State Assembly Elections in India, 1999–2000', *Asian Affairs*, (2000), p.291.

159   Nirad C. Chaudhuri, *Hinduism: a Religion to Live By.* Oxford: Oxford University Press, 1997.

160   Hansen, *The Saffron Wave*, p.229.

4   Home Writ Small: Nationalisms of Separatist Movements

1   For a pioneering study of comparative secession and a review of definitions, see Louis L. Snyder, *Global Mini-Nationalisms: Autonomy or Independence.* Westport, CT: Greenwood Press, 1982, pp.xv–xvii.

2   Christopher Lasch, *The Revolt of the Elites and the Betrayal of Democracy.* New York: W.W. Norton, 1993.

3   Philip Resnick, 'English Canada: the Nation that Dares not Speak its Name', in Kenneth McRoberts (ed.), *Beyond Quebec: Taking Stock of Canada.* Montreal: McGill-Queen's University Press, 1995, p.88.

4   Ulf Hedetoft, 'The Nation State Meets the World: National Identities in the Context of Transnationality and Cultural Globalization', Aalborg, Denmark: Center for International Studies, Aalborg University, Discussion Paper No. 2/97, p.25. The concept of 'local knowledge' comes from Clifford Geertz, *Local Knowledge.* New York: Basic Books, 1983.

5   The study was carried out in 1999 by l'Observatoire interregional du politique and l'Institut Destree and reported in *Le Soir* (Brussels), 22 April 1999, p.3.

6   Simon Jenkins, 'A Victory for Cowards', *The Times* (London), June 11, 1999.

7   A selected list includes: Christopher Bennett, *Yugoslavia's Bloody Collapse: Causes, Course and Consequences.* New York: New York University Press, 1996. Mihailo Crnobrnja, *The Yugoslav Drama.* Montreal: McGill-Queen's University Press, 1996. Thomas Cushman and Stjepan Mestrovic (eds), *This Time We Knew: Western Responses to Genocide in Bosnia.* New York: New York University Press, 1996. Bogdan Denitch, *Ethnic Nationalism: the Tragic Death of Yugoslavia.* Minneapolis, MN: University of Minnesota Press, 1994. Richard Holbrooke, *To End a War.* New York: Random House, 1998. Misha Glenny, *The Fall of Yugoslavia: the Third Balkan War.* New York: Penguin Books, 1996. Radha Kumar, *Divide and Fall? Bosnia in the Annals of Partition.* London: Verso, 1997. Branka Magas, *The Destruction of Yugoslavia: Tracking the Break-Up 1980–92.* London: Verso, 1993. David Owen, *Balkan Odyssey.* New York: Harcourt Brace, and Company, 1996. Richard H. Ullman, *The World and Yugoslavia's Wars.* New York: Council on Foreign Relations, 1996. Warren Zimmerman, *Origins of a Catastrophe: Yugoslavia and its Destroyers.* New York: Times Books, 1996. An excellent eight-part series on Bosnia that includes reviews of some of these books and others is by Mark Danner in *The New York Review of Books* from November 20, 1997 to September 24, 1998. For an insightful cultural approach, see Andrew Baruch Wachtel, *Making a Nation, Breaking a Nation: Literature and Cultural Politics in Yugoslavia.* Stanford, CA: Stanford University Press, 1998.

8   Mark Danner, 'Kosovo: The Meaning of Victory', in *New York Review of Books*, XLVI, no. 12 (July 15, 1999), p.54.

9   Howard Adelman, 'Quebec: the Morality of Secession', in Joseph H. Carens (ed.), *Is Quebec Nationalism Just? Perspectives from Anglophone Canada.* Montreal: McGill-Queen's University Press, 1995, p.165.

10 Nelson Mandela, *Long Walk to Freedom*. London: Little, Brown and Company, 1994, p.188.

11 Adrian Hastings, *The Construction of Nationhood: Ethnicity, Religion and Nationalism*. Cambridge: Cambridge University Press, 1997, p.164.

12 Ian S. Lustick, *Unsettled States, Disputed Lands: Britain and Ireland, France and Algeria, Israel and the West Bank-Gaza*. Ithaca, NY: Cornell University Press, 1993, p. 442.

13 I. William Zartman, 'Introduction: Posing the Problem of State Collapse', in Zartman (ed.), *Collapsed States: the Disintegration and Restoration of Legitimate Authority*. Boulder, CO: Lynne Rienner, 1995, p.1.

14 Zartman, 'Introduction', p.5.

15 There are few book-length studies of the modern Zulu nation. The most important is Dafnah Golan, *Inventing Shaka: Using History in the Construction of Zulu Nationalism*. Boulder, CO: Lynne Rienner, 1994.

16 Dan Wylie 'The malleable symbol of Shaka', *Johannesburg Mail and Guardian*, January 29, 1999. It reviews Carolyn Hamilton, *Terrific Majesty: the Powers of Shaka Zulu and the Limits of Historical Invention*. Cambridge, MA: Harvard University Press, 1998.

17 Quoted by Stephen Taylor, *Shaka's Children: a History of the Zulu People*. London: HarperCollins, 1995, p. 102.

18 Taylor, *Shaka's Children*, p.109.

19 Taylor, *Shaka's Children*, p.145.

20 Taylor, *Shaka's Children*, p.204.

21 Quoted by Brian Roberts, *The Zulu Kings*. London: Book Club, 1974, p.348. The reference is to John Colenso, Anglican bishop of Natal, excommunicated from the Church of England for heresy, who accepted many of the practices of the Zulus, such as polygamy.

22 On the Zulu perspective on the 1879 war, see John Laband, *Kingdom in Crisis: the Zulu Response to the British Invasion of 1879*. Durban: University of Natal Press, 1992. On the effects on Zululand of the 'peace' that followed the war, see Jeff Guy, *The Destruction of the Zulu Kingdom: the Civil War in Zululand, 1879–1884*. London: Longman, 1979. On this same subject, see Donald R. Morris, *Washing of the Spears: the Rise and Fall of the Zulu Nation*. New York: Da Capo Press, 1998.

23 Taylor, *Shaka's Children*, p.288.

24 Taylor, *Shaka's Children*, p.339.

25 See Donald L. Horowitz, *A Democratic South Africa: Constitutional Engineering in a Divided Society*. New York: Oxford University Press, 1991.

26 Albert Luthuli, *Let My People Go*. Glasgow: Fontana, 1987, p.179.

27 Gerhard Mare, *Ethnicity and Politics in South Africa*. London: Zed Books, 1993, p.67.

28 On Buthelezi see Michael Massing, 'The Chief' in *New York Review of Books*, 12 February 1987.

29 Taylor, *Shaka's Children*, p.2.

30 Horowitz, *A Democratic South Africa?* p.130.

31 'Mandela: A Tiger for our Time', *Johannesburg Mail and Guardian*, June 4, 1999.

32 Taylor, *Shaka's Children*, p.299.

33 See Gerrit Viljoen and Francois Venter, 'A Culture of Negotiation: the Politics of Inclusion in South Africa', *Harvard International Review*. 17, 4 (Fall 1995), p.80.

34 'Buthelezi Accused of Fanning Unrest', *Glasgow Herald*, 4 May 1995.

35 Suzanne Daley, 'Fear Still Accompanies Many South Africans to Polls', *New York Times* (26 May 1999).

36 See the Inkatha web site: www.ifp.org.za
37 Cited by www.ifp.org.za/emanifesto.htm
38 Leonard Thompson, *A History of South Africa*. New Haven, CT: Yale Nota Bene, 2001, p.290.
39 Horowitz, *A Democratic South Africa?* p.61.
40 Gerhard Mare and Georgina Hamilton, *An Appetite for Power: Buthelezi's Inkatha and the Politics of Loyal Resistance*. Johannesburg: Rava, 1987.
41 Mare, *Ethnicity and Politics in South Africa*, p.103.
42 Mare, *Ethnicity and Politics in South Africa*, p.78.
43 Mare, *Ethnicity and Politics in South Africa*, p.60.
44 Taylor, *Shaka's Children*, p.265.
45 Mare, *Ethnicity and Politics in South Africa*, p.63.
46 These differences are reported in Alexander Johnson, 'South Africa: the Election and the Emerging Party System', *International Affairs*, 70, no. 4 (October 1994), pp.732–3.
47 For an overview of forms of Quebec nationalism, see Leon Dion, *Quebec 1945–2000: à la recherche du Quebec*. Quebec: Les presses de l'université Laval, 1987.
48 Daniel Latouche, 'Quebec in the Emerging North American Configuration', in Robert L. Earle and John D. Wirth (eds), *Identities in North America: the Search for Community*. Stanford, CA: Stanford University Press, 1995, p. 118.
49 Michel Seymour, 'Le probleme de la nation quebecoise n'est pas son existence mais sa (non) reconnaissance', *Le Devoir* (19 September 1999).
50 See Janet Ajzenstat, *The Political Thought of Lord Durham*. Montreal: McGill-Queen's University Press, 1988.
51 *La Revue Indépendantiste* (no date given) cited by Lionel Albert, 'True Quebecers?' *Montreal Gazette* (20 September 1999), p.B3.
52 See Louis Balthazar, *Bilan du nationalisme au Quebec*. Montreal: l'Hexagone, 1990.
53 On language of education for immigrants, see Donat Taddeo and Raymond Taras, *Le débat linguistique au Quebec*. Montreal: Les Presses de l'Universite de Montreal, 1986.
54 Charles Taylor, *Reconciling the Solitudes*: Essays on Canadian Federalism and Nationalism. Montreal: McGill-Queens University Press, 1993. p.34.
55 J.F. Bosher, *The Gaullist Attack on Canada, 1967–1997*. Montreal: McGill-Queen's University Press, 1999; Frederic Bastien, *Relations particulières: la France face au Quebec après de Gaulle*. Montreal: Boreal, 1999.
56 'Rencontre avec la CIA', *L'actualité* (15 mai 2001), p.24. See also a biography of Parizeau by Pierre Duchesne, *Le croisé*. Montreal: Quebec/Amerique, 2001.
57 Fernand Dumont, *The Vigil of Quebec*. Toronto: University of Toronto Press, 1971.
58 Marcel Rioux, *Les Quebecois*. Paris: Le Seuil, 1974.
59 Leon Dion, *Nationalismes et politique au Quebec*. Montreal: Hurtubise, 1975.
60 Pierre Vallieres, *White Niggers of America: the Precocious Autobiography of a Quebec 'Terrorist'*. New York: Monthly Review Press, 1971.
61 Hubert Guindon, *Quebec Society: Tradition, Modernity and Nationhood*. Toronto: University of Toronto Press, 1988.
62 Latouche, 'Quebec in the Emerging North America', p.120.
63 Alain-G. Gagnon (ed.), *Quebec: State and Society*. Toronto: Methuen, 1984, especially the chapters by Pierre Fournier, Jorge Niosi, and Marc Renaud.
64 Francois Rocher (ed.), *Bilan quebecois du fédéralisme canadien*. Montreal: VLB Editeur, 1992.

65 Latouche, 'Quebec in the Emerging North America', p.123, summarizing the argument of Anne Legare and Nicole Morf, *La société contre l'état*. Montreal: Hurturbise, 1989.

66 Latouche, 'Quebec in the Emerging North America', p.125.

67 Latouche, 'Quebec in the Emerging North America', p.126.

68 Guy Laforest, *De la prudence: textes politiques*. Montreal: Boreal, 1993, p.171.

69 John Ralston Saul, *Reflections of a Siamese Twin: Canada at the End of the Twentieth Century*. Toronto: Penguin/Viking, 1998, p.119.

70 Gilles Duceppe, *Question d'identité*. Montreal: Lanctot Editeur, 2000, p.122.

71 Latouche, 'Quebec in the Emerging North America', p.117.

72 Latouche, 'Quebec in the Emerging North America', p.127.

73 Latouche, 'Quebec in the Emerging North America', p.131.

74 Latouche, 'Quebec in the Emerging North America', p.136.

75 Latouche, 'Quebec in the Emerging North America', p.136.

76 David J. Bercuson and Barry Cooper, *Deconfederation*. Toronto: Key Porter, 1991, p.16.

77 Kenneth McRoberts, *Misconceiving Canada: the Struggle for National Unity*. Toronto: Oxford University Press, 1997, p.255.

78 Michael Keating, *Nations Against the State: the New Politics of Nationalism in Quebec, Catalonia and Scotland*. New York: St. Martin's Press, 1965, p.65.

78 Janet Ajzenstat, 'Decline of Procedural Liberalism: the Slippery Slope to Secession', in Joseph H. Carens (ed.), *Is Quebec Nationalism Just? Perspectives from Anglophone Canada*. Montreal: McGill-Queen's University Press, 1995, p.132.

80 On the evolution of sovereigntist support in Quebec in the period 1962–94, see Jonathan Lemco, *Turmoil in the Peaceable Kingdom: the Quebec Sovereignty Movement and its Implications for Canada and the United States*. Toronto: University of Toronto Press, 1994, p.75. Also, Jean-Francois Lisée, *The Trickster: Robert Bourassa and Quebecers 1990–1992*. Toronto: Lorimer, 1994, p.360.

81 Guy Laforest, *De la prudence*, p.161.

82 Guy Bertrand, *Enough is Enough: an Attorney's Struggle for Democracy in Quebec*. Toronto: ECW Press, 1996, p. 144.

83 Quoted in Lawrence Martin, *The Antagonist: Lucien Bouchard and the Politics of Delusion*. Toronto: Penguin Books, 1997, p.256.

84 'Act respecting the process for determining the political and constitutional future of Quebec', December 6, 1994. S.Q., 1991, c.34.

85 Martin, *The Antagonist*, p.283.

86 See Ignacio Ramonet, 'Quebec et souveraineté', *Le Monde diplomatique* (Fevrier 2001).

87 Adelman, 'Quebec: the Morality of Secession', p.176.

88 Adelman, 'Quebec: the Morality of Secession', p.177.

89 'Guy Bertrand v. the Honorable Paul Begin et al', Superior Court of Quebec, September 8, 1995, published in Bertrand, *Enough is Enough*, p.150.

90 Supreme Court of Canada, 'Quebec Constitutional Amendment Reference', no. 2, December 1982, 45 N.R. 317, 331.

91 'Reference re Secession of Quebec', *Supreme Court Reports*, File No. 25506, August 20, 1998.

92 'Reference re Secession of Quebec', 'Reference by Governor in Council', Section (2).

93 'Reference re Secession of Quebec', 'Reference by Governor in Council', Section (2).

94 'Reference re Secession of Quebec', para. 66.
95 'Reference re Secession of Quebec', para. 76.
96 'Reference re Secession of Quebec', 'Reference by Governor in Council', Section (2).
97 'Reference re Secession of Quebec', paras. 123–4.
98 'Reference re Secession of Quebec', para. 112.
99 'Reference re Secession of Quebec', para. 122.
100 'Reference re Secession of Quebec', para. 126.
101 'Reference re Secession of Quebec', para. 138.
102 'Reference re Secession of Quebec', para. 136.
103 'Reference re Secession of Quebec', data cited in para. 135.
104 'Reference re Secession of Quebec', para. 154. Emphasis added.
105 United Nations General Assembly, *Declaration on the Occasion of the Fiftieth Anniversary of the United Nations*. GA Res. 50/6 (9 November 1995). Emphasis added.
106 'Reference re Secession of Quebec', para. 143.
107 European Community, *Declaration on the Guidelines on the Recognition of New States in Eastern Europe and in the Soviet Union*. 31 I.L.M. 1486 (1992).
108 'Reference re Secession of Quebec', para. 146.
109 Taylor, *Reconciling the Solitudes*, p.31.
110 Latouche, 'Quebec in the Emerging North America', p.128. Emphasis added.
111 David Gamble, 'Definition of a Quebecer bedevils the Bloc', *Montreal Gazette* (18 April 1999).
112 Laforest, *De la prudence*, p.172.
113 Philip Authier, 'Quebecers Defined', *Montreal Gazette* (12 September 1999).
114 Latouche, 'Quebec in the Emerging North America', p.138.
115 Commission des États généraux sur la langue française au Québec, 'Rapport', août 2001. See http://www.etatsgeneraux.gouv.qc.ca/
116 Letter from Stephane Dion, Federal Intergovernmental Affairs Minister, to Joseph Facal, Quebec Intergovernmental Affairs Minister, October 19, 1999. Reported in the *Montreal Gazette* (20 October 1999).
117 'Survey of Canada', *The Economist* (29 June 1991), p.3.
118 Edward Greenspon and Anthony Wilson-Smith, *Double Vision: the Inside Story of the Liberals in Power*. Toronto: Seal Books, 1997, p.324.
119 Lansing Lamont, *Breakup: the Coming End of Canada and the Stakes for America*. Toronto: Key Porter Books, 1995, p.23.
120 Lamont, *Breakup*, p.27.

5 Uninational Homes: Right-Wing Nationalism

1 For a discussion, see Sabrina P. Ramet (ed.), *The Radical Right in Central and Eastern Europe Since 1989*. University Park, PA: Pennsylvania State University Press, 1999, p.5.
2 Mark Juergensmeyer, *The New Cold War? Religious Nationalism Confronts the Secular State*. Berkeley, CA: University of California Press, 1993, p.31. For a comparative study of fundamentalisms, see Scott Appleby (ed.), *Spokesmen for the Despised*. Chicago: University of Chicago Press, 1996.
3 Charles S. Maier, *The Unmasterable Past: History, Holocaust, and German National Identity*. Cambridge, MA: Harvard University Press, 1988, p.164.

4   Maier, *The Unmasterable Past*, p.166.
5   Seymour Martin Lipset, *Political Man*. Baltimore, MD: Johns Hopkins University Press, 1981, p.489.
6   Eva Kolinsky, 'A Future for Right Extremism in Germany?' in Paul Hainsworth (ed.), *The Extreme Right in Europe and the USA*. New York: St. Martin's Press – now Palgrave Macmillan, 1992, p.78.
7   Hans-Georg Betz, *Radical Right-Wing Populism in Western Europe*. New York: St. Martin's Press, 1994, p.29. For a comparative perspective on the right-wing revival, see Peter H. Merkl and Leonard Weinberg (eds), *The Revival of Right Wing Extremism in the Nineties*. London: Frank Cass, 1997. Also, Jeffrey Kaplan and Tore Bjorgo (eds), *Nation and Race: the Developing Euro-American Racist Subculture*. Boston: Northeastern University Press, 1998. On right-wing violence, see Tore Bjorgo (ed.), *Terror from the Extreme Right*. London: Frank Cass, 1995.
8   Betz, *Radical Right-Wing Populism in Western Europe*, p.177.
9   See Jeffrey Herf, *Divided Memory: The Nazi Past in the Two Germanys*. Cambridge, MA: Harvard University Press, 1998.
10 Frederick Kempe, *Father/Land: a Personal Search for the New Germany*. New York: Putnam, 1999, p.10.
11 Rainer Munz and Ralf Ulrich, 'Too Many Foreigners? Demographic Developments, Changing Patterns of Migration and the Absorption of Immigrants: the Case of Germany, 1945–1994'. Washington, DC: Georgetown University, Center for German and European Studies, Working Paper, March 1995, p. 40.
12 Christian Joppke, *Immigration and the Nation-State: The United States, Germany, and Great Britain*. New York: Oxford University Press, 1999.
13 Christian Joppke, 'Why Liberal States Accept Unwanted Immigrants', *World Politics*, 50, no. 2 (1998), p.292.
14 Gershon Shafir, *Immigrants and Nationalists: Ethnic Conflict and Accommodation in Catalonia, the Basque Country, Latvia, and Estonia*. Albany, NY: SUNY Press, 1995, p. 14.
15 Ivan Light, 'Nationalism and Anti-Immigrant Movements in Europe and North America'. Berkeley, CA: University of California, Center for German and European Studies, Working Paper 4.3 (August 1995), p.5.
16 Benedict Anderson, 'Exodus', *Critical Enquiry*, 20 (Winter 1994), p.327.
17 Benedict Anderson, *The Spectre of Comparisons: Nationalism, Southeast Asia and the World*. London: Verso, 1998, p.74.
18 Benedict Anderson, 'Introduction', in Gopal Balakrishnan (ed.), *Mapping the Nation*. London: Verso, 1996, p.9.
19 Committee of International Relations, Group Advancement of Psychiatry, *Us and Them: the Psychology of Ethnonationalism*. New York: Mazel, 1987, p.20. Cited by Vamik Volkan, *Blood Lines: from Ethnic Pride to Ethnic Terrorism*. New York: Farrar, Straus and Giroux, 1997, p.22.
20 Samuel Huntington, 'The Erosion of American National Interest', *Foreign Affairs*, 76, no. 5 (September–October 1997), p.33.
21 Jan Nederveen Pieterse, 'Varieties of Ethnic Politics and Ethnicity Discourse', in Edwin N. Wilmsen and Patrick McAllisten (eds), *The Politics of Difference: Ethnic Premises in a World of Power*. Chicago: University of Chicago Press, 1996, p.35.
22 Nina Glick Schiller, Linda Basch, and Christina Szanton Blanc, 'From Immigrant to Transmigrant: Theorizing Transnational Migration', in *Anthropological Quarterly*, 68, no. 1 (January 1995), p.48. Quoted in Madeleine Demetriou, 'Towards Post-Nationalism? Diasporic Identities and the Political Process'. Aalborg, Denmark: Center for International Studies, Discussion Paper No. 6/99, 1999, p.2.

23 Khachig Toloyan, 'Rethinking Diaspora(s): Stateless Power in the Transnational Moment', *Diaspora*, 5, no. 1 (Spring 1996), p.30. For a study that assumes that because they are by definition transnational, immigrants should enjoy transnational rights, including citizenship, voting, and so on in home and host societies, see Yasemin N. Soysal, *Limits of Citizenship: Migrants and Postnational Membership in Europe*. Chicago: University of Chicago Press, 1994.

24 Soysal, *Limits of Citizenship*, p.143.

25 Demetriou, 'Towards Post-Nationalism?' p.9.

26 Rogers Brubaker, *Citizenship and Nationhood in France and Germany*. Cambridge, MA: Harvard University Press, 1992.

27 Alec G. Hargreaves, *Immigration, 'Race' and Ethnicity in Contemporary France*. London: Routledge, 1995, p.160.

28 Gunter Grass, *Two States – One Nation?* New York: Harcourt Brace Jovanovich, 1990.

29 Niall Ferguson, 'Uber the Hill: Why the New Germany's a Weakling', in *New Republic*, 204, no. 5 (4 February 1991), p.8.

30 Reported by Douglas B. Klusmeyer, 'Aliens, Immigrants, and Citizens: the Politics of Inclusion in the Federal Republic of Germany', *Daedalus*, 122, no. 3 (June 1993), p.89.

31 Paul Hockenos, *Free to Hate: the Rise of the Right in Post-Communist Eastern Europe*. New York: Routledge, 1993, p.28.

32 Part of this account is based on Klusmeyer, 'Aliens, Immigrants, and Citizens', pp.81ff.

33 Articles 2–5 of the Basic Law, reprinted in Elmar Hucko (ed.), *The Democratic Tradition: Four German Constitutions*. Oxford: Berg Publishers, 1989, pp.194–5.

34 See Ray Rist, *Guestworkers in Germany: the Prospects for Pluralism*. New York: Praeger, 1978. Also, Ulrich Herbert, *A History of Foreign Labor in Germany, 1880–1980*. Ann Arbor, MI: University of Michigan Press, 1990.

35 Betz, *Radical Right-Wing Populism*, p.103. See also Meredith Watts, *Xenophobia in United Germany: Generations, Modernization, and Ideology*. New York: St. Martin's Press – now Palgrave Macmillan, 1997.

36 Cited by Klusmeyer, 'Aliens, Immigrants, and Citizens', p.86.

37 Gerhard de Rham, 'Naturalization: the Politics of Citizenship Acquisition', in Zig Henry Layton (ed.), *The Political Rights of Migrant Workers in Western Europe*. Newbury Park, CA: Sage, 1990, p.182.

38 Jeffrey Peck, Mitchell Ash, and Christiane Lemke, 'Natives, Strangers, and Foreigners: Constituting Germans by Constructing Others', in Konrad H. Jarausch (ed.), *After Unity: Reconfiguring German Identities*. Providence, RI: Berghahn Books, 1997, p.78.

39 'Germany's New Citizenship Law'. http://www.bundesregierung.de/english/01/0103/04875/index.html

40 Peck *et al.*, 'Natives, Strangers, and Foreigners', p.102.

41 Riva Castoryano, *La France, l'Allemagne et leurs immigrés: negocier l'identité*. Paris: A. Colin, 1997.

42 'Germany's New Citizenship Law "A Foundation for Peace"'. http://www.bundesregierung.de/english/01/0103/04669/index.html

43 Betz, *Radical Right-Wing Populism*, p.72.

44 Barbara Marshall, 'German Migration Policies', in Gordon Smith, *et al.*, (eds), *Developments in German Politics*. Durham, NC: Duke University Press, 1992, pp. 255–6.

45 German Interior Ministry figures cited by *The Economist* (4–10 July 1998), p.45.
46 See Nicholas Fraser (ed.), *The Voice of Modern Hatred: Encounters With Europe's New Right*. New York: Overlook Press, 2001.
47 Klusmeyer, 'Aliens, Immigrants, and Citizens', p.86.
48 Jost Halfmann, 'Immigration and Citizenship in Germany: Contemporary Dilemmas', *Political Studies*, 45, no. 2 (June 1997), p.273.
49 Parlement Europeen, *Rapport elaboré au nom de la commission d'enquête sur le racisme et la xenophobie*. Luxembourg: Communautes Europeennes, 1991, p.3. Cited by Betz, *Radical Right-Wing Populism*, p.85.
50 Figures cited by Betz, *Radical Right-Wing Populism*, p.89.
51 Betz, *Radical Right-Wing Populism*, p.171.
52 Fabian Virchow, 'Racial Nationalism as a Paradigm in International Relations: the Kosovo Conflict Seen by the Far Right in Germany'. Paper presented at the Fourth Pan-European International Relations Conference, University of Kent, Canterbury, September 2001. See also Jurgen Schwab, *Deutsche Bausteine: Grundlagen nationaler Politik*. Stuttgart: DS-Verlag, 1999. Schwab was NPD spokesman in this period.
53 Jurgen R. Winkler and Siegfried Schumann, 'Radical Right-Wing Parties in Contemporary Germany', in Hans-Georg Betz and Stefan Immerfall (eds), *The New Politics of the Right: Neo-Populist Parties and Movements in Established Democracies*. New York: St. Martin's Press – now Palgrave Macmillan, 1998, p.105.
54 John Leslie, 'Re-emerging Ethnic Politics in Germany: Far Right Parties and Violence'. Berkeley, CA: University of California, Center for German and European Studies, Working Paper 6.11 (circa 1994), p.64.
55 Cited by Jonathan Kaufman, 'New Wall of Hate Tilts Germany to Right', *Boston Globe* (15 November 1992).
56 Ingo Hasselbach, *Führer-Ex: Memoirs of a Former Neo-Nazi*. New York: Random House, 1996.
57 Reported by Hockenos, *Free to Hate*, p.37.
58 Hockenos, *Free to Hate*, p.103.
59 Hockenos, *Free to Hate*, pp.32–33.
60 Jeffrey M. Peck, 'Rac(e)ing the Nation: is there a German "Home?"' in Geoff Eley and Ronald Grigor Suny (eds). *Becoming National*. New York: Oxford University Press, 1996, p.488.
61 William Safran, 'Identite(s) juive(s)', p.35.
62 Ehud Sprinzak, *Brother Against Brother: Violence and Extremism in Israeli Politics from Altalena to the Rabin Assassination*. New York: Free Press, 1999, p.7.
63 Sprinzak, *Brother Against Brother*, pp. 7–8.
64 Sprinzak, *Brother Against Brother*, p.320.
65 See Shlomo Avineri, *The Making of Modern Zionism: the Intellectual Origins of the Jewish State*. New York: Basic Books, 1981.
66 Leslie Susser, 'Between Humanism and Nationalism', *Jerusalem Post* (1 January 1990).
67 Zeev Sternhell, *The Founding Myths of Israel*. Princeton, NJ: Princeton University Press, 1998, p.342.
68 A recent biography is Ernst Pawel, *The Labyrinth of Exile: a Life of Theodor Herzl*. New York: Farrar, Straus and Giroux, 1989.
69 Seth Kulick, 'The Evolution of Secular Judaism', *The Humanist*, 53, no. 2 (March 1993), p.33.
70 Neal Ascherson, 'A Breath of Foul Air', *The Independent*, Sunday review page (11 November 1990), p. 3. For an analysis of the issue of Jewish Russophobia,

see Liah Greenfeld, 'Russophobia', *New Republic*, 202, no. 6 (5 February 1990), pp.30ff.

71 Ian S. Lustick, *For the Land and the Lord: Jewish Fundamentalism in Israel*. New York: Council on Foreign Relations Press, 1988, p.79. See also Israel Shahak and Norton Mezvinsky, *Jewish Fundamentalism in Israel*. London: Pluto Books, 1999.

72 Ya'acov Talmon, 'Uniqueness and Universality', cited by Susser, 'Between Humanism and Nationalism'.

73 See Paul R. Mendes-Flohr, (ed.), *A Land of Two Peoples: Martin Buber on Jews and Arabs*. Oxford: Oxford University Press, 1983.

74 Susser, 'Between Humanism and Nationalism'.

75 Shmuel Almog, *Nationalism and Antisemitism in Modern Europe 1815–1945*. New York: Pergamon Press, 1991.

76 David Vital, *Zionism: the Formative Years*. Oxford: Clarendon Press, 1982, p.209.

77 For a review of five 'new histories', see Charles Glass, 'The Great Lie', *London Review of Books* (30 November 2000), pp.7–10.

78 Cited by Meron Benvenisti, 'The Last Revisionist Zionist', in *Foreign Affairs*, 74, no. 1 (January– February 1995), p.171. On the use of violence see Anita Shapira, *Land and Power: the Zionist Resort to Force, 1881–1948*. Stanford, CA: Stanford University Press, 1999.

79 See Shabtai Teveth, *Ben-Gurion: the Burning Ground, 1886–1948*. New York: Houghton Mifflin, 1987. An extraordinary example of repudiation of Jewish violence aimed at fellow Jews was Begin's refusal to engage in reprisals after Ben-Gurion, in 1948, had ordered the sinking of the 'Altalena', a ship transporting arms for Irgun fighters.

80 On the assassination see Kati Marton, *A Death in Jerusalem*. New York: Pantheon Books, 1994.

81 See Yitzhak Shamir, *Summing Up: an Autobiography*. Boston: Little, Brown, 1994.

82 For an assessment of Begin's role, see Amos Perlmutter, *The Life and Times of Menachem Begin*. New York: Doubleday, 1987.

83 Sternhell, *The Founding Myths of Israel*, p. 327.

84 Jean-Paul Sartre, *Reflexions sur la question juive*. Paris: Gallimard, 1954.

85 Lustick, *For the Land and the Lord*, p.3.

86 William Safran, 'Identité(s) juive(s) à la fin du Xxe siècle', paper presented at the colloquium 'Identité(s): Multiculturalisme, Intégration?' Université Stendhal, Grenoble III, 6–9 décembre 1998, p.1.

87 Safran, 'Identité(s) juive(s)', p.6. For an eclectic study of the choice Jews in the diaspora have faced from their early existence, see Aaron Wildavsky, *Assimilation Versus Separation: Joseph the Administrator and the Politics of Religion in Biblical Israel*. New Brunswick, NJ: Transaction Publishers, 1993.

88 Akiva Orr, *Israel: Politics, Myths, and Identity Crises*. London: Pluto Press, 1994, pp.44–52.

89 Philip Roth, *Operation Shylock: a Confession*. New York: Simon and Schuster, 1993, p.32.

90 Orr, *Israel*, p.47.

91 Oren Yiftachel and Avinoam Meir, 'Frontiers, Peripheries, and Ethnic Relations in Israel: an Introduction', in Yiftachel and Meir (eds), *Ethnic Frontiers and Peripheries: Landscapes of Development and Inequality in Israel*. Boulder, CO: Westview Press, 1998, p.8.

92 Isaiah Berlin, *Against the Current*. New York: Penguin Books, 1982, p.252.

93 See Ehud Sprinzak, *Gush Emunim: the Politics of Zionist Fundamentalism in Israel*. New York: American Jewish Committee, 1986. See also Eliezer Don Yehiya, 'The Book and the Sword: the Nationalist Yeshivot and Political Radicalism in Israel', in Martin E. Marty and R. Scott Appleby (eds), *Accounting for Fundamentalisms*. Chicago: University of Chicago Press, 1994.

94 Sprinzak, *Gush Emunim*, p.78.

95 See Raphael Mergui and Philippe Simonnot, *Meir Kahane and the Far Right in Israel*. London: Al-Saqi Books, 1989, p.101.

96 For her autobiography, see Geula Cohen, *Woman of Violence: Memoirs of a Young Terrorist*. New York: Holt, Rinehart and Winston, 1966.

97 Sprinzak, *Gush Emunim*, p.118. See also Amnon Rubinstein, *The Zionist Dream Revisited: from Herzl to Gush Emunim and Back*. New York: Schocken Books, 1984.

98 Sprinzak, *Gush Emunim*, p.109.

99 Lustick, *For the Land and the Lord*, p.121.

100 Moshe Levinger, 'We and the Arabs', *Nekuda*, 36 (27 November 1981), p.15. Cited by Lustick, *For the Land and the Lord*, p.121.

101 Benjamin Ze'ev Kahane, 'A Cultural War', in Michael Ben Horin (ed.), *Baruch Hagever*. Jerusalem: Special Publication, 1995, p.256. Cited in Sprinzak, *Brother Against Brother*, p.265.

102 See Mergui and Simonnot, *Meir Kahane and the Far Right in Israel*. In addition to a lengthy interview with Kahane, the two French journalists conducted interviews with other leaders of the far right such as Yuval Neeman, Geula Cohen, Rafael Eitan, Eliezer Waldman, Moshe Levinger, and Haim Druckman.

103 Sprinzak, *Gush Emunim*, p.220.

104 On the Palestinian struggle, see Yezid Sayigh, *Armed Struggle and the Search for State: the Palestinian National Movement 1949–1993*. Oxford: Oxford University Press, 1999.

105 Benvenisti, 'The Last Revisionist Zionist'.

106 Galia Golan, 'Israel and Palestinian Statehood', in Winston A. Van Horne (ed.), *Global Convulsions: Race, Ethnicity, and Nationalism at the End of the Twentieth Century*. Albany, NY: SUNY Press, 1997, p.174.

107 Leon Wieseltier, 'Letting Go: the Shock of Recognition', *New Republic*, 209, no. 14 (4 October 1993), p.28.

108 Orr, *Israel*, pp.160–70.

109 Reported in *Jerusalem Post* (6 March 1995).

110 Palestinians comprised up to 60 percent of Jordan's population, and ethnic tensions within the country erupted in 1970 into civil war, called Black September by the PLO.

111 A 'multiculturalism bill' was introduced in the Knesset by an Israeli-Arab legislator in 1999 but failed. It would have officially turned Israel into a multicultural rather than Jewish state. See Deborah Sontag, 'Israel: Jewish or Multicultural State?' *New York Times* (December 6, 1999).

112 Sternhell, *The Founding Myths of Israel*, pp. 339–40.

113 Sprinzak, *Brother Against Brother*, p.246.

114 Sprinzak, *Brother Against Brother*, p.252.

115 Cited by Orr, *Israel*, p.49.

116 Sternhell, *The Founding Myths of Israel*, p. 345.

117 Quoted by Safran, 'Identité(s) juive(s)', p. 35, fn.73.

118 Avishai Margalit, 'Israel: Why Barak Won', *New York Review of Books*, XLVI, no. 13 (August 12, 1999), p.49.

119   Glass, 'The Great Lie', p.9.
120   Mark Juergensmeyer, *Terror in the Mind of God*. Berkeley, CA: University of California Press, 2001. On Arab suicide bombers, see Ehud Sprinzak, 'Rational Fanatics', *Foreign Policy* (Sept./Oct. 2000), pp.66–73.

6   Transnational Homes: Pan-Nationalisms

1   Arjun Appadurai, *Modernity At Large: Cultural Dimensions of Globalization*. Minneapolis, MN: University of Minnesota Press, 1996, p.160.
2   Mark Juergensmeyer, *The New Cold War? Religious Nationalism Confronts the Secular State*. Berkeley, CA: University of California Press, 1993, p.23.
3   Juergensmeyer, *The New Cold War?*, p.41.
4   Mir Zohair Husain, *Global Islamic Politics*. New York: Harper Collins, 1995, p.31.
5   See Hamilton A. Gibb, *Mohammedanism*. New York: Oxford University Press, 1995.
6   Peter Mandaville, 'Reimagining the Umma: Transnational Spaces and the Changing Boundaries of Muslim Political Community', Center for International Studies, Aalborg University, Discussion Paper No. 7/99, p.25.
7   Amos Perlmutter, 'Rage of the Arab Intellectual'. *Washington Times* (11 November 1994). For a more objective introduction to the historical evolution of Arab nationalism, see Bassam Tibi, *Arab Nationalism: a Critical Enquiry*. London: Macmillan Press, 1981.
8   Mandaville, 'Reimagining the Umma', p.17.
9   Olivier Roy, *The Failure of Political Islam*. Cambridge, MA: Harvard University Press, 1994, p.11.
10   Fatima Mernissi, *Islam and Democracy: Fear of the Modern World*. New York: Addison-Wesley, 1992, p.13.
11   I am grateful to Professor Muhammad Siddiq, Department of Near Eastern Studies at the University of California, Berkeley, for clarifying this for me.
12   Walid Khalidi, 'Arabs and the West', *Middle East Forum*, XXXII, no. 10 (December 1957), p.15.
13   Edward W. Said, *Covering Islam: How the Media and the Experts Determine How We See the Rest of the World*. New York: Pantheon Books, 1981, p.xi.
14   Said, *Covering Islam*, p.31.
15   Ernest Gellner, *Postmodernism, Reason and Religion*. London: Routledge, 1992, p.5.
16   David Lerner, *The Passing of Traditional Society: Modernizing the Middle East*. New York: Free Press 1964, p.405.
17   Tristan James Mabry, 'Modernization, Nationalism, and Islam: an Examination of Ernest Gellner's Writings on Muslim Society with reference to Indonesia and Malaysia,' *Ethnic and Racial Studies*, 21, no. 1 (January 1998), p.87.
18   Dale F. Eickelman, 'From here to modernity: Ernest Gellner on nationalism and Islamic fundamentalism', in John A. Hall (ed.), *The State of the Nation: Ernest Gellner and the Theory of Nationalism*. Cambridge: Cambridge University Press, 1998, p.262.
19   Eickelman, 'From here to modernity', p.268.
20   Mabry, 'Modernization, Nationalism, and Islam', p.65.
21   Peter Mansfield, *The Arabs*. London: Penguin, 1990, p.457.
22   Roy, *The Failure of Political Islam*, p.2.
23   Roy, *The Failure of Political Islam*, p.6.

24 Mernissi, *Islam and Democracy*, p.113.
25 Mernissi, *Islam and Democracy*, p.54.
26 John L. Esposito, *The Islamic Threat: Myth or Reality?* New York: Oxford University Press, 1993, p.186.
27 Husain, *Global Islamic Politics*, p.24. For a detailed outline of the four types of revivalists, see his chart on pp.152–7.
28 Albert Hourani, 'History', in Leonard Binder (ed.), *The Study of the Middle East: Research and Scholarship in the Humanities and the Social Sciences*. New York: John Wiley and Sons, 1976, p.117.
29 Husain, *Global Islamic Politics*, p.25.
30 Husain, *Global Islamic Politics*, p.161.
31 *ibid.*, p.183.
32 Mernissi, *Islam and Democracy*, p.146.
33 The third volume is most concerned with the rise of the Islamic trade union movement in the Dutch East Indies. See Pramoedya Ananta Toer, *Footsteps*. New York: Penguin, 1996.
34 M. Hakan Yavuz, 'Turkey's Fault Lines and the Crisis of Kemalism', *Current History*, 99, no. 633 (January 2000), p.35.
35 C. Ernest Dawn, 'The Origins of Arab Nationalism', in Rashid Khalidi, Lisa Anderson, Muhammad Muslih, and Reeva S. Simon (eds), *The Origins of Arab Nationalism*. New York: Columbia University Press, 1991, pp.3–23.
36 Mansfield, *The Arabs*, p.507.
37 John Breuilly, *Nationalism and the State*. Chicago: University of Chicago Press, 1993, p.286.
38 Roy, *The Failure of Political Islam*, p.17.
39 Mike Holt, 'Divided Loyalties: Language and Ethnic Identity in the Arab World', in Yasir Suleiman (ed.), *Language and Identity in the Middle East and North Africa*. Richmond, Surrey: Curzon Press, 1996, p.23.
40 Appadurai, *Modernity At Large*, p.167.
41 Shaul Bakhash, *The Reign of the Ayatollahs: Iran and the Islamic Revolution*. New York: Basic Books, 1990, pp. 233–4.
42 Bakhash, *The Reign of the Ayatollahs*, p.261.
43 For an introduction to post-Khomeini Iran's relations with the West, see Edward G. Shirley, 'Not Fanatics, and Not Friends', *Atlantic Monthly*, 272 (December 1993), pp. 105–12.
44 Qaddafi's Islamic manifesto was contained in his three-volume *Green Book*: *The Solution to the Problem of Democracy* (1975), *Solution of the Economic Problem: Socialism* (1977), and *Social Basis of the Third International Theory* (1979).
45 Islamic Association of Cairo University, 'Lessons from Iran', in John J. Donohue and John L. Esposito (eds), *Islam in Transition: Muslim Perspectives*. New York: Oxford University Press, 1982, p.247.
46 Roy, *The Failure of Political Islam*, p.25.
47 Esposito, *The Islamic Threat*, p.193.
48 Husain, *Global Islamic Politics*, p.214.
49 Esposito, *The Islamic Threat*, p.14.
50 Mernissi, *Islam and Democracy*, p.146.
51 Esposito, *The Islamic Threat*, p.17.
52 Edward G. Shirley, 'The Iran Policy Trap', in *Foreign Policy*, no. 96 (Fall 1994), pp.88–9.

53 Lisa Anderson, 'Democracy in the Arab World: a Critique of the Political Culture Approach', in Rex Brynen, Bahgat Korany, and Paul Noble (eds), *Political Liberalization and Democratization in the Arab World: Theoretical Perspectives*. Boulder, CO: Lynne Riener, 1995, p.78.

54 Amartya Sen, 'Human Rights and Asian Values', *New Republic* (14 & 21 July 1997) p.34.

55 Sen, 'Human Rights and Asian Values', p.34.

56 Esposito, *The Islamic Threat*, p.38.

57 Esposito, *The Islamic Threat*, p.172.

58 Mernissi, *Islam and Democracy*, p.42.

59 Mernissi, *Islam and Democracy*, p.46.

60 Michael Scott Doran, 'Somebody Else's Civil War', *Foreign Affairs*, 81, no. 1 (January/February 2002), p.23.

61 Osama bin Laden, 'Declaration of War against the Americans Occupying the Land of the Two Holy Places' (August 1996). http://www.azzam.com/html/articlesdeclaration.htm

62 Esposito, *The Islamic Threat*, p.125. For a description of radical Islamic organizations, see chapter 5.

63 Said, *Covering Islam*, p.64.

64 Esposito, *The Islamic Threat*, p.16.

65 Roy, *The Failure of Political Islam*, pp.198–9.

66 Abdelwahab El-Afendi, 'Muslim or Citizen?' *Centre for the Study of Democracy Bulletin*, 8, no. 1 (Winter 2000–2001), p.4.

67 Richard Gwyn, *Nationalism Without Walls: The Unbearable Lightness of Being Canadian*. Toronto: McLelland and Stewart, 1996, p.17.

68 Robertson Davies, *Harper's*, 1989. Cited by J. L. Granatstein, *Yankee Go Home? Canadians and Anti-Americanism*. Toronto: HarperCollins, 1996, p.283.

69 Reginald C. Stuart, 'Anti-Americanism in Canadian History', in *American Review of Canadian Studies*, 27, no. 2 (Summer 1997), p.296.

70 Stuart, 'Anti-Americanism in Canadian History', p.302.

71 Alvin Z. Rubinstein and Donald E. Smith, 'Anti-Americanism in the Third World', *Annals*, no. 497 (May 1988), p.35. See their edited volume *Anti-Americanism in the Third World: Implications for US Foreign Policy*. Westport, CT: Greenwood, 1985.

72 Paul Hollander, *Anti-Americanism: Critiques at Home and Abroad, 1965–1990*. New York: Oxford University Press, 1992, p.viii.

73 Hollander, *Anti-Americanism*, p.339.

74 Stephen Haseler, *Varieties of Anti-Americanism: Reflex and Response*. Washington, DC: Ethics and Public Policy Center, 1985, p.1.

75 Haseler, *Varieties of Anti-Americanism*, p.6.

76 Haseler, *Varieties of Anti-Americanism*, p.17.

77 Kenneth Minogue, 'Anti-Americanism: a View from London', *National Interest*, no. 3 (Spring 1986), p.48.

78 Frederick B. Pike, *Chile and the United States*. South Bend, IN: University of Notre Dame Press, 1962, p.251.

79 Granatstein, *Yankee Go Home?*, p.6.

80 Arthur P. Whitaker, *Nationalism in Latin America: Past and Present*. Gainesville, FL: University of Florida Press, 1962, p.10.

81 We recall that in *Imagined Communities* Benedict Anderson gave special emphasis to Latin America as an interpreter and then disseminator of fragmenting nationalisms.

82 Antenor Orrego, 'El nacionalismo continental', *Examen*, Mexico City (November–December 1959), pp.3–11. Cited by Whitaker, *Nationalism in Latin America*, p.62.

83 Gerhard Masur, *Nationalism in Latin America: Diversity and Unity*. New York: Macmillan, 1966, p.39.

84 Jose Marti, *Inside the Monster: Writings on the United States and American Imperialism*. New York: Monthly Review Press, 1975.

85 Lawrence E. Harrison, *The Pan-American Dream: Do Latin America's Cultural Values Discourage True Partnership with the United States and Canada?* New York: Basic Books, 1997, p. 27. Harrison's answer to the question posed in the title is a categorical yes.

86 Masur, *Nationalism in Latin America*, p.70.

87 Whitaker, *Nationalism in Latin America*, p.59.

88 A prime example was the purge of Peruvian Marxist Mariategui from the Latin American Communist conference held in Buenos Aires in 1929.

89 On the US as *caudillo*, see Roland H. Ebel, Raymond C. Taras, and James D. Cochrane, *Political Culture and Foreign Policy in Latin America: Case Studies from the Circum-Caribbean*. Albany, NY: State University of New York Press, 1988.

90 Said, *Covering Islam*, p.27.

91 Carlos Rangel, *The Latin Americans: Their Love-Hate Relationship with the United States*. New York: Harcourt Brace Jovanovich, 197, p.44.

92 The sentiment is captured in the saying 'so far from God, so near the United States'.

93 Hollander, *Anti-Americanism*, p.355.

94 Robert A. Pastor and Jorge G. Castaneda, *Limits to Friendship: The United States and Mexico*. New York: Alfred A. Knopf, 198, p.16. For studies of Mexican intellectuals' anti-American attitudes I am indebted to Mary Casey Kane, 'In the Shadow of a Giant: Intellectuals, Public Opinion, and the Yankee Image in Mexico'. Unpublished MA thesis, Center for Latin American Studies, Tulane University (23 May 2000).

95 Jorge Castaneda, 'The Choices Facing Mexico', in Susan Kaufman Purcell (ed.), *Mexico in Transition*. New York: Council on Foreign Relations Press, 1988.

96 Published in Ken Silverstein and Alexander Cockburn, 'The Killers and the Killing', *The Nation* (6 March 1995), p.306.

97 Alexander F. Watson, 'Chiapas: Implications for US–Mexico Relations'. *US Department of State Dispatch*. V, no. 7 (14 February 1994), pp.83–7.

98 Hollander, *Anti-Americanism*, p.358.

99 'Chiapas and the Americas', *The Nation* (28 March 1994), p.404.

100 Abraham F. Lowenthal, 'Latin America: Ready for Partnership?' *Foreign Affairs*, 72, no. 1 (1993), p.84.

101 The topic is discredited as a line of research for a variety of reasons. One ingenious argument against studying anti-Americanism in Latin America is that the thesis 'Latin America is anti-American' is a concoction of the CIA. It is not clear whether this argument is in itself anti-American.

102 For one study see Daniel Pipes and Adam Garfinkle, *Friendly Tyrants*. New York: St. Martin's Press, 1991.

103 Noam Chomsky, *Turning the Tide*. Boston: South End Press, 1985, p.188.

104 Carlos Rangel, *Third World Ideology and Western Reality*. New Brunswick, NJ: Transaction Books, 1986, p.ix.

105 Haseler, *The Varieties of Anti-Americanism*, p. 44.

106   Harrison, *The Pan-American Dream*, p.5.
107   Harrison, *The Pan-American Dream*, p.256.
108   Hollander, *Anti-Americanism*.
109   *New York Times* (17 December 1995).

7   Nationalisms, Homes, and Hostilities

1   Benedict Anderson, *The Spectre of Comparisons: Nationalism, Southeast Asia and the World*. London: Verso, 1998, p.2.
2   Michael Ignatieff, *The Warrior's Honor: Ethnic War and the Modern Conscience*. New York: Metropolitan Books, 1998, p. 94.
3   Ignatieff, *The Warrior's Honor*, pp.92–93.
4   See Anthony Giddens, *The Nation-State and Violence*. Berkeley, CA: University of California Press, 1990.
5   Ignatieff, *The Warrior's Honor*, p.97.
6   See Fareed Zakaria, 'The Rise of Illiberal Democracy', in *Foreign Affairs*, 76, no. 6 (November/December 1997), pp.22–43.
7   Ali A. Mazrui, 'Islamic and Western Values', *Foreign Affairs*, 76, no. 5 (September/ October 1997), pp.131–2.
8   Michael Hechter, *Containing Nationalism*. New York: Oxford University Press, 2000.
9   Michael Lind, 'National Good?' *Prospect* (October 2000), p.3.
10   Ignatieff, *The Warrior's Honor*, p.95.
11   Marc Shell, *Children of the Earth: Literature, Politics, and Nationhood*. New York: Oxford University Press, 1993, p.194.
12   Gregory Jusdanis, *The Necessary Nation*. Princeton, NJ: Princeton University Press, 2001, p.17.
13   Theodore Lowi, *The End of Liberalism: The Second Republic of the United States*. New York: W.W. Norton, 1979.
14   Julia Christeva, *Nations Without Nationalism*. New York: Columbia University Press, 1993.
15   Jusdanis, *The Necessary Nation*, p.186.
16   Kenneth R. Minogue, *Nationalism*. London: B.T. Batsford, 1967, p.16.
17   Anne McClintock, ' "No Longer in a Future Heaven": Women and Nationalism in South Africa', in *Transition*, 51 (1991), p.121. See Frantz Fanon, *Black Skin, White Masks*. London: Pluto Press, 1986.

Bibliography

This lists English-language books that address the subject of nationalism in a general or comparative way. Single-country studies of nationalism are not included.

Alter, Peter, *Nationalism*. London: Edward Arnold, 1989.

Anderson, Benedict, *Imagined Communities: Reflections on the Origin and Spread of Nationalism*. New York: Verso, 1993.

Barkey, Karen, and Mark von Hagen (eds), *After Empire: Multiethnic Societies and Nation-Building. The Soviet Union and the Russian, Ottoman, and Habsburg Empires*. Boulder, CO: Westview Press, 1997.

Barth, Frederick, *Ethnic Groups and Boundaries: the Social Organization of Cultural Differences*. London: Allen and Unwin, 1970.

Beiner, Ronald (ed.), *Theorizing Nationalism*. Albany, NY: SUNY Press, 1999.

Billig, Michael, *Banal Nationalism*. London: Sage Publications, 1997.

Birch, Anthony H., *Nationalism and National Integration*. London: Unwin Hyman, 1989.

Brass, Paul R., *Ethnicity and Nationalism: Theory and Comparison*. Newbury Park, CA: Sage Publications, 1991.

Bremmer, Ian, and Ray Taras (eds), *New States, New Politics: Building the Post-Soviet Nations*. New York: Cambridge University Press, 1997.

Breuilly, John, *Nationalism and the State*. Chicago: University of Chicago Press, 1994.

Brubaker, Rogers, *Nationalism Reframed: Nationhood and the National Question in the New Europe*. Cambridge: Cambridge University Press, 1996.

Buchanan, Allen, *Secession: the Morality of Political Divorce from Fort Sumter to Lithuania and Quebec*. Boulder, CO: Westview Press, 1991.

Buchheit, Lee C., *Secession: the Legitimacy of Self-Determination*. New Haven, CT: Yale University Press, 1978.

Calhoun, Craig, *Nationalism*. Buckingham: Open University Press, 1997.

Caplan, Richard, and John Feffer (eds), *Europe's New Nationalism: States and Minorities in Conflict*. New York: Oxford University Press, 1996.

Carr, Edward Hallett, *Nationalism and After*. London: Macmillan, 1945.

Chatterjee, Partha, *The Nation and its Fragments: Colonial and Postcolonial Histories*. Princeton, NJ: Princeton University Press, 1993.

Chazan, Naomi (ed.), *Irredentism and International Politics*. Boulder, CO: Lynne Rienner, 1991.

Clarke, Desmond M., and Charles Jones, *The Rights of Nations: Nations and Nationalism in a Changing World*. New York: St. Martin's Press – now Palgrave Macmillan, 1999.

Cobban, Alfred, *The Nation State and National Self-Determination*. London: Collins, 1969.

Connor, Walker, *Ethnonationalism: the Quest for Understanding*. Princeton, NJ: Princeton University Press, 1994.

Dahbour, Omar, and Micheline R. Ishay (eds), *The Nationalism Reader*. Atlantic Highlands, NJ: Humanities Press, 1995.

Danspeckgruber, Wolfgang (ed.), *The Self-Determination of Peoples: Community, Nation, and State in an Interdependent World*. Boulder, CO: Lynne Rienner, 2002.

Deutsch, Karl W., *Nationalism and Social Communication*. Cambridge, MA: MIT Press, 1953.

Deutsch, Karl W., and William Foltz (eds), *Nation-Building*. New York: Atherton Press, 1963.

Diamond, Larry, and Marc F. Plattner (eds), *Nationalism, Ethnic Conflict, and Democracy*. Baltimore, MD: Johns Hopkins University Press, 1994.

Doyle, Michael W, *Empires*. Ithaca, NY: Cornell University Press, 1986.

Eley, Geoff, and Ronald G. Suny (eds), *Becoming National*. New York: Oxford University Press, 1996.

Enloe, Cynthia H., *Ethnic Conflict and Political Development*. Boston, MA: Little, Brown, 1973.

Esman, Milton J., *Ethnic Politics*. Ithaca, NY: Cornell University Press, 1994.

Esman, Milton J., and Shibley Telhami (eds), *International Organizations and Ethnic Conflict*. Ithaca, NY: Cornell University Press, 1995.

Geary, Patrick J., *The Myth of Nations: the Medieval Origins of Europe*. Princeton, NJ: Princeton University Press, 2002.

Geertz, Clifford, *Old Societies and New States: the Quest for Modernity in Asia and Africa*. Glencoe, IL: Free Press, 1963.

Gellner, Ernest, *Conditions of Liberty: Civil Society and its Rivals*. London: Penguin, 1994.

Gellner, Ernest, *Encounters with Nationalism*. Oxford: Blackwell, 1994.

Gellner, Ernest, *Nations and Nationalism*. Ithaca, NY: Cornell University Press, 1983.

Gellner, Ernest, *Thought and Change*. Chicago: University of Chicago Press, 1978.

Glazer, Nathan, and Daniel P. Moynihan (eds), *Ethnicity: Theory and Experience*. Cambridge, MA: Harvard University Press, 1975.

Gottlieb, Gidon, *Nation Against State: a New Approach to Ethnic Conflicts and the Decline of Sovereignty*. New York: Council on Foreign Relations Press, 1993.

Greenfeld, Liah, *Nationalism: Five Roads to Modernity*. Cambridge, MA: Harvard University Press, 1992.

Griffiths, Stephen I., *Nationalism and Ethnic Conflict: Threats to European Security*. New York: Oxford University Press, 1993.

Gurr, Ted Robert, *Minorities at Risk: a Global View of Ethnopolitical Conflicts*. Washington, DC: United States Institute of Peace Press, 1993.

Gurr, Ted Robert, and Barbara Harff, *Ethnic Conflict in World Politics*. Boulder, CO: Westview Press, 1994.

Gurr, Ted Robert, *Peoples Versus States: Minorities at Risk in the New Century*. Washington, DC: US Institute of Peace, 2000.

Hall, John A. (ed.), *State of the Nation: Ernest Gellner and the Theory of Nationalism*. Cambridge: Cambridge University Press, 1998.

Hardt, Michael, and Antonio Negri, *Empire*. Cambridge, MA: Harvard University Press, 2000.

Hayes, Carlton J.H., *Essays on Nationalism*. New York: Macmillan, 1926.

Hayes, Carlton J.H., *The Historical Evolution of Modern Nationalism*. New York: R.R. Smith, 1931.

Hayes, Carlton, *Nationalism: a Religion*. New York: Macmillan, 1960.

Hechter, Michael, *Containing Nationalism*. New York: Oxford University Press, 2001.

Hedetoft, Ulf, and Mette Hjort (eds), *The Postnational Self: Belonging and Identity*. Minneapolis, MN: University of Minnesota Press, 2002.

Heraclides, Alexis, *The Self-determination of Minorities in International Politics*. London: Frank Cass, 1991.

Herb, Guntram H., and David H. Kaplan (eds), *Nested Identities: Nationalism, Territory, and Scale*. Lanham, MD: Rowman and Littlefield, 1999.

Hertz, Frederick, *Nationality in History and Politics: a Study of the Psychology and Sociology of National Sentiment and Character*. New York: Oxford University Press, 1944.

Hobsbawm, E.J., *Nations and Nationalism Since 1780: Programme, Myth, Reality*. New York: Cambridge University Press, 1993.

Hobson, John A., *Imperialism: a Study*. Ann Arbor, MI: University of Michigan Press, 1965.

Horowitz, Donald L., *Ethnic Groups in Conflict*. Berkeley, CA: University of California Press, 1985.

Huntington, Samuel P., *The Clash of Civilizations and the Remaking of World Order*. New York: Simon and Schuster, 1997.

Hutchinson, John, and Anthony D. Smith (eds), *Nationalism*. New York: Oxford University Press, 1994.

Hylland Eriksen, Thomas, *Ethnicity and Nationalism: Anthropological Perspectives*. London: Pluto Press, 1993.

Ignatieff, Michael, *Blood and Belonging: Journeys into the New Nationalism*. New York: Farrar, Straus, and Giroux, 1993.

Ignatieff, Michael, *The Warrior's Honor: Ethnic War and the Modern Conscience*. New York: Henry Holt, 1998.

Ignatieff, Michael, *Virtual War: Kosovo and Beyond*. New York: Henry Holt, 2000.

Jackson, Peter and Jan Penrose (eds), *Constructions of Race, Place and Nation*. London: UCL Press, 1993.

Jackson, Robert H., *Quasi-States: Sovereignty, International Relations, and the Third World*. Cambridge: Cambridge University Press, 1990.

Juergensmeyer, Mark, *The New Cold War? Religious Nationalism Confronts the Secular State*. Berkeley, CA: University of California Press, 1993.

Juergensmeyer, Mark, *Terror in the Mind of God*. Berkeley, CA: University of California Press, 2001.

Jusdanis, Gregory, *The Necessary Nation*. Princeton, NJ: Princeton University Press, 2001.

Kamenka, Eugene (ed.), *Nationalism: the Nature and Evolution of an Idea*. London: Edward Arnold, 1976.

Keating, Michael, *Nations Against the State*. Houndmills, Basingstoke: Palgrave, 2001.

Kedourie, Elie, *Nationalism*. London: Hutchison, 1960.

Kellas, James G., *The Politics of Nationalism and Ethnicity*. New York: St. Martin's Press, 1998.

Keyes, Charles F. (ed.), *Ethnic Change*. Seattle, WA: University of Washington Press, 1981.

Kohn, Hans, *The Idea of Nationalism: a Study in its Origins and Background*. New York: Collier Books, 1969.

Kohn, Hans, *Nationalism and Realism: 1852–1879*. Princeton, NJ: Van Nostrand, 1968.

Kohn, Hans, *Prophets and Peoples: Studies in Nineteenth Century Nationalisms*. London: Collier Books, 1969.

Kolsto, Pal, *Political Construction Sites: Nation-Building in Russia and the Post-Soviet States*. Boulder, CO: Westview Press, 2000.

Kupchan, Charles A. (ed.), *Nationalism and Nationalities in the New Europe*. Ithaca, NY: Cornell University Press, 1995.

Kymlicka, Will, *Multicultural Citizenship*. Oxford: Clarendon Press, 1996.

Kymlicka, Will, *Politics in the Vernacular: Nationalism, Multiculturalism, and Citizenship*. New York: Oxford University Press, 2000.

Lake, David A., and Donald Rothchild (eds), *The International Spread of Ethnic Conflict: Fear, Diffusion, and Escalation*. Princeton, NJ: Princeton University Press, 1998.

Leone, Bruno (ed.), *Nationalism*. St. Paul, MN: Greenhaven Press, 1986.

Lijphart, Arend, *Democracy in Plural Societies*. New Haven, CT: Yale University Press, 1977.

Lustick, Ian S., *Unsettled States, Disputed Lands: Britain and Ireland, France and Algeria, Israel and the West Bank-Gaza*. Ithaca, NY: Cornell University Press, 1993.

Mayall, James, *Nationalism and International Society*. Cambridge: Cambridge University Press, 1994.

Miall, Hugh (ed.), *Minority Rights in Europe: Prospects for a Transitional Regime*. New York: Council on Foreign Relations Press, 1995.

Midlarsky, Manus I. (ed.), *The Internationalization of Communal Strife*. London: Routledge, 1992.

Miller, David, *On Nationality*. Oxford: Clarendon Press, 1995.

Montville, J. (ed.), *Conflict and Peacemaking in Multiethnic Societies*. Toronto: Lexington, 1990.

Motyl, Alexander J. (ed.), *Encyclopedia of Nationalism*. New York: Academic Press, 2000.

Moynihan, Daniel Patrick, *Pandaemonium: Ethnicity in International Politics*. New York: Oxford University Press, 1994.

Niebuhr, Reinhold, *The Structure of Nations and Empires*. New York: Charles Scribner's Sons, 1959.

Nimni, Ephraim, *Marxism and Nationalism: Theoretical Origins of a Political Crisis*. Boulder, CO: Pluto Press, 1991.

O'Brien, Conor Cruise, *God Land: Reflections on Religion and Nationalism*. Cambridge, MA: Harvard University Press, 1988.

Pfaff, William, *The Wrath of Nations: Civilization and the Furies of Nationalism*. New York: Touchstone Books, 1993.

Premdas, Ralph R., S.W.R. de A. Samarasinghe, and Alan B. Anderson (eds), *Secessionist Movements in Comparative Perspective*. New York: St. Martin's – now Palgrave Macmillan, 1990.

Rothschild, Joseph, *Ethnopolitics: a Conceptual Framework*. New York: Columbia University Press, 1981.

Rudolph, Richard L., and David F. Good (eds), *Nationalism and Empire: the Habsburg Monarchy and the Soviet Union*. New York: St. Martin's, 1992.

Ryan, Stephen, *Ethnic Conflict and International Relations*. Aldershot: Dartmouth, 1990.

Said, Abdul A., and Luiz R. Simmons (eds), *Ethnicity in an International Context*. New Brunswick, NJ: Transaction Books, 1976.

Saideman, Stephen M., *The Ties that Divide: Ethnic Politics, Foreign Policy, and International Conflict*. New York: Columbia University Press, 2001.

Schulze, Hagen, *States, Nations and Nationalism*. Oxford: Blackwell, 1998.

Seers, Dudley, *The Political Economy of Nationalism*. New York: Oxford University Press, 1983.

Seton-Watson, Hugh, *Nations and States: an Enquiry into the Origins of Nations and the Politics of Nationalism*. Boulder, CO: Westview Press, 1977.

Seton-Watson, Hugh, *The New Imperialism*. Totowa, NJ: Rowman and Littlefield, 1971.

Shafer, Boyd C., *Faces of Nationalism*. New York: Harcourt, Brace, Jovanovich, 1972.

Shafer, Boyd C., *Nationalism: Myth and Reality*. New York: Harcourt, Brace and World, 1955.

Shiels, Frederick L. (ed.), *Ethnic Separatism and World Politics.* Lanham, MD: University Press of America, 1984.

Smith, Anthony D., *The Ethnic Origins of Nations.* Oxford: Basil Blackwell, 1986.

Smith, Anthony D., *The Ethnic Revival.* Cambridge: Cambridge University Press, 1981.

Smith, Anthony D., *National Identity.* Reno, NV: University of Nevada Press, 1991.

Smith, Anthony D., *Nationalism in the Twentieth Century.* New York: New York University Press, 1979.

Smith, Anthony D., *Theories of Nationalism.* New York: Holmes and Meier, 1983.

Smith, Graham (ed.), *The Nationalities Question in the Post-Soviet States.* London: Longman, 1996.

Snyder, Jack, *From Voting to Violence: Democratization and Nationalist Conflict.* New York: W.W. Norton, 2000.

Snyder, Jack, and Barbara F. Walter, *Civil War, Insecurity, and Intervention.* New York: Columbia University Press, 1999.

Snyder, Louis L., *Encyclopedia of Nationalism.* New York: Paragon House, 1990.

Snyder, Louis L., *Macro-Nationalisms: a History of the Pan-Movements.* Westport, CT: Greenwood Press, 1984.

Snyder, Louis L., *The Meaning of Nationalism.* New Brunswick, NJ: Rutgers University Press, 1954.

Spencer, Metta (ed.), *Separatism: Democracy and Disintegration.* Lanham, MD: Rowman and Littlefield, 1998.

Szporluk, Roman, *Communism and Nationalism.* New York: Oxford University Press, 1988.

Szporluk, Roman (ed.), *National Identity and Ethnicity in Russia and the New States of Eurasia.* Armonk, NY: M.E. Sharpe, 1994.

Talmon, Jacob L., *Myth of the Nation and the Vision of Revolution: Ideological Polarization in the Twentieth Century.* New Brunswick, NJ: Transaction Books, 1991.

Tamir, Yael, *Liberal Nationalism.* Princeton, NJ: Princeton University Press, 1993.

Taras, Ray (ed.), *National Identities and Ethnic Minorities in Eastern Europe.* London: Macmillan – now Palgrave Macmillan, 1997.

Teich, Mikulas, and Roy Porter, *The National Question in Europe in Historical Context.* New York: Cambridge University Press, 1993.

Wiebe, Robert H., *Who We Are: a History of Popular Nationalism.* Princeton, NJ: Princeton University Press, 2002.

Wiener, Myron, *The Global Migration Crisis: Challenge to States and to Human Rights.* New York: HarperCollins, 1995.

Young, M. Crawford, *The Politics of Cultural Pluralism.* Madison, WI: University of Wisconsin Press, 1976.

Young, M. Crawford, *The Rising Tide of Cultural Pluralism: The Nation-State at Bay?* Madison, WI: University of Wisconsin Press, 1993.

Zartman, I. William (ed.), *Collapsed States: the Disintegration and Restoration of Legitimate Authority.* Boulder, CO: Lynne Rienner, 1995.

Znaniecki, Florian, *Modern Nationalities: a Sociological Study.* Westport, CT: Greenwood Press, 1973.

Zwick, Peter, *National Communism.* Boulder, CO: Westview Press, 1983.

Index